Easy Meals
For Busy
Women

Easy Meals
For Busy
Women

Over 500 delicious step-by-step recipes

Love Food™ is an imprint of Parragon Books Ltd

Parragon
Queen Street House
4 Queen Street
Bath BA1 1HE, UK

Love Food™ and the accompanying heart device is a trade mark of
Parragon Books Ltd

ISBN 978-1-4075-0509-1

Design by Fiona Roberts
Cover artwork by Diana Birkett
Line illustrations by Victoria Mitchell
Editor: Fiona Biggs

Printed in China

Notes for the Reader

This book uses metric and imperial measurements. Follow the same units of
measurement throughout; do not mix metric and imperial. All spoon measurements
are level, unless otherwise stated: teaspoons are assumed to
be 5 ml, and tablespoons are assumed to be 15 ml. Unless otherwise stated,
milk is assumed to be whole, eggs and individual fruits such as bananas
are medium, and pepper is freshly ground black pepper.

Recipes using raw or very lightly cooked eggs should be avoided by
infants, the elderly, pregnant women, convalescents and anyone suffering
from an illness. Pregnant and breast-feeding women are advised to
avoid eating peanuts and peanut products.

Contents

❊ ❊ ❊

Introduction

It is ironic that with all the advances of twenty-first century technology we have never been so short of time. Our families tend to be far smaller than those of our grandmothers and our homes are filled with all kinds of electronic gadgetry designed to make our lives easier, yet it is increasingly difficult to find the time to prepare healthy and tasty home-cooked meals. At the same time, we have never been so well informed about the importance of a well-balanced diet. Busy mums and professional women – and those who struggle to combine the two – seem to be caught in a time trap, juggling all sorts of demands and pressures and with no obvious escape route.

Home cooking with fresh ingredients is undoubtedly the key to a healthy lifestyle. First of all, you know exactly what ingredients have gone into a dish. Not only can you avoid artificial additives, but you can keep a careful eye on quantities of fat, sugar and salt. It is a much more economical option too – the same dish purchased as a takeaway often costs up to twice as much. In addition, home cooking tastes better, has a more tempting aroma and looks more appealing. This makes a meal much more enjoyable and it has been proved that savouring your food helps the brain recognize when your body has had enough to eat. When food is merely fuel to be shovelled in, overeating and its serious health consequences are far more common.

It is all very well knowing these things, but if the effort of finding the time to cook simply adds to the stress in a hectic life, then it is hardly a healthy choice. Even deciding what to cook can be taxing. **Easy Meals for Busy Women** solves the problem. It is packed with hundreds of fabulous recipes for easy-cook meals, some of which can be prepared, cooked and served in

❖ ❖ ❖

a matter of minutes. Many others, once you have done the initial preparation, can be left to bubble gently to perfection with no further effort. Clear step-by-step instructions make the recipes simple to follow, even if you are a complete beginner. Each stage of preparation and cooking is explained in a logical and straightforward way so that an extensive, stress-free repertoire of marvellous meals will be at your fingertips in no time at all. In addition, you can count on superb results every time.

This comprehensive cookbook is not just an escape route from slaving endlessly over a hot stove, but is also an invaluable source of inspiration. When it comes to planning dinner and your mind goes completely blank, just leaf through the pages for a wealth of ideas for all courses and occasions and every age and taste.

As there is such a vast array of recipes to choose from, they have been divided into five chapters to help you find exactly the one you want. **Starters & Snacks** features both hot and cold hors d'oeuvres to tantalize your taste buds, as well as an abundance of easy-cook snacks that make great lunches or the perfect accompaniment to a well-deserved relaxing night in watching the television.

In **Soups & Salads** you will find lots of familiar favourites as well as some more unusual recipes. Home-made soup is, perhaps, the ultimate comfort food and is surprisingly easy and quick to prepare. Salad, whether an accompaniment or a main course, is always a quick and healthy option but can sometimes be boring, so you are sure to be delighted with the huge range of colourful dishes based on vegetables, fruit, rice and other grains, meat and poultry, and fish and shellfish.

From roast chicken to casseroles and from turkey to tuna, the recipes in **Main Dishes** will guarantee that you will never be short of ideas for tasty, trouble-free meals. Whether you are tempted by a vegetarian stir-fry or a succulent steak, there is the perfect dish for every occasion and season of the year.

Pasta and noodle dishes are the busy cook's best friends and **Pasta, Noodles & Rice** is a treasury of fast and fabulous recipes. From traditional Italian sauces to classic Chinese stir-fries, the range of ingredients is almost limitless and the variety of flavours is immense. Rice dishes are almost as quick to cook and just as diverse, with recipes inspired by countries as far apart as Spain and Indonesia.

Desserts & Baking is full of almost effortless sweet treats to end your perfect meal. You can indulge in chocolate, refresh with fruit, satisfy with a traditional hot pie, or impress with an elegant cheesecake. Home-made brownies, cakes, muffins and biscuits are always a delight and don't have to take up hours in the kitchen. Even the recipes for sweet and savoury breads are undemanding – and you can always go off and do something else while the dough rises.

Storecupboard Essentials

While different lifestyles mean it is impossible to say what everyone should have in their storecupboard, having a basic range of ingredients to hand will save you time when you want to cook. If your storecupboard is well stocked, you will find that you already have many of the ingredients needed in a recipe and will only need to supplement them with a few fresh items. It will also enable you to produce a few quick and simple dishes using only storecupboard items – perfect for when you do not have time, or the inclination, to shop for fresh ingredients.

Dry Ingredients

Pasta There are so many varieties of pasta available that you should stick to the ones you use regularly or you will end up with lots of half-empty packets. Spaghetti and macaroni are good basic pastas to have in your storecupboard. For a wider choice, try lasagne (sheets), cannelloni (tubes), fusilli (spirals), farfalle (bows), tagliatelle (ribbons) and conchiglie (shells).

Rice and grains A small range of different kinds of rice opens up a wide array of savoury and sweet dishes. A good basic rice to have in your storecupboard is long-grain rice. For a wider range of dishes, try basmati rice, arborio rice and brown rice. It is also useful to have both couscous and polenta in your storecupboard because they are quick to cook and are a good staple to accompany any meat or fish dishes.

Noodles Egg noodles are the most common noodles, and are often served as an accompaniment for stir-fries or other Asian dishes. They are available in various thicknesses and are very quick to cook (from 1–5 minutes). Rice noodles are available as very fine noodles; most of them only need soaking before use, but check the pack for instructions because they vary. They can be added to soups and to stir-fries.

Flour This is a very useful item to have in the storecupboard. Plain flour is used for thickening casseroles, making sauces and coating food such as escalopes of meat and chicken before cooking. Self-raising flour is used for baking cakes, biscuits and desserts. Bread flour is used for breadmaking – it can be white, brown or wholemeal. It has a higher percentage of gluten, which gives the dough its elasticity. Finally, cornflour provides a quick way to thicken sauces.

Sugar Granulated sugar is the one sugar you need on a day-to-day basis. Use it to sweeten tea or coffee, on cereals, and with fruits when they are too tart. Caster sugar is finer than granulated sugar and is better for cakes, cookies, and meringues. Icing sugar is a very finely powdered sugar, used for making icing and for sprinkling over cakes and desserts as decoration. It often turns lumpy in storage so it is essential to sift it before use. Brown sugar is a moist sugar, which is available in varying shades depending on how much molasses is present. Demerara sugar is suitable for cakes and desserts, while dark muscavado sugar is only suitable for rich cakes like Christmas cake or gingerbreads.

Nuts and seeds A few nuts, such as walnuts, almonds, pine kernels, cashew nuts and hazelnuts are useful in the storecupboard. They can be used to add extra texture and crunch to many savoury dishes, such as salads, rice and pasta, as well as baked goods, desserts and pastries. Seeds, such as sunflower and pumpkin seeds, are useful for sprinkling over salads and sesame seeds are often used to sprinkle over stir-fries and other Asian dishes.

Dried fruits Many fruits are available dried and can be used in baking and savoury dishes, such as stews and casseroles. Dried fruits can also be eaten as a healthy snack food.

Canned and Bottled Goods

Oils Good oil is important for many kitchen tasks – for frying, for brushing foods before grilling, baking and making salad dressings. Sunflower oil and groundnut oil are good all-purpose oils, which can be used for all cooking methods. Olive oil can also be used as a cooking oil, but make sure that you save your most expensive extra virgin olive oil for salad dressings or for drizzling over foods. Sesame oil is a dark, nutty oil frequently used in Chinese and Thai cooking. If used alone, it will burn easily, so it is best mixed with sunflower oil for cooking or used to flavour the food just before serving.

Beans and lentils These are a good, economical source of protein. Using canned varieties cuts out the soaking and cooking time needed for the dried versions, making them a useful convenience food. Basics for your storecupboard include borlotti beans, chickpeas and lentils. For a wider choice, try butter beans, cannellini beans and red kidney beans. They all have different shapes and colours and can be used to add bulk to casseroles, stews and soups.

Tomatoes are available in cans, whole or chopped. If you use them in casseroles, whole tomatoes will cook down. However, if you want to make a quick pasta sauce, the chopped variety is better.

Sun-dried tomatoes These are available bottled in oil or dried, in which case they need to be rehydrated before use. Snip them into salads or add them to pasta sauces to give a vibrant flavour.

❈ ❈ ❈

Chargrilled peppers in oil These are wonderful when you have no time to grill and peel peppers. They are ready to add to salads, soups and casseroles.

Other canned vegetables Canned vegetables, preserved at the peak of goodness, are wholesome and nutritious. Many vegetables are available in canned form and, unlike their fresh counterparts, they are available all year round. Keep a store for adding to sauces and stews.

Olives There is a wide variety of olives available; some are flavoured with herbs. Choose your favourites and keep them for nibbling and also for use in pastas and on pizzas.

Canned fish Anchovies are used for pizzas, salads and garnishes. They can also be added to pasta sauces and casseroles to produce a deeper flavour. Sardines make a delicious snack served with lots of buttered toast, or as an instant pâté with butter and lemon juice. Tuna is another useful standby. It is very versatile and can be eaten simply with a salad or used to make a pasta or rice dish.

Flavourings, Herbs and Spices

Garlic Garlic is an indispensable ingredient in many dishes; use it whenever its pungent aroma and flavour are needed. Buy whole heads of garlic that are plump and firm.

Onions Onions are available in yellow, white and red, in a vast range of sizes. The ordinary yellow onion is the one normally used for cooking. Red onions have a sweet, mild flavour, whereas white onions have a stronger flavour.

Chillies These are from the same family as peppers, but they are very hot. Usually the smaller the chilli, the hotter the flavour. They are available in green or red. Remove all the seeds before use unless you like a really hot dish.

Lemons and limes Lemons are one of the most popular flavourings in the kitchen. They can be used in sweet and savoury dishes and in a variety of ways, either whole, sliced, just the juice, or just the grated rind, which has an intense flavour owing to its aromatic oils. If you are using the lemon zest, try to buy the unwaxed variety. Limes are similar to lemons, but are smaller, with green skin. They can be used in many of the same ways as lemons, and are popular in Thai and South American cooking.

Mustards Mustards can be used in recipes or served as an accompaniment for steaks, beef and ham. Hot mustard has a strong, pungent flavour and quite a kick. Dijon mustard is the traditional mustard of France and is now gaining in popularity owing to its milder flavour. Wholegrain mustard does not have the strong flavour of hot mustard, but it does have a wonderful texture, which makes it a good ingredient in sauces. Mustard is also used in dressings and marinades, and dry mustard can be used in savoury baking.

Soy sauce This is a popular Chinese sauce. It is used with all Asian foods, both in cooking and at the table, and adds a salty flavour. Soy sauce comes in light and dark varieties: use the light one with shellfish and chicken, and the dark one with duck and meat.

Stock cubes or granules These are a useful storecupboard standby for when you do not have time to make fresh stock. They are available in different flavours – beef, chicken, vegetable, fish etc. The powder form is very convenient because you can add very small amounts.

Thai fish sauce (nam pla) This sauce is used in many Thai recipes. It is rather like soy sauce; it adds flavour but also brings out the flavour of the other ingredients.

Vinegars Vinegars have many uses in cooking and are most often used in dressings and marinades. Balsamic vinegar is the richest of all the vinegars, with a deep brown colour and a fruity sweet flavour. The best varieties are aged in oak barrels for up to 25 years, but can be very expensive. Wine vinegars are more everyday vinegars – red varieties are best used with foods with robust flavours, such as beef, whereas the white varities are often used in chicken and fish dishes.

Worcestershire sauce This very spicy sauce has been a favourite for many years. Add it to casserole dishes and soups for a fiery flavour.

Herbs A wide variety of fresh herbs is now available in supermarkets so you can use them all year round. Alternatively, you can grow them in your garden or on a windowsill so that you can have them really fresh. Dried and frozen herbs are available and can be useful whenever the fresh herb is not obtainable: use 1 teaspoon of dried instead of 1 tablespoon of fresh or frozen. Basil, coriander, oregano, mint, parsley, rosemary, sage and thyme are all popular herbs with a variety of uses.

Spices There is a vast range of spices available nowadays – in fact it is confusing because there are so many. It is a good idea to buy spices in small amounts because they tend to lose their flavour, especially the ready-ground ones. Useful spices include chilli powder, cinnamon, coriander, cumin, ginger, nutmeg, paprika and turmeric. It is also useful to keep a store of whole peppercorns for grinding over food to add an aromatic pungency.

Refrigerator Essentials

Butter This has a huge range of uses in cooking, and is added to sauces, cakes, pastries and biscuits. Unsalted varieties are available and are good for spreading on bread and also for baking cakes and sweet pastries.

Milk Ideal for adding to beverages and pouring over cereals. It is also essential for white sauces, desserts, batters and soups. Semi-skimmed milk is a good choice both for drinking and cooking, but try full-fat milk if you like a creamier taste.

Cream Cream is generally used to thicken and enrich soups and savoury dishes, or in decadent desserts. Double cream is good for adding to hot sauces because it does not curdle when heated. Soured cream is a useful standby, and has the added benefit that it keeps in the refrigerator for far longer than cream (up to 2 weeks).

Cheese It is a good idea to keep a small quantity of both Cheddar and Parmesan cheese in your refrigerator at all times for both cooking and eating. Cheddar is an all-purpose cheese and is available in different strengths, from mild to mature. Use it for grating and sprinkling over au gratin dishes or for incorporating into a sauce. Parmesan is also widely used both for eating and for cooking. It has a good, strong, sweet flavour and can be grated or shaved over pasta dishes or sprinkled over salad leaves. Other useful cheeses for cooking include blue cheese, mozzarella cheese and mascarpone cheese.

Eggs Eggs are one of the most versatile and nutritious foods, whether used whole or in their separate – whites and yolks – components. Always keep half a dozen eggs ready for use: you will need medium eggs for main recipes and smaller ones for cooking processes like coating and glazing. Use them to make a speedy omelette or scrambled eggs on toast for a quick meal.

Simple
starters & snacks

Mexican-Style Pizzas

4 ready-made individual pizza bases
1 tbsp olive oil
200 g/7 oz canned chopped tomatoes with garlic and herbs
2 tbsp tomato purée
200 g/7 oz canned kidney beans, drained and rinsed
115 g/4 oz sweetcorn kernels, thawed, if frozen
1–2 tsp chilli sauce
1 large red onion, shredded
100 g/3$\frac{1}{2}$ oz reduced-fat Cheddar cheese, grated
1 large green chilli, sliced into rings
2 tbsp fresh coriander, chopped
salt and pepper

❈ Preheat the oven to 220°C/425°F/Gas Mark 7. Arrange the pizza bases on a baking tray and brush them lightly with the oil.

❈ In a bowl, mix together the chopped tomatoes, tomato purée, kidney beans and sweetcorn, and add chilli sauce to taste. Season with salt and pepper.

❈ Spread the tomato and kidney bean mixture evenly over each pizza base to cover. Top each pizza with shredded onion and sprinkle with some grated cheese and a few slices of green chilli to taste. Bake in the oven for about 20 minutes until the vegetables are tender, the cheese has melted and the base is crisp and golden.

❈ Remove the pizzas from the baking tray and transfer to serving plates. Sprinkle with the chopped coriander and serve immediately.

Vegetable Calzone

DOUGH
450 g/1 lb strong white flour
2 tsp easy-blend dried yeast
1 tsp caster sugar
150 ml/5 fl oz vegetable stock
150 ml/5 fl oz passata
beaten egg, to glaze

FILLING
1 tbsp vegetable oil
1 onion, chopped
1 garlic clove, crushed
2 tbsp chopped sun-dried tomatoes
100 g/3$\frac{1}{2}$ oz spinach, chopped
3 tbsp drained canned sweetcorn kernels
25 g/1 oz French beans, cut into thirds
1 tbsp tomato purée
1 tbsp chopped oregano
50 g/1$\frac{3}{4}$ oz mozzarella cheese, sliced
salt and pepper

❈ Sift the flour into a bowl. Add the yeast and sugar and beat in the stock and passata to make a smooth dough.

❈ Knead the dough on a lightly floured surface for 10 minutes, then place in a clean, lightly oiled bowl and leave to rise in a warm place for 1 hour.

❈ Heat the oil in a frying pan and sauté the onion for 2–3 minutes. Stir in the garlic, tomatoes, spinach, sweetcorn and beans and cook for 3–4 minutes. Add the tomato purée and oregano and season well.

❈ Divide the risen dough into 4 equal portions and roll each portion out on a floured surface to form an 18-cm/7-inch circle. Spoon a quarter of the filling mixture on to one half of each circle and top with the sliced mozzarella cheese.

❈ Fold the dough over to encase the filling, pressing the edge firmly with a fork to seal. Glaze the dough with the beaten egg.

❈ Put the calzone on a lightly greased baking tray and cook in a preheated oven, 220°C/425°F/Gas Mark 7, for 25–30 minutes until risen and golden. Serve warm.

Potato-Filled Naan Breads

225 g/8 oz waxy potatoes, scrubbed and diced	85 g/3 oz baby spinach, shredded
1 tbsp vegetable oil	4 small or 2 large naan breads
1 onion, chopped	lime pickle, to serve
2 garlic cloves, crushed	
1 tsp ground cumin	**RAITA**
1 tsp ground coriander	150 ml/5 fl oz low-fat natural
$\frac{1}{2}$ tsp chilli powder	yogurt
1 tbsp tomato purée	4 tbsp diced cucumber
3 tbsp vegetable stock	1 tbsp chopped fresh mint

❊ Bring a saucepan of lightly salted water to the boil and parboil the potatoes for 10 minutes. Drain thoroughly.

❊ Heat the oil in a separate saucepan and cook the onion and garlic over a low heat, stirring frequently, for 3 minutes. Add the spices to the pan and cook for a further 2 minutes.

❊ Stir in the potatoes, tomato purée, stock and spinach. Cook for 5 minutes until the potatoes are tender.

❊ Warm the naan breads through in a preheated oven, 150°C/300°F/Gas Mark 2, for about 2 minutes.

❊ To make the raita, mix together the yogurt, cucumber and mint in a small bowl.

❊ Remove the warmed naan breads from the oven. Using a sharp knife, cut a slit into the side of each bread to make a pocket. Spoon a portion of the spicy potato mixture into each pocket.

❊ Serve the filled naan breads immediately, accompanied by the raita and lime pickle.

Refried Beans with Tortillas

2 tbsp olive oil	25 g/1 oz Cheddar cheese, grated
1 onion, finely chopped	salt and pepper
3 garlic cloves, crushed	
1 green chilli, chopped	
400 g/14 oz canned red kidney beans, drained	**RELISH**
400 g/14 oz canned pinto beans, drained	4 spring onions, chopped
	1 red onion, chopped
2 tbsp chopped coriander	1 green chilli, chopped
150 ml /5 fl oz vegetable stock	1 tbsp garlic wine vinegar
8 wheat tortillas	1 tsp caster sugar
	1 tomato, chopped

❊ Heat the oil in a large frying pan. Add the onion and sauté for 3–5 minutes. Add the garlic and chilli and cook for 1 minute.

❊ Mash the beans with a potato masher and stir into the pan with the coriander.

❊ Stir in the stock and cook the beans, stirring, for 5 minutes until soft and pulpy.

❊ Place the tortillas on a baking tray and heat through in a warm oven for 1–2 minutes.

❊ Mix together the relish ingredients.

❊ Spoon the beans into a serving dish and top with the cheese. Season well. Roll the tortillas and serve with the relish and beans.

Cheese & Onion Tartlets

PASTRY
125 g/4$^{1}/_{2}$ oz plain flour
$^{1}/_{4}$ tsp salt
75 g/2$^{3}/_{4}$ oz butter, cut into small pieces
1–2 tbsp water

FILLING
1 egg, beaten
100 ml/3$^{1}/_{2}$ fl oz single cream
50 g/1$^{3}/_{4}$ oz Red Leicester cheese, grated
3 spring onions, finely chopped
salt
cayenne pepper

❊ To make the pastry, sift the flour and salt into a mixing bowl. Rub in the butter with your fingers until the mixture resembles breadcrumbs. Stir in the water and mix to form a dough.

❊ Roll out the pastry on a lightly floured surface. Using a 7.5-cm/3-inch biscuit cutter, stamp out 12 rounds from the pastry and line a patty tin.

❊ To make the filling, whisk together the egg, cream, cheese and spring onions in a mixing jug. Season to taste with salt and cayenne pepper.

❊ Pour the filling mixture into the pastry cases and bake in a preheated oven, 180°C/350°F/Gas Mark 4, for about 20–25 minutes, or until the filling is just set. Serve the tartlets warm or cold.

Tomato & Courgette Tartlets

olive oil, for oiling and brushing
2 x 48 x 28-cm/19 x 11-inch
sheets filo pastry
1 tbsp torn fresh basil leaves,
plus extra leaves to garnish
7–8 cherry tomatoes,
thinly sliced

1 courgette, thinly sliced
2 eggs, beaten
150 ml/5 fl oz skimmed or
semi-skimmed milk
pepper
selection of salads and boiled
new potatoes, to serve

❈ Preheat the oven to 190°C/375°F/Gas Mark 5. Lightly oil 4 x 12-cm/4½-inch individual loose-based tart tins.

❈ Working quickly so that the filo pastry does not dry out, cut each sheet into 6 equal-sized pieces measuring about 16 x 14 cm/6¼ x 5½ inches. Layer 3 pieces of pastry at a time in the 4 tart tins, lightly brushing between each layer with oil. Carefully press the pastry into the sides of the tins so that the corners of the pastry squares point upwards. Arrange the tins on a large baking tray.

❈ Sprinkle two-thirds of the torn basil leaves over the pastry bases and cover with overlapping slices of tomato and courgette. Beat the eggs with the milk in a bowl and season well with pepper. Divide the egg mixture evenly between the tins and sprinkle the remaining torn basil leaves over it.

❈ Bake in the preheated oven for 20–25 minutes, or until the egg mixture has set and the pastry is crisp and golden. Serve warm or cold, garnished with basil leaves and with the selection of salads and boiled new potatoes.

Mushroom Tartlets

500 g/1 lb 2 oz filo pastry,
thawed, if frozen
115 g/4 oz butter, melted
1 tbsp hazelnut oil
4 tbsp pine kernels
350 g/12 oz mixed mushrooms,
such as button, chestnut,
oyster and shiitake

2 tsp chopped fresh parsley
225 g/8 oz soft goat's cheese
salt and pepper
sprigs of fresh parsley, to
garnish
lettuce, tomatoes, cucumber
and spring onions, to serve

❈ Cut the sheets of filo pastry into pieces about 10 cm/ 4 inches square and use them to line 4 individual tart tins, brushing each layer of pastry with melted butter. Line the tins with foil or baking paper and baking beans. Bake in a preheated oven, 200°C/400°F/Gas Mark 6, for about 6–8 minutes or until light golden brown.

❈ Remove the tarts from the oven and carefully take out the foil or baking paper and baking beans. Reduce the oven temperature to 180°C/350°F/Gas Mark 4.

❈ Put any remaining butter into a large frying pan with the oil and fry the pine kernels until golden brown. Remove from the pan and drain on kitchen paper.

❈ Add the mushrooms to the pan and cook gently, stirring frequently, for about 4–5 minutes. Add the parsley and season to taste with salt and pepper.

❈ Spoon one-quarter of the goat's cheese into the base of each tart. Divide the mushrooms equally between them and sprinkle pine kernels over the top.

❈ Return the tarts to the oven for about 5 minutes to heat through and then serve, garnished with the sprigs of parsley. Serve with the lettuce, tomatoes, cucumber and spring onions.

Mushroom Brioches

6 small brioches
5 tbsp olive oil
1 garlic clove, crushed
2 shallots, finely chopped
350 g/12 oz chestnut
mushrooms, sliced

1 tsp Dijon mustard
2 tbsp dry sherry
1 tsp chopped fresh thyme
150 ml/5 fl oz double cream
salt and pepper

❋ Preheat the oven to 200°C/400°F/Gas Mark 6. Cut the tops off the brioches and scoop out the insides of each one to make a hollow case. Brush the insides of the brioches with 3 tablespoons of the oil. Place them on a baking tray and cook in the oven for 10–12 minutes, until crisp.

❋ Meanwhile, heat the remaining oil in a saucepan. Add the garlic and shallots and cook for 3 minutes, until soft. Add the mushrooms and cook gently for 5 minutes, stirring occasionally.

❋ Stir in the mustard, sherry, thyme, cream and salt and pepper to taste, then cook for a few minutes until the mixture is slightly reduced and thickened. Spoon into the brioche cases and serve immediately.

Potato & Spinach Triangles

2 tbsp butter, melted, plus
extra for greasing
225 g/8 oz waxy potatoes,
finely diced
500 g/1 lb 2 oz baby spinach
2 tbsp water
1 tomato, deseeded and
chopped

1/4 tsp chilli powder
1/2 tsp lemon juice
225 g/8 oz (8 sheets) filo pastry,
thawed, if frozen
salt and pepper
crisp salad, to serve

❋ Lightly grease a baking tray with a little butter.

❋ Bring a saucepan of lightly salted water to the boil and cook the potatoes for 10 minutes, or until cooked through. Drain thoroughly and place in a mixing bowl.

❋ Meanwhile, put the spinach in a large saucepan with the water, cover and cook, stirring occasionally, over a low heat for 2 minutes, until wilted. Drain the spinach thoroughly, squeezing out excess moisture, and add to the potatoes. Stir in the tomato, chilli powder and lemon juice. Season to taste with salt and pepper.

❋ Lightly brush 8 sheets of filo pastry with melted butter. Spread out four of the sheets and lay a second sheet on top of each. Cut them into 20 x 10-cm/8 x 4-inch rectangles.

❋ Spoon a portion of the potato and spinach mixture on to one end of each rectangle. Fold a corner of the pastry over the filling, fold the pointed end back over the pastry strip, then fold over the remaining pastry to form a triangle.

❋ Place the triangles on the baking tray and bake in a preheated oven, 190°C/375°F/Gas Mark 5, for 20 minutes, or until golden brown.

❋ Serve the potato and spinach filo triangles either warm or cold with the salad.

Tomato & Cheese Bruschetta

4 muffins
4 garlic cloves, crushed
2 tbsp butter
1 tbsp chopped basil
4 large, ripe tomatoes
1 tbsp tomato purée
8 stoned black olives, halved
55 g/2 oz mozzarella cheese,
sliced
salt and pepper
fresh basil leaves, to garnish

DRESSING
1 tbsp extra virgin olive oil
2 tsp lemon juice
1 tsp clear honey

❖ Cut the muffins in half to give 8 thick pieces. Toast the muffin halves under a hot grill for 2–3 minutes until golden.

❖ Beat the garlic, butter and basil together and spread on to each muffin half.

❖ Cut a cross shape at the top of each tomato. Plunge the tomatoes into a bowl of boiling water – this will make the skin easier to peel. After a few minutes, pick up each tomato with a fork and peel away the skin. Chop the tomato flesh and mix with the tomato purée and olives. Divide the mixture between the muffins.

❖ Mix the dressing ingredients and drizzle over each muffin. Arrange the mozzarella cheese on top and season to taste with salt and pepper.

❖ Return the muffins to the grill for 1–2 minutes until the cheese has melted. Serve, garnished with the basil leaves.

Crostini Alla Fiorentina

❉ SERVES 4 ❉

3 tbsp olive oil	2 tbsp chopped fresh parsley
1 onion, chopped	3–4 canned anchovy fillets,
1 celery stick, chopped	finely chopped
1 carrot, chopped	2 tbsp stock or water
1–2 garlic cloves, crushed	25–40 g/1–1$\frac{1}{2}$ oz butter
125 g/4$\frac{1}{2}$ oz chicken livers	1 tbsp capers
125 g/4$\frac{1}{2}$ oz calf's, lamb's or	salt and pepper
pig's liver	chopped fresh parsley,
150 ml/5 fl oz red wine	to garnish
1 tbsp tomato purée	toasted bread, to serve

❉ Heat the oil in a frying pan over a low heat. Add the onion, celery, carrot and garlic and cook for about 4–5 minutes, or until the onion is soft.

❉ Rinse the chicken livers and pat dry on kitchen paper. Rinse the liver and pat dry. Slice into strips. Add the liver to the pan and fry for a few minutes until the strips are well sealed on all sides.

❉ Add half the wine and cook until it has mostly evaporated. Add the rest of the wine, tomato purée, half the parsley, anchovy fillets, stock, a little salt and plenty of pepper.

❉ Cover the pan and simmer, stirring occasionally, for about 15–20 minutes or until tender and most of the liquid has been absorbed.

❉ Leave the mixture to cool slightly, then either coarsely mince or put into a food processor and process to a chunky purée.

❉ Return to the pan and add the butter, capers and remaining parsley. Heat through gently until the butter melts. Adjust the seasoning, if necessary, and spoon into a bowl. Garnish with the parsley and serve warm or cold, spread on the slices of toasted bread.

Vegetable-Topped Muffins

❉ SERVES 4 ❉

1 red onion, cut into 8 wedges	**SAUCE**
1 aubergine, halved and sliced	2 tbsp butter
1 yellow pepper, deseeded	1 tbsp plain flour
and sliced	150 ml/5 fl oz milk
1 courgette, sliced	5 tbsp vegetable stock
4 tbsp olive oil	85 g/3 oz Cheddar cheese,
1 tbsp garlic vinegar	grated
2 tbsp vermouth	1 tsp wholegrain mustard
2 garlic cloves, crushed	3 tbsp chopped fresh mixed
1 tbsp chopped fresh thyme	herbs
2 tsp light brown sugar	salt and pepper
4 muffins	

❉ Arrange the onion, aubergine, yellow pepper and courgette in a shallow non-metallic dish. Mix together the oil, vinegar, vermouth, garlic, thyme and sugar and pour over the vegetables, turning to coat well. Set aside to marinate for 1 hour.

❉ Transfer the vegetables to a baking tray. Roast in a preheated oven, 200°C/400°F/Gas Mark 6, for about 20–25 minutes or until the vegetables have softened.

❉ Meanwhile, make the sauce. Melt the butter in a small saucepan and stir in the flour. Cook, stirring constantly, for 1 minute, then remove from the heat. Gradually stir in the milk and stock and return the pan to the heat. Bring to the boil, stirring constantly until thickened. Stir in the cheese, mustard and mixed herbs and season well.

❉ Cut the muffins in half and toast under a preheated grill for 2–3 minutes until golden brown, then transfer to a serving plate. Spoon the roasted vegetables on to the muffins and pour the sauce over the top. Serve immediately.

Ciabatta Rolls

4 ciabatta rolls	**FILLING**
2 tbsp olive oil	1 red pepper
1 garlic clove, crushed	1 green pepper
	1 yellow pepper
	4 radishes, sliced
	1 bunch of watercress
	115 g/4 oz cream cheese

❊ Slice the ciabatta rolls in half. Heat the oil and garlic in a saucepan. Pour the garlic and oil mixture over the cut surfaces of the rolls and set aside.

❊ Halve and deseed the peppers and place, skin side up, on a grill rack. Cook under a preheated hot grill for 8–10 minutes until just beginning to char. Remove the peppers from the grill and place in a polythene bag. When cool enough to handle, peel and thinly slice them.

❊ Arrange the radish slices on 1 half of each roll with a few watercress leaves. Spoon the cream cheese on top. Pile the roasted peppers on top of the cream cheese and top with the other half of the roll. Serve immediately.

Scrambled Tofu

75 g/2¾ oz margarine	4 ciabatta rolls
450 g/1 lb marinated firm tofu	2 tbsp chopped mixed fresh
1 red onion, chopped	herbs
1 red pepper, deseeded and	salt and pepper
chopped	fresh herbs, to garnish

❊ Melt the margarine in a frying pan and crumble the tofu into the pan.

❊ Add the onion and pepper and cook for 3–4 minutes, stirring occasionally.

❊ Meanwhile, slice the ciabatta rolls in half horizontally and toast them under a hot grill for about 2–3 minutes, turning once, until lightly golden. Remove the toasts and transfer them to a warmed serving plate.

❊ Add the herbs to the tofu mixture, stir gently to combine and season with salt and pepper.

❊ Spoon the tofu mixture on to the toast and garnish with the fresh herbs. Serve at once.

Raisin Coleslaw & Tuna-Filled Pitta Breads

85 g/3 oz grated carrot
55 g/2 oz white cabbage, thinly sliced
85 g/3 oz low-fat natural yogurt
1 tsp cider vinegar
25 g/1 oz raisins
200 g/7 oz canned tuna steak in water, drained
2 tbsp pumpkin seeds
4 wholemeal or white pitta breads
pepper
4 dessert apples, to serve

❖ Mix the carrot, cabbage, yogurt, vinegar and raisins together in a bowl. Lightly stir in the tuna and half the pumpkin seeds and season to taste with pepper.

❖ Lightly toast the pitta breads under a preheated hot grill or in a toaster, then leave to cool slightly. Using a sharp knife, cut each pitta bread in half. Divide the filling evenly between the pitta breads and sprinkle the remaining pumpkin seeds over the filling.

❖ Core and cut the apples into wedges, then serve immediately with the filled pitta breads.

Chicken Wraps

150 g/5$\frac{1}{2}$ oz low-fat natural yogurt
1 tbsp wholegrain mustard
280 g/10 oz cooked skinless, boneless chicken breast, diced
140 g/5 oz Webbs lettuce, finely shredded
85 g/3 oz cucumber, thinly sliced
2 celery sticks, sliced
85 g/3 oz black seedless grapes, halved
8 x 20-cm/8-inch soft flour tortillas
pepper

❖ Combine the yogurt and mustard in a bowl and season to taste with pepper. Stir in the chicken and toss until thoroughly coated.

❖ Put the lettuce, cucumber, celery and grapes into a separate bowl and mix well.

❖ Fold a tortilla in half and in half again to make a cone that is easy to hold. Half-fill the tortilla pocket with the salad mixture and top with some of the chicken mixture. Repeat with the remaining tortillas, salad and chicken. Serve immediately.

Chicken Pan Bagna

1 large French stick
1 garlic clove
125 ml/4 fl oz olive oil
20 g/$\frac{3}{4}$ oz canned anchovy fillets
50 g/2 oz cold roast chicken
2 large tomatoes, sliced
8 large, stoned black olives, chopped
pepper

❖ Using a sharp bread knife, cut the French stick in half lengthways and open out.

❖ Cut the garlic clove in half and rub over the bread.

❖ Sprinkle the cut surface of the bread with the oil.

❖ Drain the anchovies and set aside.

❖ Thinly slice the chicken and arrange on top of the bread. Arrange the tomatoes and drained anchovies on top of the chicken.

❖ Scatter with the olives and plenty of pepper. Sandwich the loaf back together and wrap tightly in foil until required. Cut into slices to serve.

Mixed Bean Pâté

400 g/14 oz canned mixed beans, drained
2 tbsp olive oil
juice of 1 lemon
2 garlic cloves, crushed
1 tbsp chopped fresh coriander
2 spring onions, chopped
salt and pepper
shredded spring onions, to garnish

❈ Rinse the beans thoroughly under cold running water and drain well.

❈ Transfer the beans to a food processor or blender and process until smooth. Alternatively, place the beans in a bowl and mash thoroughly by hand with a fork or potato masher.

❈ Add the oil, lemon juice, garlic, coriander and chopped spring onions and blend until fairly smooth. Season to taste with salt and pepper.

❈ Transfer the pâté to a serving bowl, cover and chill in the refrigerator for at least 30 minutes.

❈ Garnish with the shredded spring onions and serve.

Olive & Anchovy Pâté

175 g/6 oz black olives, stoned and chopped
finely grated rind and juice of 1 lemon
50 g/1 1/2 oz unsalted butter
4 canned anchovy fillets, drained and rinsed
2 tbsp extra virgin olive oil
15 g/1/2 oz ground almonds
fresh herbs, to garnish
thin slices of toast, to serve

❈ If you are making the pâté by hand, chop the olives very finely and then mash them along with the lemon rind and juice and butter, using a fork or potato masher. Alternatively, place the olives, lemon rind and juice and butter in a food processor and blend until all of the ingredients are finely chopped.

❈ Chop the drained anchovies and add them to the olive and lemon mixture. Mash the pâté by hand or blend in a food processor for 20 seconds.

❈ Gradually whisk in the olive oil and stir in the ground almonds. Place the black olive pâté in a serving bowl. Leave the pâté to chill in the refrigerator for about 30 minutes. Serve the pâté accompanied by thin pieces of toast, if wished.

Lentil Pâté

1 tbsp vegetable oil, plus extra
for greasing
1 onion, chopped
2 garlic cloves, crushed
1 tsp garam masala
$\frac{1}{2}$ tsp ground coriander
850 ml/1$\frac{1}{2}$ pints
vegetable stock
175 g/6 oz red lentils
1 small egg
2 tbsp milk
2 tbsp mango chutney
2 tbsp chopped parsley
chopped parsley, to garnish
salad leaves and toast, to serve

❖ Heat the oil in a large saucepan and sauté the onion and garlic, stirring constantly, for 2–3 minutes. Add the spices and cook for a further 30 seconds.

❖ Stir in the stock and lentils and bring the mixture to the boil. Reduce the heat and simmer for 20 minutes, until the lentils are cooked and softened. Remove the pan from the heat and drain off any excess moisture.

❖ Put the mixture in a food processor and add the egg, milk, chutney and parsley. Process until smooth.

❖ Grease and line the base of a 450-g/1-lb loaf tin and spoon in the mixture, levelling the surface. Cover and cook in a preheated oven, 200°C/400°F/Gas Mark 6, for 40–45 minutes, or until firm to the touch.

❖ Cool in the tin for 20 minutes, then transfer to the refrigerator.

❖ Turn out the pâté on to a serving plate, slice and garnish with the chopped parsley. Serve with the salad leaves and toast.

Cheese & Bean Pâté

800 g/1 lb 12 oz canned borlotti
or cannellini beans, rinsed
and drained
350 g/12 oz ricotta cheese
2 garlic cloves, roughly
chopped
4 tbsp lemon juice
115 g/4 oz butter, melted
3 tbsp chopped fresh flat-leaf
parsley

salt and pepper
sunflower oil, for oiling
sprigs of fresh flat-leaf
parsley and lemon wedges,
to garnish
cheese-flavoured focaccia
fingers, to serve

❊ Place the beans, cheese, garlic, lemon juice and melted butter in a food processor and process to a smooth purée. Add the parsley and salt and pepper to taste and process again briefly to mix.

❊ Lightly oil a plain ring mould. Scrape the mixture into the mould and smooth the surface. Cover with clingfilm and chill in the refrigerator until set.

❊ To serve, turn out the pâté on to a serving dish and fill the centre with the sprigs of parsley. Garnish with the lemon wedges and serve with the cheese-flavoured focaccia fingers.

Mushroom & Chestnut Pâté

225 g/8 oz dried chestnuts,
soaked overnight
25 g/1 oz dried ceps
4 tbsp hot water
4 tbsp Marsala or medium
sherry
1 tbsp olive oil
675 g/1 lb 8 oz chestnut
mushrooms, sliced

1 tbsp balsamic vinegar
1 tbsp chopped fresh parsley
1 tbsp soy sauce
salt and pepper
thinly sliced radish, to garnish
wholemeal toast triangles or
crusty bread, to serve

❊ Drain the chestnuts, place them in a saucepan and add cold water to cover. Bring to the boil, then reduce the heat, cover and simmer for 45 minutes, or until tender. Drain well and set aside to cool.

❊ Meanwhile, place the ceps in a bowl with the hot water and 1 tablespoon of the Marsala. Set aside to soak for 20 minutes. Drain well, reserving the soaking liquid. Pat the mushrooms dry with kitchen paper. Strain the soaking liquid through a fine sieve or coffee filter paper.

❊ Heat the oil in a large heavy-based frying pan. Add the chestnut mushrooms and cook over a low heat, stirring occasionally, for 5 minutes, or until softened.

❊ Add the ceps, the reserved soaking liquid and the vinegar. Cook, stirring constantly, for 1 minute. Increase the heat and stir in the remaining Marsala. Cook, stirring frequently, for 3 minutes. Remove the pan from the heat.

❊ Transfer the chestnuts to a food processor and process to a purée. Add the mushroom mixture and the parsley and process to a smooth paste. Add the soy sauce and salt and pepper to taste and briefly process again to mix together.

❊ Scrape the pâté into a serving bowl, cover and chill in the refrigerator. Garnish with the radish slices before serving with the toast triangles.

Walnut, Egg & Cheese Pâté

❖ SERVES 2 ❖

1 celery stick
1–2 spring onions
25 g/1 oz shelled walnuts
1 tbsp chopped fresh parsley
1 tsp chopped fresh dill or
1/2 tsp dried dill
1 garlic clove, crushed
dash of Worcestershire sauce
115 g/4 oz cottage cheese

55 g/2 oz blue cheese, such as
Stilton or Danish Blue
1 hard-boiled egg
2 tbsp butter
salt and pepper
fresh herbs, to garnish
crackers, toast or crusty bread
and crudités, to serve

❖   Finely chop the celery, slice the spring onions very thinly and chop the walnuts evenly. Place in a bowl.

❖   Add the dill and garlic and Worcestershire sauce to taste and mix well, then stir the cottage cheese evenly through the mixture.

❖   Finely grate the blue cheese into the pâté mixture. Finely chop the hard-boiled egg and stir it into the mixture. Season to taste with salt and pepper.

❖   Melt the butter and stir it into the pâté, then spoon into 1 serving dish or 2 individual dishes. Smooth the top, but do not press down firmly. Chill until set.

❖   Garnish with the fresh herbs and serve with the crackers and crudités.

Hummus with Crudités

❖ SERVES 4 ❖

175 g/6 oz canned chickpeas,
drained and rinsed
125 ml/4 fl oz tahini
2 garlic cloves
125 ml/4 fl oz lemon juice
2–3 tbsp water
1 tbsp olive oil
1 tbsp chopped fresh parsley
pinch of cayenne pepper
salt

CRUDITÉS
4 carrots, cut into thin batons
4 celery sticks, cut into thin
batons
4 radishes
1/2 small cauliflower, cut into
florets
1 green pepper, deseeded and
cut into thin batons
1 red pepper, deseeded and cut
into thin batons

❖   Place the chickpeas, tahini, garlic and lemon juice in a blender or food processor and season to taste with salt.

❖   Process the ingredients, gradually adding water to the mixture as necessary until the consistency becomes smooth and creamy. Taste, and adjust the seasoning if necessary.

❖   Transfer the mixture to a serving bowl and make a hollow in the centre with the back of a spoon. Pour the oil into the hollow, then sprinkle the hummus with the parsley and the cayenne pepper.

❖   Arrange the crudités on a large serving platter and serve immediately with the hummus.

Crudités with Coriander Dip

CRUDITÉS
115 g/4 oz baby sweetcorn cobs
115 g/4 oz young asparagus
spears
1 head of chicory, leaves
separated
1 red pepper, deseeded and
sliced
1 orange pepper, deseeded and
sliced
8 radishes, topped and tailed

CORIANDER DIP
1 tbsp hot water
1 tsp saffron threads
225 g/8 oz fat-free
fromage frais
3 tbsp chopped fresh coriander
1 tbsp chopped garlic chives
salt and pepper
sprigs of fresh coriander,
to garnish

❊ Blanch the baby sweetcorn cobs and asparagus spears in separate saucepans of boiling water for 2 minutes. Drain, plunge into iced water and drain again.

❊ Arrange all the vegetables on a serving platter and cover with a damp tea towel while you make the dip.

❊ Put the hot water into a small bowl. Lightly crush the saffron threads between your fingers and add them to the bowl. Set aside for about 3–4 minutes, until the water has turned a rich golden colour.

❊ Beat the fromage frais until it becomes smooth, then beat in the infused saffron water. Stir in the chopped coriander and chives and season to taste with salt and pepper. Serve the dip immediately with the crudités, garnished with the sprigs of coriander.

Aubergine Spread

2 large aubergines
1 tomato
1 garlic clove, chopped
4 tbsp extra virgin olive oil
2 tbsp lemon juice
2 tbsp pine kernels, lightly toasted
2 spring onions, finely chopped
salt and pepper
ground cumin and 2 tbsp finely chopped fresh flat-leaf parsley, to garnish

✿ Using a fork or metal skewer, pierce the aubergines all over. Place them on a baking tray in a preheated oven, 230°C/450°F/Gas Mark 8, and roast for 20–25 minutes until they are very soft.

✿ Use a folded tea towel to remove the aubergines from the baking tray and set them aside to cool.

✿ Place the tomato in a heatproof bowl, pour boiling water over to cover and leave for 30 seconds. Drain, then plunge into cold water to prevent it from cooking. Peel the tomato, then cut in half and scoop out the seeds with a teaspoon. Finely dice the flesh and set aside.

✿ Cut the cooled aubergines in half lengthways. Scoop out the flesh with a spoon and transfer to a food processor. Add the garlic, olive oil, lemon juice and pine kernels and season to taste with salt and pepper. Process until smooth. Alternatively, mash by hand.

✿ Scrape the mixture into a bowl and stir in the spring onions and diced tomato. Cover with clingfilm and chill for 30 minutes before serving.

✿ Garnish the dip with a pinch of the ground cumin and the parsley, then serve.

Authentic Guacamole

1 ripe tomato
2 limes
2–3 ripe small to medium avocados, or
1–2 large ones
$1/4$–$1/2$ onion, finely chopped
pinch of ground cumin
pinch of mild chilli powder
$1/2$–1 fresh green chilli, such as jalapeño or serrano, deseeded and finely chopped
1 tbsp finely chopped fresh coriander leaves, plus extra to garnish
salt (optional)
tortilla chips, to serve

✿ Place the tomatoes in a heatproof bowl, pour boiling water over to cover and leave for 30 seconds. Drain and plunge into cold water. Peel off the skins. Cut the tomatoes in half, deseed and chop the flesh.

✿ Squeeze the juice from the limes into a small bowl. Cut 1 avocado in half around the stone. Twist the 2 halves apart in opposite directions, then remove the stone with a knife. Carefully peel off the skin, dice the flesh and toss in the bowl of lime juice to prevent the flesh discolouring. Repeat with the remaining avocados. Coarsely mash the avocados with a fork.

✿ Add the onion, tomato, cumin, chilli powder, chillies and coriander to the avocados. Add salt to taste. If using as a dip for tortilla chips, do not add salt.

✿ To serve the guacamole, transfer to a serving dish, garnish with coriander and serve with the tortilla chips.

Spicy Potato Chips

❋ **SERVES 4** ❋

4 large waxy potatoes	$1/2$ tsp chilli powder
2 sweet potatoes	1 tsp garam masala
4 tbsp butter, melted	salt

❋ Cut the potatoes and sweet potatoes into slices about 1 cm/$1/2$ inch thick, then cut them into chip shapes.

❋ Place the potatoes in a large bowl of cold salted water. Set aside to soak for 20 minutes.

❋ Remove the potato slices with a slotted spoon and drain thoroughly. Pat with kitchen paper until they are completely dry.

❋ Pour the melted butter on to a baking tray. Transfer the potato slices to the baking tray.

❋ Sprinkle with the chilli powder, garam masala and salt, turning the potato slices to coat them with the mixture.

❋ Cook the chips in a preheated oven, 200°C/400°F/Gas Mark 6, turning frequently, for 40 minutes, until browned and cooked through.

❋ Drain the chips on kitchen paper to remove the excess oil and serve.

Chilli Polenta Crisps

❋ **SERVES 4** ❋

350 g/12 oz instant polenta	150 ml/5 fl oz soured cream
2 tsp chilli powder	1 tbsp chopped parsley
1 tbsp olive oil or melted butter	salt and pepper

❋ Place 1.5 litres/$2^3/4$ pints of water in a saucepan and bring to the boil. Add 2 teaspoons of salt and then add the polenta in a steady stream, stirring constantly.

❋ Reduce the heat slightly and continue stirring for about 5 minutes. It is essential to stir the polenta, otherwise it will stick and burn. The polenta should have a thick consistency at this point and should be stiff enough to hold the spoon upright in the pan.

❋ Add the chilli powder to the polenta mixture and stir well. Season to taste with a little salt and pepper.

❋ Spread out the polenta on a board or baking tray to about 4 cm/$1^1/2$ inches thick. Leave to cool and set.

❋ Cut the cooled polenta mixture into thin wedges.

❋ Heat the oil in a pan. Add the polenta wedges and fry for 3–4 minutes on each side or until golden and crispy. Alternatively, brush with melted butter and grill for 6–7 minutes until golden. Drain the cooked polenta on paper towels.

❋ Mix the soured cream with the parsley and place in a bowl.

❋ Serve the polenta chips with the soured cream and parsley dip.

Cheese & Onion Potato Patties

900 g/2 lb potatoes
1 onion, grated
50 g/1¾ oz Gruyère cheese,
grated
2 tbsp chopped fresh parsley
1 tbsp olive oil
2 tbsp butter
salt and pepper
1 spring onion, shredded and
1 small tomato, quartered,
to garnish

❖ Bring a saucepan of lightly salted water to the boil, parboil the potatoes for 10 minutes and leave to cool. Peel the potatoes and grate with a coarse grater. Place the grated potatoes in a large mixing bowl.

❖ Stir in the onion, cheese and parsley. Season well with salt and pepper. Divide the potato mixture into 4 portions of equal size and form them into cakes.

❖ Heat half of the olive oil and butter in a frying pan and cook two of the patties over a high heat for 1 minute, then reduce the heat and cook for 5 minutes, until they are golden underneath. Turn them over and cook for a further 5 minutes. Keep warm.

❖ Repeat with the other half of the oil and butter to cook the remaining 2 patties. Transfer to warmed individual serving plates, garnish with the spring onions and tomatoes and serve immediately.

Golden Vegetable Cakes

❊ SERVES 4 ❊

1 orange pepper
1 red pepper
1 yellow pepper
3 tbsp olive oil
2 tbsp red wine vinegar
1 tsp French mustard
1 tsp clear honey
salt and pepper
sprigs of fresh flat-leaf parsley,
to garnish
green vegetables, to serve

CAKES
225 g/8 oz potatoes, coarsely grated
225 g/8 oz carrots, coarsely grated
350 g/12 oz celeriac, coarsely grated
1 garlic clove, crushed
1 tbsp lemon juice
25 g/1 oz butter, melted
1 egg, beaten
1 tbsp vegetable oil

❊ Place the peppers on a baking tray and bake in a preheated oven, 190°C/375°F/Gas Mark 5, for 35 minutes, turning after 20 minutes. Cover with a tea towel and leave to cool for 10 minutes.

❊ Peel the peppers, then cut in half and discard the seeds. Thinly slice the flesh into strips and place in a shallow dish.

❊ Put the oil, vinegar, mustard, honey and seasoning in a small screw-top jar and shake well to mix. Pour over the pepper strips, mix well and marinate for 2 hours.

❊ To make the vegetable cakes, put the potatoes, carrots and celeriac in a mixing bowl and toss in the garlic and lemon juice.   Mix in the butter and the egg. Season to taste with salt and pepper. Divide the mixture into 8 and pile on to 2 baking trays lined with baking paper, forming each into a 10-cm/4-inch round. Brush with oil.

❊ Bake in a preheated oven, 220°C/425°F/Gas Mark 7, for 30–35 minutes, until the cakes are crisp around the edges and golden. Carefully transfer to a warmed serving dish. Heat the peppers and the marinade for 2–3 minutes until warmed through. Spoon the peppers over the cakes, garnish with the sprigs of parsley and serve immediately with the green vegetables.

Potato Skins with Guacamole

❊ SERVES 4 ❊

4 x 225g/8 oz baking potatoes
2 tsp olive oil
coarse sea salt and pepper
chopped fresh chives,
to garnish

GUACAMOLE DIP
175 g/6 oz ripe avocado
1 tbsp lemon juice

2 ripe, firm tomatoes. finely chopped
1 tsp grated lemon rind
100 g/3 1/2 oz low-fat soft cheese with herbs and garlic
4 spring onions, finely chopped
a few drops of Tabasco sauce
salt and pepper

❊ Bake the potatoes in a preheated oven, 200°C/400°F/Gas Mark 6, for 1 1/4 hours. Remove from the oven and allow to cool for 30 minutes. Reset the oven to 220°C/425°F/Gas Mark 7.

❊ Halve the potatoes lengthways and scoop out 2 tablespoons of the flesh. Slice in half again. Place on a baking tray and brush the flesh side lightly with the oil. Sprinkle with salt and pepper. Bake for a further 25 minutes until golden and crisp.

❊ To make the guacamole dip, mash the avocado with the lemon juice. Add the remaining ingredients and mix.

❊ Drain the potato skins on kitchen paper and transfer to a warmed serving platter. Garnish with the chives. Pile the dip into a serving bowl and serve with the potato skins.

Cheese & Potato Slices

900 g/2 lb waxy potatoes, unpeeled and thickly sliced	1$\frac{1}{2}$ tsp chilli powder
70 g/2$\frac{1}{2}$ oz fresh white breadcrumbs	2 eggs, beaten
	oil, for deep frying
40 g/1$\frac{1}{2}$ oz Parmesan cheese, freshly grated	chilli powder, for dusting (optional)

❊ Bring a saucepan of lightly salted water to the boil and cook the potatoes for about 10–15 minutes, or until just tender. Drain thoroughly.

❊ Mix the breadcrumbs, cheese and chilli powder together in a bowl, then transfer to a shallow dish. Pour the beaten eggs into a separate shallow dish.

❊ Dip the potato slices in the beaten egg and then roll them in the breadcrumbs to coat completely.

❊ Heat the oil in a large saucepan or deep-fat fryer to 180°C/350°F or until a cube of bread browns in 30 seconds. Cook the cheese and potato slices, in several batches, for 4–5 minutes or until they turn a golden brown colour.

❊ Remove the cheese and potato slices from the oil with a slotted spoon and drain thoroughly on kitchen paper. Keep the cheese and potato slices warm while you cook the remaining batches.

❊ Transfer the cheese and potato slices to warmed individual serving plates. Dust lightly with the chilli powder, if using, and serve immediately.

Cottage Potatoes

4 baking potatoes	1 tbsp tequila
2 tsp sun-dried tomato purée	1 tbsp finely chopped fresh coriander
$\frac{1}{2}$ tsp ground coriander	225 g/8 oz low-fat cottage cheese
1 tbsp olive oil	
3–4 spring onions, finely chopped	salt and pepper
1–2 fresh green chillies, deseeded and finely chopped	lime wedges and sprigs of fresh coriander, to garnish

❊ Cut a cross in the middle of each potato and prick the skins with a fork. Wrap the potatoes individually in foil and bake in a preheated oven, 200°C/400°F/Gas Mark 6, for 1 hour, or until soft and cooked through.

❊ Meanwhile, combine the sun-dried tomato purée and ground coriander in a small bowl. Season to taste with salt and pepper. Just before the potatoes are ready, heat the oil in a small saucepan and add the spring onions and chillies. Cook, stirring occasionally, for 2–3 minutes until softened. Stir in the sun-dried tomato paste mixture and tequila and cook for a further minute. Remove from the heat and stir in the chopped coriander.

❊ Place the cottage cheese in a bowl and add the tomato mixture. Stir in to blend thoroughly.

❊ Unwrap the potatoes and squeeze gently to open out the cut side. Divide the cottage cheese equally between the potatoes and serve, garnished with the lime wedges and sprigs of coriander.

Chicken & Cheese Jackets

4 large baking potatoes
225 g/8 oz cooked, skinless,
boneless chicken breasts
4 spring onions
250 g/9 oz low-fat soft cheese
or Quark
pepper
coleslaw, green salad or mixed
salad, to serve

❄ Scrub the potatoes and pat dry with absorbent kitchen paper.

❄ Prick the potatoes all over with a fork. Bake in a preheated oven, 200°C/400°F/
Gas Mark 6, for about 50 minutes until tender.

❄ Meanwhile, using a sharp knife, dice the chicken breasts and trim and thickly slice the
spring onions. Place the chicken and spring onions in a bowl.

❄ Add the low-fat soft cheese or Quark to the bowl, stir well to combine and coat the
chicken.

❄ Cut a cross through the top of each potato and pull slightly apart. Spoon the chicken
filling into the potatoes and sprinkle with pepper.

❄ Serve the chicken and cheese jackets immediately with the coleslaw.

Hash Browns

500 g/1 lb 2 oz waxy potatoes	**SAUCE**
1 carrot, diced	300 ml/10 fl oz passata
1 celery stick, diced	2 tbsp chopped fresh coriander
55 g/2 oz button mushrooms, diced	1 tbsp Worcestershire sauce
1 onion, diced	1/2 tsp chilli powder
2 garlic cloves, crushed	2 tsp brown sugar
25 g/1 oz frozen peas, thawed	2 tsp American mustard
55 g/2 oz freshly grated Parmesan cheese	5 tbsp vegetable stock
4 tbsp vegetable oil	
2 tbsp butter	
salt and pepper	

❊ Bring a saucepan of lightly salted water to the boil and cook the potatoes for 10 minutes. Drain and set aside to cool. Meanwhile, bring a separate saucepan of lightly salted water to the boil cook the carrot for 5 minutes.

❊ When the potatoes are cool enough to handle, grate them with a coarse grater.

❊ Drain the carrot and add it to the grated potatoes, with the celery, mushrooms, onion, garlic, peas and cheese. Season to taste with salt and pepper.

❊ Put all of the sauce ingredients in a small saucepan and bring to the boil. Reduce the heat to low and simmer for 15 minutes.

❊ Divide the potato mixture into 8 equal portions and shape into flattened rectangles with your hands.

❊ Heat the oil and butter in a frying pan and cook the hash browns in batches over a low heat for 4–5 minutes on each side until crisp and golden brown.

❊ Transfer the hash browns to a serving plate and serve immediately with the tomato sauce.

Filled Baked Sweet Potatoes

4 red-fleshed sweet potatoes, about 250 g/9 oz each	1 tbsp olive oil
115 g/4 oz frozen broad beans	1 tbsp balsamic vinegar
115 g/4 oz frozen sweetcorn kernels	140 g/5 oz tomatoes
115 g/4 oz fine long French beans	2 tbsp torn fresh basil leaves, plus extra leaves, to garnish
	pepper

❊ Preheat the oven to 190°C/375°F/Gas Mark 5. Scrub the sweet potatoes and pierce the skin of each with a sharp knife several times. Arrange on a baking tray and bake in the preheated oven for 1–1 1/4 hours, or until soft and tender when pierced with the point of a sharp knife. Keep warm.

❊ When the potatoes are cooked, bring a saucepan of water to the boil, add the broad beans and sweetcorn and return to the boil. Reduce the heat, cover and simmer for 5 minutes. Top and tail the French beans, cut in half and add to the pan. Return to the boil, then reduce the heat, cover and simmer for 3 minutes, or until the French beans are just tender.

❊ Blend the oil with the vinegar in a small bowl and season to taste with pepper. Drain the sweetcorn and beans, return to the pan, add the tomatoes and pour over the dressing. Add the torn basil leaves and mix well.

❊ Remove the sweet potatoes from the oven, cut in half lengthways and open up. Divide the sweetcorn and bean filling between the potatoes and serve immediately, garnished with basil leaves.

Jacket Potatoes with Pesto

❄ **SERVES 4** ❄

4 baking potatoes, about	3 tbsp chopped fresh basil
225 g/8 oz each	salt and pepper
150 ml/5 fl oz double cream	2 tbsp pine kernels
75 ml/3 fl oz vegetable stock	2 tbsp grated Parmesan
1 tbsp lemon juice	cheese
2 garlic cloves, crushed	

❄ Scrub the potatoes well and prick the skins with a fork. Rub a little salt into the skins and place on a baking tray.

❄ Cook in a preheated oven, 190°C/375°F/Gas Mark 5, for 1 hour or until the potatoes are cooked through and the skins are crisp.

❄ Remove the potatoes from the oven and cut them in half lengthways. Using a spoon, scoop the potato flesh into a mixing bowl, leaving a thin shell of potato inside the skins. Mash the potato flesh with a fork.

❄ Meanwhile, mix the cream and stock in a saucepan and simmer over a low heat for about 8–10 minutes or until reduced by half.

❄ Stir in the lemon juice, garlic and basil and season to taste with salt and pepper. Stir the mixture into the mashed potato flesh, together with the pine kernels.

❄ Spoon the mixture back into the potato shells and sprinkle the cheese on top. Return the potatoes to the oven for 10 minutes or until the cheese has browned, and serve.

Jacket Potatoes with Beans

❄ **SERVES 6** ❄

1.8 kg/4 lb potatoes	400 g/14 oz canned red kidney
4 tbsp ghee or vegetable oil	beans, drained and rinsed
1 large onion, chopped	1 tbsp lemon juice
2 garlic cloves, crushed	2 tbsp tomato purée
1 tsp turmeric	150 ml/5 fl oz water
1 tbsp cumin seeds	2 tbsp chopped fresh mint or
2 tbsp mild or medium curry	coriander
paste	salt and pepper
350 g/12 oz cherry tomatoes	
400 g/14 oz canned black-eyed	
beans, drained and rinsed	

❄ Scrub the potatoes and prick several times with a fork. Place in a preheated oven, 180°C/350°F/Gas Mark 4, and cook for 1–1¼ hours, or until the potatoes feel soft when gently squeezed.

❄ About 20 minutes before the end of cooking time, prepare the topping. Heat the ghee in a saucepan, add the onion and cook over a low heat, stirring frequently, for 5 minutes. Add the garlic, turmeric, cumin seeds and curry paste and cook gently for 1 minute.

❄ Stir in the tomatoes, black-eyed beans and red kidney beans, lemon juice, tomato purée, water and mint. Season to taste with salt and pepper, then cover and simmer over a low heat, stirring frequently, for 10 minutes.

❄ When the potatoes are cooked, cut them in half and mash the flesh lightly with a fork. Spoon the prepared bean mixture on top, place on warmed serving plates and serve immediately.

Paprika Potatoes

4 baking potatoes
125 ml/4 fl oz vegetable stock
1 onion, finely chopped
1 garlic clove, finely chopped
125 ml/4 fl oz natural yogurt
2 tsp paprika
salt and pepper

❊ Prick the potatoes with a fork and bake in a preheated oven, 200°C/400°F/Gas Mark 6, for about 1 hour, until tender.

❊ Just before the potatoes are ready, pour the stock into a saucepan and add the onion and garlic. Bring to the boil and simmer for 5 minutes.

❊ Remove the potatoes from the oven and cut a lengthways slice from the top of each. Do not switch off the oven. Using a teaspoon, carefully scoop out the flesh, leaving a shell. Stir the potato flesh into the onion mixture, then add half the yogurt and 1$^1/_2$ teaspoons of the paprika and season to taste with salt and pepper. Mix well and push through a sieve with the back of a wooden spoon.

❊ Spoon the potato mixture into the potato shells and return to the oven for 10 minutes, until heated through. Top the potatoes with the remaining yogurt, sprinkle over the remaining paprika and serve immediately.

Sweet Potato & Leek Patties

	GINGER SAUCE
900 g/2 lb sweet potatoes	2 tbsp white wine vinegar
4 tsp sunflower oil	2 tsp caster sugar
2 leeks, trimmed and finely chopped	1 red chilli, deseeded and chopped
1 garlic clove, crushed	2.5-cm/1-inch piece of fresh root ginger, cut into thin strips
2 tsp finely chopped fresh root ginger	2 tbsp ginger wine
200 g/7 oz canned sweetcorn, drained	4 tbsp vegetable stock
2 tbsp low-fat natural fromage frais	1 tsp cornflour
6 tbsp wholemeal flour	
salt and pepper	
lettuce leaves and shredded spring onions, to serve	

❄ Bring a saucepan of lightly salted water to the boil. Meanwhile, peel the potatoes, cut them into thick cubes and then cook them for 10–15 minutes, drain well and mash. Leave to cool.

❄ Heat 2 teaspoons of the oil and fry the leeks, garlic and ginger for 2–3 minutes. Stir into the potato with the sweetcorn, seasoning and fromage frais. Form into 8 patties and toss in the flour. Chill for 30 minutes. Place the patties on a preheated grill rack and lightly brush with oil. Grill the patties for 5 minutes, then turn over, brush with oil and grill for a further 5 minutes.

❄ To make the sauce, place the vinegar, sugar, chilli and ginger in a pan and simmer for 5 minutes. Stir in the wine. Blend the stock and cornflour and add to the sauce, stirring, until thickened. Serve the patties with the lettuce and spring onions, and the sauce.

Spinach Crêpes

	FILLING
90 g/3 oz wholemeal flour	1 tbsp vegetable oil
1 egg	3 spring onions, thinly sliced
150 ml/5 fl oz natural yogurt	225 g/8 oz ricotta cheese
3 tbsp water	4 tbsp natural yogurt
1 tbsp vegetable oil, plus extra for brushing	85 g/3 oz Gruyère cheese, grated
200 g/7 oz frozen leaf spinach, thawed and puréed	1 egg, lightly beaten
pinch of grated nutmeg	115 g/4 oz unsalted cashew nuts
salt and pepper	2 tbsp chopped fresh parsley
lemon wedges and sprigs of fresh coriander, to garnish	pinch of cayenne pepper

❄ Sift the flour and a pinch of salt into a bowl and tip in any bran left in the sieve. Whisk the egg with the yogurt, water and oil. Gradually pour it on to the flour, beating constantly. Stir in the spinach and season with pepper and nutmeg.

❄ To make the filling, heat the oil in a pan and fry the spring onions until translucent. Remove with a slotted spoon and drain on kitchen paper. Beat the ricotta cheese with the yogurt and half the Gruyère cheese. Beat in the egg and stir in the spring onions, the cashew nuts and the parsley. Season with salt and cayenne pepper to taste.

❄ Brush a small heavy frying pan with oil and heat. Pour in 3–4 tablespoons of the batter and tilt the pan so that it covers the base. Cook for 3 minutes until bubbles appear in the centre. Turn and cook the other side for 2 minutes until lightly browned. Slide on to a warmed plate and keep warm while you cook the remainder. The batter should make 8–12 crêpes.

❄ Spread a little filling over each crêpe and fold in half and then half again. Spoon the remaining filling into the opening.

❄ Grease a shallow, ovenproof dish and arrange the crêpes in a single layer. Sprinkle over the remaining cheese and cook in a preheated oven, 180°C/350°F/Gas Mark 4, for about 15 minutes. Serve hot, garnished with the lemon wedges and coriander.

Macaroni & Corn Crêpes

❄ SERVES 4 ❄

2 sweetcorn cobs	25 g/1 oz plain flour
4 tbsp butter	4 egg yolks
115 g/4 oz red peppers,	4 tbsp olive oil
deseeded and finely diced	salt and pepper
285 g/10 oz dried short-cut	sautéed oyster mushrooms
macaroni	and leeks, to serve
150 ml/5 fl oz double cream	

❄ Bring a saucepan of water to the boil, add the sweetcorn and cook for about 8 minutes. Drain thoroughly and refresh under cold running water for 3 minutes. Carefully cut away the kernels on to kitchen paper and set aside to dry.

❄ Melt 2 tablespoons of the butter in a frying pan. Add the peppers and cook over a low heat for 4 minutes. Drain and pat dry with kitchen paper.

❄ Bring a large saucepan of lightly salted water to the boil. Add the macaroni, bring back to the boil and cook for about 12 minutes or until tender, but still firm to the bite. Drain the macaroni thoroughly and set aside to cool in cold water until required.

❄ Beat the cream with the flour, a pinch of salt and the egg yolks in a bowl until smooth. Add the sweetcorn and peppers. Drain the macaroni and then toss into the corn and cream mixture. Season with pepper to taste.

❄ Heat the remaining butter with the oil in a large frying pan. Drop spoonfuls of the mixture into the pan and press down to form flat crêpes. Fry until golden on both sides. Drain on absorbent kitchen paper. Serve immediately with the oyster mushrooms and leeks.

Corn & Red Pepper Crêpes

❄ SERVES 4 ❄

150 g/5$\frac{1}{2}$ oz frozen sweetcorn	1 small red pepper, deseeded
kernels, thawed	and very finely chopped
4 tbsp polenta	1 small egg yolk
4 tbsp plain flour	$\frac{1}{2}$ tsp caster sugar
1 tbsp very finely chopped fresh	2 egg whites
parsley	1 tbsp olive oil

❄ Process half the sweetcorn in a food processor until finely chopped. Scrape into a bowl and add the remaining sweetcorn, polenta, flour, parsley and chopped pepper. Beat the egg yolk with the sugar in a small bowl, then add it to the sweetcorn mixture and stir thoroughly.

❄ Beat the egg whites in a clean bowl until they stand in soft peaks. Gently fold half the egg whites into the sweetcorn mixture, then fold in the remaining egg whites.

❄ Heat half the oil in a heavy frying pan. Drop spoonfuls of the batter into the pan, spacing them out well, and cook for 3 minutes, until the undersides are golden brown. Flip over the crêpes carefully with a spatula and cook the other sides for about 3 minutes until golden brown. Transfer the crêpes to a plate and keep warm while you cook the remaining batter, adding more oil to the pan if necessary. Serve immediately.

Chinese Vegetable Pancakes

1 tbsp vegetable oil
1 garlic clove, crushed
2.5-cm/1-inch piece of root
ginger, grated
1 bunch spring onions, trimmed
and shredded lengthways
100 g/3½ oz mangetout,
topped, tailed and shredded
225 g/8 oz tofu, drained and cut
into 1-cm/½-inch pieces
2 tbsp dark soy sauce, plus
extra to serve
2 tbsp hoisin sauce, plus extra
to serve
60 g/2 oz canned bamboo
shoots, drained
60 g/2 oz canned water
chestnuts, drained and sliced
100 g/3½ oz beansprouts
1 small red chilli, deseeded and
thinly sliced
1 small bunch fresh chives
12 soft Chinese pancakes

TO SERVE
shredded Chinese leaves
1 cucumber, sliced
strips of red chilli

❖ Heat the oil in a non-stick wok or a large frying pan and stir-fry the garlic and ginger for 1 minute.

❖ Add the spring onions, mangetout, tofu, soy sauce and hoisin sauce. Stir-fry for 2 minutes.

❖ Add the bamboo shoots, water chestnuts, beansprouts and sliced red chilli to the pan.

❖ Stir-fry gently for a further 2 minutes until the vegetables are just tender.

❖ Snip the chives into 2.5-cm/1-inch lengths and stir into the mixture.

❖ Heat the pancakes according to the packet instructions and keep warm.

❖ Divide the vegetables and tofu between the pancakes. Roll up and serve with the Chinese leaves, cucumber, chilli and extra sauce for dipping.

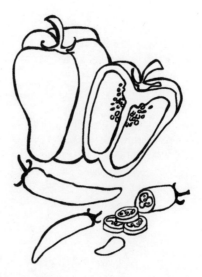

Soufflé Omelette

175 g/6 oz cherry tomatoes
225 g/8 oz mixed mushrooms,
    such as button, chestnut,
    shiitake and oyster
4 tbsp vegetable stock
small bunch of fresh thyme
4 eggs, separated

125 ml/4 fl oz water
4 egg whites
4 tsp olive oil
25 g/1 oz rocket
salt and pepper
sprigs of fresh thyme, to
    garnish

❊ Halve the tomatoes and place them in a saucepan. Wipe the mushrooms with kitchen paper, trim if necessary, and slice if large. Place the mushrooms in the pan with the tomatoes.

❊ Add the stock and thyme, still tied together, to the pan. Bring to the boil, cover and simmer for 5–6 minutes until tender. Drain, remove the thyme and discard. Keep the mixture warm.

❊ Meanwhile, separate the eggs and whisk the egg yolks with the water until foamy. In a clean, grease-free bowl, whisk the 8 egg whites until stiff and dry.

❊ Spoon the egg yolk mixture into the egg whites and, using a metal spoon, fold together until well mixed. Take care not to knock out too much of the air.

❊ For each omelette, brush a small omelette pan with 1 teaspoon of the oil and heat until hot. Pour in a quarter of the egg mixture and cook for 4–5 minutes until the mixture has set.

❊ Finish cooking the omelette under a preheated medium grill for 2–3 minutes.

❊ Transfer the omelette to a warmed serving plate. Fill the omelette with a few rocket leaves and a quarter of the mushroom and tomato mixture. Flip over the top of the omelette, garnish with the sprigs of thyme and serve.

Spanish Potato Omelette

125 ml/4 fl oz olive oil
675 g/1 lb 8 oz potatoes, sliced
1 large onion, sliced

1 large garlic clove, crushed
6 large eggs
salt and pepper

❊ Heat a 25-cm/10-inch frying pan, preferably non-stick, over a high heat. Pour in the oil and heat. Reduce the heat, add the potatoes, onion and garlic and cook for 15–20 minutes, stirring frequently, until the potatoes are tender.

❊ Beat the eggs together in a large bowl and season generously with salt and pepper. Using a slotted spoon, transfer the potatoes and onion to the bowl of eggs. Pour the excess oil left in the pan into a heatproof jug, then scrape off the crusty bits from the base of the pan.

❊ Reheat the pan. Add about 2 tablespoons of the oil reserved in the jug. Pour in the potato mixture, smoothing the vegetables into an even layer. Cook for about 5 minutes, shaking the pan occasionally, or until the base of the omelette is set.

❊ Shake the pan and use a spatula to loosen the side of the omelette. Place a large plate face down over the pan. Carefully invert the omelette onto the plate.

❊ If you are not using a non-stick pan, add 1 tablespoon of the reserved oil to the pan and swirl around. Gently slide the omelette back into the pan, cooked side up. Use the spatula to tuck down the edge. Continue cooking over a medium heat for 3–5 minutes until set.

❊ Remove the pan from the heat and slide the omelette on to a serving plate. Leave to cool for at least 5 minutes before cutting. Serve hot, warm or at room temperature.

Indian-Style Omelette

❊ **SERVES 4** ❊

1 small onion, very finely chopped
2 fresh green chillies, deseeded and finely chopped
2 tbsp finely chopped fresh coriander leaves

4 eggs
1 tsp salt
2 tbsp vegetable oil
sprigs of fresh basil, to garnish
toasted bread or crisp green salad, to serve

❊ Place the onion, chillies and coriander in a large mixing bowl and mix together.

❊ Whisk the eggs in a separate bowl. Stir the onion mixture into the eggs. Add the salt and whisk again.

❊ Heat 1 tablespoon of the oil in a large heavy-based frying pan over a medium heat. Place a ladleful of the omelette batter in the pan. Cook the omelette, turning once and pressing down with a flat spoon to make sure that the egg is cooked right through, until the omelette is just firm and golden brown.

❊ Repeat the same process with the remaining batter. Set the omelettes aside as you make them and keep warm while you make the remaining batches.

❊ Serve the omelettes hot, garnished with the sprigs of basil and accompanied by the toasted bread.

Thai-Style Omelette

❊ **SERVES 4** ❊

225 g/8 oz white crabmeat, thawed, if frozen
3 spring onions, finely chopped
1 tbsp chopped fresh coriander
1 tbsp chopped fresh chives
pinch of cayenne pepper
2 tbsp vegetable oil
2 garlic cloves, crushed
1 tsp freshly grated root ginger
1 fresh red chilli, deseeded and finely chopped

2 tbsp lime juice
2 lime leaves, shredded
2 tsp sugar
2 tsp Thai fish sauce
3 eggs
4 tbsp coconut cream
1 tsp salt
finely chopped spring onion, to garnish

❊ Put the crabmeat into a bowl and check for any small pieces of shell. Add the spring onions, coriander, chives and cayenne pepper and set aside.

❊ Heat 1 tablespoon of the vegetable oil in a small saucepan and stir-fry the garlic, ginger and chilli for 30 seconds. Add the lime juice, lime leaves, sugar and fish sauce. Simmer for 3–4 minutes until reduced. Remove from the heat and set aside to cool, then add to the crab mixture.

❊ Lightly beat the eggs with the coconut cream and salt. Heat the remaining oil in a frying pan over a medium heat. Add the egg mixture and, as it sets on the bottom, carefully pull in the edges towards the centre, allowing unset egg to run underneath.

❊ When the egg is nearly set, spoon the crab mixture down the centre. Cook for a further 1–2 minutes to finish cooking the egg, then turn the omelette out of the pan on to a serving dish. Set aside to cool, then chill in the refrigerator for 2–3 hours or overnight. Cut into 4 pieces, garnish with the spring onion and serve.

Pasta Omelette

4 tbsp olive oil
1 small onion, chopped
1 fennel bulb, thinly sliced
115 g/4 oz potato, diced
1 garlic clove, chopped
4 eggs
1 tbsp chopped fresh flat-leaf parsley
pinch of chilli powder
100 g/3 1/2 oz cooked short pasta
2 tbsp stuffed green olives, halved
salt and pepper
sprigs of fresh marjoram, to garnish
tomato salad, to serve

❈ Heat half of the oil in a heavy-based frying pan over a low heat. Add the onion, fennel and potato and cook, stirring occasionally, for 8–10 minutes, until the potato is just tender.

❈ Stir in the garlic and cook for 1 minute. Remove the pan from the heat, transfer the vegetables to a plate and set aside.

❈ Beat the eggs until they are frothy. Stir in the parsley and season with salt and pepper and a pinch of chilli powder.

❈ Heat 1 tablespoon of the remaining oil in a clean frying pan. Add half of the egg mixture to the pan, then add the cooked vegetables, pasta and half the olives. Pour in the remaining egg mixture and cook until the sides begin to set.

❈ Lift up the edges of the omelette with a fish slice to allow the uncooked egg to spread underneath. Cook, shaking the pan occasionally, until the underside is a light golden brown colour.

❈ Slide the omelette out of the pan on to a plate. Wipe the pan with kitchen paper and heat the remaining oil. Invert the omelette into the pan and cook until the other side is a golden brown colour.

❈ Slide the omelette on to a warmed serving dish and garnish with the remaining olives and the marjoram. Cut into wedges and serve with the tomato salad.

Prawn Omelette

❊ **SERVES 4** ❊

3 tbsp sunflower oil
2 leeks, trimmed and sliced
350 g/12 oz raw tiger prawns
4 tbsp cornflour
1 tsp salt

6 oz/175 g mushrooms, sliced
85 g/3 oz beansprouts
6 eggs
deep-fried leeks, to garnish
(optional)

❊ Heat the sunflower oil in a preheated wok or large frying pan. Add the sliced leeks and stir-fry for 3 minutes.

❊ Rinse the prawns under cold running water and then pat dry with absorbent kitchen paper.

❊ Mix together the cornflour and salt in a large bowl.

❊ Add the prawns to the cornflour and salt mixture and toss to coat all over.

❊ Add the prawns to the wok and stir-fry for 2 minutes or until the prawns are almost cooked through.

❊ Add the mushrooms and beansprouts to the wok and stir-fry for a further 2 minutes.

❊ Beat the eggs with 3 tablespoons of cold water. Pour the egg mixture into the wok and cook until the egg sets, carefully turning over once. Turn the omelette out on to a clean board, divide into 4 and serve hot, garnished with the deep-fried leeks, if using.

Spinach & Herb Frittata

❊ **SERVES 6–8** ❊

4 tbsp olive oil
6 spring onions, sliced
250 g/9 oz young spinach leaves, any coarse stems removed, rinsed
6 large eggs
3 tbsp finely chopped mixed fresh herbs, such as flat-leaf parsley, thyme and coriander

2 tbsp freshly grated Parmesan cheese, plus extra to garnish
salt and pepper
sprigs of fresh parsley, to garnish

❊ Heat a 25-cm/10-inch frying pan, preferably non-stick with a flameproof handle, over a medium heat. Add the oil and heat. Add the spring onions and cook for about 2 minutes. Add the spinach and cook until it just wilts.

❊ Beat the eggs in a large bowl and season to taste with salt and pepper. Using a slotted spoon, transfer the spinach and onions to the bowl of eggs and stir in the herbs. Pour the excess oil left in the pan into a heatproof jug, then scrape off the crusty sediment from the bottom of the pan.

❊ Reheat the pan. Add 2 tablespoons of the reserved oil. Pour in the egg mixture, smoothing it into an even layer. Cook, shaking the pan occasionally, for 6 minutes or until the base is set when you lift up the side with a spatula.

❊ Sprinkle the top of the frittata with the cheese. Place the pan under a preheated broiler and cook for 3 minutes or until the excess liquid is set and the cheese is golden.

❊ Remove the pan from the heat and slide the frittata on to a serving plate.

❊ Leave to stand for at least 5 minutes before cutting and garnishing with the extra cheese and the parsley. Serve hot, warm or at room temperature.

Onion & Gruyère Frittata

1 tbsp olive oil	100 g/3½ oz Gruyère cheese,
1 garlic clove, crushed	grated
2 red onions, thinly sliced	pepper
8 eggs	4 slices soda bread, to serve

❋ Heat the oil in a nonstick frying pan over a medium-low heat, add the garlic and onions and cook, stirring occasionally, for 10 minutes, or until the onions are very soft and a little caramelized.

❋ Beat the eggs with half the cheese and pepper to taste in a large bowl, pour over the onions and gently stir until the eggs are evenly distributed. Cook for 5 minutes, or until the eggs are set on the bottom.

❋ Meanwhile, preheat the grill to high. Sprinkle the remaining cheese over the frittata and place under the preheated grill until the cheese is melted. Cut the frittata into 4 wedges and serve at once with the soda bread.

Chorizo & Cheese Tortilla

2 small potatoes	8 large eggs
4 tbsp olive oil	2 tbsp cold water
1 small onion, chopped	55 g/2 oz mature Mahon,
1 red pepper, deseeded	Manchego or Parmesan
and chopped	cheese, grated
2 tomatoes, deseeded and diced	salt and pepper
140 g/5 oz chorizo sausage,	
finely chopped	

❋ Bring a small saucepan of lightly salted water to the boil and cook the potatoes for 15–20 minutes or until just tender. Drain and leave to stand until cool enough to handle, then dice.

❋ Heat the oil in a large frying pan that can safely be placed under the grill. Add the onion, pepper and tomatoes and cook over a low heat, stirring occasionally, for 5 minutes. Add the diced potatoes and chorizo and cook for an additional 5 minutes. Meanwhile, preheat the grill to high.

❋ Beat the eggs with the water and salt and pepper to taste in a large bowl. Pour the mixture into the pan and cook for 8–10 minutes or until the underside is set. Lift the edge of the tortilla occasionally to let the uncooked egg run underneath. Sprinkle the grated cheese over the tortilla and place under the hot grill for 3 minutes, or until the top is set and the cheese has melted. Serve warm or cold, cut into thin wedges.

Tomato & Potato Tortilla

1 kg/2 lb 4 oz potatoes, peeled
and cut into small cubes
2 tbsp olive oil
1 bunch spring onions, chopped
115 g/4 oz cherry tomatoes
6 eggs
3 tbsp water
2 tbsp chopped fresh parsley
salt and pepper

❖ Bring a saucepan of lightly salted water to the boil and cook the potatoes for 8–10 minutes or until tender. Drain and reserve until required.

❖ Preheat the grill to medium. Heat the oil in a large frying pan. Add the spring onions and fry until just softened. Add the potatoes and fry for 3–4 minutes until coated with oil and hot. Smooth the top and scatter over the tomatoes.

❖ Mix the eggs, water, salt and pepper and parsley together in a bowl, then pour into the frying pan. Cook over a very gentle heat for 10–15 minutes until the tortilla looks fairly set.

❖ Place the frying pan under the hot grill and cook until the top is brown and set. Leave to cool for 10–15 minutes before sliding out of the frying pan on to a chopping board. Cut into wedges and serve immediately.

46

Omelette in Tomato Sauce

❊ **SERVES 4** ❊

2 tbsp butter
1 onion, finely chopped
2 garlic cloves, chopped
4 eggs, beaten
150 ml/5 fl oz milk
75 g/2¾ oz Gruyère cheese, diced

400g/14 oz canned chopped tomatoes
1 tbsp rosemary, stalks removed
150 ml/5 fl oz vegetable stock
freshly grated Parmesan cheese, for sprinkling
fresh crusty bread, to serve

❊ Melt the butter in a large frying pan. Add the onion and garlic and cook for 4–5 minutes until soft.

❊ Beat together the eggs and milk and add the mixture to the pan.

❊ Using a spatula, raise the cooked edges of the omelette and tip any uncooked egg around the edge of the pan.

❊ Scatter over the cheese. Cook for 5 minutes, turning once, until golden on both sides. Remove the omelette from the pan and roll up.

❊ Add the tomatoes, rosemary and stock to the pan, stirring, and bring to the boil.

❊ Leave the tomato sauce to simmer for about 10 minutes until reduced and thickened.

❊ Slice the omelette into strips and add to the tomato sauce in the frying pan. Cook for 3–4 minutes or until piping hot.

❊ Sprinkle the grated cheese over the omelette strips and serve with the bread.

Basque Scrambled Eggs

❊ **SERVES 4–6** ❊

3–4 tbsp olive oil
1 large onion, finely chopped
1 large red pepper, deseeded and chopped
1 large green pepper, deseeded and chopped
2 large tomatoes, peeled, deseeded and chopped

55 g/2 oz chorizo sausage, thinly sliced, outer casing removed, if preferred
35 g/1¼ oz butter
10 large eggs, lightly beaten
salt and pepper
4–6 thick slices country-style bread, toasted, to serve

❊ Heat 2 tablespoons of the oil in a large heavy-based frying pan over a medium heat. Add the onion and peppers and cook for 5 minutes, or until the vegetables are soft but not brown. Add the tomatoes and heat through. Transfer to a heatproof plate and keep warm in a preheated low oven.

❊ Add another tablespoon of the oil to the pan. Add the chorizo and cook for 30 seconds, just to warm through and flavour the oil. Add the sausage to the reserved vegetables.

❊ Add a little extra olive oil, if necessary, to bring it back to 2 tablespoons. Add the butter and allow to melt. Season the eggs with salt and pepper, then add to the pan and scramble until cooked to the desired degree of firmness. Return the vegetables to the pan and stir through. Serve immediately with the toast.

Mexican Eggs

❄ SERVES 4 ❄

8 large eggs
2 tbsp milk
1 tsp olive oil
1 red pepper, deseeded and
thinly sliced
½ fresh red chilli

1 fresh chorizo sausage,
skinned and sliced
4 tbsp chopped fresh coriander
pepper
4 slices toasted wholemeal
bread, to serve

❄ Beat the eggs, milk and pepper to taste in a large bowl. Set aside.

❄ Heat the oil in a non-stick frying pan over a medium heat, add the red pepper and chilli and cook, stirring frequently, for 5 minutes, or until the red pepper is soft and brown in places. Add the chorizo and cook until just brown. Transfer to a warmed plate and set aside.

❄ Return the pan to the heat, add the egg mixture and cook to a soft scramble. Add the chorizo mixture, stir to combine and scatter over the coriander. Serve immediately on the toasted wholemeal bread.

Flamenco Eggs

❄ SERVES 4 ❄

4 tbsp olive oil
1 onion, thinly sliced
2 garlic cloves, finely chopped
2 small red peppers, deseeded
and chopped
4 tomatoes, peeled, deseeded
and chopped

1 tbsp chopped fresh parsley
200 g/7 oz canned sweetcorn
kernels, drained
4 eggs
salt and cayenne pepper

❄ Preheat the oven to 180°C/350°F/Gas Mark 4. Heat the olive oil in a large heavy-based frying pan. Add the onion and garlic and cook over a low heat, stirring occasionally, for 5 minutes or until soft. Add the red peppers and cook, stirring occasionally, for a further 10 minutes. Stir in the tomatoes and parsley, season to taste with salt and cayenne pepper and cook for a further 5 minutes. Stir in the sweetcorn and remove the pan from the heat.

❄ Divide the mixture between 4 individual ovenproof dishes. Make a hollow in the surface of each using the back of a spoon. Break an egg into each depression.

❄ Bake in the preheated oven for 15–25 minutes, or until the eggs have set. Serve hot.

Baked Cheese & Tomato Soufflés

6 medium tomatoes, peeled,
deseeded and chopped
1 tbsp sugar
55 g/2 oz butter, plus extra
for greasing
55 g/2 oz plain flour
300 ml/10 fl oz milk
4 large eggs, separated
225 g/8 oz mature Cheddar
cheese, grated
2 tbsp fresh thyme leaves, plus
extra to garnish

❖ Place the tomatoes in a sieve set over a bowl. Sprinkle with the sugar and leave to drain for 30–45 minutes. Preheat the oven to 180°C/350°F/Gas Mark 4.

❖ Grease and base-line 6 x 200-ml/7-fl oz ramekin dishes. Melt the butter in a saucepan and add the flour. Gradually add the milk, stirring. Bring slowly to the boil, stirring, then simmer for 2–3 minutes until thickened. Quickly stir in the egg yolks and remove from the heat. Stir in the cheese and 1 tablespoon of the thyme.

❖ Whisk the egg whites in a clean bowl until stiff, then fold into the cheese mixture. Mix together the tomatoes and the remaining thyme and divide between the ramekins.
Fill each ramekin with the soufflé mixture and stand them in a roasting tin.

❖ Half-fill the roasting tin with hot water and cook for 25–30 minutes until firm and brown. Turn the soufflés out upside down, garnish with thyme and serve.

Carrot & Potato Soufflé

2 tbsp butter, melted	2 eggs, separated
4 tbsp fresh wholemeal breadcrumbs	2 tbsp orange juice
	¼ tsp grated nutmeg
3 floury potatoes, baked in their skins	salt and pepper
	carrot curls, to garnish
2 carrots, grated	

❖ Brush the inside of an 850-ml/1½-pint soufflé dish with the butter. Sprinkle about three-quarters of the breadcrumbs over the base and sides.

❖ Cut the jacket potatoes in half and scoop the flesh into a mixing bowl.

❖ Add the carrots, egg yolks, orange juice and nutmeg to the potato flesh. Season to taste with salt and pepper.

❖ In a separate bowl, whisk the egg whites until soft peaks form, then gently fold into the potato mixture with a metal spoon until well incorporated.

❖ Gently spoon the potato and carrot mixture into the prepared soufflé dish. Sprinkle the remaining breadcrumbs over the top of the mixture.

❖ Cook in a preheated oven, 200°C/400°F/Gas Mark 6, for 40 minutes until risen and golden. Do not open the oven door during the cooking time, otherwise the soufflé will sink. Serve at once, garnished with the carrot curls.

Leek & Herb Soufflé

350 g/12 oz baby leeks	2 eggs, separated
1 tbsp olive oil	2 tbsp chopped mixed herbs
125 ml/4 fl oz vegetable stock	2 tbsp natural yogurt
50 g/1¾ oz walnuts	salt and pepper

❖ Using a sharp knife, finely chop the leeks. Heat the oil in a frying pan. Add the leeks and sauté over a medium heat, stirring occasionally, for 2–3 minutes.

❖ Add the stock to the pan, reduce the heat and simmer gently for a further 5 minutes.

❖ Place the walnuts in a food processor or blender and process until finely chopped. Add the leek mixture to the nuts and process briefly to form a purée. Transfer to a mixing bowl.

❖ Mix together the egg yolks, herbs and yogurt until thoroughly combined. Pour the egg mixture into the leek purée. Season to taste with salt and pepper and mix well.

❖ In a separate, grease-free mixing bowl, whisk the egg whites until firm peaks form.

❖ Fold the egg whites into the leek mixture. Spoon the mixture into a lightly greased 850-ml/1½-pint soufflé dish and place on a warmed baking tray.

❖ Cook in a preheated oven, 180°C/350°F/Gas Mark 4, for 35–40 minutes or until well risen and set. Serve the soufflé immediately.

Vegetable Samosas

FILLING	
2 tbsp vegetable oil	225 g/8 oz potatoes, diced
1 onion, chopped	100 g/3^1/$_2$ oz frozen peas,
^{1}/$_2$ tsp ground coriander	thawed
^{1}/$_2$ tsp ground cumin	150 g/5^1/$_2$ oz fresh spinach,
pinch of turmeric	chopped
^{1}/$_2$ tsp ground ginger	
^{1}/$_2$ tsp garam masala	**PASTRY**
1 garlic clove, crushed	350 g/12 oz filo pastry
	oil, for deep-frying

❊ To make the filling, heat the oil in a frying pan. Add the onion and sauté, stirring frequently, for 1–2 minutes until soft. Stir in all of the spices and garlic and cook for 1 minute.

❊ Add the potatoes and cook over a low heat, stirring frequently, for 5 minutes until they begin to soften.

❊ Stir in the peas and spinach and cook for a further 3–4 minutes.

❊ Lay out the filo pastry sheets out on a clean work surface and fold each sheet in half lengthways.

❊ Place 2 tablespoons of the vegetable filling at one end of each folded pastry sheet. Fold over one corner to make a triangle. Continue folding in this way to make a triangular package and seal the edges with water.

❊ Repeat with the remaining pastry and the remaining filling.

❊ Heat the oil for deep-frying to 180°C/350°F or until a cube of bread browns in 30 seconds. Fry the samosas, in batches, for 1–2 minutes until golden. Drain each batch on absorbent kitchen paper and keep warm while cooking the remainder. Serve immediately.

Vegetable-Stuffed Parathas

PASTRY	FILLING
225 g/8 oz wholemeal flour	675 g/1 lb 8 oz potatoes
(ata or chapatti flour)	^{1}/$_2$ tsp turmeric
^{1}/$_2$ tsp salt	1 tsp garam masala
200 ml/7 fl oz water	1 tsp finely chopped root ginger
100 g/3^1/$_2$ oz ghee,	1 tbsp fresh coriander leaves
plus 2–3 tbsp	3 green chillies, deseeded and
	finely chopped
	1 tsp salt

❊ To make the parathas, mix the flour, salt, water and ghee together in a bowl to form a dough. Divide the dough into 6 equal portions. Roll each portion out on to a floured work surface. Brush the middle of the dough portions with ^{1}/$_2$ teaspoon of ghee. Fold the dough portions in half, roll into a pipe-like shape, flatten with the palms of your hands, then roll around a finger to form a coil. Roll out again, using flour to dust when necessary, to form a round about 18 cm/ 7 inches in diameter.

❊ Bring a saucepan of lightly salted water to the boil, add the potatoes and cook until soft enough to be mashed.

❊ Blend the turmeric, garam masala, ginger, coriander leaves, chillies and salt in a bowl. Add the spice mixture to the mashed potato and mix well. Spread about 1 tablespoon of the spicy potato mixture on each dough portion and cover with another rolled-out piece of dough. Seal the edges well.

❊ Heat 2 teaspoons of the ghee in a heavy-based frying pan. Place the parathas gently in the pan, one by one, and fry, turning and moving them about gently with a fish slice, until golden.

❊ Remove the parathas from the pan, keep warm while cooking the remainder and serve immediately.

Vegetarian Spring Rolls

25 g/1 oz fine cellophane
noodles
2 tbsp groundnut oil
2 garlic cloves, crushed
$^1/_2$ tsp freshly grated root
ginger
55 g/2 oz oyster mushrooms,
thinly sliced
2 spring onions, finely chopped
50g/1$^3/_4$ oz beansprouts
1 small carrot, finely shredded
$^1/_2$ tsp sesame oil
1 tbsp light soy sauce
1 tbsp rice wine or dry sherry
$^1/_4$ tsp pepper
1 tbsp chopped fresh coriander
1 tbsp chopped fresh mint
24 spring-roll wrappers
$^1/_2$ tsp cornflour
groundnut oil, for deep-frying
sprigs of fresh mint, to garnish

❖ Place the noodles in a heatproof bowl, pour over enough boiling water to cover and leave them to stand for 4 minutes. Drain, rinse in cold water, then drain again. Cut or snip the noodles into 5-cm/2-inch lengths.

❖ Heat the groundnut oil in a wok or wide saucepan over a high heat. Add the garlic, ginger, oyster mushrooms, spring onions, beansprouts and carrot and stir-fry for 1 minute or until just soft.

❖ Stir in the sesame oil, soy sauce, rice wine, pepper, chopped coriander and mint, then remove the wok from the heat. Stir in the rice noodles.

❖ Arrange the spring-roll wrappers on a work surface, pointing diagonally. Mix the cornflour with 1 tablespoon water to a smooth paste and brush the edges of wrapper with it. Spoon a little filling on to the pointed side of the same wrapper. Roll the point of the wrapper over the filling, then fold the side points inwards over the filling. Continue to roll up the wrapper away from you, moistening the tip with a little more cornflour paste to secure the roll.

❖ Heat the oil in a wok or deep frying pan to 180°C/350°F or until a cube of bread browns in 30 seconds. Add the rolls, in batches, and deep-fry for 2–3 minutes each until golden and crisp.

Fried Tofu with Peanut Sauce

❖ **SERVES 4** ❖

500 g/1 lb 2 oz marinated or plain tofu	**BATTER**
2 tbsp rice vinegar	4 tbsp plain flour
2 tbsp sugar	2 eggs, beaten
1 tsp salt	4 tbsp milk
3 tbsp smooth peanut butter	1/2 tsp baking powder
1/2 tsp chilli flakes	1/2 tsp chilli powder
3 tbsp barbecue sauce	
1 litre/1 3/4 pints sunflower oil	
2 tbsp sesame oil	

❖ Cut the tofu into 2.5-cm/1-inch triangles. Set aside until required.

❖ Combine the vinegar, sugar and salt in a saucepan. Bring to the boil and then simmer for 2 minutes.

❖ Remove the sauce from the heat and add the smooth peanut butter, chilli flakes and barbecue sauce, stirring well until thoroughly blended.

❖ To make the batter, sift the plain flour into a bowl, make a well in the centre and add the eggs. Draw in the flour, adding the milk slowly. Stir in the baking powder and chilli powder.

❖ Heat both the sunflower oil and sesame oil in a deep-fat fryer or large saucepan until a light haze appears on top.

❖ Dip the tofu triangles into the batter and deep-fry until golden brown. You may need to do this in batches. Drain on absorbent kitchen paper.

❖ Transfer the tofu triangles to a serving dish and serve with the peanut sauce.

Mushroom Bites with Aïoli

❖ **SERVES 4** ❖

2 egg whites	**AÏOLI**
115 g/4 oz fresh white breadcrumbs	4 garlic cloves, crushed
2 tbsp freshly grated Parmesan cheese	2 egg yolks
1 tsp paprika	225 ml/8 fl oz extra virgin olive oil
225 g/8 oz button mushrooms	salt and pepper

❖ First make the aïoli. Put the garlic in a bowl, add a pinch of salt and mash with the back of a spoon. Add the egg yolks and beat with a whisk for 30 seconds until creamy. Beat in the oil, one drop at a time. As the mixture begins to thicken, add the oil in a steady stream, beating constantly.

❖ Season the aïoli to taste with salt and pepper, cover the bowl with clingfilm and chill in the refrigerator until required.

❖ Lightly whisk the egg whites. Combine the breadcrumbs, cheese and paprika in a bowl. Dip each mushroom into the egg whites then into the breadcrumbs. Place on a baking tray lined with baking paper.

❖ Bake in a preheated oven, 190°C/375°F/Gas Mark 5, for 15 minutes until the coating is crisp and golden. Serve immediately with the aïoli.

Deep-Fried Chilli Corn Balls

❖ **SERVES 4** ❖

6 spring onions, sliced
3 tbsp fresh coriander, chopped
225 g/8 oz canned sweetcorn kernels, drained
1 tsp mild chilli powder
1 tbsp sweet chilli sauce
25 g/1 oz desiccated coconut
1 egg
75 g/2¾ oz polenta
oil, for deep-frying
extra-sweet chilli sauce, for dipping

❖ In a large bowl, mix together the spring onions, coriander, sweetcorn, chilli powder, chilli sauce, coconut, egg and polenta until well blended.

❖ Cover the bowl with clingfilm and leave to stand for about 10 minutes.

❖ Heat the oil for deep-frying in a large preheated wok or frying pan to 180°C/350°F or until a cube of bread browns in 30 seconds.

❖ Carefully drop spoonfuls of the chilli and polenta mixture into the hot oil. Deep-fry the chilli corn balls, in batches, for 4–5 minutes or until crispy and a deep golden brown colour.

❖ Remove the chilli corn balls with a slotted spoon, transfer to absorbent kitchen paper and leave to drain thoroughly.

❖ Transfer the chilli corn balls to serving plates and serve with extra-sweet chilli sauce for dipping.

Falafel

❖ **SERVES 4** ❖

225 g/8 oz dried chickpeas
1 large onion, finely chopped
1 garlic clove, crushed
2 tbsp chopped fresh parsley
2 tsp ground cumin
2 tsp ground coriander
cayenne pepper
½ tsp baking powder
salt
oil, for deep-frying

TO SERVE
hummus
tomato wedges
pitta bread

❖ Soak the chickpeas overnight in enough cold water to cover them and allow room for expansion. Drain, then place in a saucepan, cover with fresh water and bring to the boil. Reduce the heat and simmer for 1 hour or until tender. Drain.

❖ Place the chickpeas in a food processor and blend to make a coarse paste. Add the onion, garlic, parsley, cumin, coriander, cayenne pepper and salt to taste and baking powder. Blend again to mix thoroughly.

❖ Cover and leave to rest for 30 minutes, then shape into 8 balls. Leave to rest for a further 30 minutes. Heat the oil in a wok or large saucepan to 180°C/350°F or until a cube of bread browns in 30 seconds. Gently drop in the balls and cook until golden brown. Remove from the oil and drain on a plate lined with kitchen paper.

❖ Serve hot or at room temperature with the hummus, tomato wedges and pitta bread.

Mixed Mushroom Cakes

500 g/1 lb 2 oz floury potatoes,
diced
2 tbsp butter
175 g/6 oz mixed mushrooms,
chopped
2 garlic cloves, crushed
1 small egg, beaten
1 tbsp chopped fresh chives,
plus extra to garnish
salt and pepper
flour, for dusting
oil, for frying

❖ Bring a saucepan of lightly salted water to the boil and cook the potatoes for 10 minutes or until cooked through.

❖ Drain the potatoes well, mash with a potato masher or fork and set aside.

❖ Meanwhile, melt the butter in a frying pan. Add the mushrooms and garlic and cook, stirring constantly, for 5 minutes. Drain well.

❖ Stir the mushrooms and garlic into the potatoes, together with the beaten egg and chives.

❖ Divide the mixture equally into 4 portions and shape them into round cakes. Toss the cakes in the flour until they are completely coated.

❖ Heat the oil in a frying pan. Add the potato cakes and fry over a medium heat for 10 minutes until they are golden brown, turning them over carefully halfway through.

❖ Serve the cakes immediately, garnished with chives.

Lentil Croquettes

225 g/8 oz split red lentils
1 green pepper, deseeded and finely chopped
1 red onion, finely chopped
2 garlic cloves, crushed
1 tsp garam masala
1/2 tsp chilli powder
1 tsp ground cumin
2 tsp lemon juice
2 tbsp chopped unsalted peanuts
600 ml/1 pint water
1 egg, beaten
3 tbsp plain flour
1 tsp ground turmeric
1 tsp chilli powder
4 tbsp vegetable oil
salt and pepper
salad leaves and fresh herbs, to serve

❄ Put the lentils in a large saucepan with the chopped pepper, onion, garlic, garam masala, chilli powder, ground cumin, lemon juice and peanuts. Add the water and bring to the boil. Reduce the heat and simmer gently, stirring occasionally, for about 30 minutes or until all the liquid has been absorbed.

❄ Remove the mixture from the heat and set aside to cool slightly. Beat in the egg and season to taste with salt and pepper. Set aside to cool completely.

❄ With floured hands, form the mixture into 8 rectangles or ovals.

❄ Combine the flour, turmeric and chilli powder on a small plate. Roll the croquettes in the spiced flour mixture to coat thoroughly.

❄ Heat the oil in a large frying pan. Add the croquettes, in batches, and fry, turning once, for about 10 minutes until crisp on both sides. Transfer to warmed serving plates and serve immediately with the salad leaves and herbs.

Feta Cheese Patties

2 large carrots
1 large courgette
1 small onion
55 g/2 oz feta cheese (drained weight)
4 tbsp plain flour
1/4 tsp cumin seeds
1/2 tsp poppy seeds
1 tsp medium curry powder
1 tbsp chopped fresh parsley
1 egg, beaten
2 tbsp butter
2 tbsp vegetable oil
salt and pepper
sprigs of fresh herbs, to garnish

❄ Coarsely grate the carrots, courgette, onion and feta cheese, either by hand or in a food processor.

❄ Place the flour, cumin seeds, poppy seeds, curry powder and parsley in a large bowl and stir to combine. Season to taste with salt and pepper.

❄ Add the vegetable and cheese mixture to the seasoned flour, tossing well to combine. Stir in the beaten egg.

❄ Heat the butter and oil in a large heavy-based frying pan. Place heaped tablespoonfuls of the patty mixture in the pan, flattening them slightly with the back of the spoon. Cook over a low heat for about 2 minutes on each side until crisp and golden brown. Drain the patties on kitchen paper and keep warm. Cook more patties in the same way until all the mixture is used.

❄ Serve immediately, garnished with the sprigs of herbs.

Cheese Puffs & Fiery Salsa

❖ **SERVES 8** ❖

70 g/2¹/₂ oz plain flour
50 ml/2 fl oz Spanish olive oil
150 ml/5 fl oz water
2 eggs, beaten
55 g/2 oz Manchego,
Parmesan, Cheddar or
Gouda cheese, finely grated
¹/₂ tsp paprika
sunflower oil, for deep-frying
salt and pepper

FIERY SALSA

2 tbsp Spanish olive oil
1 small onion, finely chopped
1 garlic clove, crushed
splash of dry white wine
400 g/14 oz canned chopped
 tomatoes
1 tbsp tomato purée
¹/₄–¹/₂ tsp chilli flakes
dash of Tabasco sauce
salt and pepper

❖ To make the salsa, heat the oil in a saucepan. Add the onion and fry for 5 minutes or until soft but not brown. Add the garlic and fry for a further 30 seconds. Add the wine and allow to bubble, then add all the remaining salsa ingredients to the pan and simmer, uncovered, for 10–15 minutes or until a thick sauce has formed. Spoon into a serving bowl and reserve until ready to serve.

❖ Meanwhile, prepare the cheese puffs. Sift the flour on to a plate. Place the oil and water in a saucepan and slowly bring to the boil, then remove from the heat and quickly tip in the flour all at once. Using a wooden spoon, beat the mixture until it is smooth and leaves the sides of the pan.

❖ Leave to cool for 1–2 minutes, then gradually add the eggs, beating hard after each addition and keeping the mixture stiff. Add the cheese and paprika, season to taste with salt and pepper and mix well. Store in the refrigerator.

❖ Just before serving the cheese puffs, heat the sunflower oil in a deep-fat fryer to 180°C/350°F or until a cube of bread browns in 30 seconds. Drop teaspoonfuls of the cheese puff mixture, in batches, into the hot oil and deep-fry for 2–3 minutes, turning once. They should rise to the surface of the oil and puff up. Drain well on kitchen paper.

❖ Serve the puffs hot, with the fiery tomato salsa for dipping.

Mozzarella with Radicchio

❖ **SERVES 4** ❖

500 g/1 lb 2 oz mozzarella
cheese
4 large tomatoes, sliced
2 radicchio
fresh basil leaves, to garnish

DRESSING

1 tbsp red or green pesto
6 tbsp virgin olive oil
3 tbsp red wine vinegar
handful of fresh basil leaves
salt and pepper

❖ To make the dressing, mix together the pesto, oil and vinegar.

❖ Tear the basil leaves into tiny pieces and add them to the dressing. Season.

❖ Thinly slice the cheese and arrange on 4 serving plates with the tomatoes.

❖ Leaving the root end on the radicchio, slice each one into quarters. Grill them quickly, so that the leaves singe on the outside. Place two quarters on each serving plate.

❖ Drizzle the dressing over the radicchio, cheese and tomatoes. Garnish with the basil and serve.

Baked Herb Ricotta

1 tbsp olive oil, plus extra
for drizzling
1 kg/2 lb 4 oz fresh ricotta
cheese, drained
3 eggs, lightly beaten
3 tbsp chopped fresh herbs,
such as tarragon, parsley,
dill and chives
1/2 tsp paprika, plus extra
for sprinkling
4 slices granary bread
pepper
green salad, to serve

❊ Preheat the oven to 180°C/350°F/Gas Mark 4. Brush a 1-kg/2 lb 4-oz non-stick loaf tin with the oil.

❊ Put the ricotta cheese into a bowl and beat well. Add the eggs and stir until smooth, then stir in the herbs, pepper to taste, and paprika.

❊ Spoon the mixture into the prepared tin and put into a roasting tin half-filled with water. Bake in the preheated oven for 30–40 minutes or until set. Remove from the oven and leave to cool.

❊ Meanwhile, cut the crusts off the bread and toast on each side. Cut each slice widthways to create 2 thin slices. Cut each slice diagonally into triangles. Arrange in a single layer on a baking tray and bake in the oven for 10 minutes.

❊ Turn out the baked ricotta on to a serving dish, drizzle with a little oil and sprinkle with paprika. Serve with the toast and green salad.

Stuffed Mushrooms

8 open-cup mushrooms
1 tbsp olive oil
1 small leek, chopped
1 celery stick, chopped
100 g/3$^{1}/_{2}$ oz firm tofu, diced
1 courgette, chopped
1 carrot, chopped
100 g/3$^{1}/_{2}$ oz wholemeal
breadcrumbs

2 tbsp chopped fresh basil
1 tbsp tomato purée
2 tbsp pine kernels
85 g/3 oz Cheddar cheese,
grated
150 ml/5 fl oz vegetable stock
salt and pepper
salad, to serve

✳ Carefully remove the stalks from the mushrooms and finely chop them. Set aside the cups.

✳ Heat the olive oil in a large heavy-based frying pan over a medium heat. Add the chopped mushroom stalks, leek, celery, tofu, courgette and carrot and cook, stirring constantly, for 3–4 minutes.

✳ Stir in the breadcrumbs, chopped basil, tomato purée and pine kernels. Season to taste with salt and pepper and mix thoroughly.

✳ Divide the stuffing mixture evenly between the mushroom cups and sprinkle the grated cheese over the top. Arrange the mushrooms in a shallow ovenproof dish and pour the stock around them.

✳ Cook in a preheated oven, 220°C/425°F/Gas Mark 7, for 20 minutes or until the mushrooms are cooked through and the cheese has melted. Remove the mushrooms from the dish and serve immediately with a salad.

Garlic Mushrooms

450 g/1 lb medium-cup
mushrooms
175 g/6 oz softened butter
2 garlic cloves, crushed
juice and grated rind of
$^{1}/_{2}$ lemon

2 tbsp chopped fresh parsley
salt and pepper
fresh crusty bread, to serve

✳ Preheat the oven to 220°C/425°F/Gas Mark 7. Remove the mushroom stalks and arrange the mushrooms, rounded side down, in a shallow baking dish.

✳ Mix together the butter, garlic, lemon juice and rind, parsley and salt and pepper in a bowl. Divide the garlic butter between the mushroom cups.

✳ Bake in the oven for 15–20 minutes, until the mushrooms are soft and the garlic butter is sizzling. Serve immediately with the bread.

Thai Spiced Mushrooms

❖ **SERVES 4** ❖

8 large flat mushrooms	8 baby sweetcorn cobs, sliced
3 tbsp sunflower oil	3 spring onions, chopped
2 tbsp light soy sauce	115 g/4 oz beansprouts
1 garlic clove, crushed	100 g/3½ oz firm tofu, diced
2-cm/¾-inch piece of galangal	2 tsp sesame seeds, toasted
or root ginger, grated	chopped cucumber and sliced
1 tbsp Thai green curry paste	red pepper, to serve

❖ Remove the stalks from the mushrooms and set aside. Place the cups on a baking tray. Mix 2 tablespoons of the oil with 1 tablespoon of the soy sauce and brush all over the mushroom caps.

❖ Cook the mushroom cups under a preheated grill until golden and tender, turning them over once.

❖ Meanwhile, chop the mushroom stalks finely. Heat the remaining oil in a heavy-based frying pan or wok and stir-fry the stalks with the garlic and galangal for 1 minute.

❖ Stir in the curry paste, sweetcorn and spring onions and stir-fry for 1 minute. Add the beansprouts and stir for a further minute.

❖ Add the tofu and the remaining soy sauce, then toss lightly to heat through. Spoon the mixture into the mushroom cups.

❖ Sprinkle with the sesame seeds. Serve immediately with the chopped cucumber and sliced red pepper.

Stuffed Tomatoes

❖ **SERVES 4** ❖

4 large tomatoes	2 garlic cloves, very finely
2 tbsp finely chopped fresh	chopped
basil	1 tbsp chopped fresh parsley
4 tsp olive oil	225 ml/8 fl oz vegetable stock
280 g/10 oz button mushrooms,	1 tbsp freshly grated Parmesan
very finely chopped	cheese
1 small onion, very finely	salt and pepper
chopped	sprigs of fresh basil, to garnish

❖ Slice a lid from the top of each tomato and reserve. Using a teaspoon, carefully scoop out the flesh from the tomato shells and chop. Place it in a bowl and add 1 teaspoon of the basil. Invert the tomato shells on kitchen paper to drain.

❖ Heat 1 tablespoon of the oil in a frying pan. Add the mushrooms, onion, garlic, parsley and remaining basil and season to taste with pepper. Cover and cook over a low heat for 2 minutes, then remove the lid and cook, stirring occasionally, for 8–10 minutes more. Meanwhile, bring the stock to the boil in a saucepan and cook until reduced by about three-quarters. Stir in the chopped tomato mixture and cook for a further 3–4 minutes until thickened. Push the mixture through a sieve with a wooden spoon and stir it into the mushroom mixture. Stir in the Parmesan cheese.

❖ Stand the tomatoes in an ovenproof dish and season the insides with salt. Fill each tomato with stuffing and replace the lids. Brush with the remaining oil and bake in a preheated oven, 180°C/350°F/Gas Mark 4, for about 15 minutes or until tender and cooked through. Serve the tomatoes warm, garnished with the sprigs of basil.

Pasta-Stuffed Tomatoes

4 tbsp extra virgin olive oil, plus
extra for greasing
8 beef tomatoes or large round
tomatoes
115 g/4 oz dried ditalini or other
very small pasta shapes
8 black olives, stoned and finely
chopped
2 tbsp finely chopped fresh
basil
1 tbsp finely chopped fresh
parsley
55 g/2 oz freshly grated
Parmesan cheese
salt and pepper
sprigs of fresh basil, to garnish

❖ Brush a baking tray with oil. Slice the tops off the tomatoes and reserve to use as lids. If the tomatoes will not stand up, cut a thin slice off the bottom of each tomato.

❖ Using a teaspoon, scoop out the tomato pulp and put it into a sieve, but do not pierce the tomato shells. Invert the tomato shells on to kitchen paper, pat dry and then set aside to drain.

❖ Bring a large saucepan of lightly salted water to the boil. Add the pasta, bring back to the boil and cook for 8–10 minutes or until the pasta is tender, but still firm to the bite. Drain the pasta and set aside.

❖ Put the olives, basil, parsley and cheese into a large mixing bowl and stir in the drained tomato pulp. Add the pasta to the bowl. Stir in the oil, mix together well and season to taste with salt and pepper.

❖ Spoon the pasta mixture into the tomato shells and replace the lids. Arrange the stuffed tomatoes on the prepared baking tray and bake in a preheated oven, 190°C/375°F/Gas Mark 5, for 15–20 minutes.

❖ Remove the tomatoes from the oven and set aside to cool until they are just warm.

❖ Arrange the pasta-stuffed tomatoes on a serving dish, garnish with the sprigs of basil and serve.

Thai-Style Sweetcorn Fritters

❖ SERVES 4 ❖

55 g/2 oz plain flour
1 large egg
2 tsp Thai green curry paste
5 tbsp coconut milk
400 g/14 oz canned or frozen
  sweetcorn kernels
4 spring onions
1 tbsp chopped fresh coriander
1 tbsp chopped fresh basil
salt and pepper
vegetable oil, for frying
lime wedges and chilli relish,
  to serve

❖ Place the flour, egg, curry paste, coconut milk and about half the sweetcorn in a food processor and process until a smooth thick batter forms. Pour into a bowl.

❖ Finely chop the spring onions and stir into the batter with the remaining sweetcorn, chopped coriander and basil. Season to taste with salt and pepper.

❖ Heat a small amount of oil in a wide heavy-based frying pan. Drop in tablespoonfuls of the batter and cook for 2–3 minutes until golden brown.

❖ Turn the fritters over and cook for a further 2–3 minutes until golden all over. Fry the batter in batches, making about 12–16 fritters and keeping the cooked fritters hot while you cook the remaining batter.

❖ Serve the fritters as soon as they are all cooked, with the lime wedges and a chilli relish.

Courgette Fritters

❖ MAKES 16–30 ❖

100 g/3^1/$_2$ oz self–raising flour
2 eggs, beaten
50 ml/2 fl oz milk
300 g/10^1/$_2$ oz courgettes
2 tbsp fresh thyme
1 tbsp oil
salt and pepper

❖ Sift the self-raising flour into a large bowl and make a well in the centre. Add the eggs to the well and, using a wooden spoon, gradually draw in the flour.

❖ Slowly add the milk to the mixture, stirring constantly to form a thick batter.

❖ Meanwhile, wash the courgettes. Grate the courgettes over a sheet of kitchen paper placed in a bowl to absorb some of the juices.

❖ Add the courgettes, thyme and salt and pepper to taste to the batter and mix thoroughly.

❖ Heat the oil in a large heavy-based frying pan. Taking a tablespoon of the batter for a medium-sized fritter or half a tablespoon of batter for a smaller-sized fritter, spoon the mixture into the hot oil and cook, in batches, for 3–4 minutes on each side.

❖ Remove the fritters with a slotted spoon and drain thoroughly on absorbent kitchen paper. Keep each batch of fritters warm in the oven while making the rest. Transfer to serving plates and serve hot.

Vegetable Fritters

100 g/3$\frac{1}{2}$ oz wholemeal flour
pinch of salt
pinch of cayenne pepper
4 tsp olive oil
175 ml/6 fl oz cold water
100 g/3$\frac{1}{2}$ oz broccoli florets
100 g/3$\frac{1}{2}$ oz cauliflower florets
50 g/2 oz mangetout
1 large carrot, cut into batons
1 red pepper, deseeded and sliced

2 egg whites, beaten
oil, for deep-frying

SAUCE
150 ml/5 fl oz pineapple juice
150 ml/5 fl oz vegetable stock
2 tbsp white wine vinegar
2 tbsp light brown sugar
2 tsp cornflour
2 spring onions, chopped

❖ Sift the flour and a pinch of salt into a mixing bowl and add the cayenne pepper. Make a well in the centre and gradually beat in the oil and cold water to make a smooth batter.

❖ Bring a saucepan of lightly salted water to the boil, cook the vegetables for 5 minutes and drain well.

❖ Whisk the egg whites until they form peaks and gently fold them into the flour batter.

❖ Dip the vegetables into the batter, turning to coat well. Drain off any excess batter. Heat the oil in a deep-fat fryer to 180°C/350°F or until a cube of bread browns in 30 seconds. Fry the vegetables, in batches, for 1–2 minutes, until golden. Remove from the oil with a slotted spoon and drain on kitchen paper.

❖ Place all of the sauce ingredients in a saucepan and bring to the boil, stirring, until the sauce is thickened and clear. Serve with the fritters.

Aspagarus Parcels

100 g/3$\frac{1}{2}$ oz fine tip asparagus
1 red pepper, deseeded and thinly sliced
50 g/1$\frac{3}{4}$ oz beansprouts

2 tbsp plum sauce
1 egg yolk
8 sheets filo pastry
oil, for deep-frying

❖ Place the asparagus, pepper and beansprouts in a large mixing bowl.

❖ Add the plum sauce to the vegetables and mix until well combined.

❖ Beat the egg yolk and set aside until required.

❖ Lay out the sheets of filo pastry on a clean work surface.

❖ Place a little of the asparagus and red pepper filling at the top end of each sheet. Brush the edges of the pastry with a little of the beaten egg yolk.

❖ Roll up the pastry, tucking in the ends and enclosing the filling like a spring roll. Repeat with the remaining pastry sheets.

❖ Heat the oil for deep-frying in a large preheated wok. Carefully cook the parcels, 2 at a time, in the hot oil for 4–5 minutes or until crispy.

❖ Remove the parcels with a slotted spoon and leave to drain on absorbent kitchen paper.

❖ Transfer the parcels to warmed serving plates and serve immediately.

Asparagus with Eggs & Parmesan Cheese

300 g/10½ oz asparagus,
trimmed
4 large eggs
85 g/3 oz Parmesan cheese
pepper

❊ Bring 2 saucepans of water to the boil. Add the asparagus to 1 saucepan, return to a simmer and cook for 5 minutes or until just tender.

❊ Meanwhile, reduce the heat of the second saucepan to a simmer and carefully crack in the eggs, one at a time. Poach for 3 minutes or until the whites are just set but the yolks are still soft. Remove with a slotted spoon.

❊ Drain the asparagus and divide between 4 warmed plates. Top each plate of asparagus with an egg and shave over the cheese. Season to taste with pepper and serve immediately.

Greek Onions

❖ **SERVES 6** ❖

450 g/1 lb shallots
3 tbsp olive oil
3 tbsp clear honey
2 tbsp garlic wine vinegar
3 tbsp dry white wine
1 tbsp tomato purée

2 celery sticks, sliced
2 tomatoes, deseeded and
  chopped
salt and pepper
chopped celery leaves,
  to garnish

❖ Peel the shallots. Heat the oil in a large saucepan, add the shallots and cook, stirring, for 3–5 minutes or until they begin to brown.

❖ Add the honey and cook over a high heat for a further 30 seconds, then add the vinegar and wine, stirring well.

❖ Stir in the tomato purée, celery and tomatoes and bring the mixture to the boil. Cook over a high heat for 5–6 minutes. Season to taste and leave to cool slightly.

❖ Garnish with the chopped celery leaves and serve warm. Alternatively, chill in the refrigerator before serving.

Vegetable Rolls

❖ **SERVES 4** ❖

8 large Chinese leaves

FILLING
2 baby sweetcorn cobs, sliced
1 carrot, finely chopped
1 celery stick, chopped
4 spring onions, chopped
4 water chestnuts, chopped
2 tbsp unsalted cashew nuts,
  chopped

1 garlic clove, chopped
1 tsp grated fresh root ginger
25 g/1 oz canned bamboo
  shoots, drained, rinsed and
  chopped
1 tsp sesame oil
2 tsp soy sauce

❖ Place the Chinese leaves in a large bowl and pour over boiling water to soften them. Leave them to stand for 1 minute and drain thoroughly.

❖ Mix together the baby sweetcorn cobs, chopped carrot, celery, spring onions, water chestnuts, cashew nuts, garlic, ginger and bamboo shoots in a large bowl.

❖ In a separate bowl, whisk together the sesame oil and soy sauce. Add this to the vegetables and stir well until all the vegetables are thoroughly coated in the mixture.

❖ Spread out the Chinese leaves on a chopping board and divide the filling mixture between them, carefully spooning an equal quantity of the mixture on to each leaf.

❖ Roll up the Chinese leaves, folding in the sides, to make neat parcels. Secure the parcels with cocktail sticks.

❖ Place in a small heatproof dish in a steamer, cover and cook for 15–20 minutes, until the parcels are cooked.

❖ Transfer the vegetable rolls to a warmed serving dish and serve.

Stuffed Aubergines

4 aubergines
175 g/6 oz bulgur wheat
300 ml/10 fl oz boiling water
3 tbsp olive oil
2 garlic cloves, crushed
2 tbsp pine kernels
1/2 tsp turmeric
1 tsp chilli powder
2 celery sticks, chopped
4 spring onions, chopped
1 carrot, grated
55 g/2 oz button mushrooms, chopped
2 tbsp raisins
2 tbsp chopped fresh coriander
salt
green salad, to serve

❖ Cut the aubergines in half lengthways and carefully scoop out the flesh with a teaspoon without piercing the shells. Chop the flesh and set aside. Rub the insides of the aubergines with a little salt and set aside for 20 minutes.

❖ Meanwhile, put the bulgur wheat in a large bowl and pour the boiling water over it. Set aside for about 20 minutes or until the bulgur wheat has completely absorbed the water.

❖ Heat the oil in a heavy-based frying pan. Add the garlic, pine kernels, turmeric, chilli powder, celery, spring onions, carrot, mushrooms and raisins and cook over a low heat, stirring occasionally, for 2–3 minutes.

❖ Stir in the reserved aubergine flesh and cook for a further 2–3 minutes. Add the chopped coriander, mixing well.

❖ Remove the pan from the heat and stir in the bulgur wheat. Rinse the aubergine shells under cold water and pat dry with kitchen paper.

❖ Spoon the bulgur filling into the aubergines and place in a roasting tin. Pour in a little boiling water and cook in a preheated oven, 180°C/350°F/Gas Mark 4, for about 15–20 minutes until piping hot. Remove from the oven, transfer to a warmed serving plate and serve hot with the green salad.

Aubergine Rolls

2 aubergines, thinly sliced lengthways
5 tbsp olive oil, plus extra for brushing
1 garlic clove, crushed
4 tbsp pesto
175 g/6 oz mozzarella cheese, grated
basil leaves, torn into pieces
salt and pepper
fresh basil leaves, to garnish

❖ Place the aubergine slices in a colander or on a plate and sprinkle liberally with salt. Set aside for 10–15 minutes to extract the bitter juices. Turn the slices over and repeat. Rinse thoroughly under cold running water and drain on kitchen paper.

❖ Heat the olive oil in a large frying pan and add the garlic. Add the aubergine slices, a few at a time, and fry lightly on both sides over a medium heat. Drain them on kitchen paper.

❖ Spread the pesto on 1 side of the aubergine slices. Top with the grated mozzarella and sprinkle with the torn basil leaves. Season to taste with salt and pepper. Roll up the slices and secure with wooden cocktail sticks.

❖ Lightly brush an ovenproof dish with a little olive oil and arrange the aubergine rolls in it. Place in a preheated oven, 180°C/350°F/Gas Mark 4, and bake for 8–10 minutes.

❖ Transfer the aubergine rolls to a warmed serving plate. Scatter with the basil leaves and serve immediately.

Aubergine Timbales

1 large aubergine
butter, for greasing
55 g/2 oz dried macaroni
1 tbsp vegetable oil
1 onion, chopped
2 garlic cloves, crushed
2 tbsp drained canned
sweetcorn
2 tbsp frozen peas, thawed
100 g/3 1/2 oz spinach
4 tbsp grated Cheddar cheese
1 egg, beaten
225 g/8 oz canned chopped
tomatoes
1 tbsp chopped fresh basil
salt and pepper

SAUCE
4 tbsp olive oil
2 tbsp white wine vinegar
2 garlic cloves, crushed
3 tbsp chopped basil
1 tbsp caster sugar

❖ Cut the aubergine lengthways into thin strips, using a potato peeler. Place in a bowl of salted boiling water and leave to stand for 3–4 minutes. Drain well.

❖ Grease 4 x 150-ml/5-fl oz ramekin dishes and line with the aubergine strips, leaving 2.5 cm/1 inch overlapping.

❖ Bring a saucepan of lightly salted water to the boil. Add the pasta, bring back to the boil and cook for 8–10 minutes until tender but still firm to the bite. Drain.

❖ Heat the oil in a saucepan and sauté the onion and garlic for 2–3 minutes. Stir in the sweetcorn and peas and remove the pan from the heat.

❖ Blanch the spinach, drain well, chop and reserve. Add the pasta to the onion mixture with the cheese, egg, tomatoes and basil. Season and mix. Half-fill each ramekin with some of the pasta. Place the spinach on top and then the remaining pasta mixture. Fold the aubergine over the pasta filling to cover. Put the ramekins in a roasting tin half-filled with boiling water, cover and cook in a preheated oven, 180°C/350°F/Gas Mark 4, for 20–25 minutes or until set.

❖ Meanwhile, heat all the sauce ingredients in a pan. Turn out the timbales and serve with the sauce.

Mexican Beans

500 g/1 lb 2 oz dried pinto or borlotti beans	1 onion, cut into chunks
sprig of fresh mint	salt
sprig of fresh thyme	warmed flour or corn tortillas
sprig of fresh flat-leaf parsley	and shredded spring onion, to serve

✽ Pick through the beans and remove any pieces of grit or stone. Put the beans in a bowl, cover with cold water and set aside to soak overnight. If you want to cut down on the soaking time, bring the beans to the boil, boil for 5 minutes, then remove from the heat, cover and set aside for 2 hours.

✽ Drain the beans, place in a pan and cover with fresh water. Add the herbs. Bring to the boil, then reduce the heat to very low, cover and simmer gently for about 2 hours until the beans are tender. The best way to check that they are done is to sample a bean every so often after 1¾ hours' cooking time.

✽ Add the onion chunks and continue to cook until the onion and beans are very tender.

✽ To serve as a side dish, drain, season with salt and serve in a bowl lined with the warmed tortillas, garnished with the spring onion.

Bombay Bowl

400 g/14 oz canned chickpeas	**TO GARNISH**
2 potatoes	1 tomato, sliced
1 onion	2 fresh green chillies,
2 tbsp tamarind paste	deseeded and chopped
6 tbsp water	fresh coriander leaves
1 tsp chilli powder	
2 tsp sugar	
1 tsp salt	

✽ Drain the chickpeas and place them in a bowl.

✽ Using a sharp knife, cut the potatoes into even-sized dice.

✽ Bring a saucepan of lightly salted water to the boil and cook the potatoes until until tender. Drain and set aside until required.

✽ Using a sharp knife, finely chop the onion. Set aside until required.

✽ Mix together the tamarind paste and water in a small mixing bowl.

✽ Add the chilli powder, sugar and salt to the tamarind paste mixture and stir well to combine. Pour the mixture over the chickpeas.

✽ Add the chopped onion and the diced potatoes and stir to mix. Season to taste with a little salt.

✽ Transfer the mixture to a serving bowl and garnish with the tomato, chillies and coriander.

Chickpeas with Parma Ham

1 tbsp olive oil
1 medium onion, thinly sliced
1 garlic clove, chopped
1 small red pepper, deseeded
and cut into thin strips
200 g/7 oz Parma ham,
cut into cubes

400g/14 oz canned chickpeas,
drained and rinsed
1 tbsp chopped parsley,
to garnish
crusty bread, to serve

✻ Heat the oil in a frying pan. Add the onion, garlic and pepper and cook for 3–4 minutes or until the vegetables have softened. Add the ham to the pan and fry for 5 minutes or until it is just beginning to brown.

✻ Add the chickpeas to the pan and cook, stirring, for 2–3 minutes until warmed through.

✻ Sprinkle with chopped parsley and transfer to warmed serving plates. Serve with the bread.

Chorizo & Chickpea Tapas

100 ml/3$\frac{1}{2}$ fl oz olive oil
2–3 tbsp sherry vinegar
250 g/9 oz fresh chorizo
sausage, in 1 piece
1 small Spanish onion,
finely chopped

400 g/14 oz canned chickpeas
salt and pepper
finely chopped fresh oregano or
flat-leaf parsley, to garnish
chunks of fresh bread, to serve

✻ Place 6 tablespoons of the olive oil and 2 tablespoons of the vinegar in a bowl and whisk together. Taste and add a little more vinegar, if desired. Season with salt and pepper to taste and set aside.

✻ Using a small, sharp knife, remove the casing from the chorizo sausage. Cut the meat into 5-mm/$\frac{1}{4}$-inch slices, then cut each slice into half-moon shapes.

✻ Heat the remaining olive oil in a small heavy-based frying pan over a medium–high heat. Add the onion and cook, stirring occasionally, for 2–3 minutes. Add the chorizo sausage and cook for about 3 minutes or until the sausage is cooked through.

✻ Using a slotted spoon, remove the sausage and onion and drain on crumpled kitchen paper. Transfer to the bowl with the dressing while they are still hot and stir together.

✻ Empty the chickpeas into a sieve and rinse well under cold running water; shake off the excess water. Add to the bowl with the other ingredients and stir together. Set aside to cool.

✻ Just before serving, adjust the seasoning, then spoon the tapas into a serving bowl and sprinkle with the herbs. Serve with the bread.

Chilli Bean Cakes with Avocado Salsa

55 g/2 oz pine kernels
425 g/15 oz canned mixed
beans, drained and rinsed
1/2 red onion, finely chopped
1 tbsp tomato purée
1/2 fresh red chilli, deseeded
and finely chopped
55 g/2 oz fresh brown
breadcrumbs
1 egg, beaten
1 tbsp finely chopped fresh
coriander
2 tbsp sunflower oil
1 lime, cut into quarters,
to garnish
4 toasted granary bread rolls,
to serve (optional)

SALSA
1 avocado, stoned, peeled and
chopped
100 g/3 1/2 oz tomatoes,
deseeded and chopped
2 garlic cloves, crushed
2 tbsp finely chopped fresh
coriander
1 tbsp olive oil
juice of 1/2 lime
pepper

❖ Heat a non-stick frying pan over a medium heat, add the pine kernels and cook, turning, until just browned. Tip into a bowl and set aside.

❖ Put the beans into a large bowl and roughly mash. Add the onion, tomato purée, chilli, pine kernels and half the breadcrumbs and mix well. Add half the egg and the coriander and mash together, adding a little more egg, if needed, to bind the mixture.

❖ Form the mixture into 4 flat cakes. Coat with the remaining breadcrumbs, cover and chill in the refrigerator for 30 minutes.

❖ To make the salsa, mix all the ingredients together in a serving bowl, cover and refrigerate until required.

❖ Heat the oil in a frying pan over a medium heat, add the bean cakes and cook for 4–5 minutes on each side, or until crisp and heated through. Remove from the pan and drain on kitchen paper.

❖ Serve each bean cake in a toasted granary roll, if using, with the salsa, garnished with a lime quarter.

Cured Meats & Tomatoes

4 plum tomatoes
1 tbsp balsamic vinegar
6 canned anchovy fillets,
drained and rinsed
2 tbsp capers, drained
and rinsed
125 g/4½ oz green olives,
stoned

175 g/6 oz mixed cured meats,
sliced
8 fresh basil leaves
1 tbsp extra virgin olive oil
salt and pepper
crusty bread, to serve

❋ Using a sharp knife, cut the tomatoes into even-sized slices. Sprinkle the tomato slices with the vinegar and a little salt and pepper to taste, and set aside.

❋ Chop the anchovy fillets into pieces measuring about the same length as the olives.

❋ Push a piece of anchovy and a caper into each olive.

❋ Arrange the sliced meat on 4 individual serving plates together with the tomatoes, filled olives and basil leaves.

❋ Lightly drizzle the oil over the meat, tomatoes and olives and serve with the bread.

Spare Ribs

900 g/2 lb pork spare ribs
2 tbsp dark soy sauce
3 tbsp hoisin sauce
1 tbsp Chinese rice wine or dry
sherry
pinch of Chinese five-spice
powder

2 tsp dark brown sugar
¼ tsp chilli sauce
2 garlic cloves, crushed
sprigs of fresh coriander, to
garnish (optional)

❋ Cut the spare ribs into separate pieces if they are joined together. If desired, you can chop them into 5-cm/2-inch lengths, using a cleaver.

❋ Mix together the soy sauce, hoisin sauce, rice wine, five-spice powder, sugar, chilli sauce and garlic in a large mixing bowl.

❋ Place the ribs in a shallow dish and pour over the mixture, turning to coat thoroughly. Cover with clingfilm and leave to marinate in the refrigerator, turning the ribs from time to time, for at least 1 hour.

❋ Remove the ribs from the marinade and arrange them in a single layer on a wire rack placed over a roasting tin half filled with warm water. Using a pastry brush, coat the ribs evenly with the marinade, reserving the remaining marinade.

❋ Cook in a preheated oven, 180°C/350°F/Gas Mark 4, for 30 minutes. Remove the roasting tin from the oven and turn the ribs over. Brush with the remaining marinade and return to the oven for a further 30 minutes or until cooked through. Add more hot water to the roasting tin during cooking, if required. Do not allow it to dry out as the water steams the ribs and aids in their cooking.

❋ Transfer the ribs to a warmed serving dish, garnish with the coriander and serve immediately.

Sweet & Sour Pork Ribs

2 garlic cloves, crushed
5-cm/2-inch piece of root
ginger, grated
150 ml/5 fl oz soy sauce
2 tbsp sugar
4 tbsp sweet sherry

4 tbsp tomato purée
300 g/10$\frac{1}{2}$ oz pineapple, cubed
2 kg/4 lb 8 oz pork spare ribs
3 tbsp clear honey
300 g/10$\frac{1}{2}$ oz pineapple rings,
fresh or canned, to serve

❊ Mix together the garlic, ginger, soy sauce, sugar, sherry, tomato purée and cubed pineapple in a non-porous dish.

❊ Put the spare ribs into the dish and make sure that they are coated completely with the marinade.

❊ Cover the dish with clingfilm.

❊ Leave the ribs to marinate at room temperature for 2 hours.

❊ Cook the ribs under a medium grill for 30–40 minutes, brushing with the honey after 20–30 minutes.

❊ Baste the ribs with the reserved marinade frequently until cooked.

❊ Cook the pineapple rings under the grill for about 10 minutes, turning once.

❊ Transfer the ribs to a serving dish and serve with the grilled pineapple rings on the side.

Pork & Peanut Baskets

2 sheets filo pastry, each about
42 x 28 cm/16$\frac{1}{2}$ x 11 inches
2 tbsp vegetable oil
1 garlic clove, crushed
125 g/4$\frac{1}{2}$ oz minced pork
1 tsp Thai red curry paste
2 spring onions, finely chopped

3 tbsp crunchy peanut butter
1 tbsp light soy sauce
1 tbsp chopped fresh coriander
salt and pepper
sprigs of fresh coriander,
to garnish

❊ Cut each sheet of filo pastry into 24 squares, 7 cm/ 2$\frac{3}{4}$ inches across, to make a total of 48 squares. Brush each square lightly with oil, and arrange the squares in stacks of 4 in 12 small patty tins, pointing outwards. Press the pastry down into the patty tins.

❊ Bake the pastry cases in a preheated oven, 200°C/ 400°F/Gas Mark 6, for 6–8 minutes until golden brown.

❊ Meanwhile, heat 1 tablespoon of the oil in a wok. Add the garlic and fry for 30 seconds, then stir in the pork and stir-fry over a high heat for 4–5 minutes until the meat is golden brown.

❊ Add the curry paste and spring onions and continue to stir-fry for a further minute, then stir in the peanut butter, soy sauce and chopped coriander. Season to taste with salt and pepper.

❊ Spoon the pork mixture into the filo baskets and serve hot, garnished with the coriander.

Chicken Wontons

250 g/9 oz boneless chicken breasts, skinned
60 g/2 oz mushrooms
1 garlic clove
2 shallots
1 tbsp fish sauce or mushroom ketchup
1 tbsp chopped fresh coriander
2 tbsp vegetable oil
about 50 wonton wrappers
oil, for deep-frying
sliced spring onion, to garnish
sweet chilli sauce, to serve

❖ Put the chicken, mushrooms, garlic, shallots, fish sauce and coriander into a blender or food processor. Blend for 10–15 seconds. Alternatively, finely chop all the ingredients and mix together well.

❖ Heat the vegetable oil in a wok or frying pan and add the chicken mixture. Stir-fry for about 8 minutes, breaking up the mixture as it cooks, until it browns. Transfer to a bowl and leave to cool for 10–15 minutes.

❖ Place the wonton wrappers on a clean, damp tea towel. Layering 2 wrappers together at a time, place teaspoonfuls of the chicken mixture into the middle. Dampen the edges with water, then make small pouches, pressing the edges together to seal. Repeat with the remaining wrappers until all the mixture is used.

❖ Heat the oil for deep-frying in a wok or deep-fat fryer. Fry the wontons, a few at a time, for about 2–3 minutes until golden brown. Remove the wontons from the oil with a slotted spoon and drain on kitchen paper. Keep warm while frying the remaining wontons.

❖ Transfer the wontons to a warmed serving platter and garnish with the sliced spring onion. Serve at once, accompanied by the sweet chilli sauce.

Sesame Ginger Chicken

4 wooden satay sticks, soaked in warm water
500 g/1 lb 2 oz boneless chicken breasts
sprigs of fresh mint, to garnish

MARINADE
1 garlic clove, crushed
1 shallot, very finely chopped
2 tbsp sesame oil

1 tbsp fish sauce or light soy sauce
finely grated rind of 1 lime or 1/2 lemon
2 tbsp lime juice or lemon juice
1 tsp sesame seeds
2 tsp finely grated ginger root
2 tsp chopped fresh mint
salt and pepper

❖ To make the marinade, put the crushed garlic, chopped shallot, sesame oil, fish sauce, lime rind and juice, sesame seeds, ginger and mint into a large non-metallic bowl. Season with a little salt and pepper and mix together until all the ingredients are thoroughly combined.

❖ Remove the skin from the chicken breasts and cut the flesh into chunks.

❖ Add the chicken to the marinade, stirring to coat the chicken completely in the mixture. Cover with clingfilm and chill in the refrigerator for at least 2 hours so that the flavours are absorbed.

❖ Thread the chicken on to wooden skewers. Place them on the rack of a grill pan and baste with the marinade.

❖ Place the skewers under a preheated grill for about 8–10 minutes. Turn them frequently, basting them with the remaining marinade.

❖ Serve the chicken skewers at once, garnished with sprigs of fresh mint.

Tuna-Stuffed Tomatoes

4 plum tomatoes
2 tbsp sun-dried tomato paste
2 egg yolks
2 tsp lemon juice
finely grated rind of 1 lemon
4 tbsp olive oil
115 g/4 oz canned tuna, drained

2 tbsp capers, rinsed
salt and pepper
2 sun-dried tomatoes, cut into strips, and fresh basil leaves, to garnish

❖ Halve the tomatoes and scoop out the seeds. Divide the sun-dried tomato paste between the tomato halves and spread around the inside of the skin.

❖ Place on a baking tray and roast in a preheated oven, 200°C/400°F/Gas Mark 6, for 12–15 minutes. Leave to cool slightly.

❖ In a food processor, blend the egg yolks and lemon juice with the lemon rind until smooth. Once mixed and with the motor still running slowly, add the olive oil. Stop the processor as soon as the mayonnaise has thickened. Alternatively, use a hand whisk, beating the mixture constantly until it thickens.

❖ Add the tuna and capers to the mayonnaise and season.

❖ Spoon the tuna mayonnaise mixture into the tomato shells and garnish with the sun-dried tomato strips and basil. Return to the oven for a few minutes or serve chilled.

Fish Cakes with Chilli Sauce

450 g/1 lb firm white fish, such
as hake, haddock or cod,
skinned and
roughly chopped
1 tbsp Thai fish sauce
1 tbsp red curry paste
1 kaffir lime leaf, finely
shredded
2 tbsp chopped fresh
coriander
1 egg
1 tsp brown sugar

40 g/1½ oz French beans,
thinly sliced crossways
salt
vegetable oil, for frying

SWEET AND SOUR DIPPING SAUCE
4 tbsp sugar
1 tbsp cold water
3 tbsp white rice vinegar
2 small hot fresh red chillies,
finely chopped
1 tbsp Thai fish sauce

❖ For the fish cakes, put the fish, fish sauce, curry paste, lime leaf, coriander, egg, sugar and salt into the bowl of a food processor. Process until smooth. Scrape into a bowl and stir in the beans. Set aside.

❖ To make the sauce, put the sugar, water and vinegar into a small saucepan and heat gently until the sugar has dissolved. Bring to the boil and simmer for 2 minutes. Remove from the heat, stir in the chillies and fish sauce and set aside.

❖ Heat a frying pan with enough oil to cover the base generously. Divide the fish mixture into 16 small balls. Flatten the balls into patties and fry in the hot oil for 1–2 minutes on each side until golden. Drain on kitchen paper. Serve hot with the dipping sauce.

Gravadlax

2 x 450 g/1 lb salmon fillets,
with skin on
6 tbsp roughly chopped
fresh dill
115 g/4 oz sea salt
55 g/2 oz sugar

1 tbsp white peppercorns,
roughly crushed
12 slices brown bread,
buttered, to serve
slices of lemon and sprigs
of fresh dill, to garnish

❖ Wash the salmon fillets and dry with kitchen paper. Put 1 fillet, skin side down, in a non-metallic dish.

❖ Combine the dill, sea salt, sugar and peppercorns. Spread this mixture over the first fillet of fish and place the second fillet, skin side up, on top. Put a plate, the same size as the fish, on top and put a weight on the plate (3 or 4 cans of tomatoes or similar will do).

❖ Chill in the refrigerator for 2 days, turning the fish about every 12 hours and basting with any juices that have come out of the fish.

❖ Remove the salmon from the brine and slice thinly, without slicing the skin, as you would smoked salmon. Cut the brown bread into triangles and serve with the salmon. Garnish with the lemon wedges and sprigs of dill.

Salmon Pancakes

450 g/1 lb floury potatoes, grated
2 spring onions, chopped
2 tbsp self-raising flour
2 eggs, beaten
2 tbsp vegetable oil
salt and pepper
fresh chives, to garnish

TOPPING
150 ml/5 fl oz soured cream
125 g/4^1/2 oz smoked salmon

❖   Rinse the grated potatoes under cold running water, drain and pat dry on kitchen paper. Transfer to a mixing bowl.

❖   Mix the spring onions, flour and eggs into the potatoes and season well with salt and pepper.

❖   Heat 1 tablespoon of the vegetable oil in a frying pan. Drop about 4 tablespoons of the mixture into the pan and spread each one with the back of a spoon to form a round (the mixture should make 16 pancakes). Cook for 5–7 minutes, turning once, until golden. Drain well.

❖   Heat the remaining oil and cook the remaining mixture in batches.

❖   Top the pancakes with the soured cream and smoked salmon, garnish with the chives and serve hot.

76

Butterfly Prawns

500 g/1 lb 2 oz or 16 raw tiger
prawns, peeled, leaving the
tails intact
juice of 2 limes
1 tsp cardamom seeds
2 tsp cumin seeds, ground
2 tsp coriander seeds, ground

1/2 tsp ground cinnamon
1 tsp ground turmeric
1 garlic clove, crushed
1 tsp cayenne pepper
2 tbsp oil
cucumber slices, to garnish
sweet chutney, to serve

❊ Soak 8 wooden skewers in water for 20 minutes. Cut the prawns lengthways in half down to the tail and flatten out to a symmetrical shape.

❊ Thread a prawn on to 2 wooden skewers, with the tail between them, so that, when laid flat, the skewers hold the prawn in shape. Thread another 3 prawns on to these 2 skewers in the same way.

❊ Repeat until you have 4 sets of 4 prawns each.

❊ Lay the skewered prawns in a non-porous, non-metallic dish, and sprinkle over the lime juice.

❊ Combine the spices and the oil and coat the prawns well in the mixture. Cover the prawns and chill for 4 hours.

❊ Cook in a grill pan lined with foil under a preheated grill for 6 minutes, turning once.

❊ Serve immediately, garnished with the cucumber and accompanied by the sweet chutney.

Giant Garlic Prawns

125 ml/4 fl oz olive oil
4 garlic cloves, finely chopped
2 hot fresh red chillies,
deseeded and finely chopped
450 g/1 lb cooked king prawns

2 tbsp chopped fresh flat-leaf
parsley
salt and pepper
lemon wedges, to garnish
crusty bread, to serve

❊ Heat the olive oil in a large heavy-based frying pan over a low heat. Add the garlic and chillies and cook, stirring occasionally, for 1–2 minutes until soft but not coloured.

❊ Add the prawns and stir-fry for 2–3 minutes until heated through and coated in the oil and garlic mixture.

❊ Turn off the heat and add the parsley, stirring well to mix. Season to taste with salt and pepper.

❊ Divide the prawns and the garlic-flavoured oil between warmed serving dishes, garnish with the lemon wedges and serve with the bread.

Pasta & Prawn Packets

❄ **SERVES 4** ❄

450 g/1 lb dried fettuccine	2 garlic cloves, crushed
150 ml/5 fl oz pesto	125 ml/4 fl oz dry white wine
4 tsp extra virgin olive oil	salt and pepper
750 g/1 lb 10 oz large raw	
prawns, peeled and deveined	

❄ Cut out 4 x 30-cm/12-inch squares of greaseproof paper.

❄ Bring a pan of lightly salted water to the boil. Add the pasta, bring back to the boil and cook for 2–3 minutes until just soft. Drain and set aside.

❄ Mix together the fettuccine and half of the pesto. Spread out the paper squares and put 1 teaspoon of the olive oil in the middle of each. Divide the fettuccine between the squares, then divide the prawns and place on top of the fettuccine.

❄ Mix together the remaining pesto and the garlic and spoon it over the prawns. Season each parcel to taste with salt and pepper and sprinkle with the white wine.

❄ Dampen the edges of the greaseproof paper and wrap the parcels loosely, twisting the edges to seal.

❄ Place the parcels on a baking tray and bake in a preheated oven, 200°C/400°F/Gas Mark 6, for 10–15 minutes until piping hot and the prawns have changed colour. Transfer the parcels to 4 individual serving plates and serve.

Chilli & Peanut Prawns

❄ **SERVES 4** ❄

450 g/1 lb king prawns, peeled,	10 sheets filo pastry
leaving tails intact	25 g/1 oz butter, melted
3 tbsp crunchy peanut butter	50 g/1¾ oz fine egg noodles
1 tbsp chilli sauce	oil, for frying

❄ Using a sharp knife, make a small horizontal slit across the back of each prawn. Press down on the prawns so that they lie flat.

❄ Mix together the peanut butter and chilli sauce in a small bowl until well blended. Using a pastry brush, spread a little of the sauce on to each prawn so they are evenly coated.

❄ Cut each pastry sheet in half and brush with melted butter.

❄ Wrap each prawn in a piece of pastry, tucking the edges under to fully enclose the prawn.

❄ Place the fine egg noodles in a bowl, pour over enough boiling water to cover and leave to stand for 5 minutes. Drain the noodles thoroughly. Use 2–3 cooked noodles to tie around each prawn parcel.

❄ Heat the oil in a preheated wok. Cook the prawns for 3–4 minutes, or until golden and crispy.

❄ Remove the prawns with a slotted spoon, transfer to absorbent kitchen paper and leave to drain. Transfer to serving plates and serve warm.

Prawn Fritters

350 g/12 oz potatoes
350 g/12 oz celeriac
1 carrot
1/2 small onion
225 g/8 oz peeled cooked
prawns, thawed, if frozen, and
well-drained on kitchen paper
2 1/2 tbsp plain flour
1 egg, lightly beaten
salt and pepper
vegetable oil, for frying

CHERRY TOMATO SALSA
225 g/8 oz mixed cherry
tomatoes, quartered
1/2 small mango, finely diced
1 fresh red chilli, deseeded and
finely chopped
1/2 small red onion, finely
chopped
1 tbsp chopped fresh coriander
1 tbsp chopped fresh chives
2 tbsp olive oil
2 tsp lemon juice
salt and pepper

❖ For the salsa, mix the tomatoes, mango, chilli, onion, coriander, chives, olive oil, lemon juice and seasoning. Set aside for the flavours to infuse.

❖ Using a food processor or the fine blade of a box grater, finely grate the potatoes, celeriac, carrot and onion. Mix together with the prawns, flour and egg. Season well and set aside.

❖ Divide the prawn mixture into 8 equal pieces. Press each into a greased 10-cm/4-inch metal pastry cutter (if you have only 1 cutter, you can simply shape the fritters individually).

❖ Heat a shallow layer of oil in a large frying pan. When hot, transfer the fritters, still in the cutters, to the frying pan, in 4 batches if necessary. When the oil sizzles underneath, remove the cutter. Fry gently, pressing down with a spatula, for 6–8 minutes on each side until crisp and browned and the vegetables are tender. Drain on kitchen paper and keep warm. Serve hot with the tomato salsa.

Prawns with Garlic Butter

2 tbsp olive oil
20 raw king prawns
4 garlic cloves, finely chopped
4 tbsp finely chopped fresh
flat-leaf parsley

juice of 1/2 lemon
5 tbsp dry white wine
25 g/1 oz butter, diced
sea salt and pepper

❊ Heat the oil in a large heavy-based frying pan. Add the prawns, season to taste with sea salt and pepper and cook over a medium heat for 2 minutes. Turn the prawns over, add the garlic and parsley and cook for a further 2–3 minutes, or until the prawns have changed colour.

❊ Add the lemon juice and cook, stirring constantly, until it has almost evaporated. Using a slotted spoon, transfer the prawns to a serving dish and keep warm.

❊ Pour the wine into the pan, bring to the boil and cook until reduced by about half. Whisk in the butter, a piece at a time, until the sauce has thickened. Pour some of the sauce over the prawns and reserve the rest for dipping. Serve immediately with the extra sauce.

Calamari

450 g/1 lb prepared squid
plain flour, for coating
sunflower oil, for deep-frying

salt
lemon wedges, to garnish
aïoli, to serve

❊ Slice the squid into 1-cm/1/2-inch rings and halve the tentacles if large. Rinse and dry well on kitchen paper so that they do not spit during cooking. Dust the squid rings with flour so that they are lightly coated. Do not season the flour, as Spanish cooks will tell you that seasoning squid with salt before cooking toughens it.

❊ Heat the sunflower oil in a deep-fat fryer to 180°C/350°F or until a cube of bread browns in 30 seconds. Carefully add the squid rings in batches, so that the temperature of the oil does not drop. Deep-fry for 2–3 minutes, or until golden brown and crisp all over, turning several times. Do not overcook as the squid will become tough and rubbery rather than moist and tender.

❊ Using a slotted spoon, remove the fried squid from the deep-fat fryer and drain well on kitchen paper. Keep warm in a warm oven while you deep-fry the remaining squid rings.

❊ Sprinkle the deep-fried squid rings with salt and serve piping hot, garnished with the lemon wedges for squeezing over them. Accompany with a bowl of aïoli for dipping.

Thai-Style Crab Sandwich

❈ SERVES 4 ❈

2 tbsp lime juice
2-cm/¾-inch piece of fresh
ginger root, grated
2-cm/¾-inch piece of lemon
grass, finely chopped
5 tbsp mayonnaise

2 large slices crusty bread
1 ripe avocado
150 g/5½ oz cooked crabmeat
pepper
sprigs of fresh coriander,
to garnish

❈ Mix half the lime juice with the ginger and lemon grass. Add the mayonnaise and mix well.

❈ Spread 1 tablespoon of mayonnaise smoothly over each slice of bread.

❈ Halve the avocado and remove the stone. Peel and thinly slice the flesh, then arrange the slices on the bread. Sprinkle with lime juice.

❈ Spoon the crabmeat over the avocado, then add any remaining lime juice. Spoon over the remaining mayonnaise, season with pepper, garnish with a sprig of coriander and serve immediately.

Crab Ravioli

❈ SERVES 4 ❈

450 g/1 lb crabmeat (fresh or
canned and drained)
½ red pepper, deseeded and
finely diced
125 g/4½ oz Chinese leaves,
shredded
25 g/1 oz beansprouts, roughly
chopped

1 tbsp light soy sauce
1 tsp lime juice
16 wonton wrappers
1 small egg, beaten
2 tbsp peanut oil
1 tsp sesame oil
salt and pepper

❈ Mix together the crabmeat, red pepper, Chinese leaves, beansprouts, soy sauce and lime juice. Season and leave to stand for 15 minutes.

❈ Spread out the wonton wrappers on a work surface. Spoon a little of the crabmeat mixture into the centre of each wrapper. Brush the edges with egg and fold in half, pushing out any air. Press the edges together to seal.

❈ Heat the peanut oil in a preheated wok or frying pan. Fry the ravioli, in batches, for 3–4 minutes, turning, until brown. Remove with a slotted spoon and drain on kitchen paper.

❈ Heat any remaining filling in the wok or frying pan over a gentle heat until hot. Serve the ravioli with the hot filling, sprinkled with the sesame oil.

Crab Cakes with Salsa Verde

250 g/9 oz crabmeat,
thawed, if frozen
250 g/9 oz white fish fillet, such
as cod, skinned and roughly
chopped
1 fresh red chilli, deseeded and
roughly chopped
1 garlic clove, roughly chopped
2.5-cm/1-inch piece of root
ginger, roughly chopped
1 lemon grass stalk, roughly
chopped
3 tbsp chopped fresh coriander
1 egg white
groundnut or sunflower oil,
for frying

SALSA VERDE

2 fresh green chillies, deseeded
and roughly chopped
8 spring onions, roughly chopped
2 garlic cloves, roughly chopped
1 bunch of fresh parsley
grated rind and juice of 1 lime
juice of 1 lemon
4 tbsp olive oil
1 tbsp green Tabasco sauce
salt and pepper

❄   Place the crabmeat, fish, red chilli, garlic, ginger, lemon grass, coriander and egg white in a food processor and process until thoroughly blended, then transfer to a bowl, cover with clingfilm and chill in the refrigerator for 30–60 minutes.

❄   Meanwhile, make the salsa verde. Place the green chillies, spring onions, garlic and parsley in a food processor and process until finely chopped. Transfer to a small bowl and stir in the lime rind, lime and lemon juice, olive oil and Tabasco sauce. Season to taste with salt and pepper, cover with clingfilm and leave to chill in the refrigerator until ready to serve.

❄   Heat 2 tablespoons of the groundnut oil in a non-stick frying pan. Add spoonfuls of the crab mixture, flattening them gently with a spatula and keeping them spaced well apart. Cook for 4 minutes, then turn with a spatula and cook the other side for 3 minutes, or until golden brown. Remove from the frying pan and keep warm while you cook the remaining batches, adding more oil if necessary. Transfer the crab cakes to a large serving plate and serve with the salsa verde.

Steamed Crab Cakes

❖ **SERVES 4** ❖

1–2 banana leaves	200 g/7 oz cooked crabmeat,
2 garlic cloves, crushed	flaked
1 tsp finely chopped	1 tbsp Thai fish sauce
lemon grass	2 egg whites
$^1/_2$ tsp pepper	1 egg yolk, lightly beaten
2 tbsp chopped fresh coriander	8 fresh coriander leaves
3 tbsp creamed coconut	sunflower oil, for deep-frying
1 tbsp lime juice	chilli sauce, to serve

❖ Line 8 x 100-ml/3$^1/_2$-fl oz ramekins or foil containers with the banana leaves, cutting them to shape.

❖ Mix together the garlic, lemon grass, pepper and coriander. Mash the creamed coconut with the lime juice until smooth. Stir it into the other ingredients with the crabmeat and fish sauce.

❖ In a clean dry bowl, whisk the egg whites until stiff, then lightly and evenly fold them into the crab mixture.

❖ Spoon the mixture into the ramekins or foil containers lined with banana leaves and press down lightly. Brush the tops with egg yolk and top each with a coriander leaf.

❖ Place in a steamer half-filled with boiling water, then cover with a close-fitting lid and steam for 15 minutes, or until firm to the touch. Pour off the excess liquid and remove from the ramekins or foil containers.

❖ Heat the oil to 180°C/350°F or until a cube of bread browns in 30 seconds. Add the crab cakes and deep-fry for about 1 minute, turning them over once, until golden brown. Serve hot with the chilli sauce.

Mussels in White Wine

❖ **SERVES 4** ❖

3 litres/5$^1/_4$ pints fresh mussels	good pinch of finely grated
55 g/2 oz butter	lemon rind
1 large onion, very finely	1 bouquet garni sachet
chopped	1 tbsp plain flour
2–3 garlic cloves, crushed	4 tbsp single or double cream
350 ml/12 fl oz dry white wine	2–3 tbsp chopped fresh parsley
150 ml/5 fl oz water	salt and pepper
2 tbsp lemon juice	warm crusty bread, to serve

❖ Scrub the mussels in several changes of cold water and debeard. All of the mussels must be tightly closed; if they don't close when given a sharp tap, they must be discarded.

❖ Melt half the butter in a large saucepan. Add the onion and garlic, and fry gently until soft but not coloured.

❖ Add the wine, water, lemon juice, lemon rind, bouquet garni and plenty of seasoning. Bring to the boil, then cover and simmer for 4–5 minutes.

❖ Add the mussels to the pan, cover tightly and simmer for 5 minutes, shaking the pan frequently, until all the mussels have opened. Discard any mussels that have not opened. Remove the bouquet garni.

❖ Remove the empty half shell from each mussel. Blend the remaining butter with the flour and whisk into the soup, a little at a time. Simmer gently for 2–3 minutes until slightly thickened.

❖ Add the cream and half the parsley to the soup and reheat gently. Adjust the seasoning. Ladle the mussels and soup into large warmed soup bowls, sprinkle with the remaining parsley and serve with the bread.

Mussels with Garlic Butter

800 g/1 lb 12 oz live mussels, in their shells	4 tbsp chopped fresh flat-leaf parsley, plus extra sprigs to garnish
splash of dry white wine	
1 bay leaf	2 tbsp snipped fresh chives
85 g/3 oz butter	2 garlic cloves, finely chopped
350 g/12 oz fresh white or brown breadcrumbs	salt and pepper
	lemon wedges, to serve

❈ Clean the mussels by scrubbing or scraping the shells and pulling out any beards that are attached to them. Discard any with broken shells and any that refuse to close when sharply tapped with the back of a knife. Place the mussels in a colander and rinse under cold running water.

❈ Place the mussels in a large saucepan and add a splash of wine and the bay leaf. Cook, covered, over a high heat for 5 minutes, shaking the saucepan occasionally, or until the mussels are opened. Drain the mussels and discard any that remain closed.

❈ Shell the mussels, reserving one half of each shell. Arrange the mussels, in their half-shells, in a large, shallow, ovenproof serving dish.

❈ Melt the butter and pour into a bowl. Add the breadcrumbs, parsley, chives, garlic and salt and pepper to taste and mix well together. Leave until the butter has set slightly. Using your fingers or 2 teaspoons, take a large pinch of the herb and butter mixture and use to fill each mussel shell, pressing it down well. Leave the mussels to chill until ready to serve.

❈ To serve, preheat the oven to 230°C/450°F/Gas Mark 8. Bake the mussels in the preheated oven for 10 minutes or until hot. Serve immediately, garnished with the sprigs of parsley and accompanied by the lemon wedges for squeezing over them.

Seared Scallops

450 g/1 lb scallops, without roe	3 tbsp light soy sauce
6 spring onions	50 g/1¾ oz butter, cubed
2 tbsp vegetable oil	
1 green chilli, deseeded and sliced	

❈ Rinse the scallops under cold running water, then pat dry with absorbent kitchen paper.

❈ Using a sharp knife, slice each scallop in half horizontally.

❈ Using a sharp knife, trim and slice the spring onions.

❈ Heat the oil in a large preheated wok.

❈ Add the chilli, spring onions and scallops to the wok and stir-fry over a high heat for 4–5 minutes or until the scallops are just cooked through.

❈ Add the soy sauce and butter to the scallop stir-fry and heat through until the butter melts.

❈ Transfer to warmed serving bowls and serve hot.

Grilled Sardines

12 fresh sardines
2 tbsp garlic-flavoured olive oil
coarse sea salt and pepper
lemon wedges, to serve

❖ Scrape the scales off the sardines with a knife, then, working with 1 sardine at a time, hold it firmly in one hand and snap off the head with your other hand, pulling downwards. This should remove most of the guts with the head, but use a finger to remove any innards that remain. You can then use your thumb and forefinger to grasp the top of the backbone and pull it towards you to remove. Rinse well and pat dry with kitchen paper.

❖ Preheat the grill to high and brush the grill rack with a little of the oil. Brush the sardines with the oil and arrange in a single layer on the grill rack. Sprinkle with salt and pepper to taste.

❖ Grill about 10 cm/4 inches from the heat for 3 minutes or until the skin becomes crisp. Use kitchen tongs to turn over the sardines and brush with more oil and sprinkle with salt and pepper. Continue grilling for 2–3 minutes or until the flesh flakes easily and the skin is crisp. Serve immediately with the lemon wedges.

Simple
soups & salads

Plum Tomato Soup

❖ **SERVES 4** ❖

2 tbsp olive oil
2 red onions, chopped
2 celery sticks, chopped
1 carrot, chopped
500 g/1 lb 2 oz plum tomatoes, halved
750 ml/1¼ pints vegetable stock
1 tbsp chopped fresh oregano
1 tbsp chopped fresh basil
150 ml/5 fl oz dry white wine
2 tsp caster sugar
125 g/4½ oz hazelnuts, toasted
125 g/4½ oz stoned black or green olives
handful of fresh basil leaves
1 tbsp olive oil
1 loaf ciabatta bread
salt and pepper
sprigs of fresh basil, to garnish

❖ Heat the oil in a large saucepan. Add the onions, celery and carrot and fry over a low heat, stirring frequently, until soft but not coloured.

❖ Add the tomatoes, stock, chopped herbs, wine and sugar. Bring to the boil, cover and simmer for 20 minutes.

❖ Place the toasted hazelnuts in a blender or food processor, together with the olives and basil leaves, and process until thoroughly combined but not too smooth. Alternatively, finely chop the nuts, olives and basil leaves and pound them together in a mortar with a pestle, then turn into a small bowl. Add the oil and process or beat thoroughly for a few seconds to combine. Turn the mixture into a serving bowl.

❖ Warm the ciabatta bread in a preheated oven,190°C/375°F/Gas Mark 5, for 3–4 minutes.

❖ Process the soup in a blender or a food processor, or press through a sieve until smooth. Check the seasoning. Ladle into warmed soup bowls and garnish with the sprigs of basil. Slice the warmed bread and spread with the olive and hazelnut paste. Serve with the soup.

Lentil & Tomato Soup

❖ **SERVES 4** ❖

450 g/1 lb tomatoes
1 tbsp corn or sunflower oil
1 onion, finely chopped
1 garlic glove, crushed
½ tsp ground cumin
½ tsp ground coriander
125 g/4 oz red lentils
1.2 litres/2 pints vegetable stock
salt and pepper
finely chopped fresh coriander, to garnish

❖ Using a small serrated knife make a cross in the tomato skins. Place in boiling water for 20 seconds and then plunge into cold water. Slip off the skins. Halve the tomatoes, remove the seeds and chop the flesh. Heat the oil in a saucepan. Add the onion and cook over a low heat, stirring occasionally, for 5 minutes until softened. Stir in the garlic, cumin, coriander, tomatoes and lentils and cook, stirring constantly, for 4 minutes more.

❖ Pour in the stock, bring to the boil, then simmer gently for 30–40 minutes until the lentils are tender. Season to taste with salt and pepper.

❖ Remove the pan from the heat and allow to cool slightly, then process in a blender or food processor to a purée. Transfer to a clean pan and reheat. Serve the soup immediately, garnished with the chopped coriander.

Spicy Gazpacho Soup

❖ **SERVES 4–6** ❖

1 cucumber
2 green peppers
6 ripe tomatoes
1/2 fresh hot chilli
1/2–1 onion, finely chopped
3–4 garlic cloves, chopped
4 tbsp extra virgin olive oil
1/4–1/2 tsp ground cumin
2–4 tsp sherry vinegar or a
  combination of balsamic
  vinegar and wine vinegar

4 tbsp chopped fresh coriander
2 tbsp chopped fresh parsley
300 ml/10 fl oz vegetable or
  chicken stock
600 ml/1 pint tomato juice or
  passata
salt and pepper
ice cubes, to serve

❖ Cut the cucumber in half lengthways, then cut into quarters. Remove the seeds with a teaspoon and dice the flesh. Cut the peppers in half, remove the cores and seeds, then dice the flesh.

❖ If you prefer to peel the tomatoes, place in a heatproof bowl, pour over boiling water to cover and stand for 30 seconds. Drain and plunge into cold water. The skins will then slide off easily. Cut the tomatoes in half, deseed if wished, then chop the flesh. Deseed and chop the fresh chilli.

❖ Combine half the cucumber, green pepper, tomatoes and onion in a blender or food processor with all the chilli, garlic, olive oil, cumin, vinegar, coriander and parsley. Process with enough stock for a smooth purée.

❖ Pour the puréed soup into a bowl and stir in the remaining stock and the tomato juice. Add the remaining green pepper, cucumber, tomatoes and onion, stirring well. Season to taste with salt and pepper, then cover with clingfilm and chill in the refrigerator for a few hours.

❖ Ladle the chilled soup into bowls and serve with ice cubes in each bowl.

Roasted Vegetable Soup

❖ **SERVES 6** ❖

2–3 tbsp olive oil
700 g/1 lb 9 oz ripe tomatoes,
  peeled, seeded and halved
3 large yellow peppers, halved
  and deseeded
3 courgettes, halved
  lengthways
1 small aubergine, halved
  lengthways

4 garlic cloves, halved
2 onions, cut into eighths
pinch of dried thyme
1 litre/13/4 pints vegetable
  stock
125 ml/4 fl oz single cream
salt and pepper
shredded fresh basil leaves,
  to garnish

❖ Brush a large shallow baking dish with olive oil. Laying them cut side down, arrange the tomatoes, peppers, courgettes and aubergine in one layer (use two dishes, if necessary). Tuck the garlic cloves and onion pieces into the gaps and drizzle the vegetables with olive oil. Season lightly with salt and pepper and sprinkle with the thyme.

❖ Place the vegetables in a preheated oven, 190°C/375°F/ Gas Mark 5, and bake, uncovered, for 30–35 minutes, or until soft and brown around the edges. Leave to cool, then scrape out the aubergine flesh and remove the skin from the peppers.

❖ Working in batches, put the aubergine, pepper flesh, courgettes, tomatoes, garlic and onions into a food processor and chop to the consistency of salsa or pickle; do not purée. Alternatively, place in a bowl and chop with a knife.

❖ Combine the stock with the chopped vegetable mixture in a saucepan and simmer over a medium heat for 20–30 minutes until all the vegetables are tender and the flavours have completely blended.

❖ Stir in the cream and heat the soup very gently for about 5 minutes, stirring occasionally, until hot. Taste and adjust the seasoning, if necessary. Ladle the soup into warmed bowls, garnish with the basil and serve.

Jerusalem Artichoke Soup

675 g/1 lb 8 oz Jerusalem
artichokes
5 tbsp orange juice
25 g/1 oz butter
1 leek, chopped
1 garlic clove, crushed
300 ml/10 fl oz vegetable stock
150 ml/5 fl oz milk
2 tbsp chopped coriander
150 ml/5 fl oz natural yogurt
grated orange rind, to garnish

❖ Rinse the artichokes and place in a large saucepan with 2 tablespoons of the orange juice and enough water to cover. Bring to the boil, reduce the heat and cook for 20 minutes, or until the artichokes are tender.

❖ Drain the artichokes, reserving 425 ml/15 fl oz of the cooking liquid. Leave the artichokes to cool, then peel and place in a large bowl. Mash the flesh with a potato masher.

❖ Melt the butter in a large saucepan. Add the leek and garlic and fry over a low heat, stirring frequently, for 2–3 minutes, until the leek is soft.

❖ Stir in the mashed artichoke, stock, milk, remaining orange juice and reserved cooking water. Bring to the boil, then simmer for 2–3 minutes.

❖ Remove a few pieces of leek with a slotted spoon and reserve. Process the remainder in a food processor for 1 minute until smooth. Alternatively, press through a sieve with the back of a spoon.

❖ Transfer the soup to a clean saucepan and stir in the reserved leeks, coriander and yogurt and heat through. Transfer to individual soup bowls, garnish with the orange rind and serve.

Pumpkin Soup

about 1 kg/2 lb 4 oz pumpkin
40 g/1$\frac{1}{2}$ oz butter or
margarine
1 onion, thinly sliced
1 garlic clove, crushed
900 ml/1$\frac{1}{2}$ pints vegetable
stock
$\frac{1}{2}$ tsp ground ginger
1 tbsp lemon juice
3–4 thinly pared strips of
orange rind (optional)

1–2 bay leaves or 1 bouquet
garni
300 ml/10 fl oz milk
salt and pepper
4–6 tablespoons single or
double cream, natural yogurt
or fromage frais and some
snipped chives, to garnish

❉ Peel the pumpkin, remove the seeds and then cut the flesh into 2.5-cm/1-inch cubes.

❉ Melt the butter in a large heavy-based saucepan. Add the onion and garlic and fry over a low heat until soft but not coloured.

❉ Add the pumpkin and toss with the onion for 2–3 minutes.

❉ Add the stock and bring to the boil over a medium heat. Season to taste with salt and pepper and add the ginger, lemon juice, strips of orange rind, if using, and bay leaves or bouquet garni. Cover and simmer over a low heat for about 20 minutes, until the pumpkin is tender.

❉ Discard the orange rind, if using, and the bay leaves or bouquet garni. Cool the soup slightly, then press through a sieve or process in a food processor until smooth. Pour into a clean saucepan.

❉ Add the milk and reheat gently. Adjust the seasoning. Garnish with a swirl of cream and the chives, and serve.

Carrot, Apple & Celery Soup

900 g/2 lb carrots, finely diced
1 onion, chopped
3 celery sticks, sliced
1 litre/1$\frac{3}{4}$ pints vegetable stock
3 apples
2 tbsp tomato purée

1 bay leaf
2 tsp caster sugar
$\frac{1}{4}$ large lemon
salt and pepper
shredded celery leaves,
to garnish

❉ Place the carrots, onion and celery in a large heavy-based saucepan and add the stock. Bring to the boil, reduce the heat, cover and simmer for 10 minutes.

❉ Peel, core and dice 2 of the apples. Add the apple, the tomato purée, bay leaf and sugar to the pan and bring to the boil over a medium heat. Reduce the heat, half-cover with a lid and simmer for 20 minutes. Remove the bay leaf.

❉ Meanwhile, wash, core and cut the remaining apple into thin slices, without peeling.

❉ Place the apple slices in a small pan and squeeze over the lemon juice. Heat the apple slices gently and simmer for 1–2 minutes until tender.

❉ Drain the apple slices and set aside until required.

❉ Place the carrot and apple mixture in a blender or food processor and process until smooth. Alternatively, press the mixture through a sieve with the back of a wooden spoon.

❉ Gently reheat the soup, if necessary, and season to taste with salt and pepper. Ladle the soup into warmed bowls and serve topped with the reserved apple slices and shredded celery leaves.

Broccoli & Potato Soup

2 tbsp olive oil	1 litre/1¾ pints vegetable stock
2 potatoes, diced	150 ml/5 fl oz double cream
1 onion, diced	pinch of paprika, plus extra for
225 g/8 oz broccoli florets	sprinkling
125 g/4½ oz blue cheese,	salt and pepper
crumbled	

❄ Heat the oil in a large saucepan and add the diced potatoes and onion. Sauté gently for 5 minutes, stirring constantly.

❄ Reserve a few broccoli florets for the garnish and add the remaining broccoli to the pan. Add the cheese and stock.

❄ Bring to the boil, then reduce the heat, cover the pan and simmer for 25 minutes until the potatoes are tender.

❄ Transfer the soup to a food processor or blender in 2 batches and process until the mixture is a smooth purée.

❄ Return the purée to a clean saucepan and stir in the cream and the paprika. Season to taste with salt and pepper.

❄ Blanch the reserved broccoli florets in a little boiling water for about 2 minutes, then drain with a slotted spoon.

❄ Pour the soup into warmed bowls and garnish with the broccoli florets and a sprinkling of paprika. Serve immediately.

Cauliflower & Broccoli Soup

3 tbsp vegetable oil	300 ml/10 fl oz vegetable stock
1 red onion, chopped	75 g/2¾ oz Gruyère cheese,
2 garlic cloves, crushed	grated
300 g/10½ oz cauliflower	pinch of paprika
florets	150 ml/5 fl oz single cream
300 g/10½ oz broccoli florets	paprika and Gruyère cheese
1 tbsp plain flour	shavings, to garnish
600 ml/1 pint milk	

❄ Heat the vegetable oil in a large heavy-based saucepan. Add the onion, garlic, cauliflower florets and broccoli florets and sauté over a low heat, stirring constantly, for about 3–4 minutes. Sprinkle the flour over the vegetables and cook, stirring constantly, for a further minute.

❄ Gradually stir in the milk and stock and bring to the boil, stirring constantly. Reduce the heat and simmer for 20 minutes.

❄ Remove about a quarter of the vegetables with a slotted spoon and set aside. Put the remaining soup in a food processor or blender and process for about 30 seconds, until smooth. Alternatively, press the vegetables through a sieve with the back of a wooden spoon. Transfer the soup to a clean saucepan.

❄ Return the reserved vegetable pieces to the soup. Stir in the grated cheese, paprika and single cream and heat through over a low heat, without boiling, for about 2–3 minutes, or until the cheese starts to melt.

❄ Ladle the soup into warmed individual serving bowls, garnish with the cheese shavings and dust with the paprika. Serve immediately.

Parsnip Soup with Ginger

2 tsp olive oil
1 large onion, chopped
1 large leek, sliced
800 g/1 lb 12 oz parsnips, sliced
2 carrots, thinly sliced
4 tbsp grated root ginger
2–3 garlic cloves, finely chopped
grated rind of $\frac{1}{2}$ orange
1.4 litres/$2\frac{1}{2}$ pints water
225 ml/8 fl oz orange juice
salt and pepper
snipped fresh chives or slivers
of spring onion, to garnish

❖ Heat the olive oil in a large saucepan over a medium heat. Add the onion and leek and cook, stirring occasionally, for about 5 minutes until soft.

❖ Add the parsnips, carrots, ginger, garlic, orange rind, water and a pinch of salt. Reduce the heat, cover the pan and simmer, stirring occasionally, for about 40 minutes until the vegetables are soft.

❖ Remove from the heat and set aside to cool slightly, then transfer to a blender or food processor and process to a smooth purée, in batches if necessary.

❖ Return the soup to the pan and stir in the orange juice. Add a little water or more orange juice, if you prefer a thinner consistency. Taste and adjust the seasoning with salt and pepper.

❖ Simmer for about 10 minutes to heat through. Ladle into warmed bowls, garnish with the chives and serve immediately.

Creamy Sweetcorn Soup

1 large onion, chopped	1 tbsp cornflour
300 g/10½ oz potatoes, diced	3 tbsp cold water
1 litre/1¾ pints skimmed milk	4 tbsp low-fat natural yogurt
1 bay leaf	salt and pepper
½ tsp freshly grated nutmeg	100 g/3½ oz lean ham, diced,
450 g/1 lb sweetcorn kernels,	and 2 tbsp snipped fresh
canned or frozen, drained or	chives, to garnish
thawed	

❖ Place the onion and potato in a large saucepan and pour over the milk.

❖ Add the bay leaf, nutmeg and half the sweetcorn to the pan. Bring to the boil, cover and simmer over a low heat for 15 minutes until the potato is softened. Stir the soup occasionally and keep the heat low so that the milk does not burn on the base of the pan.

❖ Remove and discard the bay leaf and set the liquid aside to cool for about 10 minutes. Transfer to a blender and process for a few seconds. Alternatively, rub the soup through a sieve.

❖ Pour the smooth liquid into a saucepan. Blend the cornflour with the cold water to make a paste and stir it into the soup.

❖ Bring the soup back to the boil, stirring until it thickens, and add the remaining sweetcorn. Heat through for 2–3 minutes until piping hot.

❖ Remove the soup from the heat and season to taste with salt and pepper. Add the yogurt and stir until it is thoroughly blended.

❖ Ladle the creamy sweetcorn soup into warmed bowls and serve, garnished with the diced ham and snipped chives.

Cheese & Vegetable Chowder

25 g/1 oz butter	1 large potato, finely diced
1 large onion, finely chopped	3–4 sprigs of fresh thyme or
1 large leek, split lengthways	⅛ tsp dried thyme
and thinly sliced	1 bay leaf
1–2 garlic cloves, crushed	350 ml/12 fl oz single cream
55 g/2 oz plain flour	300 g/10½ oz mature Cheddar
1.2 litres/2 pints vegetable stock	cheese, grated
3 carrots, finely diced	salt and pepper
2 celery sticks, finely diced	chopped fresh parsley,
1 turnip, finely diced	to garnish

❖ Melt the butter in a large heavy-based saucepan over a medium–low heat. Add the onion, leek and garlic. Cover and cook for about 5 minutes, stirring frequently, until the vegetables are starting to soften.

❖ Stir the flour into the vegetables and cook for 2 minutes. Add a little of the stock and stir, scraping the bottom of the pan to mix in the flour. Bring to the boil, stirring frequently, and slowly stir in the rest of the stock.

❖ Add the carrots, celery, turnip, potato, thyme and bay leaf. Reduce the heat, cover the pan and cook the soup gently for about 35 minutes, stirring occasionally, until the vegetables are tender. Remove the bay leaf and the thyme sprigs and discard.

❖ Stir in the cream and simmer over a very low heat for 5 minutes. Add the cheese a handful at a time, stirring constantly for 1 minute after each addition to make sure it is completely melted.

❖ Taste the soup and adjust the seasoning, adding salt if needed, and pepper to taste.

❖ Ladle the soup into warmed bowls, sprinkle with the parsley and serve.

Spicy Lentil & Carrot Soup

❖ **SERVES 4** ❖

125 g/4^1/$_2$ oz split red lentils
1.2 litres/2 pints vegetable stock
350 g/12 oz carrots, sliced
2 onions, chopped
225 g/8 oz canned chopped tomatoes
2 garlic cloves, chopped
2 tbsp ghee or oil
1 tsp ground cumin

1 tsp ground coriander
1 fresh green chilli, deseeded and chopped, or 1 tsp minced chilli
^{1}/$_2$ tsp turmeric
1 tbsp lemon juice
300 ml/10 fl oz milk
salt
2 tbsp chopped fresh coriander
natural yogurt, to serve

❖ Place the lentils in a sieve and rinse well under cold running water. Drain and place in a large saucepan, together with 900 ml/1^1/$_2$ pints of the stock, the carrots, onions, tomatoes and garlic. Bring the mixture to the boil, reduce the heat, cover and simmer for 30 minutes, or until the vegetables and lentils are tender.

❖ Meanwhile, heat the ghee or oil in a small saucepan. Add the cumin, ground coriander, chilli and turmeric and fry over a low heat for 1 minute. Remove from the heat and stir in the lemon juice. Season to taste with salt.

❖ Process the soup in batches in a blender or food processor. Return the soup to the large pan, add the spice mixture and the remaining stock and simmer over a low heat for 10 minutes.

❖ Add the milk, taste and adjust the seasoning, if necessary. Stir in the chopped coriander and reheat gently. Serve hot with a swirl of yogurt.

Curried Courgette Soup

❖ **SERVES 4** ❖

2 tsp butter
1 large onion, finely chopped
900 g/2 lb courgettes, sliced
450 ml/16 fl oz vegetable stock
1 tsp curry powder

125 ml/4 fl oz soured cream
salt and pepper
soured cream and croûtons, to garnish

❖ Melt the butter in a saucepan over a medium heat. Add the onion and cook for 3 minutes until it begins to soften.

❖ Add the courgettes, stock and curry powder, and salt if using unsalted stock. Bring the soup to the boil, reduce the heat, cover and cook for about 25 minutes until the vegetables are tender.

❖ Allow the soup to cool slightly, then transfer it to a blender or food processor, working in batches if necessary. Purée the soup until just smooth, but still with green flecks. (If using a food processor, strain off the cooking liquid and reserve. Purée the soup solids with enough cooking liquid to moisten them, then combine with the remaining liquid.)

❖ Return the soup to the pan and stir in the soured cream. Reheat gently over a low heat just until hot, but be careful not to allow the soup to boil.

❖ Taste and adjust the seasoning, if needed. Ladle the soup into warmed bowls and serve, garnished with a swirl of soured cream and the croûtons.

Spinach Soup

1 tbsp olive oil
1 onion, halved and thinly sliced
1 leek, split lengthways and thinly sliced
1 potato, finely diced
1 litre/1¾ pints water
2 sprigs fresh marjoram or ¼ tsp dried marjoram
2 sprigs fresh thyme, or ¼ tsp dried thyme
1 bay leaf
400 g/14 oz young spinach
freshly grated nutmeg
salt and pepper
4 tbsp single cream, to serve

❈ Heat the oil in a heavy-based saucepan over a medium heat. Add the onion and leek and cook, stirring occasionally, for about 3 minutes until they are just beginning to soften.

❈ Add the potato, water, marjoram, thyme and bay leaf and season with a pinch of salt. Bring to the boil, reduce the heat, cover and cook gently for about 25 minutes until the vegetables are tender. Remove the bay leaf and the herb stems.

❈ Add the spinach and continue cooking for 3–4 minutes, stirring frequently, just until it is completely wilted. Remove the pan from the heat and set aside to cool slightly.

❈ Transfer the soup to a blender or food processor and process to a smooth purée, working in batches if necessary. (If using a food processor, strain off the cooking liquid and reserve. Process the soup solids with enough cooking liquid to moisten them, then combine with the remaining liquid.)

❈ Return the soup to the pan and thin with a little more water, if wished. Season to taste with salt and pepper and nutmeg. Place over a low heat and simmer until reheated. Ladle the soup into warmed bowls and swirl a tablespoonful of cream into each serving.

Chilled Watercress Soup

1 tbsp olive oil	1 bay leaf
3 large leeks, thinly sliced	175 g/6 oz watercress, washed
350 g/12 oz potatoes,	and dried
finely diced	175 ml/6 fl oz single cream
600 ml/1 pint vegetable stock	salt and pepper
450 ml/16 fl oz water	watercress leaves, to garnish

❈ Heat the oil in a heavy-based saucepan over a medium heat. Add the sliced leeks and cook for about 3 minutes, stirring frequently, until they begin to soften.

❈ Add the potatoes, stock, water and bay leaf. Add salt if the stock is unsalted. Bring to the boil, then reduce the heat, cover the pan and cook gently for about 25 minutes, until the vegetables are tender. Remove the bay leaf and discard it.

❈ Add the watercress and continue to cook for a further 2–3 minutes, stirring frequently, until the watercress is completely wilted.

❈ Allow the soup to cool slightly, then transfer to a blender or food processor and purée until smooth, working in batches if necessary. (If using a food processor, strain off the cooking liquid and reserve. Purée the soup solids with enough cooking liquid to moisten them, then combine with the remaining liquid.)

❈ Put the soup into a large bowl and then stir in half the cream. Season with salt, if needed, and plenty of pepper. Leave to cool to room temperature.

❈ Refrigerate until cold. Taste and adjust the seasoning, if necessary. Ladle into chilled bowls, drizzle the remaining cream on top and garnish with the watercress leaves. Serve at once.

Pear & Watercress Soup

	CROÛTONS
4 pears	2–3 slices day-old bread
1 bunch of watercress	2 tbsp olive oil
850 ml/1½ pints vegetable	
stock	
juice of ½ lemon	
salt and pepper	
125 ml/4 fl oz double cream	

❈ Core the pears and slice them lengthways. Set aside about one third of the watercress. Place the remaining leaves with the stalks in a heavy-based saucepan and add the pears and stock. Bring to the boil, reduce the heat and simmer for 15 minutes.

❈ Remove the pan from the heat, leave to cool slightly, then add the reserved watercress. Pour into a blender or food processor and process until smooth. Pour the soup through a fine-mesh sieve into a bowl, stir in the lemon juice and season to taste.

❈ To make the croûtons, cut the day-old bread into 5-mm/¼-inch squares. Heat the olive oil in a heavy-based frying pan and add the bread cubes. Cook, tossing and stirring constantly until evenly coloured. Drain on kitchen paper.

❈ If serving hot, stir in the cream and transfer the soup to a clean saucepan. Heat gently until warmed through, then serve immediately, garnished with the croûtons. If serving cold, let the soup cool before you stir in the cream, then cover with clingfilm and chill in the refrigerator.

Asparagus Soup

❋ SERVES 4 ❋

1 bunch asparagus, about 350 g/12 oz, or 2 packs mini asparagus, about 150 g/5$\frac{1}{2}$ oz each	3 tbsp plain flour
	$\frac{1}{4}$ tsp ground coriander
	1 tbsp lemon juice
	450 ml/16 fl oz milk
700 ml/1$\frac{1}{4}$ pints vegetable stock	4–6 tbsp double or single cream
60 g/2 oz butter or margarine	salt and pepper
1 onion, chopped	

❋ Wash and trim the asparagus, discarding the lower, woody part of the stem. Cut the remainder into short lengths, keeping aside a few tips to use as a garnish. Mini asparagus does not need to be trimmed.

❋ Cook the tips in the minimum of boiling salted water for 5–10 minutes. Drain and set aside.

❋ Put the asparagus in a saucepan with the stock, bring to the boil, cover and simmer for about 20 minutes, until soft. Drain and reserve the stock.

❋ Melt the butter in a saucepan. Add the onion and fry over a low heat until soft, but only barely coloured. Stir in the flour and cook for 1 minute, then gradually whisk in the reserved stock and bring to the boil.

❋ Simmer for 2–3 minutes, until thickened, then stir in the cooked asparagus, seasoning, coriander and lemon juice. Simmer for 10 minutes, then cool a little and either press through a sieve with the back of a spoon or process in a blender or food processor until smooth.

❋ Pour into a clean saucepan, add the milk and reserved asparagus tips and bring to the boil. Simmer for 2 minutes. Stir in the cream, reheat gently and serve.

Leek, Potato & Carrot Soup

❋ SERVES 3 ❋

1 leek, about 175 g/6 oz	salt and pepper
1 tbsp sunflower oil	chopped fresh parsley, to garnish
1 garlic clove, crushed	
700 ml/1$\frac{1}{4}$ pints vegetable stock	**PURÉED SOUP**
1 bay leaf	5–6 tbsp milk
$\frac{1}{4}$ tsp ground cumin	1–2 tbsp double cream, crème fraîche or soured cream
175 g/6 oz potatoes, diced	
125 g/4$\frac{1}{2}$ oz coarsely grated carrot	

❋ Trim off and discard some of the coarse green part of the leek, then slice thinly and rinse thoroughly in cold water. Drain well.

❋ Heat the oil in a heavy-based saucepan. Add the leek and garlic, and fry over a low heat for about 2–3 minutes, until soft, but barely coloured. Add the vegetable stock, bay leaf and cumin and season to taste with salt and pepper. Bring the mixture to the boil, stirring constantly.

❋ Add the diced potatoes to the saucepan, cover and simmer over a low heat for 10–15 minutes. Keep a careful eye on the soup during the cooking time to make sure the potato cooks until it is just tender, but not broken up. Add the grated carrot to the pan and simmer the soup for a further 2–3 minutes. Adjust the seasoning if necessary, discard the bay leaf and serve the soup in warmed bowls, sprinkled liberally with the chopped parsley.

❋ To make a puréed soup, first process the leftovers (about half the original soup) in a blender or food processor, or press through a sieve with the back of a wooden spoon until smooth, and then return to a clean saucepan with the milk. Bring to the boil and simmer for 2–3 minutes.

❋ Adjust the seasoning and stir in the cream before serving the soup in warmed bowls, sprinkled with the parsley.

Beetroot & Potato Soup

1 onion, chopped
350 g/12 oz potatoes, diced
1 small Bramley apple, peeled,
cored and grated
3 tbsp water
1 tsp cumin seeds
500 g/1 lb 2 oz cooked beetroot,
peeled and diced
1 bay leaf
pinch of dried thyme
1 tsp lemon juice
600 ml/1 pint hot vegetable
stock
salt and pepper
6 tbsp soured cream, to serve
sprigs of fresh dill, to garnish

❖ Place the onion, potatoes, apple and water in a large bowl. Cover and cook in a microwave oven on HIGH power for 10 minutes.

❖ Stir in the cumin seeds and cook on HIGH power for 1 minute.

❖ Stir in the beetroot, bay leaf, thyme, lemon juice and stock. Cover and cook on HIGH power for 12 minutes, stirring halfway through. Set aside, uncovered, for 5 minutes.

❖ Remove and discard the bay leaf. Strain the vegetables and reserve the liquid in a jug.

❖ Place the vegetables with a little of the reserved liquid in a food processor or blender and process to a smooth and creamy purée. Alternatively, either mash the vegetables with a potato masher or press through a sieve.

❖ Pour the vegetable purée into a clean bowl with the reserved liquid and mix well. Season to taste with salt and pepper. Cover and cook on HIGH power for 4–5 minutes until piping hot.

❖ Serve the soup in warmed bowls. Swirl 1 tablespoon of soured cream into each serving and garnish with a few sprigs of dill.

French Onion Soup

1 tbsp butter	200 ml/7 fl oz dry white wine
2 tbsp olive oil	2 litres/3$\frac{1}{2}$ pints vegetable
1 kg/2 lb 4 oz large yellow	stock
onions, halved and sliced into	3 tbsp Cognac or brandy
half-circles	6 slices French stick
3 large garlic cloves, finely	200 g/7 oz Gruyère cheese,
chopped	grated
2 tbsp plain flour	salt and pepper

❖ Melt the butter with the oil in a large heavy-based saucepan over a medium heat. Add the onions and cook, covered, for 10–12 minutes until they soften, stirring occasionally. Add the garlic and sprinkle with salt and pepper.

❖ Reduce the heat a little and continue cooking, uncovered, for 30–35 minutes, or until the onions turn a deep, golden brown, stirring from time to time until they start to colour, then stirring more frequently and scraping the bottom of the pan as they begin to stick.

❖ Sprinkle the flour over the onions and stir to blend. Stir in the wine and bubble for 1 minute. Pour in the stock and bring to the boil, scraping the bottom of the pan and stirring to combine well. Reduce the heat to low, add the Cognac and simmer gently, stirring occasionally, for 45 minutes.

❖ Put 6 soup bowls to warm. Toast the bread on one side under a preheated hot grill. Turn over and top with the cheese, dividing it evenly between the slices. Grill until the cheese bubbles and melts.

❖ Place a piece of cheese toast in each of the 6 warmed bowls, then ladle the hot soup over. Serve at once.

Provençal Garlic Soup

1.2 litres/2 pints chicken stock	salt and pepper
3 garlic bulbs, separated into	sprigs of fresh thyme, to
cloves and peeled	garnish
6 sprigs fresh thyme	
6 fresh sage leaves	**CROÛTES**
1 bunch of parsley	1 French stick, sliced
2 bay leaves	25 g/1 oz butter, melted
pinch of saffron threads	25 g/1 oz freshly grated
3 egg yolks	Parmesan cheese
3 tbsp extra virgin olive oil	

❖ Pour the stock into a large saucepan and add the garlic, thyme, sage, parsley, bay leaves and saffron. Bring to the boil, stirring occasionally, then reduce the heat, partially cover and simmer gently for 40 minutes.

❖ Just before the soup is ready, make the croûtes. Toast the bread slices on one side under a preheated hot grill. Brush the untoasted sides with the melted butter and sprinkle with the cheese. Place under the grill until the cheese has melted and is bubbling.

❖ Meanwhile, whisk the egg yolks in a heatproof bowl until thickened, then gradually whisk in the oil, one drop at a time, until fully combined. Add 1 tablespoon of the egg mixture to the soup, whisking constantly, then season to taste with salt and pepper. Strain the soup into the egg mixture, whisking constantly. Ladle into warmed bowls, garnish with the sprigs of thyme and serve immediately with the croûtes.

Pepper & Chilli Soup

225 g/8 oz red peppers, deseeded and sliced
1 onion, sliced
2 garlic cloves, crushed
1 green chilli, chopped
300 ml/10 fl oz passata
600 ml/1 pint vegetable stock
2 tbsp chopped basil
salt and pepper
sprigs of fresh basil, to garnish

❉ Put the sliced red peppers in a large saucepan with the onion, garlic and chilli. Add the passata and the vegetable stock and bring to the boil, stirring well.

❉ Reduce the heat to a simmer and continue to cook the vegetables for 20 minutes, or until the peppers have softened. Drain, reserving the liquid and vegetables separately.

❉ Using the back of a spoon, press the vegetables through a sieve. Alternatively, process in a food processor until smooth.

❉ Return the vegetable purée to a clean saucepan with the reserved cooking liquid. Add the basil, season and heat through until hot. Garnish the soup with fresh basil sprigs and serve immediately.

Fresh Mushroom Soup

40 g/1$\frac{1}{2}$ oz butter
700 g/1 lb 9 oz mushrooms, sliced
1 onion, finely chopped
1 shallot, finely chopped
25 g/1 oz plain flour
2–3 tbsp dry white wine or sherry
1.4 litres/2$\frac{1}{2}$ pints vegetable stock
150 ml/5 fl oz single cream
2 tbsp chopped fresh parsley
lemon juice (optional)
salt and pepper
4 tbsp soured cream or crème fraîche, to garnish

❉ Melt half the butter in a large frying pan over a medium heat. Add the mushrooms and season with salt and pepper. Cook for about 8 minutes until they are golden brown, stirring occasionally at first, then more often after they start to colour. Remove the pan from the heat.

❉ Melt the remaining butter in a saucepan over a medium heat, add the onion and shallot and cook for 2–3 minutes until just soft. Stir the flour into the pan and continue cooking for 2 minutes. Add the wine and stock and stir well.

❉ Set aside about one quarter of the mushrooms. Add the remainder to the pan. Reduce the heat, cover and cook gently for 20 minutes, stirring occasionally.

❉ Allow the soup to cool slightly, then transfer to a blender or food processor and purée until smooth, working in batches, if necessary. (If using a food processor, strain off the cooking liquid and reserve. Purée the soup solids with enough cooking liquid to moisten them, then combine with the remaining liquid.)

❉ Return the soup to the pan and stir in the reserved mushrooms, the cream and parsley. Cook for about 5 minutes to heat through. Taste and adjust the seasoning, adding a few drops of lemon juice, if wished. Ladle into warmed bowls and garnish with the soured cream.

Creamy Mushroom & Tarragon Soup

50 g/1¾ oz butter
1 onion, chopped
700 g/1 lb 9 oz button
mushrooms, roughly chopped
850 ml/1½ pints vegetable
stock
3 tbsp chopped fresh tarragon,
plus extra to garnish
150 ml/5 fl oz crème fraîche
salt and pepper

❊ Melt half the butter in a large saucepan. Add the onion and fry gently for 10 minutes, until soft. Add the remaining butter and the mushrooms and stir-fry for 5 minutes, or until the mushrooms are browned.

❊ Stir in the stock and tarragon, bring to the boil, then reduce the heat and leave to simmer gently for 20 minutes. Transfer to a food processor or blender and process until smooth. Return the soup to the pan.

❊ Stir in the crème fraîche and add salt and pepper to taste. Reheat the soup gently until hot. Ladle into warmed serving bowls and garnish with chopped tarragon. Serve immediately.

Minestrone

1 tbsp olive oil
1 onion, finely chopped
1 leek, halved lengthways and thinly sliced
2 garlic cloves, finely chopped
400 g/14 oz canned chopped tomatoes
1 carrot, finely diced
1 small turnip, finely diced
1 small potato, finely diced
125 g/4$\frac{1}{2}$ oz peeled celeriac, finely diced
250 g/9 oz peeled pumpkin, finely diced

700 ml/1$\frac{1}{4}$ pints water
1 litre/1$\frac{3}{4}$ pints vegetable stock
400 g/14 oz canned cannellini or borlotti beans, drained and rinsed
100 g/3$\frac{1}{2}$ oz leafy cabbage, such as cavolo nero
85 g/3 oz small dried pasta shapes or broken spaghetti
salt and pepper
freshly grated Parmesan cheese, to serve

❊ Heat the oil in a large saucepan over a medium heat. Add the onion, leek and garlic to the pan and cook for 3–4 minutes, stirring occasionally, until they are slightly soft.

❊ Add the tomatoes, carrot, turnip, potato, celeriac, pumpkin, water and stock to the pan. Bring to the boil, stirring occasionally.

❊ Stir in the beans and cabbage. Season the soup lightly with salt and pepper. Reduce the heat and simmer, partially covered, for about 50 minutes until all the vegetables are tender.

❊ Meanwhile, bring a saucepan of lightly salted water to the boil. Add the pasta and cook until it is just tender. Drain and add the pasta to the cooked soup.

❊ Taste the soup and adjust the seasoning. Ladle into warmed bowls and serve with the cheese sprinkled over the top.

Chickpea & Tomato Soup

2 tbsp olive oil
2 leeks, sliced
2 courgettes, diced
2 garlic cloves, crushed
800 g/1 lb 12 oz canned chopped tomatoes
1 tbsp tomato purée
1 fresh bay leaf

850 ml/1$\frac{1}{2}$ pints chicken stock
400 g/14 oz canned chickpeas, drained and rinsed
225 g/8 oz spinach
freshly-grated Parmesan cheese and warmed sun-dried tomato bread, to serve

❊ Heat the oil in a large saucepan, add the leeks and courgettes and cook briskly for 5 minutes, stirring constantly.

❊ Add the garlic, tomatoes, tomato purée, bay leaf, stock and chickpeas.

❊ Bring to the boil and simmer for 5 minutes.

❊ Finely shred the spinach, add to the soup and cook for 2 minutes. Season to taste.

❊ Discard the bay leaf. Serve the soup immediately with the cheese and the warmed sun-dried tomato bread.

Mixed Bean Soup

1 tbsp vegetable oil
1 red onion, halved and sliced
100 g/3½ oz potato, diced
1 carrot, diced
1 leek, sliced
1 fresh green chilli, sliced
3 garlic cloves, crushed
1 tsp ground coriander
1 tsp chilli powder
1 litre/1¾ pints vegetable stock
450 g/1 lb mixed canned beans, such as red kidney, borlotti, black-eyed or flageolet, drained and rinsed
salt and pepper
2 tbsp chopped fresh coriander, to garnish

❄ Heat the oil in a large saucepan and add the onion, potato, carrot and leek. Cook, stirring occasionally, for 2 minutes until the vegetables are slightly soft.

❄ Add the chilli and garlic and cook for a further minute.

❄ Stir in the ground coriander, chilli powder and stock.

❄ Bring the soup to the boil, reduce the heat and cook for 20 minutes or until the vegetables are tender.

❄ Stir in the beans, season to taste and cook, stirring occasionally, for a further 10 minutes.

❄ Ladle the soup into warmed bowls, garnish with the chopped coriander and serve.

Red Bean Soup

175 g/6 oz dried red kidney beans, soaked overnight
1.7 litres/3 pints water
1 large ham bone or bacon knuckle
2 carrots, chopped
1 large onion, chopped
2 celery sticks, thinly sliced
1 leek, trimmed, washed and sliced
1–2 bay leaves
2 tbsp olive oil
2–3 tomatoes, peeled and chopped
1 garlic clove, crushed
1 tbsp tomato purée
60 g/2 oz arborio rice
125–175 g/4–6 oz green cabbage, finely shredded
salt and pepper

❄ Drain the beans and place them in a saucepan with enough water to cover. Bring to the boil, then boil for 15 minutes to remove any harmful toxins. Reduce the heat and simmer for 45 minutes.

❄ Drain the beans and put into a clean saucepan with the water, ham bone, carrots, onion, celery, leek, bay leaves and oil. Bring to the boil, then cover and simmer for 1 hour or until the beans are very tender.

❄ Discard the bay leaves and bone, reserving any ham pieces from the bone. Remove a small cupful of the beans and reserve. Purée or liquidize the soup in a food processor or blender, or push through a coarse sieve, and transfer to a clean saucepan.

❄ Add the tomatoes, garlic, tomato purée and rice and season. Bring back to the boil and simmer for about 15 minutes or until the rice is tender.

❄ Add the cabbage and the reserved beans and ham, and continue to simmer for 5 minutes. Adjust the seasoning and serve very hot. If liked, a piece of toasted crusty bread may be put in the base of each soup bowl before ladling in the soup. Serve very hot.

Vegetable Soup with Cannellini Beans

❖ SERVES 4 ❖

1 small aubergine
2 large tomatoes
1 potato, peeled
1 carrot, peeled
1 leek
425 g/15 oz canned cannellini
beans
850 ml/1 1/2 pints hot vegetable
or chicken stock
2 tsp dried basil
10 g/1/2 oz dried ceps, soaked
for 10 minutes in enough
warm water to cover
50 g/1 3/4 oz vermicelli
3 tbsp pesto
freshly grated Parmesan
cheese, to serve (optional)

❖ Slice the aubergine into rings about 10 mm/1/2 inch thick, then cut each ring into 4.

❖ Cut the tomatoes and potato into small dice. Cut the carrot into sticks about 2.5 cm/ 1 inch long and cut the leek into rings.

❖ Place the cannellini beans and their liquid in a large saucepan. Add the aubergine, tomatoes, potatoes, carrot and leek, stirring to mix.

❖ Add the stock to the pan and bring to the boil. Reduce the heat and leave to simmer for 15 minutes.

❖ Add the basil, ceps, their soaking liquid and the vermicelli and simmer for 5 minutes or until all the vegetables are tender.

❖ Remove the pan from the heat and stir in the pesto.

❖ Serve with the cheese, if using.

Bean & Pasta Soup

225 g/8 oz dried haricot beans, soaked overnight, drained and rinsed
4 tbsp olive oil
2 large onions, sliced
3 garlic cloves, chopped
400 g/14 oz canned chopped tomatoes
1 tsp dried oregano
1 tsp tomato purée
850 ml/1½ pints water
90 g/3 oz dried small pasta shapes, such as fusilli or conchigliette
125 g/4½ oz sun-dried tomatoes, drained and thinly sliced
1 tbsp chopped fresh coriander or flat-leaf parsley
salt and pepper
2 tbsp freshly grated Parmesan cheese

❊ Put the soaked beans into a large saucepan, cover with cold water and bring to the boil. Boil rapidly for 15 minutes to remove any harmful toxins. Drain the beans in a colander.

❊ Heat the oil in a saucepan over a medium heat and fry the onions until they are just beginning to change colour. Stir in the garlic and cook for 1 further minute. Stir in the chopped tomatoes, oregano and the tomato purée and pour on the water. Add the drained beans, bring to the boil and cover the pan. Simmer for about 45 minutes or until the beans are almost tender.

❊ Add the pasta, season to taste with salt and pepper and stir in the sun-dried tomatoes. Return the soup to the boil, partially cover the pan and continue cooking for 10 minutes, or until the pasta is nearly tender.

❊ Stir in the coriander. Taste the soup and adjust the seasoning if necessary. Transfer to a warmed soup tureen to serve. Sprinkle with the cheese and serve hot.

Brown Lentil & Pasta Soup

4 rashers streaky bacon, cut into small squares
1 onion, chopped
2 garlic cloves, crushed
2 sticks celery, chopped
50 g/1¾ oz farfalline or spaghetti, broken into small pieces
400 g/14 oz canned brown lentils, drained
1.2 litres/2 pints hot ham or vegetable stock
2 tbsp chopped fresh mint

❊ Place the bacon in a large frying pan together with the onions, garlic and celery. Dry-fry for 4–5 minutes, stirring, until the onion is tender and the bacon is just beginning to brown.

❊ Add the pasta to the pan and cook, stirring, for about 1 minute to coat the pasta in the oil.

❊ Add the lentils and the stock and bring to the boil. Reduce the heat and leave to simmer for 12–15 minutes or until the pasta is tender.

❊ Remove the pan from the heat and stir in the chopped fresh mint.

❊ Transfer the soup to warmed soup bowls and serve immediately.

Spicy Lentil Soup

❈ **SERVES 4** ❈

115 g/4 oz red lentils
2 tsp vegetable oil
1 large onion, finely chopped
2 garlic cloves, crushed
1 tsp ground cumin
1 tsp ground coriander
1 tsp garam masala
2 tbsp tomato purée
1 litre/1¾ pints vegetable stock

350 g/12 oz canned sweetcorn, drained
salt and pepper

TO SERVE
low-fat natural yogurt
chopped fresh parsley
warmed pitta bread

❈ Rinse the red lentils thoroughly under cold running water. Drain well and set side.

❈ Heat the oil in a large non-stick saucepan and fry the onion and garlic gently until soft but not brown.

❈ Stir in the cumin, coriander, garam masala, tomato purée and 4 tablespoons of the stock. Mix well and simmer gently for 2 minutes.

❈ Add the lentils and pour in the remaining stock. Bring to the boil, reduce the heat, cover and simmer for 1 hour until the lentils are tender and the soup thickened. Stir in the sweetcorn and heat through for 5 minutes. Season to taste with salt and pepper.

❈ Ladle into warmed soup bowls and top each with a spoonful of the yogurt and a sprinkling of the parsley. Serve with the warmed pitta bread.

Broad Bean & Mint Soup

❈ **SERVES 4** ❈

2 tbsp olive oil
1 red onion, chopped
2 garlic cloves, crushed
450 g/1 lb potatoes, diced
500 g/1 lb 2 oz broad beans, thawed, if frozen

850 ml/1½ pints vegetable stock
2 tbsp freshly chopped mint
natural yogurt and sprigs of fresh mint, to garnish

❈ Heat the oil in a large saucepan. Add the onion and garlic and sauté for 2–3 minutes, until softened.

❈ Add the potatoes to the pan and cook, stirring constantly, for 5 minutes.

❈ Stir in the beans and the stock, then cover the pan and simmer for 30 minutes, or until the beans and potatoes are tender.

❈ Remove a few vegetables with a slotted spoon and set aside. Place the remainder of the soup in a food processor or blender and process until smooth.

❈ Transfer the soup to a clean saucepan and add the reserved vegetables and chopped mint. Stir thoroughly and heat through gently.

❈ Transfer the soup to a warmed tureen or individual serving bowls. Garnish with swirls of yogurt and sprigs of mint and serve immediately.

Parisian Pea Soup

25 g/1 oz butter
2 shallots, finely chopped
450 g/1 lb peas
2 Little Gem or 1 small cos or
Webbs lettuce, shredded
1.2 litres/2 pints vegetable
stock
pinch of freshly grated nutmeg
salt and pepper

❖ Shell the peas. Melt the butter in a large saucepan. Add the shallots and cook over a medium heat, stirring occasionally, for 5 minutes, until softened.

❖ Add the peas, shredded lettuce and stock to the pan and season to taste with the nutmeg and salt and pepper. Bring to the boil, cover and simmer for 10–15 minutes until the peas are tender.

❖ Remove the pan from the heat and allow to cool slightly. Pour into a blender or food processor and process to a purée. Transfer the soup to a clean saucepan and heat through gently before serving.

Sweet Potato Soup

350 g/12 oz sweet potatoes
1 acorn squash
4 shallots
olive oil, for brushing
5–6 garlic cloves, unpeeled
850 ml/1½ pints vegetable stock
snipped fresh chives and 125 ml/4 fl oz single cream, to garnish

❉ Cut the sweet potatoes, squash and shallots in half lengthways. Brush the cut sides with oil.

❉ Put the vegetables, cut sides down, in a shallow roasting tin. Add the garlic cloves. Roast in a preheated oven, 190°C/375°F/Gas Mark 5, for about 40 minutes until tender and light brown.

❉ When cool, scoop the flesh from the potato and squash halves and put in a saucepan with the shallots. Remove the garlic peel and add the soft insides to the other vegetables.

❉ Add the stock and a pinch of salt. Bring just to the boil, reduce the heat and simmer, partially covered, for about 30 minutes, stirring occasionally, until the vegetables are very tender.

❉ Allow the soup to cool slightly, then transfer to a blender or food processor and purée until smooth, working in batches, if necessary. (If using a food processor, strain off the cooking liquid and reserve. Purée the soup solids with enough cooking liquid to moisten them, then combine with the remaining liquid.)

❉ Return the soup to the pan and stir in the cream, reserving a little to garnish. Season to taste, then simmer for 5–10 minutes until completely heated through. Ladle into warmed bowls, garnish with the chives and a swirl of cream and serve.

Garlic & Potato Soup

1 large bulb of garlic with large cloves, peeled
2 tsp olive oil, plus extra for brushing
2 large leeks, thinly sliced
1 large onion, finely chopped
500 g/1 lb 2 oz potatoes, diced
1.2 litres/2 pints vegetable stock
1 bay leaf
150 ml/5 fl oz single cream
freshly grated nutmeg
lemon juice, optional
salt and pepper
snipped fresh chives or parsley, to garnish

❉ Put the garlic cloves in a baking dish, lightly brush with oil and bake in a preheated oven, 180°C/350°F/Gas Mark 4, for about 20 minutes until golden.

❉ Heat the oil in a large saucepan over a medium heat. Add the leeks and onion, cover and cook for about 3 minutes, stirring frequently, until they begin to soften.

❉ Add the potatoes, roasted garlic, stock and bay leaf. Season with salt (unless the stock is salty already) and pepper. Bring to the boil, reduce the heat, cover and cook gently for about 30 minutes, until the vegetables are tender. Remove the bay leaf.

❉ Allow the soup to cool slightly, then transfer to a blender or food processor and purée until smooth, working in batches if necessary. (If using a food processor, strain off the cooking liquid and reserve. Purée the soup solids with enough cooking liquid to moisten them, then combine with the remaining liquid.)

❉ Return the soup to the pan and stir in the cream and a generous grating of nutmeg. Taste and adjust the seasoning, if necessary, adding a few drops of lemon juice, if using. Reheat over a low heat. Ladle into warmed soup bowls, garnish with the chives and serve.

Chicken & Tomato Soup

60 g/2 oz unsalted butter
1 large onion, chopped
500 g/1 lb 2 oz chicken, very finely shredded
600 ml/1 pint chicken stock
6 medium tomatoes, finely chopped
pinch of bicarbonate of soda
1 tbsp caster sugar
150 ml/5 fl oz double cream
salt and pepper
fresh basil leaves, to garnish
croûtons, to serve

❊ Melt the butter in a large saucepan and sauté the onion and shredded chicken for 5 minutes.

❊ Add 300 ml/10 fl oz of the stock to the pan, with the tomatoes and bicarbonate of soda.

❊ Bring the soup to the boil and simmer for 20 minutes.

❊ Allow the soup to cool, then blend in a food processor.

❊ Return the soup to the pan, add the remaining stock, season and add the sugar. Pour the soup into a tureen and add a swirl of double cream. Serve the soup with the croûtons and garnish with the basil.

Chicken & Sweetcorn Soup

1 skinless, boneless chicken breast, about 175 g/6 oz
2 tbsp sunflower oil
2–3 spring onions, thinly sliced diagonally
1 small or 1/2 large red pepper, thinly sliced
1 garlic clove, crushed
125 g/41/2 oz baby sweetcorn, thinly sliced
1 litre/13/4 pints chicken stock
200 g/7 oz can of sweetcorn niblets, well drained
2 tbsp sherry
2–3 tsp bottled sweet chilli sauce
2–3 tsp cornflour
2 tomatoes, quartered and deseeded, then sliced
salt and pepper
chopped fresh coriander or parsley, to garnish

❊ Cut the chicken breast into 4 strips lengthways, then cut each strip into narrow slices across the grain.

❊ Heat the oil in a wok or frying pan, swirling it around until it is really hot.

❊ Add the chicken and stir-fry for 3–4 minutes, moving it around the wok until it is well sealed all over and almost cooked through.

❊ Add the spring onions, pepper and garlic, and stir-fry for 2–3 minutes. Add the baby sweetcorn and stock and bring to the boil.

❊ Add the sweetcorn niblets, sherry, sweet chilli sauce and salt to taste, and simmer for 5 minutes, stirring from time to time.

❊ Blend the cornflour with a little cold water. Add to the soup and bring to the boil, stirring until the sauce is thickened. Add the tomato slices, season to taste and simmer for 1–2 minutes.

❊ Serve the soup hot, sprinkled with the coriander.

Chicken Soup with Almonds

1 large or 2 small boneless
skinned chicken breasts
1 tbsp sunflower oil
4 spring onions, thinly sliced
diagonally
1 carrot, cut into julienne strips
700 ml/1¼ pints chicken stock
finely grated rind of ½ lemon
40 g/1½ oz ground almonds
1 tbsp light soy sauce
1 tbsp lemon juice
25 g/1 oz flaked almonds,
toasted
salt and pepper

❄ Cut each breast into 4 strips lengthways, then slice very thinly across the grain to give shreds of chicken.

❄ Heat the oil in a wok, swirling it around until really hot.

❄ Add the spring onions and cook for 2 minutes, then add the chicken and toss it for 3–4 minutes until sealed and almost cooked through, stirring all the time. Add the carrot strips and stir.

❄ Add the stock to the wok and bring to the boil. Add the lemon rind, ground almonds, soy sauce, lemon juice and plenty of seasoning. Bring back to the boil and simmer, uncovered, for 5 minutes, stirring from time to time.

❄ Adjust the seasoning, add most of the toasted flaked almonds and continue to cook for a further 1–2 minutes.

❄ Serve the soup very hot, in individual bowls, sprinkled with the remaining flaked almonds.

Lemon & Chicken Soup

60 g/2 oz butter
8 shallots, thinly sliced
2 carrots, thinly sliced
2 celery sticks, thinly sliced
225 g/8 oz boned chicken
  breasts, finely chopped
3 lemons
1.2 litres/2 pints chicken stock

225 g/8 oz dried spaghetti,
  broken into small pieces
150 ml/5 fl oz double cream
salt and white pepper
sprigs of fresh parsley and
  3 lemon slices, halved,
  to garnish

❊ Melt the butter in a large saucepan. Add the shallots, carrots, celery and chicken and cook over a low heat, stirring occasionally, for 8 minutes.

❊ Thinly pare the lemons and blanch the lemon rind in boiling water for 3 minutes. Squeeze the juice from the lemons.

❊ Add the lemon rind and juice to the pan, together with the stock. Bring slowly to the boil over a low heat and simmer for 40 minutes, stirring occasionally.

❊ Add the spaghetti to the pan and cook for 15 minutes. Season to taste with salt and pepper and add the cream. Heat through, but do not allow the soup to boil or it will curdle.

❊ Pour the soup into a tureen or individual bowls, garnish with the parsley and half slices of lemon and serve immediately.

Chicken & Asparagus Soup

225 g/8 oz fresh asparagus
850 ml/1½ pints chicken stock
150 ml/5 fl oz dry white wine
1 sprig fresh parsley
1 sprig fresh dill
1 sprig fresh tarragon
1 garlic clove

55 g/2 oz vermicelli rice
  noodles
350 g/12 oz lean cooked
  chicken, finely shredded
1 small leek
salt and white pepper

❊ Wash the asparagus and trim away the woody ends. Cut each spear into pieces 4 cm/1½ inches long.

❊ Pour the stock and wine into a large saucepan and bring to the boil over a medium heat.

❊ Wash the herbs and tie them together with clean string. Peel the garlic clove and add, with the herbs, to the pan. Add the asparagus and noodles. Reduce the heat, cover and simmer for 5 minutes.

❊ Stir in the chicken and season to taste with salt and pepper. Simmer gently for a further 3–4 minutes until heated through.

❊ Trim the leek, slice it down the centre and wash under running water to remove any dirt. Shake dry and shred very finely.

❊ Remove the herbs and garlic from the pan and discard. Ladle the soup into warmed bowls, sprinkle with the shredded leek and serve immediately.

Chicken & Pasta Broth

❉ SERVES 6 ❉

350 g/12 oz boneless chicken
breasts
2 tbsp sunflower oil
1 medium onion, diced
250 g/9 oz carrots, diced
250 g/9 oz cauliflower florets
850 ml/1 1/2 pints chicken stock

2 tsp dried mixed herbs
125 g/4 1/2 oz small pasta
shapes
salt and pepper
freshly grated Parmesan
cheese, for sprinkling
crusty bread, to serve

❉ Using a sharp knife, finely dice the chicken, discarding any skin.

❉ Heat the oil in a large saucepan and quickly sauté the chicken and vegetables until they are lightly coloured.

❉ Stir in the stock and herbs. Bring to the boil and add the pasta shapes. Return to the boil, cover and simmer for 10 minutes, stirring occasionally to prevent the pasta shapes sticking together.

❉ Season to taste with salt and pepper and sprinkle with the cheese. Serve with the bread.

Chicken & Chickpea Soup

❉ SERVES 4 ❉

25 g/1 oz butter
3 spring onions, chopped
2 garlic cloves, crushed
1 sprig fresh marjoram, finely
chopped
350 g/12 oz boned chicken
breasts, diced
1.2 litres/2 pints chicken stock
350 g/12 oz canned chickpeas,
drained

1 bouquet garni
1 red pepper, diced
1 green pepper, diced
115 g/4 oz small dried pasta
shapes, such as elbow
macaroni
salt and white pepper
croûtons, to garnish

❉ Melt the butter in a large saucepan. Add the spring onions, garlic, marjoram and chicken and cook, stirring frequently, over a medium heat for 5 minutes.

❉ Add the stock, chickpeas and bouquet garni and season to taste with salt and pepper.

❉ Bring the soup to the boil, reduce the heat and simmer for about 2 hours.

❉ Add the diced peppers and pasta to the pan, then simmer the soup for a further 20 minutes.

❉ Transfer the soup to a warmed tureen. To serve, ladle the soup into individual serving bowls and serve immediately, garnished with the croûtons.

Lamb & Rice Soup

150 g/5$\frac{1}{2}$ oz lean lamb
50 g/1$\frac{3}{4}$ oz rice
850 ml/1$\frac{1}{2}$ pints lamb stock
1 leek, sliced
1 garlic clove, thinly sliced
2 tsp light soy sauce
1 tsp rice wine vinegar
1 medium open-cup
mushroom, thinly sliced
salt

❖ Using a sharp knife, trim any fat from the lamb and cut the meat into thin strips. Set aside until required.

❖ Bring a large saucepan of lightly salted water to the boil and add the rice. Bring back to the boil, stir once, reduce the heat and cook for 10–15 minutes, until tender.

❖ Drain the rice, rinse under cold running water, drain again and set aside until required.

❖ Meanwhile, put the stock in a large saucepan and bring to the boil.

❖ Add the lamb strips, leek, garlic, soy sauce and vinegar to the stock in the pan. Reduce the heat, cover and leave to simmer for 10 minutes, or until the lamb is tender and cooked through.

❖ Add the mushroom slices and the rice to the pan and cook for a further 2–3 minutes, or until the mushroom is completely cooked through.

❖ Ladle the soup into 4 individual warmed soup bowls and serve immediately.

Chinese Potato & Pork Broth

1 litre/1¾ pints chicken stock	1 tsp sesame oil
2 large potatoes, diced	1 carrot, cut into very thin strips
2 tbsp rice wine vinegar	1 tsp chopped ginger root
2 tbsp cornflour	3 spring onions, thinly sliced
4 tbsp water	1 red pepper, sliced
125 g/4½ oz pork fillet, sliced	225 g/8 oz canned bamboo
1 tbsp light soy sauce	shoots, drained

❈ Put the stock, potatoes and 1 tablespoon of the vinegar in a saucepan and bring to the boil. Reduce the heat until the stock is just simmering.

❈ Mix the cornflour with the water, then stir into the hot stock.

❈ Bring the stock back to the boil, stirring until thickened, then reduce the heat until it is just simmering again.

❈ Place the pork slices in a dish and season with the remaining vinegar, the soy sauce and the sesame oil.

❈ Add the pork slices, carrot strips and ginger to the stock and cook for 10 minutes. Stir in the spring onions, red pepper and bamboo shoots. Cook for a further 5 minutes. Pour the soup into warmed bowls and serve immediately.

Lentil, Potato & Ham Soup

300 g/10½ oz Puy lentils	1 litre/1¾ pints chicken stock
2 tsp butter	225 g/8 oz potatoes, diced
1 large onion, finely chopped	1 tbsp tomato purée
2 carrots, finely chopped	115 g/4 oz smoked ham,
1 garlic clove, finely chopped	finely diced
450 ml/16 fl oz water	salt and pepper
1 bay leaf	chopped fresh parsley,
¼ tsp dried sage or rosemary	to garnish

❈ Rinse and drain the lentils and remove any small stones.

❈ Melt the butter in a large saucepan or flameproof casserole over a medium heat. Add the onion, carrots and garlic, cover and fry, stirring occasionally, for about 4–5 minutes until the onion is slightly softened.

❈ Add the lentils with the water, bay leaf and sage or rosemary. Bring to the boil, reduce the heat, cover and simmer for 10 minutes.

❈ Add the stock, potatoes, tomato purée and ham. Bring back to a simmer. Cover and continue simmering for 25–30 minutes or until the vegetables are tender.

❈ Season to taste with salt and pepper and remove and discard the bay leaf. Ladle into warmed bowls, garnish with the parsley and serve immediately.

Spanish Chorizo Soup

❈ **SERVES 4** ❈

2 tbsp olive oil
3 large potatoes, cubed
2 red onions, quartered
1 garlic clove, crushed
1 litre/1¾ pints pork or
   vegetable stock
150 g/5½ oz Savoy cabbage,
   shredded
50 g/1¾ oz chorizo sausage,
   sliced
salt and pepper
paprika, to garnish

❈   Heat the oil in a large saucepan and add the potatoes, onions and garlic. Sauté gently for 5 minutes, stirring constantly.

❈   Add the stock and bring to the boil. Reduce the heat and cover the pan. Simmer the vegetables for about 20 minutes until the potatoes are tender.

❈   Process the soup in a food processor or blender in 2 batches for 1 minute each. Transfer the puréed soup to a clean saucepan.

❈   Add the cabbage and chorizo sausage to the pan and cook for a further 7 minutes. Season to taste.

❈   Ladle the soup into warmed soup bowls, garnish with a sprinkling of paprika and serve.

Beef Soup with Rice

❈ **SERVES 4** ❈

350 g/12 oz lean beef, such as
   rump or sirloin
1 litre/1¾ pints beef stock
1 cinnamon stick, broken in 2
2 star anise
2 tbsp dark soy sauce
2 tbsp dry sherry
3 tbsp tomato purée
115 g/4 oz canned water
chestnuts, drained and sliced
175 g/6 oz cooked white rice
1 tsp finely grated orange rind
6 tbsp orange juice
salt and pepper
strips of orange rind and
   2 tbsp snipped fresh chives,
   to garnish

❈   Carefully trim away any fat from the beef. Cut the beef into thin strips and then place in a large saucepan.

❈   Pour in the beef stock and add the cinnamon, star anise, soy sauce, sherry, tomato purée and water chestnuts. Bring to the boil over a medium heat, skimming off any foam that rises to the surface with a flat ladle or skimmer. Cover the pan, reduce the heat and simmer gently for about 20 minutes or until the beef strips are tender.

❈   Skim the soup with a flat ladle again to remove any more foam. Remove and discard the 2 pieces of cinnamon stick and the star anise and blot the surface of the soup with absorbent kitchen paper to remove as much fat as possible.

❈   Stir in the rice, orange rind and orange juice. Season to taste with salt and pepper. Heat through for 2–3 minutes before ladling into warmed bowls. Serve garnished with the strips of orange rind and snipped chives.

Beef & Vegetable Soup

225 g/8 oz tomatoes
2 corn cobs
1 litre/1¾ pints beef stock
1 carrot, thinly sliced
1 onion, chopped
1–2 small waxy potatoes, diced
¼ cabbage, thinly sliced
¼ tsp ground cumin
¼ tsp mild chilli powder
¼ tsp paprika
225 g/8 oz cooked beef, cut into
bite-sized pieces
3–4 tbsp chopped fresh
coriander (optional)
hot salsa of your choice,
to serve

❋ To peel the tomatoes, place them in a heatproof bowl, pour in enough boiling water to cover and stand for 30 seconds. Drain and plunge into cold water. The skins will then slide off easily. Chop the tomatoes.

❋ Using a large knife, cut the corn cobs into 2.5-cm/1-inch pieces.

❋ Place the stock in a saucepan with the tomatoes, carrot, onion, potatoes and cabbage. Bring to the boil, then reduce the heat and simmer for 10–15 minutes or until the vegetables are tender.

❋ Add the corn cob pieces, the cumin, chilli powder, paprika and beef. Bring back to the boil over a medium heat and cook until heated through.

❋ Ladle into warmed soup bowls and serve sprinkled with the coriander, if using, with a salsa of your choice handed round separately.

Beef Noodle Soup

225 g/8 oz lean beef	850 ml/1$\frac{1}{2}$ pints beef stock
1 garlic clove, crushed	3 baby corn cobs, sliced
2 spring onions, chopped	$\frac{1}{2}$ leek, shredded
3 tbsp soy sauce	125 g/4$\frac{1}{2}$ oz broccoli,
1 tsp sesame oil	cut into florets
225 g/8 oz egg noodles	pinch of chilli powder

❄ Using a sharp knife, cut the beef into thin strips and place in a bowl with the garlic, spring onions, soy sauce and sesame oil.

❄ Combine the ingredients in the bowl, turning the beef to coat. Cover and set aside to marinate in the refrigerator for 30 minutes.

❄ Bring a saucepan of lightly salted wter to the boil, add the noodles and cook for 3–4 minutes. Drain thoroughly and set aside.

❄ Put the beef stock in a large saucepan and bring to the boil. Add the beef, with the marinade, the corn, leek and broccoli. Cover and simmer over a low heat for 7–10 minutes or until the beef and vegetables are tender and cooked through.

❄ Stir in the noodles and chilli powder and cook for a further 2–3 minutes.

❄ Transfer the soup to warmed bowls and serve immediately.

Veal & Wild Mushroom Soup

450 g/1 lb veal, thinly sliced	140 g/5 oz oyster and shiitake
450 g/1 lb veal bones	mushrooms, roughly chopped
1.2 litres/2 pints water	150 ml/5 fl oz double cream
1 small onion	100 g/3$\frac{1}{2}$ oz dried vermicelli
6 peppercorns	1 tbsp cornflour
1 tsp cloves	3 tbsp milk
pinch of mace	salt and pepper

❄ Put the veal bones and water into a large saucepan. Bring to the boil and lower the heat. Add the onion, peppercorns, cloves and mace and simmer for about 3 hours, until the veal stock is reduced by one third.

❄ Strain the stock, skim off any fat on the surface with a slotted spoon and pour into a clean saucepan. Add the veal meat to the pan.

❄ Add the mushrooms and cream, bring to the boil over a low heat and then leave to simmer for 12 minutes, stirring occasionally.

❄ Meanwhile, bring a saucepan of lightly salted water to the boil, add the vermicelli and cook for 10 minutes or until tender but still firm to the bite. Drain and keep warm.

❄ Mix the cornflour and milk to form a smooth paste. Stir into the soup to thicken. Season to taste with salt and pepper and, just before serving, add the vermicelli. Transfer the soup to a warmed tureen and serve immediately.

Provençal Fish Soup

1 tbsp olive oil
2 onions, finely chopped
1 small leek, thinly sliced
1 small carrot, finely chopped
1 celery stick, finely chopped
1 small fennel bulb, finely
  chopped (optional)
3 garlic cloves, finely chopped
225 ml/8 fl oz dry white wine
400 g/14 oz canned tomatoes

1 bay leaf
pinch of fennel seeds
2 strips of orange rind
1/4 tsp saffron threads
1.2 litres/2 pints water
350 g/12 oz white fish fillets,
  skinned
salt and pepper
croûtons, to serve (optional)

❖ Heat the oil in a large saucepan over a medium heat. Add the onions and cook, stirring occasionally, for about 5 minutes until softened. Add the leek, carrot, celery, fennel, if using, and garlic and continue cooking for 4–5 minutes until the leek is wilted.

❖ Add the wine and simmer for 1 minute. Add the tomatoes, bay leaf, fennel seeds, orange rind, saffron and water. Bring just to the boil, reduce the heat, cover and simmer gently, stirring occasionally, for 30 minutes.

❖ Add the fish and cook for a further 20–30 minutes until it flakes easily. Remove the bay leaf and orange rind.

❖ Remove the pan from the heat and set aside to cool slightly, then transfer to a blender or food processor and process to a smooth purée, working in batches if necessary. (If using a food processor, strain off the cooking liquid and reserve. Purée the soup solids with enough cooking liquid to moisten them, then combine with the remaining liquid.)

❖ Return the soup to the pan. Taste and adjust the seasoning, if necessary, and simmer for 5–10 minutes until heated through. Ladle the soup into warmed bowls and sprinkle with the croûtons, if using. Serve the soup immediately.

Mussel & Potato Soup

750 g/1 lb 10 oz mussels
2 tbsp olive oil
100 g/3½ oz unsalted butter
2 slices rindless fatty bacon,
  chopped
1 onion, chopped
2 garlic cloves, crushed
60 g/2 oz plain flour
450 g/1 lb potatoes, thinly
  sliced

100 g/3 ½ oz dried
  conchigliette
300 ml/10 fl oz double cream
1 tbsp lemon juice
2 egg yolks
salt and pepper
2 tbsp finely chopped fresh
  parsley and lemon wedges,
  to garnish

❖ Debeard the mussels and scrub them under cold water for 5 minutes. Discard any mussels that do not close immediately when sharply tapped.

❖ Bring a large pan of water to the boil, add the mussels, oil and a little pepper. Cook until the mussels open. Discard any mussels that remain closed.

❖ Drain the mussels, reserving the cooking liquid. Remove the mussels from their shells.

❖ Melt the butter in a large saucepan, add the bacon, onion and garlic and cook for 4 minutes. Carefully stir in the flour. Measure 1.2 litres/2 pints of the reserved cooking liquid and stir it into the pan. Add the potatoes to the pan and simmer for 5 minutes. Add the conchigliette and simmer for a further 10 minutes.

❖ Add the cream and lemon juice, season to taste with salt and pepper, then add the mussels to the pan.

❖ Blend the egg yolks with 1–2 tablespoons of the remaining cooking liquid, stir into the pan and cook for 4 minutes.

❖ Ladle the soup into 4 warmed individual soup bowls, garnish with the parsley and lemon wedges and serve immediately.

Spicy Prawn Soup

2 tbsp tamarind paste
4 red chillies, very finely chopped
2 cloves garlic, crushed
2.5-cm/1-inch piece of root ginger, peeled and very finely chopped
4 tbsp fish sauce
2 tbsp palm sugar or caster sugar
1.2 litres/2 pints fish stock
8 lime leaves
100 g/3 1/2 oz carrots, very thinly sliced
350 g/12 oz sweet potato, diced
100 g/3 1/2 oz baby corn cobs, halved
3 tbsp fresh coriander, roughly chopped
100g/3 1/2 oz cherry tomatoes, halved
225 g/8 oz fantail prawns

❈ Place the tamarind paste, chillies, garlic, ginger, fish sauce, sugar and stock in a preheated wok or large heavy frying pan. Roughly tear the lime leaves and add to the wok. Bring to the boil, stirring constantly to blend the flavours.

❈ Reduce the heat and add the carrot, sweet potato and baby corn cobs to the mixture in the wok.

❈ Leave the soup to simmer, uncovered, for about 10 minutes, or until the vegetables are just tender.

❈ Stir the coriander, cherry tomatoes and prawns into the soup and heat through for 5 minutes.

❈ Transfer the soup to a warmed soup tureen or individual serving bowls and serve hot.

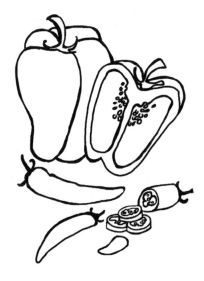

119

Hot & Sour Soup

350 g/12 oz raw or cooked
prawns, in their shells
1 tbsp vegetable oil
1 lemon grass stalk, roughly
chopped
2 kaffir lime leaves, shredded
1 fresh green chilli, deseeded
and chopped
1.2 litres/2 pints chicken or
fish stock

1 lime
1 tbsp Thai fish sauce
1 fresh red bird's-eye chilli,
deseeded and thinly sliced
1 spring onion, thinly sliced
salt and pepper
1 tbsp finely chopped fresh
coriander, to garnish

❄ Peel the prawns and reserve the shells. Devein the
prawns, cover with clingfilm and chill.

❄ Heat the oil in a large saucepan. Add the prawn shells
and stir-fry for 3–4 minutes until they turn pink. Add the
lemon grass, lime leaves, chilli and stock. Pare a thin strip
of rind from the lime and grate the rest. Add the pared rind
to the pan.

❄ Bring to the boil, then reduce the heat, cover and simmer
for about 20 minutes.

❄ Strain the liquid and pour it back into the pan. Squeeze
the juice from the lime, add to the pan with the fish sauce
and season to taste with salt and pepper.

❄ Bring the mixture to the boil. Reduce the heat, add the
prawns and simmer for 2–3 minutes.

❄ Add the thinly sliced chilli and spring onion. Sprinkle with
the coriander and lime rind and serve immediately.

Prawn Gumbo

1 large onion, finely chopped
2 rashers lean bacon, finely
chopped (optional)
1–2 garlic cloves, crushed
2 tbsp olive oil
1 large or 2 small red peppers,
finely chopped or coarsely
minced
850 ml/1$\frac{1}{2}$ pints fish or
vegetable stock
1 fresh or dried bay leaf
1 blade mace
good pinch of ground allspice
40 g/1$\frac{1}{2}$ oz long-grain rice

1 tbsp white wine vinegar
125–175 g/4$\frac{1}{2}$–6 oz okra,
trimmed and very thinly
sliced
90–125 g/3–4$\frac{1}{2}$ oz peeled
prawns
1 tbsp anchovy essence
2 tsp tomato purée
1–2 tbsp chopped fresh parsley
salt and pepper
whole prawns and sprigs of
fresh parsley, to garnish

❄ Gently fry the onion, bacon, if using, and garlic in the
oil in a large saucepan for 4–5 minutes until soft. Add the
peppers to the pan and continue to fry gently for a couple of
minutes.

❄ Add the stock, bay leaf, mace, allspice, rice, vinegar and
seasoning and bring to the boil. Cover and simmer gently for
about 20 minutes, giving an occasional stir, until the rice is
just tender.

❄ Add the okra, prawns, anchovy essence and tomato
purée, cover and simmer gently for about 15 minutes until
the okra is tender and the mixture slightly thickened.

❄ Discard the bay leaf and mace and adjust the seasoning.
Stir in the parsley and serve each portion garnished with a
whole prawn and a sprig of parsley.

Thai Prawn & Scallop Soup

1 litre/1¾ pints fish stock
juice of ½ lime
2 tbsp rice wine or sherry
1 leek, sliced
2 shallots, finely chopped
1 tbsp grated fresh root ginger
1 fresh red chilli, deseeded and
finely chopped

225 g/8 oz raw prawns, peeled
and deveined
225 g/8 oz live scallops,
shucked and cleaned
1½ tbsp chopped fresh
flat-leaf parsley, plus extra
to garnish
salt and pepper

❉ Put the stock, lime juice, rice wine, leek, shallots, ginger and chilli in a large saucepan. Bring to the boil over a high heat, then reduce the heat, cover and simmer for 10 minutes.

❉ Add the prawns, scallops and parsley, season to taste with salt and pepper and cook for 1–2 minutes.

❉ Remove the saucepan from the heat and ladle the soup into warmed serving bowls. Garnish with chopped parsley and serve.

Clam & Sorrel Soup

900 g/2 lb live clams, scrubbed
1 onion, finely chopped
150 ml/5 fl oz dry white wine
50 g/1¾ oz butter
1 small carrot, finely diced
2 shallots, finely diced
1 celery stick, finely diced

2 bay leaves
150 ml/5 fl oz double cream
25 g/1 oz loosely packed
shredded sorrel
pepper
sprigs of fresh dill, to garnish

❉ Put the clams into a large saucepan with the onion and wine. Cover and cook over a high heat for 3–4 minutes until the clams have opened. Strain, reserving the cooking liquid, but discarding the onion. Leave the clams until they are cool enough to handle. Remove from their shells.

❉ Melt the butter in a clean saucepan over a low heat. Add the carrot, shallots and celery and cook very gently for 10 minutes until softened, but not coloured. Add the reserved cooking liquid and bay leaves and simmer for a further 10 minutes.

❉ Meanwhile, roughly chop the clams, if large. Add to the soup with the cream and sorrel. Simmer for a further 2–3 minutes until the sorrel has collapsed. Season with pepper and ladle into 4 warmed soup bowls. Garnish with a few sprigs of dill and serve immediately.

Sweetcorn & Crab Soup

2 tbsp vegetable or
groundnut oil
4 garlic cloves, finely chopped
5 shallots, finely chopped
2 lemon grass stalks,
finely chopped
2.5-cm/1-inch piece of root
ginger, finely chopped
1 litre/1¾ pints chicken stock
400 g/14 oz canned
coconut milk
225 g/8 oz frozen sweetcorn
kernels
350 g/12 oz canned crabmeat,
drained and flaked
2 tbsp Thai fish sauce
juice of 1 lime
1 tsp palm sugar or soft light
brown sugar
bunch of fresh coriander,
chopped, to garnish

❊ Heat the oil in a large frying pan over a low heat, add the garlic, shallots, lemon grass and ginger and cook, stirring occasionally, for 2–3 minutes until softened. Add the stock and coconut milk and bring to the boil. Add the sweetcorn, reduce the heat and simmer gently for 3–4 minutes.

❊ Add the crabmeat, fish sauce, lime juice and sugar and simmer gently for 1 minute. Ladle into warmed bowls, garnish with the coriander and serve immediately.

Yellow Pepper Salad

4 rashers streaky bacon, chopped
2 yellow peppers
8 radishes, washed and trimmed
1 celery stick, finely chopped
3 plum tomatoes, cut into wedges
3 tbsp olive oil
1 tbsp fresh thyme
salt and pepper

❖ Dry-fry the chopped bacon in a frying pan for 4–5 minutes or until crispy. Remove the bacon from the frying pan, set aside and leave to cool until required.

❖ Using a sharp knife, halve and deseed the peppers. Slice the peppers into long strips.

❖ Using a sharp knife, halve the radishes and cut them into wedges.

❖ Mix together the peppers, radishes, celery and tomatoes and toss the mixture in the oil and thyme. Season to taste with a little salt and pepper.

❖ Transfer the salad to serving plates and garnish with the reserved crispy bacon pieces.

Coconut Couscous Salad

350 g/12 oz precooked couscous
175 g/6 oz dried apricots
1 small bunch fresh chives
2 tbsp desiccated coconut
1 tsp ground cinnamon
salt and pepper
shredded mint leaves, to garnish

DRESSING
1 tbsp olive oil
2 tbsp unsweetened orange juice
$1/2$ tsp finely grated orange rind
1 tsp wholegrain mustard
1 tsp clear honey
2 tbsp chopped fresh mint leaves

❖ Soak the couscous according to the instructions on the packet. Bring a large saucepan of water to the boil. Transfer the couscous to a steamer or large sieve lined with muslin and place over the water. Cover and steam as directed. Remove from the heat, place in heatproof bowl and set aside to cool.

❖ Slice the apricots into thin strips and place in a small bowl. Using scissors, snip the chives over the apricots.

❖ When the couscous is cool, mix in the apricots, chives, coconut and cinnamon. Season well.

❖ To make the dressing, mix all the ingredients together and season. Pour over the couscous and mix until well combined. Cover and leave to chill for 1 hour to allow the flavours to develop. Serve the salad garnished with the mint.

Artichoke Salad

250 ml/9 fl oz bottle of
artichokes in oil, drained
4 small tomatoes
25 g/1 oz sun-dried tomatoes,
cut into strips
25 g/1 oz black olives, halved
and stoned
25 g/1 oz Parma ham,
cut into strips
1 tbsp chopped fresh basil

DRESSING
3 tbsp olive oil
1 tbsp wine vinegar
1 small garlic clove, crushed
1/2 tsp mustard
1 tsp clear honey
salt and pepper

❉ Drain the artichokes thoroughly, then cut them into quarters and place in a bowl.

❉ Cut each tomato into 6 wedges and place in the bowl with the sun-dried tomatoes, olives and ham.

❉ To make the dressing, put all the ingredients into a screw-top jar and shake vigorously until the ingredients are thoroughly blended.

❉ Pour the dressing over the salad and toss well together. Transfer the salad to individual plates and sprinkle with the basil.

French Bean & Carrot Salad

350 g/12 oz French beans
225 g/8 oz carrots
1 red onion
1 red pepper

DRESSING
2 tbsp extra virgin olive oil
1 tbsp red wine vinegar
2 tsp sun-dried tomato paste
1/4 tsp caster sugar
salt and pepper

❉ Top and tail the beans and blanch them in boiling water for 4 minutes until just tender. Drain and rinse under cold water until they are cool. Drain again thoroughly.

❉ Transfer the drained beans to a large salad bowl.

❉ Peel the carrots and cut them into thin matchsticks, using a mandolin if you have one.

❉ Peel the onion and cut it into thin slices.

❉ Halve and deseed the pepper and cut the flesh into thin strips.

❉ Add the carrot, pepper and onion to the beans and toss to mix.

❉ To make the dressing, place the oil, vinegar, sun-dried tomato paste and sugar in a small screw-top jar and season to taste with salt and pepper. Shake vigorously to mix.

❉ Pour the dressing over the vegetables and serve immediately or chill in the refrigerator until required.

Green & White Salad

2 large potatoes, unpeeled and
sliced
2 green eating apples, diced
1 tsp lemon juice
25 g/1 oz walnut pieces
125 g/4^1/$_2$ oz goat's cheese,
cubed
150 g/5^1/$_2$ oz rocket
salt

DRESSING
2 tbsp olive oil
1 tbsp red wine vinegar
1 tsp clear honey
1 tsp fennel seeds

❉ Bring a large saucepan of lightly salted water to the boil, add the potatoes and cook for 15 minutes,until tender. Drain and set aside to cool. Transfer the cooled potatoes to a serving bowl.

❉ Toss the diced apples in the lemon juice, drain and stir them into the cold potatoes.

❉ Add the walnut pieces, cheese and rocket, then toss the salad to mix.

❉ In a small bowl, whisk the dressing ingredients together until well combined and pour the dressing over the salad. Serve immediately.

Spinach & Orange Salad

❈ SERVES 4 ❈

225 g/8 oz baby spinach leaves
2 large oranges
1/2 red onion, chopped

DRESSING
3 tbsp extra virgin olive oil
2 tbsp freshly squeezed orange juice
2 tsp lemon juice
1 tsp clear honey
1/2 tsp wholegrain mustard
salt and pepper

❈ Wash the spinach leaves under cold running water and dry them thoroughly on absorbent kitchen paper. Remove any tough stalks and tear the larger leaves into smaller pieces.

❈ Slice the top and bottom off each orange with a sharp knife, then remove the peel and pith. Carefully slice between the membranes of the orange to remove the segments. Reserve any juices for the salad dressing. (Working over a small bowl may be the easiest way of doing this.)

❈ Mix together the spinach leaves and orange segments and arrange them in a serving dish. Scatter the chopped onion over the salad.

❈ To make the dressing, whisk together the olive oil, orange juice, lemon juice, honey and mustard in a small bowl. Season to taste with salt and pepper.

❈ Pour the dressing over the salad just before serving. Toss the salad well to coat the leaves with the dressing.

Roasted Pepper Salad

❈ SERVES 4 ❈

4 large mixed red, green and yellow peppers
4 tbsp olive oil
1 large red onion, sliced
2 garlic cloves, crushed

4 tomatoes, peeled and chopped
pinch of sugar
1 tsp lemon juice
salt and pepper

❈ Halve and deseed the peppers.

❈ Place the peppers, skin side up, under a preheated hot grill. Cook until the skins char. Rinse under cold water and remove the skins.

❈ Trim off any thick membranes and slice thinly.

❈ Heat the oil in a frying pan and fry the onion and garlic until softened. Add the peppers and tomatoes and fry over a low heat for 10 minutes.

❈ Remove from the heat, add the sugar and lemon juice, and season to taste. Serve immediately or leave to cool (the flavours will develop as the salad cools).

Roasted Vegetable Salad

6 tbsp olive oil	3 red onions, quartered
2 aubergines	6 plum tomatoes, quartered
1 yellow pepper, deseeded and quartered	6 fresh basil leaves
1 red pepper, deseeded and quartered	**DRESSING**
1 orange pepper, deseeded and quartered	4 tbsp olive oil
	1 tbsp red wine vinegar
6 shallots	1 garlic clove, finely chopped
	salt and pepper

❊ Preheat the oven to 230°C/450°F/Gas Mark 8. Pour the oil into a large roasting tin. Add the aubergines, peppers, shallots, onions and tomatoes and toss to coat. Roast in the preheated oven for 20 minutes, turning occasionally. Transfer the peppers, shallots, onions and tomatoes to a serving platter with a slotted spoon.

❊ Return the aubergines to the oven and roast, turning once, for a further 15 minutes. Remove from the oven and leave until cool enough to handle, then cut into bite-sized pieces and add to the vegetable platter.

❊ To make the dressing, mix the oil, vinegar and garlic together, whisking well with a fork. Season to taste with salt and pepper and pour over the vegetables. Leave to cool until just warm, then sprinkle the vegetables with the basil leaves and serve.

Red Hot Slaw

1/2 small red cabbage	**DRESSING**
1 large carrot	3 tbsp mayonnaise
2 red-skinned apples	3 tbsp natural yogurt
1 tbsp lemon juice	1 garlic clove, crushed
1 medium red onion	1 tsp paprika
100 g/3½ oz Cheddar cheese, grated	1–2 tsp chilli powder
	pinch of cayenne pepper (optional)
fresh red chilli strips and carrot strips, to garnish	salt and pepper

❊ Cut the red cabbage in half and remove the central core. Finely shred the leaves and place in a large bowl. Peel and coarsely grate or finely shred the carrot and mix it into the cabbage.

❊ Core the apples and finely dice, leaving on the skins. Place in another bowl and toss in the lemon juice to help prevent the apple turning brown. Mix the apple into the cabbage and carrot.

❊ Peel and finely shred or grate the onion. Stir into the other vegetables with the cheese and mix together.

❊ To make the dressing, mix together the mayonnaise, yogurt, garlic and paprika in a small bowl. Add chilli powder to taste and the cayenne pepper, if using – remember that this will add more spice to the dressing. Season to taste with salt and pepper.

❊ Add the dressing to the vegetables and toss well to mix. Cover and leave to chill in the refrigerator for 1 hour to allow the flavours to develop.

❊ Serve garnished with the strips of chilli and carrot.

Carrot & Nut Coleslaw

1 large carrot, grated
1 small onion, finely chopped
2 celery sticks, chopped
1/4 small hard white cabbage, shredded
1 tbsp chopped parsley
4 tbsp sesame oil
1/2 tsp poppy seeds
60 g/2 oz cashew nuts
2 tbsp white wine vinegar or cider vinegar
salt and pepper
sprigs of fresh parsley, to garnish

❖ In a large salad bowl, mix together the carrot, onion, celery and cabbage. Stir in the chopped parsley and season to taste with salt and pepper.

❖ Heat the sesame oil in a saucepan with a lid. Add the poppy seeds and cover the pan. Cook over a medium–high heat until the seeds start to make a popping sound. Remove from the heat and set aside to cool.

❖ Spread out the cashew nuts on a baking tray. Place them under a medium–hot grill and toast until lightly browned, being careful not to burn them. Leave to cool.

❖ Add the vinegar to the oil and poppy seeds, then pour the dressing over the carrot mixture. Add the cooled cashew nuts. Toss together to coat well.

❖ Garnish the salad with the sprigs of parsley and serve immediately.

Tomato & Basil Salad

500 g/1 lb 2 oz tiny new or
salad potatoes, scrubbed
4–5 extra large tomatoes
2 kiwi fruit
1 onion, very thinly sliced
2 tbsp roughly chopped fresh
basil leaves
fresh basil leaves, to garnish

DRESSING
4 tbsp virgin olive oil
2 tbsp balsamic vinegar
1 garlic clove, crushed
2 tbsp mayonnaise or soured
cream
salt and pepper

❄ Bring a saucepan of lightly salted water to the boil and cook the potatoes in their skins for about 10–15 minutes or until just tender. Drain the potatoes thoroughly.

❄ To make the dressing, whisk together the oil, vinegar, garlic and salt and pepper to taste until completely emulsified. Transfer half of the dressing to another bowl and whisk in the mayonnaise.

❄ Add the creamy dressing to the warm potatoes and toss thoroughly, then leave until cold.

❄ Wipe the tomatoes and thinly slice. Peel the kiwi fruit and cut into thin slices. Layer the tomatoes with the kiwi fruit, slices of onion and chopped basil in a fairly shallow dish, leaving a space in the centre for the potatoes.

❄ Spoon the potatoes in their dressing into the centre of the tomato salad.

❄ Drizzle a little of the dressing over the tomatoes, or serve separately in a bowl or jug. Garnish the salad with the basil leaves. Cover the dish with clingfilm and chill until ready to serve.

Cucumber Salad

1 cucumber
1 tsp salt
1 small red onion
1 garlic clove, crushed

$^1/_2$ tsp chilli paste
2 tsp Thai fish sauce
1 tbsp lime juice
1 tsp sesame oil

❄ Trim the cucumber and coarsely grate the flesh. Place it in a sieve over a bowl, sprinkle with the salt and set aside to drain for about 20 minutes. Discard the liquid and rinse the cucumber.

❄ Peel and finely chop the onion, then add it to the cucumber. Toss to mix. Spoon the mixture into 4 individual bowls or a large serving bowl.

❄ Mix together the garlic, chilli paste, fish sauce, lime juice and sesame oil, then spoon the dressing over the salad. Cover the salad tightly with clingfilm and chill in the refrigerator before serving.

Mushroom Salad

150 g/5½ oz firm button mushrooms	5 anchovy fillets, drained and chopped
4 tbsp virgin olive oil	1 tbsp fresh marjoram
1 tbsp lemon juice	salt and pepper

❊ Gently wipe each mushroom with a damp cloth in order to remove any excess dirt.

❊ Thinly slice the mushrooms, using a sharp knife.

❊ To make the dressing, mix together the oil and lemon juice.

❊ Pour the dressing mixture over the mushrooms. Toss together so that the mushrooms are completely coated with the lemon juice and oil.

❊ Stir the chopped anchovy fillets into the mushrooms.

❊ Season the mushroom mixture to taste with pepper and garnish with the marjoram.

❊ Leave the mushroom salad to stand for about 5 minutes before serving so that all the flavours can be absorbed.

❊ Season the mushroom salad with a little salt and serve.

Italian Pasta Salad

2 tbsp pine kernels	salt and pepper
175 g/6 oz dried fusilli	sprigs of fresh basil, to garnish
1 tbsp olive oil	
6 tomatoes	**DRESSING**
225 g/8 oz mozzarella cheese	6 tbsp extra virgin olive oil
1 large avocado	2 tbsp white wine vinegar
2 tbsp lemon juice	1 tsp wholegrain mustard
3 tbsp chopped fresh basil	pinch of sugar

❊ Spread out the pine kernels on a baking tray and toast them under a preheated grill for 1–2 minutes. Remove and set aside to cool.

❊ Bring a large saucepan of lightly salted water to the boil. Add the pasta, bring back to the boil and cook for 8–10 minutes or until tender, but still firm to the bite. Drain the pasta and refresh in cold water. Drain again and set aside to cool.

❊ Thinly slice the tomatoes and the cheese.

❊ Cut the avocado in half lengthways, carefully remove the stone, then peel. Cut the flesh into thin slices lengthways and sprinkle with lemon juice to prevent discoloration.

❊ To make the dressing, whisk together the oil, vinegar, mustard and sugar in a small bowl and season to taste with salt and pepper.

❊ Arrange the tomatoes, cheese and avocado alternately in overlapping slices on a large serving platter, leaving room in the centre.

❊ Toss the pasta with half the dressing and the chopped basil and season to taste with salt and pepper. Spoon the pasta into the centre of the platter and pour over the remaining dressing. Sprinkle over the pine kernels, garnish with the sprigs of basil and serve immediately.

Vegetable & Pasta Salad

2 small aubergines, thinly
sliced
1 large onion, sliced
2 large beef tomatoes, peeled
and cut into wedges
1 red pepper, deseeded and
sliced
1 fennel bulb, thinly sliced
2 garlic cloves, sliced
3 tbsp olive oil
175 g/6 oz small pasta shapes
85 g/3 oz feta cheese, crumbled
a few fresh basil leaves, torn
salt and pepper
salad leaves, to serve

DRESSING
5 tbsp olive oil
juice of 1 orange
1 tsp grated orange rind
¼ tsp paprika
4 canned anchovies, finely
chopped

❖ Place the aubergine slices in a colander, sprinkle with salt and set them aside for about 1 hour to draw out some of the bitter juices. Rinse under cold running water to remove the salt, then drain. Toss on kitchen paper to dry.

❖ Arrange the aubergines, onion, tomatoes, pepper, fennel and garlic in a single layer in an ovenproof dish, sprinkle with the oil and season. Bake in a preheated oven, 220°C/450°F/ Gas Mark 7, for 45 minutes until the vegetables begin to brown. Remove from the oven and set aside to cool.

❖ Bring a large saucepan of lightly salted water to the boil. Add the pasta, bring back to the boil and cook for 10 minutes until tender, but still firm to the bite. Drain and turn into a bowl.

❖ To make the dressing, mix together the oil, orange juice, orange rind and paprika. Stir in the finely chopped anchovies and season to taste with pepper. Pour the dressing over the pasta while it is still hot and toss well. Set aside the pasta to cool.

❖ To assemble the salad, line a shallow serving dish with the salad leaves and arrange the cold roasted vegetables in the centre. Spoon the pasta in a ring around the vegetables and scatter over the feta cheese and basil leaves.

Pasta Salad & Vinaigrette

225 g/8 oz fusilli	**VINAIGRETTE**
4 tomatoes	15 g/¹/₂ oz basil leaves
50 g/1³/₄ oz black olives	1 clove garlic
25 g/1 oz sun-dried tomatoes	2 tbsp grated Parmesan
in oil	cheese
2 tbsp pine kernels	4 tbsp extra virgin olive oil
2 tbsp grated Parmesan	2 tbsp lemon juice
cheese	salt and pepper
fresh basil leaves, to garnish	

❖ Bring a saucepan of lightly salted boiling water to the boil and cook the pasta for 8–10 minutes or until just tender. Drain the pasta, rinse under cold water, then drain again thoroughly. Place the pasta in a large bowl.

❖ To make the vinaigrette, place the basil leaves, garlic, cheese, oil and lemon juice in a food processor. Season with salt and pepper to taste. Process until the leaves are well chopped and the ingredients are combined. Alternatively, finely chop the basil leaves by hand and combine with the other vinaigrette ingredients. Pour the vinaigrette over the pasta and toss to coat.

❖ Cut the tomatoes into wedges. Stone and halve the olives. Slice the sun-dried tomatoes. Place the pine kernels on a baking tray and toast under the grill until golden.

❖ Add the tomatoes (fresh and sun-dried) and the olives to the pasta and mix.

❖ Transfer the pasta to a serving dish, scatter over the pine kernels and cheese and garnish with a few basil leaves.

Pasta Salad & Mixed Cabbage

250 g/9 oz dried short-cut	2 large apples, diced
macaroni	250 g/9 oz cooked smoked
5 tbsp olive oil	bacon or ham, diced
1 large red cabbage, shredded	8 tbsp wine vinegar
1 large white cabbage,	1 tbsp sugar
shredded	salt and pepper

❖ Bring a saucepan of lightly salted water to the boil. Add the macaroni and 1 tablespoon of the oil and cook for 8–10 minutes or until tender, but still firm to the bite. Drain the pasta, then refresh in cold water. Drain again and set aside.

❖ Bring a large saucepan of lightly salted water to the boil. Add the shredded red cabbage and cook for 5 minutes. Drain the cabbage thoroughly and set aside to cool.

❖ Bring a large saucepan of lightly salted water to the boil. Add the shredded white cabbage and cook for 5 minutes. Drain the cabbage thoroughly and set aside to cool.

❖ In a large bowl, mix together the pasta, red cabbage and apple. In a separate bowl, mix together the white cabbage and bacon or ham.

❖ In a small bowl, mix together the remaining oil, the vinegar and the sugar and season to taste with salt and pepper. Pour the dressing over each of the 2 cabbage mixtures and, finally, mix them all together. Serve immediately.

Goat's Cheese & Penne Salad

250 g/9 oz dried penne	1 bunch of watercress,
5 tbsp olive oil	trimmed
1 head radicchio, torn into	2 tbsp lemon juice
pieces	3 tbsp garlic vinegar
1 Webbs lettuce, torn into	4 tomatoes, quartered
pieces	1 small onion, sliced
7 tbsp chopped walnuts	1 large carrot, grated
2 ripe pears, cored and diced	250 g/9 oz goat's cheese, diced
1 sprig fresh basil	salt and pepper

❁ Bring a large saucepan of lightly salted water to the boil. Add the penne and 1 tablespoon of the oil and cook for 8–10 minutes or until tender but still firm to the bite. Drain the pasta, refresh under cold running water, drain thoroughly again and set aside to cool.

❁ Place the radicchio and Webbs lettuce in a large salad bowl and mix together well. Top with the pasta, walnuts, pears, basil and watercress.

❁ Mix together the lemon juice, the remaining oil and the vinegar in a measuring jug. Pour the mixture over the salad ingredients and toss to coat the salad leaves well.

❁ Add the tomato quarters, onion slices, grated carrot and diced goat's cheese and toss together, using 2 forks, until well mixed. Leave the salad to chill in the refrigerator for about 1 hour before serving.

Pink Grapefruit Salad

1/2 cos lettuce	**DRESSING**
1/2 oak leaf lettuce	4 tbsp olive oil
2 pink grapefruit	1 tbsp white wine vinegar
2 ripe avocados	salt and pepper
175 g/6 oz dolcelatte cheese,	
thinly sliced	
sprigs of fresh basil, to garnish	

❁ Arrange the lettuce leaves on 4 serving plates or in a salad bowl.

❁ Remove the peel and pith from the grapefruit with a sharp serrated knife, catching the grapefruit juice in a bowl.

❁ Segment the grapefruit by cutting down each side of the membrane. Remove all the membrane. Arrange the segments on the serving plates.

❁ Peel, stone and slice the avocados, dipping them in the grapefruit juice to prevent discoloration. Arrange the slices on the salad with the cheese.

❁ To make the dressing, combine any remaining grapefruit juice with the oil and vinegar. Season to taste with salt and pepper, mixing well to combine.

❁ Drizzle the dressing over the individual plates of salad. Garnish with the sprigs of basil and serve at once.

Hot & Spicy Rice Salad

2 tsp vegetable oil
1 onion, finely chopped
1 fresh red chilli, deseeded and
finely chopped
8 cardamom pods
1 tsp turmeric
1 tsp garam masala
350 g/12 oz basmati rice, rinsed
700 ml/1¼ pints boiling water
1 orange pepper, deseeded and
chopped
225 g/8 oz cauliflower, divided
into small florets
4 ripe tomatoes, peeled,
deseeded and chopped
125 g/4½ oz seedless raisins
salt and pepper
25 g/1 oz toasted flaked
almonds, to garnish
raita of natural yogurt, onion,
cucumber and mint, to serve

❖ Heat the oil in a large non-stick saucepan. Add the onion, chilli, cardamom pods, turmeric and garam masala to the pan and fry over a low heat for 2–3 minutes until the vegetables are just softened.

❖ Stir in the rice, boiling water, chopped pepper and cauliflower. Season to taste with salt and pepper.

❖ Cover the pan with a tight-fitting lid and bring the mixture to the boil. Reduce the heat and simmer for 15 minutes without lifting the lid.

❖ Uncover the pan and fork through the rice. Stir in the tomatoes and raisins.

❖ Cover the pan again, turn off the heat and leave for a further 15 minutes. Discard the cardamom pods.

❖ Pile the salad on to a warmed serving platter and garnish with a sprinkling of the toasted flaked almonds.

❖ Serve the rice salad immediately, accompanied by the raita.

Mango & Wild Rice Salad

❖ **SERVES 4** ❖

85 g/3 oz wild rice
150 g/5½ oz basmati rice
3 tbsp hazelnut oil
1 tbsp sherry vinegar
1 ripe mango
3 celery sticks
85 g/3 oz ready-to-eat dried
apricots, chopped
55 g/2 oz flaked almonds,
toasted
2 tbsp chopped fresh coriander
or mint
salt and pepper
sprigs of fresh coriander or
mint, to garnish

❖ Cook the wild rice and basmati rice in separate saucepans of lightly salted water. Cook the wild rice for 45–50 minutes and the basmati rice for 10–12 minutes. Drain, rinse well and drain again. Place all the rice in a large bowl.

❖ Whisk together the oil and vinegar and season to taste with salt and pepper. Pour over the rice and toss well.

❖ Cut the mango in half lengthways, as close to the stone as possible. Remove and discard the stone.

❖ Peel the skin from the mango and cut the flesh into slices.

❖ Thinly slice the celery and add to the cooled rice with the mango, apricots, almonds and chopped herbs. Toss together and transfer to a serving dish.

❖ Garnish the salad with the sprigs of coriander and serve.

Red Rice Salad

❖ **SERVES 8** ❖

1 tbsp olive oil
200 g/7 oz red rice
600 ml/1 pint water
400 g/14 oz canned red kidney
beans, drained and rinsed
1 small red pepper, deseeded
and diced
1 small red onion, finely
chopped
2 small cooked beetroots (not
in vinegar), peeled and diced
6–8 red radishes, thinly sliced
2–3 tbsp chopped fresh chives
salt and pepper
fresh chives, to garnish

DRESSING
2 tbsp creamed horseradish
1 tbsp Dijon mustard
1 tsp sugar
50 ml/2 fl oz red wine vinegar
125 ml/4 fl oz extra virgin
olive oil

❖ Put the oil and rice in a heavy-based saucepan and place over a medium heat. Add the water and 1 teaspoon of salt. Bring to the boil, reduce the heat, cover and simmer gently until the rice is tender and all the water has been absorbed. (There are several varieties of red rice, all differing in cooking times, so follow the packet instructions.) Remove the pan from the heat and set aside to cool to room temperature.

❖ To make the dressing, put the horseradish, mustard and sugar into a small bowl and whisk thoroughly to combine. Whisk in the vinegar, then gradually whisk in the oil to form a smooth dressing.

❖ In a large bowl, combine the kidney beans, red pepper, onion, beetroots, radishes and chives and toss together. Season to taste with salt and pepper.

❖ Using a fork, fluff the rice into the bowl with the vegetables. Pour over the dressing and toss well. Cover and leave the salad to stand for about 1 hour. Spoon into a large shallow serving bowl, garnish with the chives and serve immediately.

Tabbouleh

175 g/6 oz quinoa
600 ml/1 pint water
10 vine-ripened cherry
tomatoes, deseeded and
chopped
7.5-cm/3-inch piece of
cucumber, diced

3 spring onions, finely chopped
juice of $1/2$ lemon
2 tbsp extra virgin olive oil
4 tbsp chopped fresh mint
4 tbsp chopped fresh coriander
4 tbsp chopped fresh parsley
salt and pepper

❊ Put the quinoa into a medium-sized saucepan and cover with the water. Bring to the boil, then reduce the heat, cover and simmer over a low heat for 15 minutes. Drain if necessary.

❊ Leave the quinoa to cool slightly before combining with the remaining ingredients in a salad bowl. Adjust the seasoning before serving.

Chinese Salad Nests

POTATO NESTS
450 g/1 lb floury potatoes,
grated
125 g/$4^1/2$ oz cornflour,
vegetable oil, for frying
fresh chives, to garnish

SALAD
125 g/$4^1/2$ oz pineapple, cubed
1 green pepper, cut into strips
1 carrot, cut into thin strips
50 g/$1^3/4$ oz mangetout,
thickly sliced

4 baby sweetcorn cobs, halved
lengthways
25 g/1 oz beansprouts
2 spring onions, sliced

DRESSING
1 tbsp clear honey
1 tsp light soy sauce
1 garlic clove, crushed
1 tsp lemon juice

❊ To make the nests, rinse the potatoes several times in cold water. Drain well on kitchen paper so they are completely dry. This is to prevent the potatoes spitting when they are cooked in the fat. Place the potatoes in a mixing bowl. Add the cornflour, mixing well to coat the potatoes.

❊ Half fill a wok with vegetable oil and heat until smoking. Line a 15-cm/6-inch diameter wire sieve with a quarter of the potato mixture and press another sieve of the same size on top.

❊ Lower the sieves into the oil and cook for 2 minutes until the potato nest is golden brown and crisp. Remove from the wok, allowing the excess oil to drain off.

❊ Repeat 3 more times to use up all of the mixture and make a total of 4 nests. Leave to cool.

❊ Mix the salad ingredients together, then spoon into the potato baskets.

❊ Mix the dressing ingredients together in a bowl. Pour the dressing over the salad, garnish with the chives and serve immediately.

Beansprouts with Vegetables

450 g/1 lb beansprouts
2 fresh red chillies, deseeded and finely chopped
1 red pepper, deseeded and thinly sliced
1 green pepper, deseeded and thinly sliced
60 g/2 oz water chestnuts, quartered
1 celery stick, sliced
Chinese roasted meats and noodles, to serve

MARINADE
3 tbsp rice wine vinegar
2 tbsp light soy sauce
2 tbsp chopped chives
1 garlic clove, crushed
pinch of Chinese curry powder

❉ Place the beansprouts, chillies, peppers, water chestnuts and celery in a large bowl and mix well to combine all the ingredients.

❉ To make the marinade, mix together the vinegar, soy sauce, chives, garlic and curry powder in a bowl.

❉ Pour the marinade over the prepared vegetables. Toss to mix the vegetables thoroughly in the marinade.

❉ Cover the salad with clingfilm and leave to chill in the refrigerator for at least 3 hours.

❉ Drain the vegetables thoroughly, transfer to a serving dish and serve with the roasted meats and noodles.

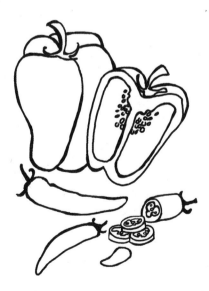

Alfalfa & Beetroot Salad

100 g/3^1/$_2$ oz baby spinach
85 g/3 oz alfalfa sprouts
2 celery sticks, sliced
4 cooked beetroot, cut into 8
wedges

DRESSING
4 tbsp olive oil
4^1/$_2$ tsp garlic wine vinegar
1 garlic clove, crushed
2 tsp clear honey
1 tbsp chopped fresh chives

❉ If the spinach leaves are large, tear them into smaller pieces (cutting them would bruise them). Place the spinach and alfalfa sprouts in a large bowl and mix together.

❉ Add the celery and mix well. Toss in the beetroot and mix again.

❉ To make the dressing, mix the oil, vinegar, garlic, honey and chives in a small bowl.

❉ Pour the dressing over the salad, toss well and serve immediately.

Red & Green Salad

3 tbsp extra virgin olive oil
juice of 1 orange
1 tsp caster sugar
1 tsp fennel seeds

650 g/1 lb 7 oz cooked beetroot
115 g/4 oz fresh baby spinach
leaves
salt and pepper

❉ Cut the beetroot into bite-sized cubes. Heat the oil in a small heavy-based saucepan. Add the orange juice, sugar and fennel seeds and season to taste with salt and pepper. Stir until the sugar has dissolved.

❉ Add the beetroot to the pan and stir gently to coat with the dressing. Remove the pan from the heat.

❉ Arrange the spinach leaves in a salad bowl. Spoon the warmed beetroot on top and serve.

Potato & Beetroot Salad

1 lb/450 g waxy potatoes, diced
4 small cooked beetroot, sliced
1/2 small cucumber, thinly
sliced
2 large dill pickles, sliced
1 red onion, halved and sliced
sprigs of fresh dill, to garnish

DRESSING
1 garlic clove, crushed
2 tbsp olive oil
2 tbsp red wine vinegar
2 tbsp chopped fresh dill
salt and pepper

❋ Bring a saucepan of lightly salted water to the boil and cook the potatoes for 15 minutes or until tender. Drain and leave to cool.

❋ When cool, mix the potatoes and beetroot together in a bowl and set aside.

❋ Line a salad platter with the slices of cucumber, dill pickles and red onion.

❋ Spoon the potato and beetroot mixture into the centre of the platter.

❋ In a small bowl, whisk all the dressing ingredients together, then pour it over the salad.

❋ Serve the potato and beetroot salad immediately, garnished with the sprigs of dill.

Potato & Apple Salad

900 g/2 lb baby new potatoes
2 green eating apples
4 spring onions, chopped

4 celery sticks, chopped
150 ml/5 fl oz mayonnaise
salt and pepper

❋ Bring a saucepan of lightly salted water to the boil and cook the potatoes for 15 minutes or until tender. Drain well and place in a salad bowl.

❋ Core and chop the apples and add them to the salad bowl with the spring onions and celery.

❋ Add the mayonnaise to the potato and apple mixture and season to taste with salt and pepper.

❋ Stir well to mix, then set aside to cool and allow the flavours to develop. Serve the salad at room temperature.

Indian Potato Salad

4 medium floury potatoes, diced
75 g/2¾ oz small broccoli
florets
1 small mango, diced
4 spring onions, sliced
salt and pepper
small cooked spiced
poppadoms, to serve

DRESSING
½ tsp ground cumin
½ tsp ground coriander
1 tbsp mango chutney
150 ml/5 fl oz low-fat natural
yogurt
1 tsp chopped ginger root
2 tbsp chopped fresh coriander

❖ Bring a saucepan of lightly salted water to the boil and cook the potatoes for 10 minutes or until tender. Drain and place in a mixing bowl.

❖ Meanwhile, bring another saucepan of lightly salted water to the boil and blanch the broccoli florets for 2 minutes. Drain the broccoli well and add to the potatoes in the bowl.

❖ When the potatoes and broccoli have cooled, add the mango and spring onions. Season to taste with salt and pepper and mix well to combine.

❖ In a small bowl, stir all the dressing ingredients together.

❖ Spoon the dressing over the potato mixture and mix together carefully, taking care not to break up the potatoes and broccoli.

❖ Serve the salad immediately, accompanied by the poppadoms.

Herby Potato Salad

500 g/1 lb 2 oz new potatoes
16 vine-ripened cherry
tomatoes, halved
70 g/2½ oz black olives,
stoned and coarsely chopped
4 spring onions, finely sliced

2 tbsp chopped fresh mint
2 tbsp chopped fresh parsley
2 tbsp chopped fresh coriander
juice of 1 lemon
3 tbsp extra virgin olive oil
salt and pepper

❄ Bring a saucepan of lightly salted water to the boil and cook the potatoes for 15 minutes or until tender. Drain, then leave to cool slightly before peeling off the skins. Cut into halves or quarters, depending on the size of the potato, then combine with the tomatoes, olives, spring onions and herbs in a salad bowl.

❄ Mix the lemon juice and oil together in a small bowl or jug and pour over the potato salad. Season to taste with salt and pepper before serving.

Sweet Potato & Bean Salad

1 sweet potato
4 baby carrots, halved
4 tomatoes
4 celery sticks, chopped
225 g/8 oz canned borlotti
beans, drained and rinsed
115 g/4 oz mixed salad leaves,
such as frisée, rocket,
radicchio and oakleaf lettuce

1 tbsp sultanas
4 spring onions, finely chopped

DRESSING
1 tbsp clear honey
6 tbsp low-fat natural yogurt
salt and pepper

❄ Peel and dice the sweet potato. Bring a saucepan of lightly salted water to the boil and cook the sweet potato for 15 minutes or until tender. Drain, transfer to a bowl and reserve until required.

❄ Cook the carrots in a separate saucepan of boiling water for 1 minute. Drain thoroughly and add to the sweet potato. Cut the tops off the tomatoes and scoop out the seeds. Chop the flesh and add to the bowl with the celery and beans. Mix well.

❄ To make the dressing, whisk all the dressing ingredients together in a small bowl, and set aside.

❄ Line a large serving bowl with the mixed salad leaves. Spoon the sweet potato and bean mixture on top, then sprinkle with the sultanas and spring onions. Spoon over the dressing and serve immediately.

Potato, Apple & Bean Salad

225 g/8 oz new potatoes,
scrubbed and quartered
225 g/8 oz mixed canned
beans, such as red kidney,
flageolet and borlotti, drained
and rinsed
1 red eating apple, diced and
tossed in 1 tbsp lemon juice
1 small yellow pepper, diced
1 shallot, sliced

½ fennel bulb, sliced
looseleaf lettuce leaves

DRESSING
1 tbsp red wine vinegar
2 tbsp olive oil
½ tbsp American mustard
1 garlic clove, crushed
2 tsp chopped fresh thyme

❊ Bring a saucepan of lightly salted water to the boil and cook the potatoes for 15 minutes or until tender. Drain and transfer to a mixing bowl.

❊ Add the potatoes to the mixed beans with the diced apple and yellow pepper, and the sliced shallots and fennel. Mix well, taking care not to break up the potatoes.

❊ In a bowl, whisk all the dressing ingredients together.

❊ Pour the dressing over the potato salad.

❊ Line a plate or salad bowl with the lettuce leaves and spoon the potato mixture into the centre. Serve the salad immediately.

Potatoes in Italian Dressing

750 g/1 lb 10 oz waxy potatoes
1 shallot
2 tomatoes
1 tbsp chopped fresh basil
salt

DRESSING
1 tomato, peeled and finely
    chopped
4 black olives, stoned and finely
    chopped
4 tbsp olive oil
1 tbsp wine vinegar
1 garlic clove, crushed
salt and pepper

❊ Bring a saucepan of lightly salted water to the boil and cook the potatoes for 15 minutes or until tender.

❊ Drain the potatoes well, chop roughly and put into a bowl.

❊ Chop the shallot. Cut the tomatoes into wedges and add the shallot and tomatoes to the potatoes.

❊ To make the Italian dressing, put all the ingredients into a screw-top jar and mix together thoroughly.

❊ Pour the Italian dressing over the potato mixture and toss thoroughly to coat the vegetables.

❊ Transfer the salad to a serving dish and sprinkle with the basil.

Minted Fennel Salad

1 fennel bulb
lemon juice
2 small oranges
1 small or ½ a large cucumber
1 tbsp chopped mint
1 tbsp virgin olive oil
2 hard-boiled eggs, to garnish

❖ Using a sharp knife, trim the outer leaves from the fennel. Thinly slice the fennel bulb into a bowl of water and sprinkle with the lemon juice.

❖ Grate the rind of the oranges over a bowl. Using a sharp knife, pare away the orange peel, then segment the orange by carefully slicing between each line of pith. Do this over the bowl in order to retain the juice.

❖ Using a sharp knife, cut the cucumber into 12-mm/½-inch rounds and then cut each round into quarters. Add the cucumber to the fennel and orange mixture together with the mint.

❖ Pour the oil over the salad and toss well.

❖ Shell and quarter the eggs and use to garnish the salad. Serve at once.

Aubergine Salad

500 g/1 lb 2 oz aubergines
4 tbsp salt
1 tbsp olive oil
1 large onion, chopped
1 garlic clove, crushed
150 ml/5 fl oz vegetable stock
400 g/14 oz canned chopped
  tomatoes
2 tbsp tomato purée
1 tsp ground cinnamon

2 tsp caster sugar
1 tbsp chopped fresh coriander
1 tbsp lemon juice
425 g/15 oz canned chickpeas,
  drained
pepper
sprigs of fresh coriander,
  to garnish
warmed pitta bread and lemon
  wedges, for serving

❈ Cut the aubergines into 1-cm/½-inch slices and then dice. Layer them in a bowl, sprinkling well with salt as you go. Set aside for 30 minutes for the bitter juices to drain out.

❈ Transfer to a colander and rinse well under cold running water to remove the salt. Drain thoroughly and pat dry with kitchen paper.

❈ Heat the oil in a large non-stick frying pan, add the onion and garlic and fry over a low heat, stirring occasionally, for 2–3 minutes until slightly soft.

❈ Pour in the stock and bring to the boil. Add the aubergines, tomatoes, tomato purée, cinnamon, sugar and pepper. Mix well and simmer gently, uncovered, for 20 minutes until soft. Remove from the heat and set aside to cool completely.

❈ Stir in the chopped coriander, lemon juice and chickpeas, cover and chill for 1 hour.

❈ Garnish with the sprigs of coriander and serve with the warmed pitta bread and lemon wedges.

Mixed Bean Salad

400 g/14 oz canned flageolet
  beans, drained
400 g/14 oz canned red kidney
  beans, drained
400 g/14 oz canned butter
  beans, drained
1 small red onion, thinly sliced
175 g/6 oz French beans,
  topped and tailed
1 red pepper, halved and
  deseeded
salt

DRESSING
4 tbsp olive oil
2 tbsp sherry vinegar
2 tbsp lemon juice
1 tsp light muscovado sugar
1 tsp chilli sauce (optional)

❈ Put the canned beans in a large mixing bowl. Add the onion and mix together.

❈ Cut the French beans in half, bring a saucepan of lightly salted water to the boil and cook the beans for about 8 minutes until just tender. Refresh under cold water and drain again. Add to the mixed beans and onions.

❈ Place the pepper halves, cut side down, on a grill rack and cook under a preheated medium grill until the skin blackens and chars. Leave the peppers to cool slightly then put them into a polythene bag for about 10 minutes. Peel away the skin from the peppers and discard. Roughly chop the pepper flesh and add it to the beans.

❈ To make the dressing, place the oil, vinegar, lemon juice, sugar and chilli sauce, if using, in a screw-top jar and shake vigorously.

❈ Pour the dressing over the mixed bean salad and toss well. Leave to chill in the refrigerator until required.

Tomato & Artichoke Salad

❖ **SERVES 4–6** ❖

4 ripe plum tomatoes, cut into wedges
115 g/4 oz baby plum tomatoes, halved
400 g/14 oz canned artichoke hearts, drained
400 g/14 oz canned butter beans, drained and rinsed
2 tbsp sunflower or groundnut oil
4 tbsp Thai sweet chilli dipping sauce
juice of 1/2 lime
pepper
fresh crusty bread, to serve

❖ Place the fresh and canned tomatoes in a large bowl. Cut the artichoke hearts in half, then add to the bowl of tomatoes. Add the butter beans and gently stir together.

❖ Mix the oil, chilli dipping sauce and lime juice together in a small bowl. Season to taste with pepper and pour over the salad. Toss gently until the salad is coated with the dressing.

❖ Cover and leave to marinate for 1 hour before serving with the bread.

Paw-Paw Salad

❖ **SERVES 4** ❖

DRESSING
4 tbsp olive oil
1 tbsp fish sauce or light soy sauce
2 tbsp lime or lemon juice
1 tbsp dark muscovado sugar
1 tsp finely chopped fresh red or green chilli

SALAD
1 crisp lettuce
1/4 small white cabbage
2 paw-paws
2 tomatoes
25 g/1 oz roasted peanuts, roughly chopped
4 spring onions, trimmed and thinly sliced
fresh basil leaves, to garnish

❖ To make the dressing, whisk together the oil, fish sauce, lime juice, sugar and chilli. Set aside, stirring occasionally to dissolve the sugar.

❖ Shred the lettuce and white cabbage, then toss together and arrange on a large serving plate.

❖ Peel the paw-paws and slice them in half. Scoop out the seeds, then slice the flesh thinly. Arrange on top of the lettuce and cabbage.

❖ Soak the tomatoes in a bowl of boiling water for 1 minute, then lift out and peel. Remove the seeds and chop the flesh. Arrange on the salad leaves.

❖ Scatter the peanuts and spring onions over the top. Whisk the dressing and pour over the salad. Garnish with the basil leaves and serve at once.

Grapefruit & Coconut Salad

125 g/4$\frac{1}{2}$ oz grated coconut
2 tsp light soy sauce
2 tbsp lime juice
2 tbsp water
2 tsp sunflower oil
1 garlic clove, halved
1 onion, finely chopped
2 large ruby grapefruits, peeled and segmented
90 g/3 oz alfalfa sprouts

❖ Toast the coconut in a dry frying pan over a low heat, stirring constantly, for about 3 minutes, or until golden brown. Transfer the toasted coconut to a bowl.

❖ Add the soy sauce, lime juice and water to the toasted coconut and mix together well.

❖ Heat the oil in a saucepan and fry the garlic and onion until soft. Stir the onion into the coconut mixture. Remove and discard the garlic.

❖ Divide the grapefruit segments between 4 plates. Sprinkle each with a quarter of the alfalfa sprouts, spoon over a quarter of the coconut mixture and serve.

Melon & Strawberry Salad

1/2 Webbs lettuce, shredded
1 small honeydew melon
225 g/8 oz strawberries, sliced
5-cm/2-inch piece of
  cucumber, thinly sliced
sprigs of fresh mint, to garnish

DRESSING
200 ml/7 fl oz natural yogurt
5-cm/2-inch piece of
  cucumber, peeled
a few fresh mint leaves
1/2 tsp finely grated lime or
  lemon rind
pinch of caster sugar
3–4 ice cubes

❊ Arrange the lettuce on 4 serving plates.

❊ Cut the melon lengthways into quarters. Scoop out the seeds and cut through the flesh down to the skin at 2.5-cm/1-inch intervals. Cut the melon close to the skin and detach the flesh.

❊ Place the chunks of melon on the beds of lettuce with the strawberries and cucumber slices.

❊ To make the dressing, put the yogurt, cucumber, mint leaves, lime rind, sugar and ice cubes into a blender or food processor. Blend together for about 15 seconds until smooth. Alternatively, finely chop the cucumber and mint, crush the ice cubes and combine with the other ingredients.

❊ Serve the salad with a little dressing poured over it. Garnish with the sprigs of mint.

Melon & Mango Salad

1 cantaloupe melon
60 g/2 oz each black and green
  grapes, halved and seeded
1 large mango
1 bunch of watercress, trimmed
Webbs lettuce leaves, shredded
2 tbsp olive oi
1 tbsp cider vinegar

1 passion fruit
salt and pepper

SWEET DRESSING
150 ml/5 fl oz low-fat thick
  natural yogurt
1 tbsp clear honey
1 tsp grated root ginger

❊ Halve the melon and scoop out the seeds. Slice, peel and cut into chunks. Mix with the grapes.

❊ Slice the mango on each side of its large flat stone. On each mango half, slash the flesh into a criss-cross pattern down to, but not through, the skin. Push the skin from underneath to turn the mango halves inside out. Now remove the flesh and add to the melon mixture.

❊ Arrange the watercress and lettuce on 4 serving plates.

❊ Mix together the olive oil and cider vinegar with a little salt and pepper. Drizzle over the watercress and lettuce.

❊ To make the sweet dressing for the melon, mix together the yogurt, honey and ginger.

❊ Divide the melon mixture between the 4 plates and spoon over the yogurt dressing.

❊ Scoop the seeds out of the passion fruit and sprinkle them over the salads. Serve immediately or chill in the refrigerator until required.

Noodle & Mango Salad

250 g/9 oz thread egg noodles
2 tbsp groundnut oil
4 shallots, sliced
2 cloves garlic, crushed
1 red chilli, deseeded and sliced
1 red pepper, deseeded and sliced
1 green pepper, deseeded and sliced

1 ripe mango, sliced into thin strips
25 g/1 oz salted peanuts, chopped

DRESSING
4 tbsp peanut butter
100 ml/3^1/2 fl oz coconut milk
1 tbsp tomato purée

❊   Place the egg noodles in a large dish or bowl. Pour over enough boiling water to cover the noodles and leave to stand for 10 minutes.

❊   Heat the oil in a large preheated wok or frying pan.

❊   Add the shallots, garlic, chilli and pepper slices to the wok and stir-fry for 2–3 minutes.

❊   Drain the egg noodles thoroughly in a colander. Add the drained noodles and mango slices to the wok and heat through for about 2 minutes.

❊   Transfer the noodle and mango salad to warmed serving dishes and scatter with the chopped peanuts.

❊   To make the dressing, mix together the peanut butter, coconut milk and tomato purée, then spoon over the salad. Serve immediately.

Egg Noodle Salad

225 g/8 oz dried egg noodles
2 tsp sesame oil
1 carrot
115 g/4 oz beansprouts
^{1}/2 cucumber
2 spring onions, finely shredded
150 g/5^1/2 oz cooked turkey breast meat, shredded into thin slivers
peanuts and chopped fresh basil, to garnish

DRESSING
5 tbsp coconut milk
3 tbsp lime juice
1 tbsp light soy sauce
2 tsp Thai fish sauce
1 tsp chilli oil
1 tsp sugar
2 tbsp chopped fresh coriander

❊   Cook the noodles in boiling water for 4 minutes, or according to the package instructions. Plunge them into a bowl of cold water to prevent any further cooking, then drain and toss in the oil.

❊   Use a vegetable peeler to shave off thin ribbons from the carrot. Bring a saucepan of lightly salted water to the boil and blanch the carrot and beansprouts for 30 seconds, then plunge into cold water for 30 seconds. Drain well. Shave thin ribbons of cucumber with the vegetable peeler.

❊   Place the carrots, beansprouts, cucumber, spring onions and turkey in a large bowl. Add the noodles and toss thoroughly to mix.

❊   Place all the dressing ingredients in a screw-top jar and shake vigorously to mix evenly.

❊   Add the dressing to the noodle mixture and toss. Pile the salad on to a serving dish. Sprinkle with the peanuts and basil and serve cold.

Potato & Tuna Salad

450 g/1 lb new potatoes, scrubbed and quartered
1 green pepper, sliced
50 g/1¾ oz canned sweetcorn, drained
1 red onion, sliced
300 g/10½ oz canned tuna in brine, drained and flaked
2 tbsp chopped stoned black olives
salt and pepper
lime wedges, to garnish

DRESSING
2 tbsp low-fat mayonnaise
2 tbsp soured cream
1 tbsp lime juice
2 garlic cloves, crushed
finely grated rind of 1 lime

❉ Bring a saucepan of lightly salted water to the boil and cook the potatoes for 15 minutes until tender. Drain and leave to cool in a mixing bowl.

❉ Gently stir in the green pepper, sweetcorn and onion.

❉ Spoon the potato mixture into a large serving bowl and arrange the tuna and olives over the top.

❉ Season the salad generously with salt and pepper.

❉ To make the dressing, mix together the mayonnaise, soured cream, lime juice, garlic and lime rind in a bowl.

❉ Spoon the dressing over the tuna and olives, garnish with the lime wedges and serve.

149

Sweet & Sour Fish Salad

❊ **SERVES 4** ❊

225 g/8 oz trout fillets
225 g/8 oz white fish fillets
(such as haddock or cod)
300 ml/10 fl oz water
1 stalk lemon grass
2 lime leaves
1 large red chilli
1 bunch spring onions,
trimmed and shredded
115 g/4 oz fresh pineapple
flesh, diced
1 small red pepper, deseeded
and diced

1 bunch watercress, washed
and trimmed
snipped fresh chives,
to garnish

DRESSING
1 tbsp sunflower oil
1 tbsp rice wine vinegar
pinch of chilli powder
1 tsp clear honey
salt and pepper

❊ Rinse the fish, place in a frying pan and pour over the water. Bend the lemon grass in half to bruise it and add to the pan with the lime leaves. Prick the chilli with a fork and add to the pan. Bring to the boil and simmer for 7–8 minutes. Let cool.

❊ Drain the fish fillet thoroughly, flake the flesh away from the skin and place in a bowl. Gently stir in the spring onions, pineapple and pepper.

❊ Arrange the watercress on 4 serving plates and spoon the cooked fish mixture on top.

❊ To make the dressing, mix all the ingredients together and season well. Spoon over the fish and serve, garnished with the chives.

Tuna, Bean & Anchovy Salad

❊ **SERVES 4** ❊

500 g/1 lb 2 oz tomatoes
200 g/7 oz canned tuna,
drained
2 tbsp chopped fresh parsley
1/2 cucumber
1 small red onion, sliced
225 g/8 oz cooked French
beans

1 small red pepper, deseeded
1 small crisp lettuce
6 tbsp Italian-style dressing
3 hard-boiled eggs
55 g/2 oz canned anchovies,
drained
12 black olives, stoned

❊ Cut the tomatoes into wedges, flake the tuna and put both into a bowl with the parsley.

❊ Cut the cucumber into slices. Slice the onion. Add the cucumber and onion to the bowl.

❊ Cut the beans in half, chop the pepper and add both to the bowl with the lettuce leaves. Pour over the dressing and toss to mix, then spoon into a salad bowl. Shell the eggs and cut into quarters, arrange over the top with the anchovies and scatter with the olives.

Lentil & Tuna Salad

2 ripe tomatoes
1 small red onion
3 tbsp virgin olive oil
1 tbsp lemon juice
1 tsp wholegrain mustard
1 garlic clove, crushed
1/2 tsp cumin powder

1/2 tsp ground coriander
400 g/14 oz canned lentils,
    drained
185 g/6 1/2 oz canned tuna,
    drained
2 tbsp fresh coriander, chopped
pepper

❊ Using a sharp knife, deseed the tomatoes and chop them into fine dice.

❊ Using a sharp knife, finely chop the red onion.

❊ To make the dressing, whisk together the oil, lemon juice, mustard, garlic, cumin powder and ground coriander in a small bowl. Set aside until required.

❊ Mix together the onion, tomatoes and lentils in a large bowl.

❊ Flake the tuna and stir it into the onion, tomato and lentil mixture.

❊ Stir in the chopped coriander.

❊ Pour the dressing over the lentil and tuna salad and season with pepper. Serve at once.

Prawn Salad

250 g/9 oz fine egg noodles
3 tbsp sunflower oil
1 tbsp sesame oil
1 tbsp sesame seeds
150 g/5 1/2 oz beansprouts
1 ripe mango, sliced

6 spring onions, sliced
75 g/2 3/4 oz radishes, sliced
350 g/12 oz cooked peeled
    prawns
2 tbsp light soy sauce
1 tbsp sherry

❊ Place the egg noodles in a large bowl and pour over enough boiling water to cover. Leave to stand for 10 minutes.

❊ Drain the noodles thoroughly and pat dry with kitchen paper.

❊ Heat the sunflower oil in a large wok or frying pan and stir-fry the noodles for 5 minutes, tossing frequently.

❊ Remove the wok from the heat and add the sesame oil, sesame seeds and bean sprouts, tossing to mix well.

❊ In a separate bowl, mix together the mango, spring onions, radishes and prawns. Stir in the soy sauce and sherry and mix until thoroughly combined.

❊ Toss the prawn mixture with the noodles and transfer to a serving dish. Alternatively, arrange the noodles around the edge of a serving plate and pile the prawn mixture into the centre. Serve immediately, as this salad is best eaten warm.

Smoked Salmon, Asparagus & Avocado Salad

200 g/7 oz asparagus spears
1 large avocado
1 tbsp lemon juice
large handful of rocket leaves
225 g/8 oz smoked salmon
1 red onion, finely sliced
1 tbsp chopped fresh flat-leaf parsley, plus extra sprigs to garnish
1 tbsp snipped fresh chives
lemon wedges, to garnish
wholemeal bread, to serve

DRESSING
1 garlic clove, chopped
4 tbsp extra virgin olive oil
2 tbsp white wine vinegar
1 tbsp lemon juice
pinch of sugar
1 tsp mustard

❖ Bring a large saucepan of lightly salted water to the boil, add the asparagus and blanch for 4 minutes. Drain and plunge into cold water, then drain again. Set aside to cool.

❖ To make the dressing, combine all the dressing ingredients in a small bowl and stir together well. Halve, peel and stone the avocado and cut into bite-sized pieces. Brush with the lemon juice to prevent discoloration.

❖ To assemble the salad, arrange the rocket on individual serving plates and top with the asparagus and avocado. Cut the smoked salmon into strips and arrange over the top of the salads, then scatter over the onion and herbs. Drizzle over the dressing, then garnish with parsley and the lemon wedges. Serve with the bread.

Lobster Salad

450 g/1 lb waxy potatoes,
scrubbed and sliced
225 g/8 oz cooked lobster meat
150 ml/5 fl oz mayonnaise
2 tbsp lime juice
finely grated rind of 1 lime
1 tbsp chopped fresh parsley

2 tbsp olive oil
2 tomatoes, deseeded and
diced
2 hard-boiled eggs, quartered
1 tbsp quartered stoned green
olives
salt and pepper

❈ Bring a saucepan of lightly salted water to the boil and cook the potatoes for 15 minutes until tender. Drain and reserve.

❈ Remove the lobster meat from the shell and then separate it into large pieces.

❈ In a bowl, mix together the mayonnaise, 1 tablespoon of the lime juice, half the lime rind and half the parsley, then set aside.

❈ In a separate bowl, whisk the remaining lime juice with the oil and pour the dressing over the potatoes. Arrange the potatoes on a serving plate.

❈ Top with the lobster meat, tomatoes, eggs and olives. Season to taste and sprinkle with the reserved parsley.

❈ Spoon the mayonnaise on to the centre of the salad, top with the remaining lime rind and serve.

Coronation Salad

1 red pepper
60 g/2 oz sultanas
1 celery stick, sliced
125 g/4$\frac{1}{2}$ oz sweetcorn kernels
1 Granny Smith apple, diced
125 g/4$\frac{1}{2}$ oz white seedless
grapes, washed and halved
250 g/9 oz cooked basmati rice
55 g/2 oz cooked peeled
prawns (optional)

1 cos lettuce, washed and
drained
1 tsp paprika, to garnish

DRESSING
4 tbsp low-fat mayonnaise
2 tsp mild curry powder
1 tsp lemon juice
1 tsp paprika
pinch of salt

❈ Deseed and chop the red pepper.

❈ Combine the sultanas, red pepper, celery, sweetcorn, apple and grapes in a large bowl. Stir in the rice and the prawns, if using.

❈ For the dressing, put the mayonnaise, curry powder, lemon juice, paprika and salt into a small bowl and mix well.

❈ Pour the dressing over the salad and gently mix until evenly coated.

❈ Line the serving plate with the lettuce leaves and spoon on to the salad. Sprinkle over the paprika and serve.

Pasta & Chicken Medley

❖ SERVES 2 ❖

125–150 g/4¹/2–5¹/2 oz dried
pasta shapes, such as twists
or bows
1 tbsp oil
2 tbsp mayonnaise
2 tsp pesto
1 tbsp soured cream or natural
fromage frais
175 g/6 oz cooked skinless,
boneless chicken meat
1–2 celery sticks

125 g/4¹/2 oz seedless black
grapes
1 large carrot, trimmed
salt and pepper
celery leaves, to garnish

FRENCH DRESSING
1 tbsp wine vinegar
3 tbsp extra virgin olive oil
salt and pepper

❖ To make the French dressing, whisk all the ingredients together until smooth.

❖ Bring a saucepan of lightly salted water to the boil and cook the pasta with the oil for 8–10 minutes until just tender. Drain thoroughly, rinse and drain again. Transfer to a bowl and mix in 1 tablespoon of the French dressing while hot; set aside until cold.

❖ Combine the mayonnaise, pesto and soured cream in a bowl, and season to taste.

❖ Cut the chicken into narrow strips. Cut the celery diagonally into narrow slices. Reserve a few grapes for a garnish, then halve the rest. Cut the carrot into narrow julienne strips.

❖ Add the chicken, the celery, the halved grapes, the carrot and the mayonnaise mixture to the pasta, and toss thoroughly. Check the seasoning, adding more salt and pepper if necessary.

❖ Arrange the pasta mixture on two plates and garnish with the reserved black grapes and the celery leaves.

Chicken & Grape Salad

❖ SERVES 4 ❖

500 g/1 lb 2 oz cooked skinless,
boneless chicken breasts
2 celery sticks, thinly sliced
250 g/9 oz black grapes
55 g/2 oz flaked almonds,
toasted
pinch of paprika
sprigs of fresh coriander or
flat-leaf parsley, to garnish

CURRY SAUCE
150 ml/5 fl oz low-fat
mayonnaise
125 g/4¹/2 oz low-fat fromage
frais
1 tbsp clear honey
1 tbsp curry paste

❖ Cut the chicken into fairly large pieces and transfer to a bowl with the sliced celery.

❖ Halve the grapes, remove the seeds and add the fruit to the bowl.

❖ To make the curry sauce, mix the mayonnaise with the fromage frais, honey and curry paste until blended.

❖ Pour the curry sauce over the salad and mix together carefully until thoroughly coated.

❖ Transfer to a shallow serving dish and sprinkle with the toasted almonds and paprika.

❖ Garnish the salad with the sprigs of coriander and serve.

Chinese Chicken Salad

225 g/8 oz skinless, boneless chicken breasts
2 tsp light soy sauce
1 tsp sesame oil
1 tsp sesame seeds
2 tbsp vegetable oil
125 g/4 1/2 oz beansprouts
1 red pepper, deseeded and thinly sliced
1 carrot, cut into matchsticks
3 baby sweetcorn cobs, sliced
snipped chives and carrot matchsticks, to garnish

SAUCE
2 tsp rice wine vinegar
1 tbsp light soy sauce
dash of chilli oil

❖ Place the chicken breasts in a shallow glass dish. Mix together the soy sauce and sesame oil and pour over the chicken. Sprinkle with the sesame seeds and set aside for 20 minutes, turning the chicken over occasionally.

❖ Remove the chicken from the marinade and cut the meat into thin slices.

❖ Heat the vegetable oil in a preheated wok or large frying pan. Add the chicken and fry for 4–5 minutes until cooked through and golden brown on both sides. Remove the chicken from the wok with a slotted spoon, set aside and leave to cool.

❖ Add the beansprouts, pepper, carrot and baby sweetcorn to the wok and stir-fry for 2–3 minutes. Remove from the wok with a slotted spoon, set aside and leave to cool.

❖ To make the sauce, mix together the vinegar, soy sauce and chilli oil.

❖ Arrange the chicken and vegetables together on a serving plate. Spoon the sauce over the salad, garnish with the chives and carrot matchsticks and serve.

Roast Chicken Salad

❄ **SERVES 4** ❄

250 g/9 oz young spinach leaves
handful of fresh parsley leaves
1/2 cucumber, thinly sliced
90 g/3 1/4 oz walnuts, toasted and chopped
350 g/12 oz boneless lean roast chicken, thinly sliced
2 red apples
1 tbsp lemon juice

sprigs of fresh flat-leaf parsley, to garnish
orange wedges, to serve

DRESSING
2 tbsp extra virgin olive oil
juice of 1 orange
finely grated rind of 1/2 orange
1 tbsp crème fraîche

❄ Wash and drain the spinach and parsley leaves, if necessary, then arrange on a large serving platter. Top with the cucumber and walnuts. Arrange the chicken slices on top of the leaves.

❄ Core the apples, then cut them in half. Cut each half into slices and brush with the lemon juice to prevent discoloration. Arrange the apple slices over the salad.

❄ Place all the dressing ingredients in a screw-top jar, screw on the lid tightly and shake well until thoroughly combined. Drizzle the dressing over the salad, garnish with the sprigs of parsley and serve immediately with the orange wedges.

Chargrilled Chicken Salad

❄ **SERVES 4** ❄

2 skinless, boneless chicken breasts
1 red onion
oil, for brushing
1 avocado, peeled and stoned
1 tbsp lemon juice
125 ml/4 fl oz low-fat mayonnaise

1/4 tsp chilli powder
1/2 tsp pepper
1/4 tsp salt
4 tomatoes, quartered
1/2 loaf sun-dried tomato-flavoured focaccia bread
green salad, to serve

❄ Using a sharp knife, cut the chicken breasts into 1-cm/1/2-inch strips.

❄ Cut the onion into 8 pieces, held together at the root. Rinse under cold running water and then brush with oil.

❄ Purée or mash the avocado and lemon juice together. Whisk in the mayonnaise. Add the chilli powder, pepper and salt.

❄ Put the chicken and onion under a hot grill and grill for 3–4 minutes on each side. Combine the chicken, onion, tomatoes and avocado mixture together.

❄ Cut the bread in half twice, so that you have quarter-circle-shaped pieces, then in half horizontally. Toast under the hot grill for about 2 minutes on each side.

❄ Spoon the chicken mixture on to the toasts and serve with the green salad.

Thai-Style Chicken Salad

400 g/14 oz small new
potatoes, scrubbed and
halved lengthways
200 g/7 oz baby sweetcorn
cobs, sliced
150 g/5¹/2 oz beansprouts
3 spring onions, trimmed and
sliced
4 cooked, skinless chicken
breasts, sliced
1 tbsp chopped lemon grass
2 tbsp chopped fresh coriander

salt and pepper
lime wedges and fresh
coriander leaves, to garnish

DRESSING
6 tbsp chilli oil or sesame oil
2 tbsp lime juice
1 tbsp light soy sauce
1 tbsp chopped fresh coriander
1 small, red chilli, deseeded
and finely chopped

❈ Bring two saucepans of water to the boil. Put the potatoes into one saucepan and cook for 15 minutes until tender. Put the sweetcorn cobs into the other saucepan and cook for 5 minutes until tender. Drain the potatoes and corn well and leave to cool.

❈ When the vegetables are cool, transfer them to a large serving dish. Add the beansprouts, spring onions, chicken, lemon grass and coriander and season with salt and pepper.

❈ To make the dressing, put all the ingredients into a screw-top jar and shake well. Alternatively, put them into a bowl and mix together well. Drizzle the dressing over the salad and garnish with the lime wedges and coriander leaves. Serve at once.

Hot & Sour Duck Salad

2 heads crisp salad lettuce,
washed and separated into
leaves
2 shallots, thinly sliced
4 spring onions, chopped
1 celery stick, finely sliced into
julienne strips
5-cm/2-inch piece of
cucumber, cut into julienne
strips
125 g/4¹/2 oz beansprouts
200 g/7 oz canned water
chestnuts, drained and sliced
4 duck breast fillets, roasted
and sliced
slices of orange, to serve

DRESSING
3 tbsp fish sauce
1¹/2 tbsp lime juice
2 garlic cloves, crushed
1 red chilli pepper, deseeded
and very finely chopped
1 green chilli pepper, deseeded
and very finely chopped
1 tsp palm or demerara sugar

❈ Place the lettuce leaves into a large mixing bowl. Add the shallots, spring onions, celery, cucumber, bean sprouts and water chestnuts. Toss well to mix. Place the mixture on a large serving platter.

❈ Arrange the duck breast slices on top of the salad in an attractive overlapping pattern.

❈ To make the dressing, put the fish sauce, lime juice, garlic, chillies and sugar into a small saucepan. Heat gently, stirring constantly. Taste and adjust the piquancy if liked by adding more lime juice, or add more fish sauce to reduce the sharpness.

❈ Drizzle the warm salad dressing over the duck salad and serve immediately with the slices of orange.

Potato & Sausage Salad

450 g/1 lb waxy potatoes
1 raddichio or lollo rosso
lettuce
1 green pepper, sliced
175 g/6 oz Italian sausage,
sliced
1 red onion, halved and sliced
125 g/4^{1}/2 oz sun-dried
tomatoes, sliced
2 tbsp shredded fresh basil

DRESSING
1 tbsp balsamic vinegar
1 tsp tomato purée
2 tbsp olive oil
salt and pepper

❖ Bring a saucepan of lightly salted water to the boil and cook the potatoes for 20 minutes until cooked through. Drain and leave to cool.

❖ Line a large serving platter with the lettuce leaves.

❖ Slice the cooled potatoes and arrange them in layers on the lettuce-lined serving platter together with the green pepper, Italian sausage, onion, sun-dried tomatoes and fresh basil.

❖ In a small bowl, whisk together the vinegar, tomato purée and oil and season to taste with salt and pepper. Pour the dressing over the potato salad and serve immediately.

Walnut, Pear & Bacon Salad

4 rashers streaky bacon
75 g/2³/4 oz walnut halves
2 Red William pears, cored and
sliced lengthways
1 tbsp lemon juice
175 g/6 oz watercress, tough
stalks removed

DRESSING
3 tbsp extra-virgin olive oil
2 tbsp lemon juice
¹/2 tsp clear honey
salt and pepper

❈ Preheat the grill to high. Arrange the bacon on a foil-lined grill pan and cook under the preheated grill until well-browned and crisp. Set aside to cool, then cut into 1-cm/¹/2-inch pieces.

❈ Meanwhile, heat a dry frying pan over a medium heat and lightly toast the walnuts, shaking the pan frequently, for 3 minutes, or until lightly browned. Set aside to cool.

❈ Toss the pears in the lemon juice to prevent discoloration. Put the watercress, walnuts, pears and bacon into a salad bowl.

❈ To make the dressing, whisk the oil, lemon juice and honey together in a small bowl or jug. Season to taste with salt and pepper, then pour over the salad. Toss well to combine and serve.

Serrano Ham with Figs

¹/2 small galia melon, peeled
and sliced
12 very thin slices of Serrano
ham, cut into strips
6 ripe fresh figs, trimmed and
quartered
150 g/5¹/2 oz white mushrooms

1 avocado
3 tbsp lemon juice
4 tbsp olive oil
pepper
sprigs of fresh flat-leaf parsley,
to garnish

❈ Divide the melon, ham and figs between 4 serving plates. Wipe the mushrooms clean with a damp cloth, then slice them thickly and scatter them over the top.

❈ Using a knife, cut the avocado in half and remove the stone. Remove and discard the skin, and cut the flesh into slices. Brush the slices with 1 tablespoon of the lemon juice to prevent discoloration, then arrange them over the top of the salad.

❈ In a separate bowl, pour in the remaining lemon juice and all the oil and stir until thoroughly mixed. Season with pepper. Pour the mixture over the salad, ensuring that all the salad ingredients are well coated. Garnish with the sprigs of parsley and serve.

Beef & Peanut Salad

½ head Chinese leaves
1 large carrot
125 g/4½ oz radishes
100 g/3½ oz baby sweetcorn
350 g/12 oz lean beef
1 tbsp groundnut oil
1 red chilli, deseeded and finely chopped
1 clove garlic, finely chopped
1 tbsp dark soy sauce

25 g/1 oz fresh peanuts (optional)
sliced red chilli, to garnish

DRESSING

1 tbsp smooth peanut butter
1 tsp caster sugar
2 tbsp light soy sauce
1 tbsp sherry vinegar
salt and pepper

❊ Finely shred the Chinese leaves and arrange on a platter. Peel the carrot and cut into matchsticks.

❊ Wash, trim and quarter the radishes, and halve the baby sweetcorn lengthwise. Arrange these ingredients around the edge of the dish and set aside.

❊ Trim the beef and slice into fine strips. Heat the oil in a non-stick wok or large frying pan and stir-fry the chilli, garlic and beef for 5 minutes. Add the dark soy sauce and stir-fry for a further 1–2 minutes until tender and cooked through.

❊ Meanwhile, make the dressing. Place all of the ingredients in a small bowl and blend them together until smooth.

❊ Place the hot cooked beef in the centre of the salad ingredients. Spoon over the dressing and sprinkle with a few peanuts, if using.

❊ Garnish the salad with the chilli slices and serve immediately.

Roast Beef Salad

❊ SERVES 4 ❊

750 g/1lb 10 oz beef fillet, trimmed of any visible fat
2 tsp Worcestershire sauce
3 tbsp olive oil
400 g/14 oz French beans
100 g/3½ oz small pasta, such as orecchiette
2 red onions, finely sliced
1 large head radicchio
50 g/1¾ oz green olives, stoned

50 g/1¾ oz shelled hazelnuts, whole
pepper

DRESSING

1 tsp Dijon mustard
2 tbsp white wine vinegar
5 tbsp olive oil

❊ Preheat the oven to 220°C/425°F/Gas Mark 7. Rub the beef with pepper to taste and Worcestershire sauce. Heat 2 tablespoons of the oil in a small roasting tin over a high heat, add the beef and sear on all sides. Transfer to the preheated oven and roast for 30 minutes. Remove and leave to cool.

❊ Bring a large saucepan of water to the boil, add the beans and cook for 5 minutes, or until just tender. Remove with a slotted spoon and refresh the beans under cold running water. Drain and put into a large bowl.

❊ Return the bean cooking water to the boil, add the pasta and cook for 11 minutes or until tender. Drain, return to the saucepan and toss with the remaining oil.

❊ Add the pasta to the beans with the onions, radicchio leaves, olives and hazelnuts in a serving dish or salad bowl and arrange some thinly sliced beef on top.

❊ Whisk the dressing ingredients together in a separate bowl, then pour over the salad and serve immediately with extra sliced beef.

Steak Salad

50 g/1¾ oz dried oyster
mushrooms
600 g/1 lb 5 oz rump steak
1 tbsp vegetable oil
1 red pepper, deseeded and
thinly sliced
40 g/1½ oz roasted cashew
nuts
red and green lettuce leaves,
to serve
fresh mint leaves, to garnish

DRESSING
2 tbsp sesame oil
2 tbsp fish sauce
2 tbsp sweet sherry
2 tbsp oyster sauce
1 tbsp lime juice
1 fresh red chilli, deseeded and
finely chopped

❖ Place the mushrooms in a bowl, cover with boiling water and leave to stand for 20 minutes. Drain and cut into thin slices.

❖ To make the dressing, place the sesame oil, fish sauce, sherry, oyster sauce, lime juice and chilli in a bowl and whisk to combine.

❖ Grill the beef, either on a griddle pan or under the grill, turning once, for 5 minutes or until browned on both sides and rare in the middle, or cook longer if desired.

❖ Slice the steak into thin strips and place in a bowl with the mushrooms, pepper and nuts. Add the dressing and toss together.

❖ Arrange the lettuce on a large serving platter and place the beef mixture on top. Garnish with the mint. Serve at room temperature.

Simple
main dishes

Meatloaf

1 thick slice crustless white bread	1 tsp dried herbs
	salt and pepper
675 g/1 lb 8 oz fresh beef, pork or lamb mince	
1 small egg	**TO SERVE**
1 tbsp finely chopped onion	tomato sauce or gravy
1 beef stock cube, crumbled	mashed potatoes
	freshly cooked French beans

❄ Preheat the oven to 180°C/350°F/Gas Mark 4.

❄ Put the bread into a small bowl and add enough water to soak. Leave to stand for 5 minutes, then drain and squeeze well to get rid of all the water.

❄ Combine the bread with all the other ingredients in a bowl. Shape into a loaf, then place on a baking tray or in an ovenproof dish. Put the meatloaf in the oven and cook for 30–45 minutes until the juices run clear when it is pierced with a cocktail stick.

❄ Serve in slices with the tomato sauce, mashed potatoes and French beans.

Beef Goulash

2 tbsp vegetable oil	175 g/6 oz mushrooms, sliced
1 large onion, chopped	600 ml/1 pint beef stock
1 garlic clove, crushed	1 tbsp cornflour
750 g/1 lb 10 oz lean stewing steak	1 tbsp water
2 tbsp paprika	4 tbsp low-fat natural yogurt
425 g/15 oz canned chopped tomatoes	paprika, for sprinkling
	salt and pepper
2 tbsp tomato purée	chopped fresh parsley, to garnish
1 large red pepper, deseeded and chopped	long-grain rice and wild rice, to serve

❄ Heat the oil in a large frying pan and cook the onion and garlic for 3–4 minutes.

❄ Cut the steak into chunks and cook over a high heat for 3 minutes until brown all over. Add the paprika and stir well, then add the chopped tomatoes, tomato purée, pepper and mushrooms. Cook for 2 minutes, stirring frequently.

❄ Pour in the beef stock. Bring to the boil, then reduce the heat. Cover and simmer for $1\frac{1}{2}$–2 hours until the meat is tender.

❄ Blend the cornflour with the water, then add to the pan, stirring until thickened and smooth. Cook for 1 minute, then season to taste with salt and pepper.

❄ Put the yogurt in a serving bowl and sprinkle with a little paprika.

❄ Transfer the beef goulash to a warmed serving dish, garnish with the parsley and serve with the rice and yogurt.

Pizzaiola Steak

❊ **SERVES 4** ❊

800 g/1 lb 12 oz canned peeled
tomatoes or 750 g/1 lb 10 oz
fresh tomatoes
4 tbsp olive oil
2–3 garlic cloves, crushed
1 onion, finely chopped
1 tbsp tomato purée
1 1/2 tsp chopped fresh
marjoram or oregano or
3/4 tsp dried marjoram or
oregano

4 thin sirloin or rump steaks
2 tbsp chopped fresh parsley
1 tsp sugar
salt and pepper
sprigs of fresh herbs, to
garnish (optional)
sauté potatoes, to serve

❊   If using canned tomatoes, purée them in a food processor, then sieve to remove the seeds. If using fresh tomatoes, peel, remove the seeds and finely chop.

❊   Heat half of the oil in a pan and fry the garlic and onions very gently for about 5 minutes, or until softened.

❊   Add the tomatoes, seasoning, tomato purée and chopped herbs to the pan. If using fresh tomatoes add 4 tablespoons water, then simmer very gently for 8–10 minutes, stirring occasionally.

❊   Meanwhile, trim the steaks, if necessary, and season. Heat the remaining oil in a frying pan and fry the steaks quickly on both sides to seal, then continue until cooked to your liking – 2 minutes for rare, 3–4 minutes for medium, or 5 minutes for well done. Alternatively, cook the steaks under a hot grill after brushing lightly with oil.

❊   When the sauce has thickened a little, adjust the seasoning and stir in the chopped parsley and sugar.

❊   Pour off the excess fat from the pan containing the steaks and add the tomato sauce. Reheat gently and serve at once, with the sauce spooned over and around the steaks. Garnish with the sprigs of herbs, if using. Serve immediately, accompanied by the sauté potatoes.

Steak in a Wine Marinade

❊ **SERVES 4** ❊

4 rump steaks, about
250 g/9 oz each
600 ml/1 pint red wine
1 onion, quartered
2 tbsp Dijon mustard

2 garlic cloves, crushed
salt and pepper
4 large field mushrooms
olive oil, for brushing

❊   Snip through the fat strip on the steaks in 3 places, so that the steak retains its shape when grilled.

❊   Combine the wine, onion, mustard, garlic and salt and pepper. Lay the steaks in a shallow non-porous dish and pour over the marinade. Cover and chill in the refrigerator for 2–3 hours.

❊   Remove the steaks from the refrigerator 30 minutes before you intend to cook them to let them come to room temperature. This is especially important if the steak is thick, so that it cooks more evenly and is not well done on the outside and raw in the middle.

❊   Sear both sides of the steak – about 1 minute on each side – under a hot grill. If the steak is about 2.5 cm/1 inch thick, keep it under the grill and cook for about 4 minutes on each side. This will give a medium-rare steak – cook it more or less, to suit your taste. If the steak is a thicker cut, move it further away from the heat. To test the readiness of the meat while cooking, simply press it with your finger – the more the meat yields, the less it is cooked.

❊   Brush the mushrooms with the oil and cook them alongside the steak for 5 minutes, turning once.

❊   Remove the steaks and set aside to rest for 1–2 minutes before serving. Slice the mushrooms and serve immediately with the meat.

Ginger Beef with Chilli

SERVES 4

4 lean beef steaks, such as rump, sirloin or fillet, 100 g/4 oz each
2 tbsp ginger wine
2.5-cm/1-inch piece of root ginger, finely chopped
1 garlic clove, crushed
1 tsp ground chilli
1 tsp vegetable oil
salt and pepper
fresh red chilli strips, to garnish

TO SERVE

freshly cooked noodles
2 spring onions, shredded

RELISH

225 g/8 oz fresh pineapple
1 small red pepper
1 fresh red chilli
2 tbsp light soy sauce
1 piece of stem ginger in syrup, drained and chopped

Trim any excess fat from the steaks, if necessary. Using a meat mallet or covered rolling pin, pound the steaks until they are 1 cm/½ inch thick. Season to taste on both sides with salt and pepper and place in a shallow dish.

Combine the ginger wine, fresh ginger, garlic and chilli and pour over the meat. Cover with clingfilm and chill for 30 minutes.

Meanwhile, make the relish. Peel and finely chop the pineapple and place it in a bowl. Halve, deseed and finely chop the pepper and chilli. Stir into the pineapple with the soy sauce and stem ginger. Cover with clingfilm and chill until required.

Brush a griddle pan with the oil and heat until very hot. Drain the beef and add to the pan, pressing down to seal. Reduce the heat and cook for 5 minutes. Turn the steaks over and cook for a further 5 minutes.

Drain the steaks on kitchen paper and transfer to warmed serving plates. Garnish with chilli strips and serve with the noodles, spring onions and relish.

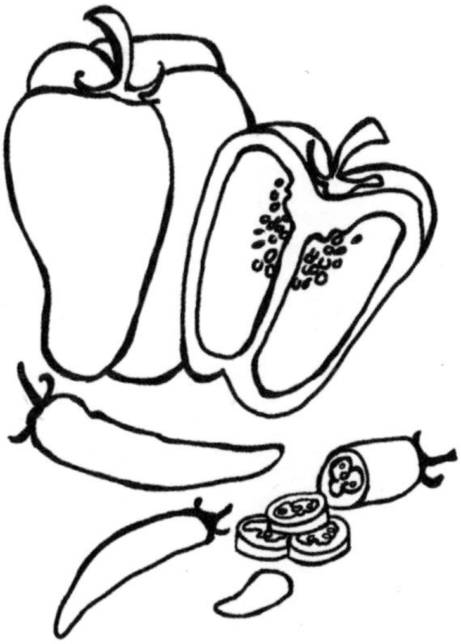

Beef Olives in Rich Gravy

❊ **SERVES 4** ❊

8 ready prepared beef olives
4 tbsp chopped fresh parsley
4 garlic cloves, finely chopped
125 g/4 1/2 oz smoked
streaky bacon, rinded and
finely chopped
grated rind of 1/2 small orange
2 tbsp olive oil
300 ml/10 fl oz dry red wine

1 bay leaf
1 tsp sugar
60 g/2 oz stoned black olives,
drained
salt and pepper
slices of orange and
chopped fresh parsley,
to garnish

❊ Unroll the beef olives and flatten out as thinly as possible using a meat tenderizer or mallet. Trim the edges to neaten them.

❊ Mix together the parsley, garlic, bacon, orange rind and salt and pepper to taste. Spread this mixture evenly over each beef olive.

❊ Roll up each beef olive tightly, then secure with a cocktail stick. Heat the oil in a frying pan and fry the beef on all sides for 10 minutes.

❊ Drain the beef olives, reserving the pan juices, and keep warm. Pour the wine into the juices, add the bay leaf, sugar and seasoning. Bring to the boil and boil rapidly for 5 minutes to reduce slightly, stirring.

❊ Return the cooked beef to the pan along with the olives and heat through for a further 2 minutes. Discard the bay leaf and cocktail sticks.

❊ Transfer the beef olives and gravy to a serving dish, and serve garnished with the orange slices and parsley.

Classic Beef Fajitas

❊ **SERVES 4–6** ❊

700 g/1 lb 9 oz steak,
cut into strips
6 garlic cloves, chopped
juice of 1 lime
pinch of mild chilli powder
pinch of paprika
pinch of ground cumin
1–2 tbsp extra virgin olive oil

TO SERVE
12 flour tortillas
vegetable oil, for greasing
1–2 avocados, stoned,
peeled, sliced and tossed
with lime juice
125 ml/4 fl oz soured cream

PICO DE GALLO SALSA
8 ripe tomatoes, diced
3 spring onions, sliced
1–2 fresh green chillies, such
as jalapeño or serrano,
deseeded and chopped
3–4 tbsp chopped fresh
coriander
5–8 radishes, diced
ground cumin
salt and pepper

❊ Combine the beef with half the garlic, half the lime juice, the chilli powder, paprika, cumin and olive oil. Add salt and pepper, mix well and marinate for at least 30 minutes at room temperature or up to overnight in the refrigerator.

❊ To make the pico de gallo salsa, put the tomatoes in a bowl with the spring onions, chillies, coriander and radishes. Season to taste with cumin and salt and pepper. Set aside.

❊ Heat the tortillas in a lightly greased non-stick frying pan. Wrap in foil, as you work, to keep them warm.

❊ Stir-fry the meat in a little oil over a high heat until browned and just cooked through.

❊ Serve the sizzling hot meat with the warmed tortillas, the pico de gallo salsa, avocado and soured cream for each person to make his or her own rolled up fajitas.

Beef in Beer

few sprigs of fresh parsley
1 tbsp sunflower or corn oil
500 g/1 lb 2 oz lean stewing
steak, trimmed of all visible
fat and cut into 2.5-cm/
1-inch cubes
1 onion, chopped

200 g/7 oz chestnut
mushrooms, cut in half
4 tsp dark muscovado sugar
350 ml/12 fl oz beef stock
300 ml/10 fl oz dark beer or
stout
salt and pepper

❊ Using a sharp knife, finely chop the parsley and reserve until required. Heat the sunflower oil in a large, heavy-based frying pan. Add the stewing steak and cook, stirring frequently, for 10 minutes, or until browned all over. Using a slotted spoon, transfer the meat to a large flameproof casserole dish.

❊ Add the onion to the frying pan and cook over a low heat, stirring occasionally, for 3 minutes. Add the mushrooms and sugar and cook, stirring occasionally, for 10 minutes. Transfer to the casserole with a slotted spoon.

❊ Add the stock, beer and reserved parsley to the casserole and season to taste with salt and pepper. Bring to the boil, cover and simmer over a very low heat for $1^{1}/_{2}$–2 hours, or until tender. Serve hot.

Beef & Beans

2 tsp cornflour
2 tbsp dark soy sauce
2 tsp peanut oil
450 g/1 lb rump or fillet steak,
cut into 2.5-cm/1-inch pieces
2 tbsp vegetable oil
3 garlic cloves, crushed
1 small onion, cut into eighths
225 g/8 oz thin French beans,
halved

25 g/1 oz unsalted cashew nuts
25 g/1 oz canned bamboo
shoots, drained and rinsed
2 tsp dark soy sauce
2 tsp Chinese rice wine or
dry sherry
125 ml/4 fl oz beef stock
2 tsp cornflour
4 tsp water
salt and pepper

❊ To make the marinade, mix together the cornflour, soy sauce and peanut oil.

❊ Place the steak in a shallow glass bowl. Pour the marinade over the steak, turn to coat thoroughly, cover and leave to marinate in the refrigerator for at least 30 minutes.

❊ Meanwhile, heat the oil in a preheated wok. Add the garlic, onion, beans, cashew nuts and bamboo shoots and stir-fry for 2–3 minutes.

❊ Remove the steak from the marinade, drain, add to the wok and stir-fry for 3–4 minutes.

❊ Mix the soy sauce, rice wine and stock together. Blend the cornflour with the water and add to the soy sauce mixture, mixing to combine.

❊ Stir the mixture into the wok and bring the sauce to the boil, stirring until thickened and clear. Reduce the heat and leave to simmer for 2–3 minutes. Season to taste and serve immediately.

Beef Teriyaki

❖ **SERVES 4** ❖

450 g/1 lb extra-thin lean
beef steaks
8 spring onions, cut into
short lengths
1 yellow pepper, deseeded
and cut into chunks
green salad, to serve

TERIYAKI SAUCE
1 tsp cornflour
2 tbsp dry sherry
2 tbsp white wine vinegar
3 tbsp soy sauce
1 tbsp dark muscovado sugar
1 garlic clove, crushed
$1/2$ tsp ground cinnamon
$1/2$ tsp ground ginger

❖ Place the meat in a shallow non-metallic dish. To make the sauce, combine the cornflour with the sherry to form a smooth paste, then stir in the vinegar, soy sauce, sugar, garlic, cinnamon and ginger. Pour the sauce over the meat, turn to coat and set aside to marinate for at least 2 hours.

❖ Remove the meat from the sauce, draining well. Pour the sauce into a small saucepan.

❖ Cut the meat into thin strips and thread these, concertina-style, on to pre-soaked wooden skewers, alternating each strip of meat with pieces of spring onion and yellow pepper.

❖ Gently heat the sauce until it is just simmering, stirring occasionally.

❖ Barbecue the kebabs over hot coals for 5–8 minutes, turning and basting the beef and vegetables occasionally with the reserved teriyaki sauce.

❖ Arrange the skewers on serving plates and pour the remaining sauce over the kebabs. Serve immediately with the green salad.

Meatballs with Tomato Relish

1 onion, finely chopped
2 garlic cloves, finely chopped
2 slices bread, crusts removed
500 g/1 lb 2 oz lean beef, minced
1 cooked baby beetroot, chopped
pinch of paprika
2 tsp finely chopped
fresh thyme

1 egg
salt and pepper
sprigs of fresh thyme, to
garnish

TOMATO RELISH
150 ml/5 fl oz passata
2 tsp creamed horseradish

❈ Preheat the oven to 230°C/450°F/Gas Mark 8. To make
the tomato relish, mix the passata and horseradish together
in a small bowl. Cover and reserve until required.

❈ Place the onion, garlic and 2 teaspoons of water in a
small saucepan and simmer over a low heat for 5 minutes.
Increase the heat, bring to the boil and cook until all the
water has evaporated. Remove from the heat.

❈ Meanwhile, tear the bread into pieces and place in a
small bowl. Add enough cold water just to cover and leave
to soak for 5 minutes. Squeeze the excess water from the
bread and place in a bowl with the minced beef, onion and
garlic mixture, beetroot, paprika, thyme and egg. Season to
taste with salt and pepper and mix thoroughly.

❈ Form the mixture into 24 small balls between the palms
of your hands. Thread 3 balls on to each of 8 skewers and
place on a baking tray. Bake in the preheated oven for
10 minutes, or until well browned. Transfer to a serving
dish, garnish with a few sprigs of thyme and serve with the
tomato relish.

Lamb with Rosemary

500 g/1 lb 2 oz lean lamb fillet
4 tbsp redcurrant jelly
1 tbsp chopped fresh rosemary
1 garlic clove, crushed
450 g/1 lb potatoes, diced
450 g/1 lb leeks, sliced
150 ml/5 fl oz fresh
vegetable stock

4 tsp low-fat natural
fromage frais
salt and pepper
freshly steamed vegetables,
to serve
chopped fresh rosemary
and fresh redcurrants,
to garnish

❈ Put the lamb in a shallow baking tin. Blend 2 tablespoons
of the redcurrant jelly with the rosemary, garlic and
seasoning. Brush over the lamb and cook in a preheated oven,
230°C/450°F/Gas Mark 8, brushing occasionally with any
cooking juices, for 30 minutes.

❈ Meanwhile, place the potatoes in a saucepan and cover
with water. Bring to the boil, and cook for 8 minutes until
softened. Drain well.

❈ Put the leeks in a saucepan with the stock. Cover and
simmer for 7–8 minutes or until soft. Drain, reserving the
cooking liquid.

❈ Place the potatoes and leeks in a bowl and mash with
a potato masher. Season and stir in the fromage frais.
Transfer to a warmed platter and keep warm.

❈ In a saucepan, melt the remaining redcurrant jelly and
stir in the leek cooking liquid. Boil for 5 minutes.

❈ Slice the lamb and arrange over the mash. Spoon the
sauce over the top. Garnish the lamb with the rosemary and
redcurrants and serve with the freshly steamed vegetables.

Roman Pan-Fried Lamb

❋ **SERVES 4** ❋

1 tbsp oil	150 ml/5 fl oz lamb or
15 g/1/2 oz butter	vegetable stock
600 g/1 lb 5 oz lamb	1 tsp sugar
(shoulder or leg), cut into	50 g/13/4 oz black olives,
2.5-cm/1-inch chunks	stoned and halved
4 garlic cloves, peeled	2 tbsp chopped parsley,
3 sprigs thyme, stalks removed	to garnish
6 canned anchovy fillets	mashed potato, to serve
150 ml/5 fl oz red wine	

❋ Heat the oil and butter in a large frying pan. Add the lamb and cook for 4–5 minutes, stirring, until the meat is brown all over.

❋ Using a pestle and mortar, grind together the garlic, thyme and anchovies to make a smooth paste.

❋ Add the wine and stock to the pan. Stir in the garlic and anchovy paste together with the sugar.

❋ Bring the mixture to the boil, reduce the heat, cover and simmer for 30–40 minutes or until the lamb is tender. For the last 10 minutes of the cooking time, remove the lid to allow the sauce to reduce slightly.

❋ Stir the olives into the sauce and mix to combine.

❋ Transfer the lamb and the sauce to a serving bowl and garnish with the parsley. Serve with the mashed potato.

Turkish Lamb Stew

❋ **SERVES 2** ❋

350 g/12 oz lean boneless lamb	11/2 tsp tomato purée
1 large or 2 small onions	1 bay leaf
1 garlic clove, crushed	1/2 tsp dried sage
1/2 red, yellow or green	1/2 tsp dried dill
pepper, roughly diced	350 g/12 oz potatoes
300 ml/10 fl oz stock	6–8 black olives,
1 tbsp balsamic vinegar	halved and stoned
2 tomatoes, peeled and	salt and pepper
roughly chopped	fresh crusty bread, to serve

❋ Cut the piece of lamb into cubes of about 2 cm/3/4 inch, discarding any excess fat or gristle.

❋ Place in a non-stick saucepan with no extra fat and heat gently until the fat runs and the meat begins to seal.

❋ Cut the onion into 8 wedges. Add to the lamb with the garlic and fry for a further 3–4 minutes.

❋ Add the red pepper, stock, vinegar, tomatoes, tomato purée, bay leaf, sage, dill and seasoning. Cover and simmer gently for 30 minutes.

❋ Peel the potatoes and cut into 2-cm/3/4-inch cubes. Add to the stew and stir well. If necessary, add a little more boiling stock or water if it seems a little dry. Cover the pan again and simmer for a further 25–30 minutes, or until tender.

❋ Add the olives and adjust the seasoning. Simmer for a further 5 minutes and serve with the bread.

Lamb Meatballs

450 g/1 lb minced lamb
3 garlic cloves, crushed
2 spring onions, finely chopped
1/2 tsp chilli powder
1 tsp Chinese curry powder
1 tbsp chopped fresh parsley
25 g/1 oz fresh white
breadcrumbs
1 egg, beaten
3 tbsp vegetable oil
125 g/4 1/2 oz Chinese leaves,
shredded
1 leek, sliced
1 tbsp cornflour
2 tbsp water
300 ml/10 fl oz lamb stock
1 tbsp dark soy sauce
shredded leek, to garnish

❖ Mix the lamb, garlic, spring onions, chilli powder, curry powder, parsley and breadcrumbs together in a bowl. Work the egg into the mixture, bringing it together to form a firm mixture. Roll into 16 small, even-sized balls.

❖ Heat the oil in a preheated wok. Add the Chinese leaves and leek and stir-fry for 1 minute. Remove from the wok with a slotted spoon and set aside.

❖ Add the meatballs to the wok and fry in batches, turning gently, for 3–4 minutes, or until golden brown all over.

❖ Mix the cornflour and water together to form a smooth paste and set aside. Pour the stock and soy sauce into the wok and cook for 2–3 minutes. Stir in the cornflour paste. Bring to the boil and cook, stirring constantly, until the sauce is thickened and clear.

❖ Return the Chinese leaves and leek to the wok and cook for 1 minute, until heated through. Arrange the Chinese leaves and leek on a warmed serving dish, top with the meatballs, garnish with the shredded leek and serve immediately.

171

Lamb Tagine

1 tbsp sunflower or corn oil
1 onion, chopped
350 g/12 oz boneless lamb, trimmed of all visible fat and cut into 2.5-cm/1-inch cubes
1 garlic clove, finely chopped
600 ml/1 pint vegetable stock
grated rind and juice of 1 orange
1 tsp clear honey
1 cinnamon stick
1-cm/¹/2-inch piece of root ginger, finely chopped
1 aubergine
4 tomatoes, peeled and chopped
115 g/4 oz dried apricots
2 tbsp chopped fresh coriander
salt and pepper
freshly cooked couscous, to serve

❈ Heat the sunflower oil in a large heavy-based frying pan or flameproof casserole. Add the onion and lamb cubes and cook over a medium heat, stirring frequently, for 5 minutes, or until the meat is lightly browned all over. Add the garlic, stock, orange rind and juice, honey, cinnamon stick and ginger. Bring to the boil, then reduce the heat, cover and simmer for 45 minutes.

❈ Using a sharp knife, halve the aubergine lengthways and thinly slice. Add to the frying pan with the chopped tomatoes and apricots. Cover and cook for a further 45 minutes, or until the lamb is tender.

❈ Stir in the coriander, season to taste with salt and pepper and serve immediately, straight from the frying pan, with the couscous.

Lamb Couscous

2 red onions, sliced
juice of 1 lemon
1 large red pepper, deseeded and thickly sliced
1 large green pepper, deseeded and thickly sliced
1 large orange pepper, deseeded and thickly sliced
pinch of saffron strands
1 cinnamon stick, broken
1 tbsp clear honey
300 ml/10 fl oz vegetable stock
2 tsp olive oil
350 g/12 oz lean lamb fillet, trimmed and sliced
1 tsp harissa
200 g/7 oz canned chopped tomatoes
425 g/15 oz canned chickpeas, drained
350 g/12 oz precooked couscous
2 tsp ground cinnamon
salt and pepper

❈ Toss the onions in the lemon juice and transfer to a saucepan. Stir in the peppers, saffron, cinnamon stick and honey. Pour in the stock, bring to the boil, cover and simmer for 5 minutes.

❈ Meanwhile, heat the oil in a frying pan and gently fry the lamb for 3–4 minutes until brown all over.

❈ Using a draining spoon, transfer the lamb to the pan with the onions and peppers. Season and stir in the harissa, tomatoes and chickpeas. Mix thoroughly, bring back to the boil and simmer, uncovered, for 20 minutes.

❈ Soak the couscous, following the packet instructions. Bring a pan of water to the boil. Put the couscous in a steamer or sieve lined with muslin over the pan of boiling water. Cover and steam.

❈ Transfer the couscous to a serving platter and dust with the ground cinnamon. Discard the cinnamon stick and spoon the stew over the couscous.

Curried Stir-Fried Lamb

450 g/1 lb potatoes, diced
450 g/1 lb lean lamb, diced
2 tbsp medium-hot curry paste
3 tbsp sunflower oil
1 onion, sliced
1 aubergine, diced
2 garlic cloves, crushed

1 tbsp grated root ginger
150 ml/5 fl oz lamb or
  beef stock
salt
2 tbsp chopped fresh
  coriander, to garnish

❉ Bring a large saucepan of lightly salted water to the boil. Add the potatoes and cook for 10 minutes. Remove the potatoes from the saucepan with a slotted spoon and drain thoroughly.

❉ Meanwhile, place the lamb in a large mixing bowl. Add the curry paste and mix well until the lamb is evenly coated in the paste.

❉ Heat the sunflower oil in a large preheated wok.

❉ Add the onion, aubergine, garlic and ginger to the wok and stir-fry for about 5 minutes.

❉ Add the lamb to the wok and stir-fry for a further 5 minutes.

❉ Add the stock and cooked potatoes to the wok, bring to the boil and simmer for 30 minutes, or until the lamb is tender and cooked through.

❉ Transfer the stir-fry to warmed serving dishes and garnish with the coriander. Serve immediately.

Lamb Kebabs with Herbs

❉ SERVES 4 ❉

1 kg/2 lb 4 oz lean leg of lamb,
  trimmed of fat
3 tbsp olive oil
1 tbsp red wine vinegar
juice of 1/2 lemon
3 tbsp low-fat natural yogurt
1 tbsp dried oregano
2 large garlic cloves, crushed
2 dried bay leaves, crumbled
4 fresh bay leaves
2 tbsp chopped parsley
salt and pepper

SAUCE
300 ml/10 fl oz low-fat natural
  yogurt
1 garlic clove, crushed
1/4 tsp salt
1/2 small cucumber, peeled
  and finely chopped
3 tbsp finely chopped mint
pinch of paprika

❉ Cut the lamb into cubes about 4–5 cm/1 1/2–2 inches square. Pat dry with kitchen paper to ensure that the meat stays crisp and firm on the outside when grilled.

❉ Whisk together the oil, vinegar, lemon juice and yogurt. Stir in the oregano, garlic and crumbled bay leaves and season. Place the meat in the marinade and stir until coated in the mixture. Cover and place in the refrigerator for at least 2 hours.

❉ Meanwhile, make the sauce. Place the yogurt in a large bowl. Stir in the garlic, salt, cucumber and mint. Cover with clingfilm and set aside in the refrigerator until required.

❉ Heat the grill to high. With a slotted spoon, lift the meat from the marinade and shake off any excess liquid. Divide the meat into 4 equal portions. Thread the meat and the bay leaves on to 4 skewers. Grill the kebabs for about 4 minutes on each side, basting frequently with the marinade. At this stage the meat should be crisp on the outside and slightly pink on the inside. If you prefer lamb well done, cook the kebabs for a little longer.

❉ Sprinkle the kebabs with the parsley and serve at once. Sprinkle the paprika over the sauce and serve chilled, as an accompaniment.

Pork with Fennel & Aniseed

4 lean pork chops,
125 g/4$^{1}/_{2}$ oz each
60 g/2 oz brown rice, cooked
1 tsp orange rind, grated
4 spring onions, trimmed
and finely chopped
$^{1}/_{2}$ tsp aniseed
1 tbsp olive oil
1 fennel bulb, trimmed
and thinly sliced
450 ml/16 fl oz unsweetened
orange juice
1 tbsp cornflour
2 tbsp Pernod
salt and pepper
fennel fronds, to garnish
cooked vegetables, to serve

❖ Trim away any excess fat from the pork chops. Using a small sharp knife, make a slit in the centre of each chop to create a pocket.

❖ Mix the rice, orange rind, spring onions, seasoning and aniseed together in a bowl.

❖ Push the rice mixture into the pocket of each chop, then press gently to seal.

❖ Heat the oil in a frying pan and fry the pork chops on each side for 2–3 minutes until lightly browned.

❖ Add the sliced fennel and orange juice to the pan, bring to the boil and simmer for 15–20 minutes until the meat is tender and cooked through. Remove the pork and fennel with a slotted spoon and transfer to a serving plate.

❖ Blend the cornflour and Pernod together in a small bowl. Add the cornflour mixture to the pan and stir into the pan juices. Cook for 2–3 minutes, stirring, until the sauce thickens.

❖ Pour the Pernod sauce over the pork chops, garnish with the fennel fronds and serve with the cooked vegetables.

Pork with Lemon & Garlic

450 g/1 lb pork fillet
50 g/1¾ oz chopped almonds
2 tbsp olive oil
100 g/3½ oz Parma ham, finely chopped
2 garlic cloves, chopped

1 tbsp fresh oregano, chopped
finely grated rind of 2 lemons
4 shallots, finely chopped
200 ml/7 fl oz ham or chicken stock
1 tsp sugar

❈ Using a sharp knife, cut the pork into 4 equal pieces. Place the pork between sheets of greaseproof paper and pound each piece with a meat mallet to flatten.

❈ Cut a horizontal slit in each piece of pork to make a pocket.

❈ Place the almonds on a baking tray. Lightly toast the almonds under a medium–hot grill for 2–3 minutes or until golden.

❈ Mix the almonds with 1 tablespoon of the oil, the ham, garlic, oregano and the finely grated rind of 1 lemon. Spoon the mixture into the pockets of the pork.

❈ Heat the remaining oil in a large frying pan. Add the shallots and cook for 2 minutes.

❈ Add the pork to the pan and cook for 2 minutes on each side or until brown all over.

❈ Add the stock to the pan, bring to the boil, cover and leave to simmer for 45 minutes or until the pork is tender. Remove the meat from the pan, set aside and keep warm.

❈ Add the remaining lemon rind and the sugar to the pan, boil for 3–4 minutes or until reduced and syrupy. Pour the lemon sauce over the pork and serve immediately.

Pork Chops & Spicy Beans

3 tbsp vegetable oil
4 lean pork chops, rind removed
2 onions, peeled and thinly sliced
2 garlic cloves, peeled and crushed
2 fresh green chillies, seeded and chopped, or 1–2 tsp minced chilli
2.5-cm/1-inch piece of root ginger, peeled and chopped

1½ tsp cumin seeds
1½ tsp ground coriander
600 ml/1 pint stock or water
2 tbsp tomato purée
½ aubergine, trimmed and cut into 1-cm/½-inch dice
salt and pepper
400 g/14 oz canned red kidney beans, drained
4 tbsp double cream
sprigs of fresh coriander, to garnish

❈ Heat the oil in a large frying pan, add the pork chops and fry until sealed and brown on both sides. Remove from the pan and set aside until required.

❈ Add the sliced onions, garlic, chillies, ginger and spices and fry gently for 2 minutes. Stir in the stock, tomato purée and aubergine and season with salt and pepper.

❈ Bring the mixture to the boil, place the pork chops on top, then cover and simmer gently over medium heat for 30 minutes.

❈ Remove the chops for a moment and stir the red kidney beans and cream into the mixture. Return the chops to the pan, cover and heat through gently for 5 minutes.

❈ Taste and adjust the seasoning, if necessary. Serve hot, garnished with the sprigs of coriander.

Pork Chops with Sage

2 tbsp flour	15 g/$\frac{1}{2}$ oz butter
1 tbsp chopped fresh	2 red onions, sliced into rings
sage or 1 tsp dried sage	1 tbsp lemon juice
4 lean boneless pork chops,	2 tsp caster sugar
trimmed of excess fat	4 plum tomatoes, quartered
2 tbsp olive oil	salt and pepper

❋ Mix the flour, sage and salt and pepper to taste on a plate. Lightly dust the pork chops on both sides with the seasoned flour.

❋ Heat the oil and butter in a frying pan, add the chops and cook them for 6–7 minutes on each side until cooked through. Drain the chops, reserving the pan juices, and keep warm.

❋ Toss the onions in the lemon juice and fry along with the sugar and tomatoes for 5 minutes until tender.

❋ Serve the pork with the tomato and onion mixture and a green salad.

Stuffed Pork with Parma Ham

500 g/1 lb 2 oz piece of	**OLIVE PASTE**
lean pork fillet	125 g/4$\frac{1}{2}$ oz stoned black
small bunch of fresh basil	olives
leaves	4 tbsp olive oil
2 tbsp freshly grated	2 garlic cloves, peeled
Parmesan cheese	
2 tbsp sun-dried tomato paste	
6 thin slices Parma ham	
1 tbsp olive oil	
salt and pepper	

❋ Trim away any excess fat and membrane from the pork fillet. Slice the pork lengthways down the middle, taking care not to cut all the way through.

❋ Open out the pork and season the inside. Lay the basil leaves down the centre. Mix the cheese and sun-dried tomato paste and spread over the basil.

❋ Press the pork back together. Wrap the ham around the pork, overlapping, to cover. Place on a rack in a roasting tin, seam side down, and brush with oil. Bake in a preheated oven, 190°C/375°F/Gas Mark 5, for 30–40, minutes depending on thickness, until cooked through. Allow to stand for 10 minutes.

❋ For the olive paste, place all the ingredients in a blender or food processor and blend until smooth. Alternatively, for a coarser paste, finely chop the olives and garlic and mix with the oil.

❋ Drain the cooked pork and thinly slice. Serve with the olive paste.

Pork with Apples & Berries

500 g/1 lb 2 oz piece lean pork
fillet
2 tsp sunflower oil
150 ml/5 fl oz fresh vegetable
stock
150 ml/5 fl oz dry rosé wine
1 tbsp chopped fresh thyme
1 tbsp clear honey
2 green eating apples, cored
and sliced, and tossed in
1 tbsp lemon juice
175 g/6 oz prepared fresh or
frozen blackberries, or
213 g/7$\frac{1}{2}$ oz canned
blackberries in natural
juice, drained
2 tsp cornflour mixed with
4 tsp cold water
salt and pepper
freshly cooked vegetables,
to serve

❋ Trim away any fat and silvery skin from the pork and cut into 1-cm/$\frac{1}{2}$-inch slices, taking care to keep the slices a good shape.

❋ Heat the oil in a non-stick frying pan, add the pork slices and fry for 4–5 minutes until brown all over. Using a slotted spoon, transfer the pork to kitchen paper. Reserve the pan juices.

❋ Pour the stock and wine into the pan with the juices and add the thyme and honey. Mix well, bring to a simmer and add the pork and apples. Continue to simmer, uncovered, for 5 minutes.

❋ Add the blackberries, season to taste and simmer for a further 5 minutes.

❋ Stir in the cornflour mixture until thickened. Serve with the freshly cooked vegetables.

Pork with Orange Sauce

4 tbsp freshly squeezed orange juice
4 tbsp red wine vinegar
2 garlic cloves, finely chopped
4 pork steaks, trimmed of all visible fat
olive oil, for brushing
pepper

GREMOLATA
3 tbsp finely chopped fresh parsley
grated rind of 1 lime
grated rind of $\frac{1}{2}$ lemon
1 garlic clove, very finely chopped

❖ Mix the orange juice, vinegar and garlic together in a shallow non-metallic dish and season to taste with pepper. Add the pork, turning to coat. Cover and leave in the refrigerator to marinate for up to 3 hours.

❖ Meanwhile, mix all the gremolata ingredients together in a small mixing bowl, cover with clingfilm and leave to chill in the refrigerator until required.

❖ Heat a non-stick griddle pan and brush lightly with olive oil. Remove the pork from the marinade, reserving the marinade, add to the pan and cook over a medium–high heat for 5 minutes on each side, or until the juices run clear when the meat is pierced with a skewer.

❖ Meanwhile, pour the marinade into a small saucepan and simmer over a medium heat for 5 minutes, or until slightly thickened. Transfer the pork to a serving dish, pour the orange sauce over it and sprinkle with the gremolata. Serve immediately.

Tangy Pork Fillet

400 g/14 oz lean pork fillet
3 tbsp orange marmalade
grated rind and juice of 1 orange
1 tbsp white wine vinegar
dash of Tabasco sauce
salt and pepper
cooked rice and mixed salad leaves, to serve

SAUCE
1 tbsp olive oil
1 small onion, chopped
1 small green pepper, deseeded and thinly sliced
1 tbsp cornflour
150 ml/5 fl oz orange juice

❖ Place a large piece of double thickness foil in a shallow dish. Put the pork in the centre of the foil and season.

❖ Heat the marmalade, orange rind and juice, vinegar and Tabasco sauce in a small saucepan, stirring until the marmalade melts and the ingredients combine. Pour the mixture over the pork and wrap the meat in foil, making sure that the parcel is well sealed so that the juices cannot run out. Place under a preheated medium grill and cook for about 25 minutes, turning the parcel occasionally.

❖ For the sauce, heat the oil and cook the onion for 2–3 minutes. Add the pepper and cook for 3–4 minutes.

❖ Remove the pork from the foil and place on the grill rack. Pour the juices into the pan with the sauce.

❖ Grill the pork for a further 10–20 minutes, turning, until cooked through and golden on the outside.

❖ In a small bowl, mix the cornflour with a little orange juice to form a paste. Add to the sauce with the remaining cooking juices. Cook, stirring, until the sauce thickens. Slice the pork, spoon over the sauce and serve with the rice and mixed salad leaves.

Pork with Plums

450 g/1 lb pork fillet
1 tbsp cornflour
2 tbsp light soy sauce
2 tbsp Chinese rice wine
4 tsp light brown sugar
pinch of ground cinnamon
5 tsp vegetable oil
2 garlic cloves, crushed
2 spring onions, chopped
4 tbsp plum sauce
1 tbsp hoisin sauce
150 ml/5 fl oz water
dash of chilli sauce
fried plum quarters and spring onions, to garnish

✻ Cut the pork fillet into thin slices.

✻ Combine the cornflour, soy sauce, rice wine, sugar and cinnamon in a small bowl.

✻ Place the pork in a shallow dish and pour the cornflour mixture over it. Toss the meat in the marinade until it is completely coated. Cover and leave to marinate for at least 30 minutes.

✻ Remove the pork from the dish, reserving the marinade.

✻ Heat the oil in a preheated wok or large frying pan. Add the pork and stir-fry for 3–4 minutes, until a light golden colour.

✻ Stir in the garlic, spring onions, plum sauce, hoisin sauce, water and chilli sauce. Bring the sauce to the boil. Reduce the heat, cover and leave to simmer for 8–10 minutes, or until the pork is cooked through and tender.

✻ Stir in the reserved marinade and cook, stirring, for about 5 minutes.

✻ Transfer the pork stir-fry to a warmed serving dish and garnish with the fried plum quarters and spring onions. Serve immediately.

Basque Pork & Beans

200 g/7 oz dried cannellini beans, soaked in cold water overnight
olive oil, for frying
600 g/1 lb 4 oz boneless leg of pork, cut into 5-cm/2-inch chunks
1 large onion, sliced
3 large garlic cloves, crushed
400 g/14 oz canned chopped tomatoes
2 green peppers, deseeded and sliced
finely grated rind of 1 large orange
salt and pepper
finely chopped fresh parsley, to garnish

✻ Drain the cannellini beans and put in a large saucepan with fresh water to cover. Bring to the boil and boil rapidly for 10 minutes. Reduce the heat and simmer for 20 minutes. Drain and set aside.

✻ Add enough oil to cover the base of a frying pan in a very thin layer. Heat the oil over a medium heat, add a few pieces of the pork and fry on all sides until brown. Remove from the pan and set aside. Repeat with the remaining pork.

✻ Add 1 tablespoon oil to the frying pan, if necessary, then add the onion and cook for 3 minutes. Stir in the garlic and cook for a further 2 minutes. Return the pork to the pan.

✻ Add the tomatoes and bring to the boil. Reduce the heat, stir in the pepper slices, orange rind and the drained beans. Season to taste with salt and pepper.

✻ Transfer the contents of the pan to a casserole. Cover the casserole and cook in a preheated oven, 180°C/350°F/Gas Mark 4, for 45 minutes until the beans and pork are tender. Sprinkle with the parsley and serve immediately straight from the casserole.

Spicy Pork with Prunes

1.5 kg/3 lb 5 oz pork joint, such
as leg or shoulder
juice of 2–3 limes
10 garlic cloves, chopped
3–4 tbsp mild chilli powder
4 tbsp vegetable oil
2 onions, chopped
500 ml/18 fl oz chicken stock
25 small tart tomatoes,
roughly chopped
25 prunes, stoned
1–2 tsp sugar
pinch of ground cinnamon
pinch of mixed spice
pinch of ground cumin
salt
warmed corn tortillas, to serve

❃ Combine the pork with the lime juice, garlic, chilli powder, 2 tablespoons of the oil and salt. Set aside to marinate in the refrigerator overnight.

❃ Remove the pork from the marinade. Wipe the pork dry with kitchen paper and reserve the marinade. Heat the remaining oil in a flameproof casserole and brown the pork evenly until just golden. Add the onions, the reserved marinade and stock. Cover and cook in a preheated oven, 180°C/350°F/Gas Mark 4, for about 2–3 hours until tender.

❃ Spoon off the fat from the surface of the cooking liquid and add the tomatoes. Continue to cook for about 20 minutes until the tomatoes are tender. Mash the tomatoes into a coarse purée. Add the prunes and sugar, then adjust the seasoning, adding cinnamon, mixed spice and cumin to taste, as well as extra chilli powder, if wished.

❃ Increase the oven temperature to 200°C/400°F/Gas Mark 6 and return the meat and sauce to the oven for a further 20–30 minutes or until the meat has browned on top and the juices have thickened.

❃ Remove the meat from the casserole and set aside for a few minutes. Carefully carve it into thin slices and spoon the sauce over the top. Serve warm with the tortillas.

Oat-Crusted Chicken Pieces

25 g/1 oz rolled oats
1 tbsp chopped fresh rosemary
4 skinless chicken quarters
1 egg white, lightly beaten

150 g/5^1/$_2$ oz natural fromage frais
2 tsp wholegrain mustard
salt and pepper
grated carrot salad, to serve

❊ Combine the oats, rosemary and salt and pepper.

❊ Brush each piece of chicken evenly with a little egg white, then coat in the oat mixture.

❊ Place the chicken pieces on a baking tray and bake in a preheated oven, 200°C/400°F/Gas Mark 6, for about 40 minutes. Test to see if the chicken is cooked by inserting a skewer into the thickest part – the juices should run clear without a trace of pink.

❊ Combine the fromage frais and mustard and season to taste with salt and pepper.

❊ Serve the chicken, hot or cold, with the sauce and a grated carrot salad.

Garlic Chicken Cushions

4 part-boned chicken breasts
115 g/4 oz frozen spinach, thawed
150 g/5^1/$_2$ oz low-fat ricotta cheese
2 garlic cloves, crushed
1 tbsp olive oil
1 onion, chopped
1 red pepper, deseeded and sliced

425 g/15 oz canned chopped tomatoes
6 tbsp wine or chicken stock
10 stuffed olives, sliced
salt and pepper
sprigs of fresh flat-leaf parsley, to garnish
pasta, to serve

❊ Make a slit between the skin and meat on 1 side of each chicken breast. Lift the skin to form a pocket, being careful to leave the skin attached to the other side.

❊ Put the spinach into a sieve and press out the water with a spoon. Mix with the ricotta, half the garlic and salt and pepper.

❊ Carefully spoon the spinach mixture under the skin of each chicken breast, then secure the edge of the skin with cocktail sticks.

❊ Heat the oil in a frying pan, add the onion and cook for 1 minute, stirring. Add the remaining garlic and the red pepper and cook for 2 minutes. Stir in the tomatoes, wine, olives and salt and pepper. Set the sauce aside and chill the chicken if preparing in advance.

❊ Bring the sauce to the boil, pour into an ovenproof dish and arrange the chicken breasts on top in a single layer.

❊ Cook, uncovered, in a preheated oven, 200°C/400°F/Gas Mark 6, for about 35 minutes until the chicken is golden and cooked through. Test by making a slit in 1 of the chicken breasts with a skewer to make sure the juices run clear.

❊ Spoon a little of the sauce over the chicken breasts, then transfer to serving plates and garnish with the parsley. Serve with the pasta.

Parma-Wrapped Chicken

❖ **SERVES 4** ❖

4 chicken breasts, skin removed
100 g/3 1/2 oz soft cheese, flavoured with herbs and garlic

8 slices Parma ham
150 ml/5 fl oz red wine
150 ml/5 fl oz chicken stock
1 tbsp brown sugar

❖ Using a sharp knife, make a horizontal slit along the length of each chicken breast to form a pocket.

❖ Beat the cheese with a wooden spoon to soften it. Spoon the cheese into the pocket of the chicken breasts.

❖ Wrap 2 slices of ham around each chicken breast and secure firmly in place with a length of string.

❖ Pour the wine and chicken stock into a large frying pan and bring to the boil. When the mixture is just starting to boil, add the sugar and stir well to dissolve.

❖ Add the chicken breasts to the mixture in the frying pan. Leave to simmer for 12–15 minutes or until the chicken is tender and the juices run clear when a skewer is inserted into the thickest part of the meat.

❖ Remove the chicken from the pan, set aside and keep warm.

❖ Reheat the sauce and boil until reduced and thickened. Remove the string from the chicken and cut into slices. Pour the sauce over the chicken to serve.

Chicken with Two Sauces

❖ **SERVES 4** ❖

2 tbsp olive oil
2 medium onions, finely chopped
2 garlic cloves, crushed
2 red peppers, chopped
pinch of cayenne pepper
2 tsp tomato purée
2 yellow peppers, chopped
pinch of dried basil

4 lean skinless, boneless chicken breasts
150 ml/5 fl oz dry white wine
150 ml/5 fl oz chicken stock
bouquet garni
salt and pepper
fresh herbs, to garnish

❖ Heat 1 tablespoon of the olive oil in each of 2 medium saucepans. Place half the chopped onions, 1 of the garlic cloves, the red peppers, cayenne pepper and tomato purée in 1 of the pans. Place the remaining onion and garlic, the yellow peppers and basil in the other pan.

❖ Cover each pan and cook over a very low heat for 1 hour until the peppers are very soft. If either mixture becomes dry, add a little water. Transfer the contents of the first pan to a food processor and process, then sieve. Repeat with the contents of the other pan.

❖ Return the sauces to the pans and season with salt and pepper. Gently reheat the sauces while the chicken is cooking.

❖ Put the chicken breasts into a frying pan and add the wine and stock. Add the bouquet garni and bring the liquid to a simmer over a medium–low heat. Cook the chicken for about 20 minutes until tender and cooked through.

❖ To serve, put a pool of each sauce on to 4 individual serving plates, slice the chicken breasts and arrange them on the plates. Garnish with the fresh herbs and serve immediately.

Thai Stir-Fried Chicken

3 tbsp sesame oil
350 g/12 oz skinless, boneless
chicken breast, thinly sliced
8 shallots, sliced
2 garlic cloves, finely chopped
2 tsp grated fresh root ginger
1 fresh green chilli, deseeded
and finely chopped
1 red pepper, deseeded
and thinly sliced
1 green pepper, deseeded
and thinly sliced
3 courgettes, thinly sliced
2 tbsp ground almonds
1 tsp ground cinnamon
1 tbsp oyster sauce
20 g/³⁄₄ oz creamed
coconut, grated
salt and pepper

❖ Heat the sesame oil in a preheated wok or heavy-based frying pan. Add the chicken, season to taste with salt and pepper and stir-fry over a medium heat for about 4 minutes.

❖ Add the shallots, garlic, ginger and chilli and stir-fry for a further 2 minutes.

❖ Add the peppers and courgettes and stir-fry for about 1 minute.

❖ Stir in the almonds, cinnamon, oyster sauce and creamed coconut and season to taste with salt and pepper. Stir-fry for 1 minute to heat through and then serve immediately.

183

Chicken Peperonata

8 chicken thighs
2 tbsp wholemeal flour
2 tbsp olive oil
1 small onion, thinly sliced
1 garlic clove, crushed
1 large red pepper, deseeded
and thinly sliced
1 large yellow pepper,
deseeded and thinly sliced

1 large green pepper,
deseeded and thinly sliced
400 g/14 oz canned chopped
tomatoes
1 tbsp chopped fresh oregano
salt and pepper
fresh oregano, to garnish
crusty wholemeal bread,
to serve

❖ Remove the skin from the chicken thighs and toss the meat in the flour.

❖ Heat the oil in a wide frying pan and fry the chicken over a medium heat until sealed and lightly browned, then remove from the pan.

❖ Add the onion to the pan, reduce the heat and cook, stirring occasionally, for about 5 minutes until soft, but not brown. Add the garlic, pepper slices, tomatoes and oregano, then bring to the boil, stirring constantly.

❖ Arrange the chicken on top of the vegetables, season to taste with salt and pepper, then cover the pan tightly and simmer for 20–25 minutes or until the chicken is completely cooked and tender.

❖ Taste and adjust the seasoning, if necessary. Transfer the chicken to a plate. Spoon the vegetables on to a warmed serving platter and top with the chicken. Garnish with the oregano and serve immediately with the bread.

Springtime Chicken Cobbler

1 tbsp vegetable oil
8 skinless chicken drumsticks
1 small onion, sliced
350 g/12 oz baby carrots
2 baby turnips
125 g/4$\frac{1}{2}$ oz broad beans or
peas
1 tsp cornflour
300 ml/10 fl oz chicken stock
2 bay leaves
salt and pepper

TOPPING
250 g/9 oz plain wholemeal flour
2 tsp baking powder
2 tbsp soft sunflower
margarine
2 tsp dry wholegrain mustard
55 g/2 oz mature Cheddar
cheese, grated
milk, to mix, plus extra for
brushing
sesame seeds, for sprinkling

❖ Heat the oil in a large heavy-based pan and fry the chicken, turning occasionally, until golden brown. Drain well and place in a casserole. Add the onion to the pan and cook, stirring occasionally, for 2–3 minutes until softened.

❖ Cut the carrots and turnips into even-sized pieces. Add to the casserole with the onions and beans or peas.

❖ Blend the cornflour with a little of the stock, then stir in the rest and heat gently, stirring until boiling. Pour into the casserole and add the bay leaves. Season to taste with salt and pepper.

❖ Cover tightly and bake in a preheated oven, 200°C/400°F/ Gas Mark 6, for 50–60 minutes or until the chicken juices run clear when pierced with a skewer.

❖ For the topping, sift the flour and baking powder. Mix in the margarine with a fork. Stir in the mustard, cheese and enough milk to mix to a fairly soft dough.

❖ Roll out and cut 16 rounds with a 4-cm/1$\frac{1}{2}$-inch cutter. Uncover the casserole, arrange the scone rounds on top of the chicken, then brush with milk and sprinkle with the sesame seeds. Return to the oven and bake for 20 minutes or until the topping is golden and firm.

Roast Chicken

250 g/9 oz parsnips, chopped
2 small carrots, chopped
25 g/1 oz fresh breadcrumbs
1/4 tsp freshly grated nutmeg
1 tbsp chopped fresh parsley,
    plus extra, for garnish
1.5 kg/3 lb chicken
1 bunch fresh parsley
1/2 onion

2 tbsp butter, softened
4 tbsp olive oil
500 g/1 lb 2 oz new potatoes,
    scrubbed
500 g/1 lb 2 oz baby carrots,
    topped and tailed
salt and pepper

❊ To make the stuffing, put the parsnips and chopped carrots into a pan, half cover with water and bring to the boil. Reduce the heat, cover and simmer until tender. Drain well, then process in a blender or food processor to a smooth purée. Transfer the purée to a bowl and set aside to cool.

❊ Mix the breadcrumbs, nutmeg and parsley into the purée and season to taste with salt and pepper.

❊ Put the stuffing into the neck end of the chicken and push a little under the skin over the breast meat. Secure the flap of skin with a small metal skewer or cocktail stick.

❊ Place the bunch of parsley and the onion inside the cavity of the chicken, then place the chicken in a large roasting tin.

❊ Spread the butter over the skin and season with salt and pepper, cover with foil and place in a preheated oven, 190°C/375°F/Gas Mark 5, for 30 minutes.

❊ Meanwhile, heat the oil in a frying pan, and lightly brown the potatoes.

❊ Transfer the potatoes to the roasting tin and add the baby carrots. Baste the chicken and continue to cook for a further hour, basting the chicken and vegetables after 30 minutes. Remove the foil for the last 20 minutes to allow the skin to crisp. Garnish the vegetables with chopped parsley and serve immediately with the chicken.

Chicken with Lime Stuffing

1 chicken, weighing 2.25 kg/5 lb
225 g/8 oz courgettes
25 g/1 oz butter
juice of 1 lime
oil, for brushing
lime slices and shreds of lime
    rind, to garnish

STUFFING
90 g/3 oz courgettes
90 g/3 oz low-fat soft cheese
finely grated rind of 1 lime
2 tbsp fresh breadcrumbs
salt and pepper

❊ To make the stuffing, top and tail and coarsely grate the courgettes and mix with the cheese, lime rind, breadcrumbs, salt and pepper.

❊ Carefully ease the skin away from the breast of the chicken with the fingertips, taking care not to split it.

❊ Push the stuffing under the skin, to cover the breast evenly.

❊ Place in a roasting tin, brush with oil and roast in a preheated oven, 190°C/375°F/Gas Mark 5, for 20 minutes per 500 g/1 lb 2 oz plus 20 minutes, or until the chicken juices run clear when pierced with a skewer.

❊ Meanwhile, top and tail the remaining courgettes and cut into long, thin strips with a potato peeler or sharp knife. Sauté in the butter and lime juice until just tender, then serve with the chicken. Garnish the chicken with the lime slices and shreds of lime rind and serve immediately.

Pot-Roast Orange Chicken

2 tbsp sunflower oil
1 chicken, weighing about
1.5 kg/3 lb 5 oz
2 large oranges
2 small onions, quartered
500 g/1 lb 2 oz small
whole carrots or thin carrots,
cut into 5-cm/2-inch lengths
150 ml/5 fl oz orange juice
2 tbsp brandy
2 tbsp sesame seeds
1 tbsp cornflour
salt and pepper

❊ Heat the oil in a large flameproof casserole and fry the chicken, turning occasionally until evenly browned.

❊ Cut one orange in half and place half inside the cavity of the chicken. Place the chicken in a large, deep casserole. Arrange the onions and carrots around the chicken. Season with salt and pepper and pour over the orange juice.

❊ Cut the remaining orange into thin wedges and tuck around the chicken, among the vegetables.

❊ Cover and cook in a preheated oven, 180°C/350°F/Gas Mark 4, for about $1^1/_2$ hours, or until the chicken juices run clear when pierced, and the vegetables are tender. Remove the lid and sprinkle with the brandy and sesame seeds. Return to the oven for 10 minutes.

❊ To serve, lift the chicken on to a large platter and add the vegetables. Skim any excess fat from the juices. Blend the cornflour with 1 tablespoon cold water, then stir into the juices and bring to the boil, stirring all the time. Adjust to taste, then serve the sauce with the chicken.

Roast Chicken with Ginger

3-cm/1¼-inch piece of root
ginger, finely chopped
2 garlic cloves, finely chopped
1 small onion, finely chopped
1 lemon grass stalk, finely
chopped
½ tsp salt
1 tsp black peppercorns

1.5 kg/3 lb 5 oz chicken
1 tbsp coconut cream
2 tbsp lime juice
2 tbsp clear honey
1 tsp cornflour
2 tsp water
stir-fried vegetables,
to serve

❋ Put the ginger, garlic, onion, lemon grass, salt and peppercorns in a mortar and crush with a pestle to form a smooth paste.

❋ Cut the chicken in half lengthways, using poultry shears or strong kitchen scissors. Spread the paste all over the chicken, both inside and out. Loosen the breast skin and gently spread the paste underneath. Transfer the chicken to a large plate, cover with clingfilm and set aside in the refrigerator to marinate overnight or at least for several hours.

❋ Heat the coconut cream, lime juice and honey in a small saucepan, stirring until smooth. Brush a little of the mixture evenly over the chicken.

❋ Place the chicken halves on a rack over a roasting tin half-filled with boiling water. Roast in a preheated oven, 180°C/350°F/Gas Mark 4, basting occasionally with the lime and honey mixture, for about 1 hour or until the chicken is a rich golden brown and the juices run clear when the thickest part is pierced with a skewer.

❋ Boil the water from the roasting tin to reduce it to about 100 ml/3½ fl oz. Blend the cornflour and water and stir into the reduced liquid. Bring gently to the boil, then stir until slightly thickened and clear. Serve the chicken with the sauce and stir-fried vegetables.

Spanish Chicken with Garlic

2–3 tbsp plain flour
cayenne pepper
4 chicken quarters, patted dry
about 4 tbsp olive oil
20 large garlic cloves,
each halved and green
core removed

1 large bay leaf
450 ml/16 fl oz chicken stock
4 tbsp dry white wine
salt and pepper
chopped fresh parsley,
to garnish

❋ Put about 2 tablespoons of the flour in a bag and season to taste with cayenne pepper and salt and pepper. Add a chicken piece and shake until it is lightly coated with the flour, shaking off the excess. Repeat with the remaining pieces, adding more flour and seasoning, if necessary.

❋ Heat 3 tablespoons of the oil in a large frying pan. Add the garlic cloves and fry for about 2 minutes, stirring, to flavour the oil. Remove with a slotted spoon and set aside.

❋ Add the chicken pieces to the pan, skin side down, and fry for 5 minutes or until the skin is golden brown. Turn and fry for a further 5 minutes, adding an extra 1–2 tablespoons of oil if necessary.

❋ Return the garlic to the pan. Add the bay leaf, stock and wine and bring to the boil. Reduce the heat, cover and simmer for 25 minutes or until the chicken is tender and the garlic cloves are very soft.

❋ Transfer the chicken to a serving platter and keep warm. Bring the cooking liquid to the boil and boil until reduced to about 250 ml/9 fl oz. Adjust the seasoning if necessary.

❋ Spoon the sauce over the chicken pieces and sprinkle the garlic cloves around it. Garnish with the parsley and serve.

Rustic Chicken & Orange Pot

8 skinless chicken drumsticks
1 tbsp wholemeal flour
1 tbsp olive oil
2 medium red onions
1 garlic clove, crushed
1 tsp fennel seeds
1 bay leaf
finely grated rind and juice
of 1 small orange
400 g/14 oz canned chopped
tomatoes

400 g/14 oz canned cannellini
or flageolet beans, drained
salt and pepper

TOPPING
3 thick slices wholemeal bread,
crusts removed
2 tsp olive oil

❋ Toss the chicken in the flour to coat evenly. Heat the oil in a non-stick frying pan. Add the chicken and cook over a fairly high heat, turning frequently, until golden brown. Transfer to a large casserole.

❋ Slice the onions into thin wedges. Add to the pan and cook over a medium heat for a few minutes until lightly browned. Stir in the garlic, then add the onions and garlic to the casserole.

❋ Add the fennel seeds, bay leaf, orange rind and juice, tomatoes and beans and season to taste with salt and pepper.

❋ Cover tightly and cook in a preheated oven, 190°C/375°F/ Gas Mark 5, for 30–35 minutes until the chicken juices are clear and not pink when pierced through the thickest part with a skewer.

❋ To make the topping, cut the bread into small dice and toss in the oil. Remove the lid from the casserole and sprinkle the bread cubes on top of the chicken. Bake for a further 15–20 minutes until the bread is golden and crisp. Serve immediately straight from the casserole.

Chicken & Plum Casserole

2 rashers lean back bacon,
rinds removed, trimmed and
chopped
1 tbsp sunflower oil
450 g/1 lb skinless, boneless
chicken thighs, cut into
4 equal strips
1 garlic clove, crushed
175 g/6 oz shallots, halved
225 g/8 oz plums, halved or
quartered (if large)
and stoned

1 tbsp light muscovado sugar
150 ml/5 fl oz dry sherry
2 tbsp plum sauce
450 ml/16 fl oz chicken stock
2 tsp cornflour mixed with
4 tsp cold water
2 tbsp flat-leaf parsley,
chopped, to garnish
crusty bread, to serve

❋ In a large non-stick frying pan, dry-fry the bacon for 2–3 minutes until the juices run out. Remove the bacon from the pan with a slotted spoon, set aside and keep warm.

❋ In the same frying pan, heat the oil and fry the chicken with the garlic and shallots for 4–5 minutes, stirring occasionally, until well browned.

❋ Return the bacon to the pan and stir in the plums, sugar, sherry, plum sauce and stock.

❋ Bring to the boil and simmer for 20 minutes until the plums are soft and the chicken is cooked through. Add the cornflour mixture to the pan and cook, stirring, for a further 2–3 minutes until thickened.

❋ Spoon the casserole on to warmed serving plates and garnish with the parsley. Serve the casserole with the bread.

Chicken & Chilli Bean Pot

2 tbsp plain flour
1 tsp chilli powder
8 chicken thighs or
4 chicken legs
3 tbsp vegetable oil
2 garlic cloves, crushed
1 large onion, chopped
1 green or red pepper,
deseeded and chopped
300 ml/10 fl oz chicken stock
350 g/12 oz tomatoes, chopped
400 g/14 oz canned red kidney
beans, rinsed and drained
2 tbsp tomato purée
salt and pepper

❖ Combine the flour and chilli powder in a shallow dish and add salt and pepper to taste. Rinse the chicken, but do not dry. Dip the chicken into the seasoned flour, turning to coat it on all sides.

❖ Heat the oil in a large, deep frying pan or flameproof casserole and add the chicken. Cook over a high heat, turning the pieces frequently, for 3–4 minutes until browned all over.

❖ Lift the chicken out of the pan or casserole with a slotted spoon and drain on kitchen paper.

❖ Add the garlic, onion and chopped pepper to the pan and cook over a medium heat, stirring occasionally, for 2–3 minutes until softened.

❖ Add the stock, tomatoes, kidney beans and tomato purée, stirring well. Bring to the boil, then return the chicken to the pan. Reduce the heat, cover and simmer for about 30 minutes until the chicken is tender. Taste and adjust the seasoning, if necessary, and serve.

189

Jamaican Chicken Stew

2 tsp sunflower oil	425 g/15 oz canned chopped
4 chicken drumsticks	tomatoes
4 chicken thighs	300ml/10 fl oz chicken stock
1 medium onion	60 g/2 oz split lentils
750-g/1 lb 10-oz piece of	350 g/12 oz canned sweetcorn
squash or pumpkin, peeled	kernels
1 green pepper	garlic salt and cayenne pepper
2.5-cm/1-inch piece of root	fresh crusty bread, to serve
ginger, finely chopped	

❖ Heat the oil in a large flameproof casserole and fry the chicken pieces, turning frequently, until they are golden all over.

❖ Peel and slice the onion.

❖ Using a sharp knife, cut the squash or pumpkin into dice.

❖ Deseed and slice the green pepper.

❖ Drain any excess fat from the casserole and add the onion, pumpkin and green pepper. Gently fry for a few minutes. Add the ginger, tomatoes, stock and lentils. Season with the garlic salt and cayenne pepper.

❖ Cover and place in a preheated oven, 190°C/375°F/Gas Mark 5, for about 1 hour, until the vegetables are tender and the juices from the chicken run clear.

❖ Add the corn and cook for a further 5 minutes. Season to taste and serve with the bread.

Chicken with Green Olives

3 tbsp olive oil	175 g/6 oz tomatoes, peeled
25 g/1 oz butter	and halved
4 chicken breasts, part boned	150 ml/5 fl oz dry white wine
1 large onion, finely chopped	175 g/6 oz stoned green olives
2 garlic cloves, crushed	4–6 tbsp double cream
2 red, yellow or green peppers,	400 g/14 oz dried pasta
deseeded and cut into large	salt and pepper
pieces	chopped fresh flat-leaf parsley,
250 g/9 oz button mushrooms,	to garnish
sliced or quartered	

❖ Heat 2 tablespoons of the oil and the butter in a frying pan. Add the chicken breasts and fry until golden brown all over. Remove the chicken from the pan.

❖ Add the onion and garlic to the pan and fry over a medium heat until beginning to soften. Add the peppers and mushrooms and cook for 2–3 minutes.

❖ Add the tomatoes and season to taste with salt and pepper. Transfer the vegetables to a casserole and arrange the chicken on top.

❖ Add the wine to the pan and bring to the boil. Pour the wine over the chicken. Cover and cook in a preheated oven, 180°C/350°F/Gas Mark 4, for 50 minutes.

❖ Add the olives to the casserole and mix in. Pour in the cream, cover and return to the oven for 10–20 minutes.

❖ Meanwhile, bring a large saucepan of lightly salted water to the boil. Add the pasta and the remaining oil and cook for 8–10 minutes or until tender, but still firm to the bite. Drain the pasta well and transfer to a serving dish.

❖ Arrange the chicken on top of the pasta, spoon over the sauce, garnish with the parsley and serve immediately. Alternatively, place the pasta in a large serving bowl and serve separately.

Pan-Cooked Chicken

4 chicken breasts, part boned	2 tsp plain flour
25 g/1 oz butter	400 g/14 oz canned artichoke
2 tbsp olive oil	halves, drained and halved
2 red onions, cut into wedges	salt and pepper
2 tbsp lemon juice	chopped fresh parsley,
150 ml/5 fl oz dry white wine	to garnish
150 ml/5 fl oz chicken stock	

❊ Season the chicken to taste with salt and pepper. Heat the oil and half the butter in a large frying pan. Add the chicken and fry for 4–5 minutes on each side until lightly golden. Remove from the pan using a slotted spoon.

❊ Toss the onion in the lemon juice, and add to the pan. Gently fry, stirring, for 3–4 minutes until just beginning to soften.

❊ Return the chicken to the pan. Pour in the wine and stock, bring to the boil, cover and gently simmer for 30 minutes.

❊ Remove the chicken from the pan, reserving the cooking juices, and keep warm. Bring the juices to the boil, and boil rapidly for 5 minutes.

❊ Blend the remaining butter with the flour to form a paste. Reduce the juices to a simmer and spoon the paste into the pan, stirring until thickened.

❊ Adjust the seasoning according to taste, stir in the artichoke hearts and cook for a further 2 minutes. Pour the mixture over the chicken and garnish with the parsley.

Potato, Leek & Chicken Pie

225 g/8 oz waxy potatoes,	2^1/$_2$ tbsp plain flour
cubed	300 ml/10 fl oz milk
5 tbsp butter	1 tbsp Dijon mustard
1 skinless chicken breast	2 tbsp chopped fresh sage
fillet, about 175 g/6 oz, cubed	225 g/8 oz filo pastry,
1 leek, sliced	thawed, if frozen
150 g/5^1/$_2$ oz chestnut	3 tbsp butter, melted
mushrooms, sliced	salt and pepper

❊ Bring a saucepan of lightly salted water to the boil and cook the potato cubes for 5 minutes. Drain and set aside.

❊ Melt the butter in a frying pan and cook the chicken cubes for 5 minutes or until browned all over.

❊ Add the leek and mushrooms and cook for 3 minutes, stirring. Stir in the flour and cook for 1 minute, stirring constantly. Gradually stir in the milk and bring to the boil. Add the mustard, sage and potato cubes and simmer for 10 minutes.

❊ Meanwhile, line a deep pie dish with half the sheets of filo pastry. Spoon the sauce into the dish and cover with 1 sheet of pastry. Brush the pastry with butter and lay another sheet on top. Brush this sheet with butter.

❊ Cut the remaining filo pastry into strips and fold them on to the top of the pie to create a ruffled effect. Brush the strips with melted butter and cook in a preheated oven, 180°C/350°F/Gas Mark 4, for 45 minutes or until golden brown and crisp. Serve hot.

Chicken Tikka

4 skinless, boneless
chicken breasts
1/2 tsp salt
4 tbsp lemon or lime juice
vegetable oil, for brushing

MARINADE

150 ml/5 fl oz low-fat natural
yogurt
2 garlic cloves, crushed
2.5-cm/1-inch piece of root
ginger grated
1 tsp ground cumin
1 tsp chilli powder
1/2 tsp ground coriander
1/2 tsp ground turmeric

SAUCE

150 ml/5 fl oz low-fat natural
yogurt
1 tsp mint sauce

❖ Cut the chicken into 2.5-cm/1-inch cubes. Sprinkle with the salt and the lemon juice. Set aside for 10 minutes.

❖ To make the marinade, combine all the ingredients in a small bowl until well mixed.

❖ Thread the cubes of chicken on to skewers. Brush the marinade over the chicken. Cover and set aside to marinate in the refrigerator for at least 2 hours, preferably overnight. Cook the chicken skewers under a preheated hot grill, brushing with oil and turning frequently, for 15 minutes or until cooked through.

❖ Meanwhile, combine the yogurt and mint sauce to make the sauce and serve with the chicken.

Skewered Chicken Spirals

❖ SERVES 4 ❖

4 skinless, boneless chicken breasts	large handful of fresh basil leaves
1 garlic clove, crushed	salt and pepper
2 tbsp tomato purée	vegetable oil, for brushing
4 rashers smoked back bacon	green salad, to serve

❖ Spread out a piece of chicken between two sheets of clingfilm and beat firmly with a rolling pin or meat mallet to flatten the chicken to an even thickness. Repeat with the remaining chicken breasts.

❖ Combine the garlic and tomato purée and spread the mixture over the chicken. Lay a bacon rasher over each, then sprinkle with the basil. Season to taste with salt and pepper.

❖ Roll up each piece of chicken firmly, then cut into thick slices. Thread the slices on to 4 skewers, making sure the skewer holds the chicken in a spiral shape.

❖ Brush lightly with oil and cook under a preheated grill for about 10 minutes, turning once. Serve hot with the salad.

Sweet & Sour Drumsticks

❖ SERVES 4 ❖

8 chicken drumsticks	1 tbsp Worcestershire sauce
4 tbsp red wine vinegar	1 garlic clove
2 tbsp tomato purée	pinch of cayenne pepper
2 tbsp soy sauce	salt and pepper
2 tbsp clear honey	crisp salad leaves, to serve

❖ Skin the chicken drumsticks if desired and slash 2–3 times with a sharp knife. Put the chicken drumsticks into a shallow non-metallic dish, arranging them in a single layer.

❖ Combine the vinegar, tomato purée, soy sauce, honey, Worcestershire sauce and garlic in a bowl. Season to taste with cayenne pepper and salt and pepper. Pour the mixture over the chicken, turning to coat. Cover and set aside in the refrigerator to marinate for 1 hour.

❖ Cook the drumsticks under a preheated grill for about 20 minutes, brushing with the glaze several times during cooking until the chicken is well browned and the juices run clear when the thickest part is pierced with a skewer.

❖ Transfer the drumsticks to a warmed serving dish and serve immediately with the salad leaves.

Spicy Coriander Chicken

❋ SERVES 4 ❋

4 skinless boneless chicken breast portions
2 garlic cloves, peeled
1 fresh green chilli, deseeded
2-cm/³⁄₄-inch piece of ginger
4 tbsp chopped fresh coriander
rind of 1 lime, finely grated
3 tbsp lime juice
2 tbsp light soy sauce
1 tbsp caster sugar
175 ml/6 fl oz coconut milk
plain boiled rice and a cucumber and radish salad, to serve

❋ Using a sharp knife, cut 3 deep slashes into the skinned side of each chicken breast portion. Place them in a single layer in a wide non-metallic dish.

❋ Put the garlic, chilli, ginger, coriander, lime rind, lime juice, soy sauce, sugar and coconut milk in a food processor and process to a smooth purée.

❋ Spread the purée over both sides of the chicken portions, coating them evenly. Cover the dish with clingfilm and set aside to marinate in the refrigerator for about 1 hour.

❋ Lift the chicken from the marinade, drain off the excess and place in a grill pan. Cook under a preheated grill for 12–15 minutes until thoroughly and evenly cooked.

❋ Meanwhile, pour the remaining marinade into a saucepan and bring to the boil. Reduce the heat and simmer for several minutes to heat thoroughly. Remove the pan from the heat.

❋ Place the chicken breast portions on warmed individual serving plates and pour over the sauce. Serve immediately accompanied by the rice and the cucumber and radish salad.

Green Chicken Curry

❋ SERVES 4 ❋

6 boneless, skinless chicken thighs
400 ml/14 fl oz coconut milk
2 garlic cloves, crushed
2 tbsp Thai fish sauce
2 tbsp Thai green curry paste
12 baby aubergines
3 fresh green chillies, finely chopped
3 kaffir lime leaves, shredded
4 tbsp fresh coriander, chopped
boiled rice, to serve

❋ Cut the chicken into bite-sized pieces. Pour the coconut milk into a large saucepan or wok and bring to the boil over a high heat.

❋ Add the chicken, garlic and fish sauce to the pan and bring back to the boil. Reduce the heat and simmer gently for about 30 minutes or until the chicken is just tender.

❋ Remove the chicken from the mixture with a slotted spoon. Set aside and keep warm.

❋ Stir the green curry paste into the pan until fully incorporated, then add the aubergines, chillies and lime leaves and simmer for 5 minutes.

❋ Return the chicken to the pan and bring to the boil. Season to taste with salt and pepper, then stir in the coriander. Serve the curry immediately with the rice.

Spicy Peanut Chicken

300 g/10½ oz skinless, boneless chicken breast
2 tbsp groundnut oil
125 g/4½ oz shelled peanuts
1 fresh red chilli, sliced
1 green pepper, deseeded and cut into strips
1 tsp sesame oil
fried rice, to serve

SAUCE
150 ml/5 fl oz chicken stock
1 tbsp Chinese rice wine or dry sherry
1 tbsp light soy sauce
1½ tsp light brown sugar
2 garlic cloves, crushed
1 tsp grated root ginger
1 tsp rice wine vinegar

❖ Trim any fat from the chicken and cut the meat into 2.5-cm/1-inch cubes. Set aside until required.

❖ Heat the groundnut oil in a preheated wok or frying pan.

❖ Add the peanuts to the wok and stir-fry for 1 minute. Remove the peanuts with a slotted spoon and set aside.

❖ Add the chicken to the wok and cook for 1–2 minutes.

❖ Stir in the chilli and green pepper and cook for 1 minute. Remove from the wok with a slotted spoon and set aside.

❖ Put half of the peanuts in a food processor and process until almost smooth. If necessary, add a little stock to form a softer paste. Alternatively, place them in a polythene bag and crush them with a rolling pin.

❖ To make the sauce, add the chicken stock, rice wine, soy sauce, sugar, garlic, ginger and vinegar to the wok.

❖ Heat the sauce without boiling and stir in the peanut purée, the remaining peanuts, the chicken, chilli and green pepper. Mix well until all the ingredients are thoroughly combined.

❖ Sprinkle the sesame oil into the wok, stir and cook for 1 minute. Transfer the spicy peanut chicken to a warmed serving dish and serve hot with the fried rice.

Garlic & Lime Chicken

4 large skinless, boneless
chicken breasts
50 g/1³/₄ oz garlic butter,
softened
3 tbsp chopped fresh coriander
1 tbsp sunflower oil

finely grated zest and juice of
2 limes, plus extra zest,
to garnish
25 g/1 oz palm sugar
boiled rice and lemon wedges,
to serve

❈   Place each chicken breast between 2 sheets of clingfilm and pound with a rolling pin until flattened to a thickness of about 1 cm/¹/₂ inch.

❈   Mix together the garlic butter and coriander and spread over each flattened chicken breast. Roll up like a Swiss roll and secure with a cocktail stick.

❈   Heat the sunflower oil in a preheated wok or heavy-based frying pan.

❈   Add the chicken rolls to the wok and cook, turning, for 15–20 minutes or until cooked through.

❈   Remove the chicken from the wok and transfer to a board. Cut each chicken roll into slices.

❈   Add the lime zest and juice and sugar to the wok and heat gently, stirring, until the sugar has dissolved. Increase the heat and allow to bubble for 2 minutes.

❈   Arrange the chicken on warmed serving plates and spoon the pan juices over to serve.

❈   Garnish the garlic and lime chicken with lime zest, and serve with the rice and lemon wedges.

Turkey Escalopes & Sausage

1 tbsp olive oil
6 canned anchovy fillets,
drained
1 tbsp capers, drained
1 tbsp fresh rosemary, stalks
removed
finely grated rind and juice of
1 orange

75 g/2³/₄ oz Italian sausage,
diced
3 tomatoes, peeled and
chopped
4 turkey or veal escalopes,
each about 125 g/4¹/₂ oz
salt and pepper
crusty bread or cooked polenta,
to serve

❈   Heat the oil in a large frying pan. Add the anchovies, capers, fresh rosemary, orange rind and juice, Italian sausage and tomatoes to the pan and cook for 5–6 minutes, stirring occasionally.

❈   Meanwhile, place the escalopes between sheets of greasproof paper. Pound the meat with a meat mallet or the end of a rolling pin to flatten it.

❈   Add the meat to the mixture in the frying pan. Season to taste with salt and pepper, cover and cook for 3–5 minutes on each side, slightly longer if the meat is thicker.

❈   Transfer to serving plates and serve with the bread.

Turkey with Orange Sauce

4 turkey breast steaks,
about 140 g/5 oz each
55 g/2 oz butter
2 tbsp olive oil
6 tbsp chicken stock

3–4 tbsp orange juice
1 tbsp chopped fresh chervil
salt and pepper
slices of orange and sprigs of
fresh chervil, to garnish

❊ Place each turkey breast steak in turn between
2 sheets of clingfilm and beat with the side of a rolling pin
or the flat surface of a meat mallet until about 5 mm/
1/4 inch thick. Season to taste with salt and pepper.

❊ Melt half the butter with the oil in a large griddle pan. Add
half the turkey steaks and cook over a high heat, turning
once, for 3–4 minutes, or until lightly browned on both sides.
Remove from the pan, add the remaining turkey steaks, 1 at
a time, and cook in the same way. Keep warm.

❊ Pour the stock into the pan and bring to the boil, stirring and
scraping up any sediment from the base of the pan. Add
3 tablespoons of the orange juice, the remaining butter and the
chervil, then reduce the heat to a simmer.

❊ Return all the turkey steaks, with any meat juices, to
the griddle pan. Simmer gently for 1 minute on each side.
Taste and adjust the seasoning, adding more orange juice
if necessary. Serve immediately, garnished with the orange
slices and sprigs of chervil.

Duck with Pineapple

4 duck breasts
1 tsp Chinese five-spice
powder
1 tbsp cornflour
1 tbsp chilli oil
225 g/8 oz baby onions, peeled
2 cloves garlic, crushed

100 g/3 1/2 oz baby sweetcorn
cobs
175 g/6 oz canned pineapple
chunks
6 spring onions, sliced
100 g/3 1/2 oz beansprouts
2 tbsp plum sauce

❊ Remove any skin from the duck breasts. Cut the duck
into thin slices.

❊ Mix the five-spice powder and the cornflour. Toss the
duck in the mixture until well coated.

❊ Heat the oil in a preheated wok. Stir-fry the duck for
10 minutes, or until just begining to crisp around the edges.
Remove from the wok and set aside.

❊ Add the onions and garlic to the wok and stir-fry for
5 minutes or until soft. Add the baby sweetcorn and stir-fry
for a further 5 minutes. Add the pineapple, spring onions
and beansprouts and stir-fry for 3–4 minutes. Stir in the
plum sauce.

❊ Return the cooked duck to the wok and toss until well
mixed. Transfer to warmed serving dishes and serve hot.

Duck with Broccoli & Peppers

1 egg white
2 tbsp cornflour
450 g/1 lb skinless, boneless duck meat
vegetable oil, for deep-frying
1 red pepper, seeded and diced
1 yellow pepper, seeded and diced
125 g/4¹/₂ oz small broccoli florets
1 garlic clove, crushed
2 tbsp light soy sauce
2 tsp Chinese rice wine or dry sherry
1 tsp light brown sugar
125 ml/4 fl oz chicken stock
2 tsp sesame seeds

❋ In a mixing bowl, beat together the egg white and cornflour.

❋ Using a sharp knife, cut the duck into 2.5-cm/1-inch cubes and stir into the egg white mixture. Leave to stand for 30 minutes.

❋ Heat the oil for deep-frying in a preheated wok or heavy-based frying pan until a cube of bread browns in 30 seconds.

❋ Remove the duck from the egg white mixture, add to the wok and fry in the oil for 4–5 minutes, until crisp. Remove the duck from the oil with a slotted spoon and drain on kitchen paper.

❋ Add the peppers and broccoli to the wok and fry for 2–3 minutes. Remove with a slotted spoon and drain on kitchen paper.

❋ Pour all but 2 tablespoons of the oil from the wok and return to the heat. Add the garlic and stir-fry for 30 seconds. Stir in the soy sauce, Chinese rice wine, sugar and stock and bring to the boil.

❋ Stir in the duck and the reserved vegetables and cook for 1–2 minutes.

❋ Carefully spoon the duck and vegetables on to a warmed serving dish and sprinkle with the sesame seeds. Serve immediately.

Noisettes of Salmon

4 salmon steaks
4 tbsp butter, softened
1 garlic clove, crushed
2 tsp mustard seeds
2 tbsp chopped fresh thyme
1 tbsp chopped fresh parsley
2 tbsp vegetable oil
4 tomatoes, peeled, deseeded
  and chopped
salt and pepper
new potatoes and green
  vegetables or salad, to serve

❖ Carefully remove the central bone from the salmon steaks and cut the steaks in half crossways. Curl each piece around to form a medallion and tie with string. Blend together the butter, garlic, mustard seeds, thyme and parsley and season to taste with salt and pepper. Set aside.

❖ Heat the oil in a griddle pan or frying pan and brown the salmon noisettes on both sides, in batches if necessary. Drain thoroughly on kitchen paper and set aside to cool.

❖ Cut 4 pieces of baking paper into 30-cm/12-inch squares. Place 2 salmon noisettes on top of each square and top with a little of the flavoured butter and tomato. Draw up the edges of the paper and fold together to enclose the fish. Place on a baking tray.

❖ Cook the parcels in a preheated oven, 200°C/400°F/Gas Mark 6, for about 10–15 minutes or until the salmon is cooked through. Serve immediately with the new potatoes and a green vegetable of your choice.

Poached Salmon

❖ SERVES 4 ❖

1 small onion, sliced
1 small carrot, sliced
1 celery stick, sliced
1 bay leaf
pared rind and juice of $1/2$ orange
a few stalks of parsley
5–6 black peppercorns
700 ml/1$1/4$ pints water
4 salmon steaks, about
  350 g/12 oz each
salt
salad leaves, to serve
lemon twists, to garnish

SAUCE
1 large avocado, peeled, halved
  and stoned
125 ml/4 fl oz low-fat natural
  yogurt
grated zest and juice of
  $1/2$ orange
a few drops of hot red pepper
  sauce
salt and pepper

❖ Put the onion, carrot, celery, bay leaf, orange rind and juice, parsley sprigs, salt and peppercorns in a saucepan just large enough to take the salmon steaks in a single layer. Pour on the water, cover the pan and bring to the boil. Simmer the stock for 20 minutes.

❖ Arrange the salmon steaks in the pan, return the stock to the boil and simmer for 3 minutes. Cover the pan, remove from the heat and leave the salmon to cool in the stock.

❖ Roughly chop the avocado and place it in a blender or food processor with the yogurt and the orange zest and juice. Process until smooth, then season to taste with salt and pepper and hot pepper sauce.

❖ Remove the salmon steaks from the stock (reserve it to make fish soup or a sauce), skin them and pat dry with kitchen paper.

❖ Cover the serving dish with the salad leaves, arrange the salmon steaks on top and spoon a little of the sauce into the centre of each one. Garnish the fish with the lemon twists, and serve the remaining sauce separately.

Spicy Grilled Salmon

❈ **SERVES 4** ❈

4 salmon steaks, about
175–225 g/6–8 oz each
lime slices, to garnish

MARINADE
4 garlic cloves
2 tbsp extra virgin olive oil
pinch of mixed spice
pinch of ground cinnamon
juice of 2 limes

1–2 tsp marinade from canned
chipotle chillies
1/4 tsp ground cumin
pinch of sugar
salt and pepper

TO SERVE
tomato wedges
3 spring onions, finely chopped
shredded lettuce

❈ To make the marinade, finely chop the garlic and place in a bowl with the olive oil, mixed spice, cinnamon, lime juice, chipotle marinade, cumin and sugar. Add salt and pepper and stir.

❈ Coat the salmon with the marinade, then place in a non-metallic dish. Marinate for at least 1 hour.

❈ Transfer the salmon to a grill pan and cook under a preheated grill for 3–4 minutes on each side.

❈ To serve, mix the tomato wedges with the spring onions. Place the salmon on individual serving plates and arrange the tomato salad and shredded lettuce beside it. Garnish with the lime slices and serve immediately.

Stir-Fried Salmon with Leeks

❈ **SERVES 4** ❈

450 g/1 lb salmon fillet,
skinned
2 tbsp sweet soy sauce
2 tbsp tomato ketchup
1 tsp rice wine vinegar
1 tbsp demerara sugar

1 clove garlic, crushed
4 tbsp corn oil
450 g/1 lb leeks, thinly
shredded
finely chopped red chillies,
to garnish

❈ Using a sharp knife, cut the salmon into slices. Place the slices of salmon in a shallow non-metallic dish.

❈ Mix together the soy sauce, tomato ketchup, vinegar, sugar and garlic.

❈ Pour the mixture over the salmon, toss well and leave to marinate for about 30 minutes.

❈ Meanwhile, heat 3 tablespoons of the corn oil in a large preheated wok.

❈ Add the leeks to the wok and stir-fry over a medium–high heat for about 10 minutes, or until the leeks become crispy and tender.

❈ Using a slotted spoon, carefully remove the leeks from the wok and transfer to warmed serving plates.

❈ Add the remaining oil to the wok. Add the salmon and the marinade to the wok and cook for 2 minutes.

❈ Remove the salmon from the wok and spoon over the leeks, garnish with the chillies and serve immediately.

Sesame Salmon with Cream

750 g/1 lb 10 oz salmon or pink
trout fillets
2 tbsp light soy sauce
3 tbsp sesame seeds
3 tbsp sunflower oil
4 spring onions, thinly
sliced diagonally
2 large courgettes, diced,
or 5-cm/2-inch piece
of cucumber, diced
grated rind of $^1/_2$ lemon
1 tbsp lemon juice
$^1/_2$ tsp turmeric
6 tbsp fish stock or water
3 tbsp double cream or
fromage frais
salt and pepper
curly endive, to garnish

❊ Skin the fish and cut into strips about 4 x 2 cm/1$^1/_2$ x $^3/_4$ inches. Pat dry on kitchen paper. Season lightly, then brush with the soy sauce and sprinkle all over with the sesame seeds.

❊ Heat 2 tablespoons of the oil in a wok. Add the pieces of fish and stir-fry for 3–4 minutes until lightly browned all over. Remove with a fish slice, drain on kitchen paper and keep warm.

❊ Heat the remaining oil in the wok and add the spring onions and courgettes and stir-fry for 1–2 minutes. Add the lemon rind, lemon juice, turmeric, stock and seasoning and bring to the boil for 1 minute. Stir in the cream.

❊ Return the fish pieces to the wok and toss gently in the sauce until they are really hot. Garnish with the curly endive and serve.

Tuna & Vegetable Stir-Fry

225 g/8 oz carrots	2 tbsp fish sauce
1 onion	15 g/1/2 oz palm sugar
175 g/6 oz baby sweetcorn cobs	finely grated zest and juice of 1 orange
2 tbsp corn oil	2 tbsp sherry
175 g/6 oz mangetout	1 tsp cornflour
450 g/1 lb fresh tuna	rice or noodles, to serve

❖ Using a sharp knife, cut the carrots into thin sticks, slice the onion and halve the baby sweetcorn.

❖ Heat the corn oil in a large preheated wok or frying pan.

❖ Add the onion, carrots, mangetout and baby sweetcorn to the wok and stir-fry for 5 minutes.

❖ Using a sharp knife, thinly slice the tuna.

❖ Add the tuna slices to the wok and stir-fry for about 2–3 minutes, or until the tuna turns opaque.

❖ Mix together the fish sauce, palm sugar, orange zest and juice, sherry and cornflour.

❖ Pour the mixture over the tuna and vegetables and cook for 2 minutes, or until the juices thicken. Serve the stir-fry with the rice.

Tuna Fish Cakes

225 g/8 oz potatoes, cubed	vegetable oil, for frying
1 tbsp olive oil	salt and pepper
1 large shallot, finely chopped	
1 garlic clove, finely chopped	**QUICK TOMATO SAUCE**
1 tsp fresh thyme leaves	2 tbsp olive oil
400 g/14 oz canned tuna in olive oil, drained	400 g/14 oz canned chopped tomatoes
grated rind of 1/2 lemon	1 garlic clove, crushed
1 tbsp chopped fresh parsley	1/2 tsp sugar
2–3 tbsp plain flour	grated rind of 1/2 lemon
1 egg, lightly beaten	1 tbsp chopped fresh basil
115 g/4 oz fresh breadcrumbs	salt and pepper

❖ For the tuna fish cakes, bring a saucepan of lightly salted water to the boil and cook the potatoes for 12–15 minutes until tender. Mash, leaving a few lumps, and set aside.

❖ Heat the oil in a small frying pan and gently cook the shallot gently for 5 minutes until soft. Add the garlic and thyme leaves and cook for an additional minute. Allow to cool slightly, then add to the potatoes with the tuna, lemon rind, parsley and seasoning. Mix together well but leave some texture.

❖ Form the mixture into 6–8 cakes. Dip the cakes first in the flour, then the egg and, finally, the breadcrumbs to coat. Chill for 30 minutes.

❖ For the tomato sauce, put the olive oil, tomatoes, garlic, sugar, lemon rind and basil into a saucepan, season to taste with salt and pepper and bring to the boil. Cover and simmer for 30 minutes. Uncover and simmer for 15 minutes until thickened.

❖ Heat enough oil in a frying pan to cover the base generously. Fry the fish cakes in batches for 3–4 minutes each side until golden and crisp. Drain on kitchen paper while you fry the remaining fish cakes. Serve hot with the tomato sauce.

Sea Bass with Artichokes

❖ SERVES 6 ❖

1.75 kg/4 lb baby artichokes
2½ tbsp fresh lemon juice, plus the cut halves of the lemon
150 ml/5 fl oz olive oil, plus extra for brushing
10 garlic cloves, thinly sliced
1 tbsp chopped fresh thyme, plus extra to garnish
6 x 115 g/4 oz sea bass fillets
1 tbsp olive oil
salt and pepper
crusty bread, to serve

❖ Peel away the tough outer leaves of each artichoke until the heart is revealed. Slice off the pointed top at about halfway between the point and the top of the stem. Cut off the stem and pare off what is left of the dark green leaves surrounding the bottom of the artichoke.

❖ Submerge the prepared artichokes in water containing the cut halves of the lemon to prevent discoloration. When all the artichokes have been prepared, turn them choke side down and thinly slice.

❖ Warm the oil in a large saucepan and add the sliced artichokes, garlic, thyme, lemon juice and seasoning. Cover and cook the artichokes over a low heat for 20–30 minutes, without colouring, until tender.

❖ Meanwhile, brush the sea bass fillets with oil and season well. Cook on a preheated griddle pan for 3–4 minutes on each side until just tender.

❖ Divide the stewed artichokes between serving plates and top each with a sea bass fillet. Garnish with thyme and serve with the bread.

Sea Bass with Ratatouille

❖ SERVES 4 ❖

2 large sea bass, filleted
olive oil, for brushing
salt and pepper

RATATOUILLE
1 large aubergine
2 medium courgettes
1 tbsp sea salt
4 tbsp olive oil
1 medium onion, roughly chopped
2 garlic cloves, crushed
½ red pepper, deseeded and roughly chopped
½ green pepper, deseeded and roughly chopped
2 large tomatoes, peeled and chopped
1 tbsp chopped fresh basil

DRESSING
5 tbsp roughly chopped fresh basil
2 garlic cloves, roughly chopped
4 tbsp olive oil
1 tbsp lemon juice
salt and pepper

❖ To make the ratatouille, roughly chop the aubergine and courgettes. Put them in a colander with the salt and set aside to drain for 30 minutes. Rinse thoroughly and pat dry on kitchen paper. Set aside.

❖ Heat the oil in a large pan and add the onion and garlic. Cook over a low heat, stirring occasionally, for 10 minutes until soft. Add the peppers, aubergine and courgettes. Season to taste and stir well. Cover and simmer very gently for 30 minutes until all the vegetables are soft. Add the tomatoes and cook for a further 15 minutes.

❖ Meanwhile make the dressing. Put the basil, garlic and half the oil into a food processor and process until finely chopped. Add the remaining oil, lemon juice and seasoning.

❖ Season the sea bass fillets and brush with a little oil. Cook in a hot frying pan, skin side down, for 2–3 minutes until the skin is brown and crispy. Turn the fish and cook for a further 2–3 minutes until just cooked through.

❖ To serve, stir the basil into the ratatouille then divide between 4 serving plates. Top with the fish and spoon around the dressing.

Blackened Fish

4 white fish steaks, such
as cod, conger eel, shark
or catfish
1 tbsp paprika
1 tsp dried thyme
1 tsp cayenne pepper
1 tsp freshly ground black
pepper
$1/2$ tsp freshly ground white
pepper
$1/2$ tsp salt
$1/4$ tsp mixed spice
2 tbsp unsalted butter
3 tbsp sunflower oil

❊ Rinse the fish steaks and pat them dry with absorbent kitchen paper.

❊ Combine the paprika, thyme, cayenne pepper, black pepper, white pepper, salt and mixed spice in a shallow dish.

❊ Place the butter and oil in a small saucepan and heat, stirring occasionally, until the butter melts.

❊ Brush the butter mixture liberally all over the fish steaks, on both sides.

❊ Dip the fish into the spice mixture until well coated on both sides.

❊ Cook the fish under a preheated grill, brushing frequently with the butter mixture, until cooked through and tender. Serve immediately.

Fish Baked with Lime

1 kg/2 lb 4 oz white fish fillets, such as bass, plaice or cod
1 lime, halved
3 tbsp extra virgin olive oil
1 large onion, finely chopped
3 garlic cloves, finely chopped
2–3 pickled jalapeño chillies, chopped
6–8 tbsp chopped fresh coriander
salt and pepper
lemon and lime wedges, to serve

❄ Place the fish fillets in a bowl and sprinkle with salt and pepper. Squeeze the juice from the lime over the fish.

❄ Heat the oil in a frying pan. Add the onion and garlic and cook for about 2 minutes, stirring frequently, until soft. Remove from the heat.

❄ Place a third of the onion mixture and a little of the chillies and coriander in the bottom of a shallow ovenproof dish or roasting tin. Arrange the fish on top. Top with the remaining onion mixture, chillies and coriander.

❄ Bake in a preheated oven, 180°C/350°F/Gas Mark 4, for 15–20 minutes or until the fish has become slightly opaque and firm to the touch. Serve immediately, with lemon and lime wedges for squeezing over the fish.

Gingered Monkfish

450 g/1 lb monkfish
1 tbsp grated root ginger
2 tbsp sweet chilli sauce
1 tbsp corn oil
100 g/3$\frac{1}{2}$ oz fine asparagus
3 spring onions, sliced
1 tsp sesame oil

❄ Remove any membrane from the monkfish. Using a sharp knife, slice the monkfish into thin flat rounds. Set aside until required.

❄ Mix together the ginger and the sweet chilli sauce in a small bowl until thoroughly blended. Brush the ginger and chilli sauce mixture over the monkfish pieces, using a pastry brush.

❄ Heat the corn oil in a large preheated wok or heavy-based frying pan.

❄ Add the monkfish pieces, asparagus and chopped spring onions to the wok and cook over a medium heat for about 5 minutes, constantly stirring very gently so the fish pieces do not break up.

❄ Remove the wok from the heat, drizzle the sesame oil over the stir-fry and toss gently to combine.

❄ Transfer the monkfish to warmed serving plates and serve immediately.

Monkfish with Coconut

450 g/1 lb monkfish tails
225 g/8 oz uncooked peeled prawns
desiccated coconut, toasted, to garnish (optional)

MARINADE
1 tsp sunflower oil
1/2 small onion, finely grated
1 tsp grated root ginger
150 ml/5 fl oz canned coconut milk
2 tbsp chopped, fresh coriander

❄ To make the marinade, heat the oil in a wok or saucepan and fry the onion and ginger for 5 minutes until just soft but not brown.

❄ Add the coconut milk to the wok and bring to the boil. Boil rapidly for about 5 minutes or until reduced to the consistency of single cream.

❄ Remove the pan from the heat and allow to cool completely.

❄ When cooled, stir the coriander into the coconut milk and pour into a shallow dish.

❄ Cut the fish into bite-sized chunks and stir gently into the coconut mixture, together with the prawns. Leave to chill for 1–4 hours.

❄ Thread the fish and prawns on to skewers and discard any remaining marinade. Grill the skewers under a preheated hot grill for 10–15 minutes, turning frequently. Garnish with toasted coconut, if using.

Monkfish with Caper Sauce

750 g/1 lb 10 oz monkfish tail
finely grated rind and juice of 1 small lemon
2 tbsp olive oil
a small bunch of fresh bay leaves
1 small lemon, cut into wedges,
green salad, to serve

SAUCE
6 tbsp olive oil
1 garlic clove, finely chopped
finely grated rind and juice 1 small lemon
1 tbsp chopped fresh parsley
2 tbsp capers, drained and chopped
3 anchovy fillets, finely chopped
pepper

❄ Wash and pat dry the monkfish using kitchen paper. Carefully trim away the grey membrane and slice either side of the central bone to give 2 thick fillets.

❄ Cut the monkfish into 2.5-cm/1-inch cubes and place in a shallow dish. Toss in the lemon rind and juice and the oil.

❄ Drain the fish, reserving the juices, and thread on to bamboo skewers, threading a few bay leaves and wedges of lemon in between the fish cubes.

❄ Preheat the grill to medium. Place the skewers on a rack and cover the ends of the skewers with foil to prevent them burning. Brush with some of the reserved juices and cook for 3 minutes. Turn over, brush again and cook for a further 3–4 minutes until tender and cooked through.

❄ Meanwhile, mix together all the ingredients for the caper sauce and set aside.

❄ Drain the skewers and transfer to warmed serving plates. Serve with the sauce and the salad.

Steamed Yellow Fish Fillets

500 g/1 lb 2 oz firm fish fillets, such as red snapper, sole or monkfish
1 dried red bird's-eye chilli
1 small onion, chopped
3 garlic cloves, chopped
2 sprigs fresh coriander
1 tsp coriander seeds
$1/2$ tsp turmeric
$1/2$ tsp pepper
1 tbsp Thai fish sauce
2 tbsp coconut milk
1 small egg, beaten
2 tbsp rice flour
fresh red and green chilli strips, to garnish
soy sauce, to serve

❖ Remove any skin from the fish and cut the fillets diagonally into long 2-cm/¾-inch strips.

❖ Place the dried chilli, onion, garlic, coriander and coriander seeds in a mortar and grind with a pestle to a smooth paste.

❖ Add the turmeric, pepper, fish sauce, coconut milk and beaten egg, stirring well to mix.

❖ Dip the fish strips into the paste mixture, then into the rice flour to coat lightly.

❖ Bring the water in the base of a steamer to the boil, then arrange the fish strips in the top of the steamer. Cover and steam for about 12–15 minutes until the fish is just firm.

❖ Transfer to a serving plate, garnish with the chilli strips and serve with the soy sauce.

Baked Lemon Sole

❋ **SERVES 8–10** ❋

2 garlic cloves
4 lemon sole fillets, about 6 oz/175 g each
1 shallot, finely chopped
2 sprigs fresh lemon thyme, plus extra to garnish
2 sprigs fresh lemon balm, plus extra to garnish
grated rind and juice of 1 lemon
2 tbsp extra virgin olive oil
salt and pepper

❋ Preheat the oven to 350°F/180°C/Gas Mark 4. Using a sharp knife, thinly slice the garlic and set aside.

❋ Arrange the sole fillets in a single layer in the base of a large ovenproof dish and sprinkle with the shallot. Place the reserved garlic slices and the herb sprigs on top of the fillets and season to taste with salt and pepper. Mix the lemon juice and olive oil together in a small measuring jug and pour it over the fish.

❋ Bake in the preheated oven for 15 minutes, or until the fish flakes easily when tested with a fork. Sprinkle with the lemon rind, garnish with herbs and serve immediately.

Sole Fillets in Marsala

❋ **SERVES 4** ❋

1 tbsp peppercorns, crushed
8 sole fillets
100 ml/3$\frac{1}{2}$ fl oz Marsala
150 ml/5 fl oz double cream

STOCK
600 ml/1 pint water
bones and skin from the sole fillets
1 onion, peeled and halved
1 carrot, peeled and halved
3 fresh bay leaves

SAUCE
1 tbsp olive oil
15 g/$\frac{1}{2}$ oz butter
4 shallots, finely chopped
100 g/ 3$\frac{1}{2}$ oz baby button mushrooms, wiped and halved

❋ To make the stock, place the water, fish bones and skin, onion, carrot and bay leaves in a large saucepan and bring to the boil.

❋ Reduce the heat and leave the mixture to simmer for 1 hour or until the stock has reduced to about 150 ml/ 5 fl oz. Drain the stock through a fine sieve, discarding the bones and vegetables, and set aside.

❋ To make the sauce, heat the oil and butter in a frying pan. Add the shallots and cook, stirring, for 2–3 minutes or until just soft.

❋ Add the mushrooms to the frying pan and cook, stirring, for a further 2–3 minutes or until they are just beginning to brown.

❋ Add the peppercorns and sole fillets to the pan in batches. Fry the sole fillets for 3–4 minutes on each side or until golden brown. Remove the fish with a fish slice, set aside and keep warm while you cook the remainder.

❋ Pour the wine and stock over the last fillet and leave to simmer for 3 minutes. Remove the fish with a fish slice, set aside and keep warm. Increase the heat and boil the mixture in the pan for about 5 minutes or until the sauce has reduced and thickened. Pour in the cream and heat through. Pour the sauce over the fish and serve.

Sole & Smoked Salmon Rolls

❋ **SERVES 4** ❋

60 g/2 oz fresh wholemeal breadcrumbs
½ tsp grated lime rind
1 tbsp lime juice
60 g/2 oz low-fat soft cheese
4 x 125 g/4½ oz sole fillets
60 g/2 oz smoked salmon
150 ml/5 fl oz fresh fish stock
150 ml/5 fl oz low-fat natural yogurt
1 tbsp chopped fresh chervil
salt and pepper
fresh chervil, to garnish
selection of freshly steamed vegetables and lime wedges, to serve

❋ In a mixing bowl, combine the breadcrumbs, lime rind and juice, soft cheese and seasoning to form a soft stuffing mixture.

❋ Skin the sole fillets by inserting a sharp knife in between the skin and flesh at the tail end. Holding the skin in your fingers and keeping it taut, strip the flesh away from the skin.

❋ Halve the sole fillets lengthways. Place strips of smoked salmon over the skinned side of each fillet, trimming the salmon as necessary.

❋ Spoon one-eighth of the stuffing on to each fish fillet and press down along the fish with the back of a spoon. Carefully roll up from the head to the tail end. Place, seam side down, in an ovenproof dish and pour in the stock. Bake in a preheated oven, 190°C/375°F/Gas Mark 5, for 15 minutes.

❋ Using a fish slice, transfer the fish to a warmed serving plate, cover and keep warm. Pour the cooking juices into a saucepan and add the yogurt and chopped chervil. Season to taste and heat gently without boiling. Garnish the fish rolls with the chervil and serve with the yogurt sauce, steamed vegetables and lime wedges.

Sardine & Potato Bake

❋ **SERVES 4** ❋

1 kg/2 lb 4 oz potatoes
1 kg/2 lb 4 oz sardines, thawed, if frozen
1 tbsp olive oil, plus extra for oiling
1 onion, chopped
2–3 garlic cloves, crushed
400 g/14 oz canned peeled tomatoes, partly drained and chopped
2 tbsp chopped fresh parsley
1–2 tbsp chopped fresh Italian herbs, such as oregano, thyme, rosemary and marjoram
150 ml/5 fl oz dry white wine
salt and pepper

❋ Put the potatoes in a saucepan of lightly salted water, bring to the boil, cover and simmer for 10 minutes, then drain. When cool enough to handle, cut into slices about 5 mm/¼ inch thick.

❋ To gut and clean the sardines, cut off their heads and tails and then slit open the length of the belly. Turn the fish over so the skin is facing upwards and press firmly along the backbone to loosen the bones. Turn over again and carefully remove the backbone. Wash the fish in cold water, drain well and dry them on kitchen paper.

❋ Heat the oil in a frying pan and fry the onion and garlic until soft but not coloured.

❋ Arrange the potatoes in a well-oiled ovenproof dish and sprinkle with the onions, parsley and plenty of salt and pepper to taste.

❋ Lay the open sardines over the potatoes, skin side down, then cover with the tomatoes and the rest of the herbs. Pour in the wine and season with salt and pepper.

❋ Cook, uncovered, in a preheated oven, 190°C/180°F/Gas Mark 5, for about 40 minutes until the fish is tender. If the casserole seems to be drying out, add another couple of tablespoons of wine. Serve hot.

Sardines, Olives & Tomatoes

❊ SERVES 4 ❊

12 fresh sardines, gutted and
cleaned
fresh basil leaves
4 plum tomatoes
8 stoned black olives
15 g/1/2 oz butter
1 tbsp olive oil
2 tbsp lemon juice
salt and pepper

TO GARNISH
sliced plum tomatoes
sliced olives
sprig of fresh basil

❊ Season the sardines inside and out with salt and pepper to taste. Insert 1–2 basil leaves inside the cavity of each fish. Using a sharp knife, make a few slashes in the body of each fish.

❊ Cut the tomatoes and olives into slices and transfer to a large bowl. Tear 4 basil leaves into small pieces and toss them together with the tomatoes and olives.

❊ Divide the tomato and olive mixture among 4 large sheets of foil, and place 3 sardines on top of each individual portion.

❊ Melt the butter and oil together in a small saucepan. Stir in the lemon juice and pour the mixture over the fish.

❊ Wrap the fish in the foil. Grill under a preheated medium grill for 15–20 minutes until the fish is firm and cooked through.

❊ Transfer the fish to serving plates and remove the foil. Garnish the fish with the slices of tomato and olive and the sprig of basil. Serve at once.

Curried Prawns

350 g/12 oz small courgettes
450 g/1 lb cooked tiger prawns
5 tbsp vegetable oil
4 garlic cloves, finely chopped
5 tbsp chopped fresh coriander
1 fresh green chilli, deseeded
and finely chopped
1/2 tsp ground turmeric
1 1/2 tsp ground cumin

pinch of cayenne pepper
200 g/7 oz canned chopped
tomatoes
1 tsp grated root ginger
1 tbsp lemon juice
salt
lime wedges, to garnish
steamed basmati rice, to serve

❊ Cut the courgettes into batons. Put into a colander, sprinkle with a little salt and set aside for 30 minutes. Rinse, drain and pat dry. Spread out the prawns on kitchen paper to drain.

❊ Heat the oil in a wok or frying pan over a high heat. Add the garlic. As soon as the garlic begins to brown, add the courgettes, coriander, chilli, turmeric, cumin, cayenne pepper, tomatoes, ginger, lemon juice and salt to taste. Stir well and bring to the boil.

❊ Cover and simmer over a low heat for about 5 minutes. Uncover and add the prawns.

❊ Increase the heat to high and simmer for about 5 minutes until the liquid is reduced to a thick sauce. Serve with the basmati rice, garnished with the lime wedges.

Prawns in Green Sauce

2 tbsp vegetable oil
3 onions, chopped
5 garlic cloves, chopped
5–7 ripe tomatoes, diced
175–225 g/6–8 oz French
beans, cut into 5-cm/2-inch
pieces, blanched for 1 minute
1/4 tsp ground cumin
pinch of mixed spice
pinch of ground cinnamon

1/2–1 canned chipotle chilli in
adobo marinade, with some
of the marinade
450 ml/16 fl oz fish stock or
water mixed with a fish
stock cube
450 g/1 lb raw prawns, peeled
sprigs of fresh coriander, to
garnish
lime wedges, to serve

❊ Heat the oil in a large pan. Add the onions and garlic and cook over a low heat, stirring occasionally, for about 5–10 minutes until softened. Add the tomatoes and cook for 2 minutes.

❊ Add the French beans, cumin, mixed spice, cinnamon, chipotle chilli and marinade and fish stock. Bring to the boil, then reduce the heat and simmer for a few minutes to combine the flavours.

❊ Add the prawns and cook, stirring gently, for 1–2 minutes only, then remove the pan from the heat and set the prawns aside to steep in the hot liquid to finish cooking. They are cooked when they have turned a bright pink colour.

❊ Serve the prawns immediately, garnished with the sprigs of coriander and accompanied by the lime wedges.

Chilli-Marinated Prawns

❊ SERVES 4 ❊

650 g/1 lb 7 oz large prawns, peeled
1/2 tsp ground cumin
1/2 tsp mild chilli powder
1/2 tsp paprika
2 tbsp orange juice
grated rind of 1 orange
2 tbsp extra virgin olive oil
2 tbsp chopped fresh coriander, plus extra to garnish
2 ripe avocados
1/2 onion, finely chopped
1/4 fresh green or red chilli, deseeded and chopped
juice of 1/2 lime
salt and pepper

❊ Combine the prawns with the cumin, chilli powder, paprika, orange juice, orange rind, oil and half the coriander. Season to taste with salt and pepper.

❊ Thread the prawns on to metal skewers, or bamboo skewers soaked in cold water for 30 minutes.

❊ Cut the avocados in half around the stone. Twist apart, then remove the stone with a knife. Carefully peel off the skin, then dice the flesh. Immediately combine the avocados with the remaining coriander, onion, chilli and lime juice. Season with salt and pepper and set aside.

❊ Place the prawns on a foil-lined grill pan under a hot grill and cook for only a few minutes on each side.

❊ Serve the prawns immediately, garnished with coriander and accompanied by the avocado sauce.

Hot & Sweet Prawns

❊ SERVES 4 ❊

500 g/1 lb 2 oz raw prawns
3 tbsp sesame oil
2 tbsp lime juice
1 tbsp chopped fresh coriander

SAUCE
4 tbsp light malt vinegar
2 tbsp fish sauce or light soy sauce
2 tbsp water
2 tbsp light muscovado sugar
2 garlic cloves, crushed
2 tsp grated ginger root
1 red chilli, deseeded and finely chopped
2 tbsp chopped fresh coriander
salt

❊ Peel and devein the prawns, leaving the tails intact. Skewer the prawns on wooden skewers that have been soaked in warm water for 20 minutes.

❊ Mix together the sesame oil, lime juice and coriander in a shallow bowl. Lay the skewered prawns in this mixture. Cover and chill in the refrigerator for 30 minutes, turning once, so that the prawns absorb the marinade.

❊ Meanwhile, make the sauce. Heat the vinegar, fish sauce, water, sugar and salt to taste until boiling. Remove from the heat and leave to cool.

❊ Mix together the garlic, ginger, chilli and coriander in a small serving bowl. Add the cooled vinegar mixture and stir until well combined.

❊ Place the prawns on a foil-lined grill pan under a preheated grill for about 6 minutes, turning once and basting often with the marinade, until cooked.

❊ Transfer to a warmed serving platter and serve with the dipping sauce.

Fried Prawns with Cashew Nuts

2 garlic cloves, crushed
1 tbsp cornflour
pinch of caster sugar
450 g/1 lb raw tiger prawns
4 tbsp vegetable oil
1 leek, sliced
125 g/4½ oz broccoli florets
1 orange pepper,
deseeded and diced
75 g/2¾ oz unsalted
cashew nuts

SAUCE
175 ml/6 fl oz fish stock
1 tbsp cornflour
dash of chilli sauce
2 tsp sesame oil
1 tbsp Chinese rice wine

❖ Mix together the garlic, cornflour and sugar in a bowl.

❖ Peel and devein the prawns. Stir the prawns into the mixture to coat thoroughly.

❖ Heat the oil in a preheated wok and add the prawn mixture. Stir-fry over a high heat for 20–30 seconds until the prawns turn pink. Remove the prawns from the wok with a slotted spoon, drain on absorbent kitchen paper and set aside until required.

❖ Add the leek, broccoli and diced pepper to the wok and stir-fry for 2 minutes.

❖ To make the sauce, place the fish stock, cornflour, chilli sauce to taste, the sesame oil and rice wine in a small bowl. Mix until thoroughly combined.

❖ Add the sauce to the wok, together with the cashew nuts. Return the prawns to the wok and cook for 1 minute to heat through.

❖ Transfer the prawn stir-fry to a warmed serving dish and serve immediately.

213

Seafood Stew

225 g/8 oz clams
700 g/1 lb 9 oz mixed fish,
such as sea bass, skate,
red snapper, rock fish and
any Mediterranean fish you
can find
12–18 raw tiger prawns
about 3 tbsp olive oil
1 large onion, finely chopped
2 garlic cloves, very finely
chopped

2 tomatoes, halved, deseeded
and chopped
700 ml/1¼ pints fish stock
1 tbsp tomato purée
1 tsp fresh thyme leaves
pinch of saffron threads
pinch of sugar
salt and pepper
finely chopped fresh parsley,
to garnish

❊ Soak the clams in a bowl of lightly salted water for 30 minutes. Rinse them under cold running water and lightly scrub to remove any sand from the shells. Discard any broken clams or open clams that do not shut when firmly tapped with the back of a knife, as these will be unsafe to eat.

❊ Prepare the fish as necessary, removing any skin and bones, then cut into bite-sized chunks.

❊ To prepare the prawns, break off the heads. Peel and devein the prawns, leaving the tails intact, if wished. Set all the seafood aside.

❊ Heat the oil in a large pan. Add the onion and cook for 5 minutes, stirring. Add the garlic and cook for about another 2 minutes until the onion is soft, but not brown.

❊ Add the tomatoes, stock, tomato purée, thyme leaves, saffron threads and sugar, then bring to the boil, stirring to dissolve the tomato purée. Reduce the heat, cover and simmer for 15 minutes. Season to taste with salt and pepper.

❊ Add the seafood and simmer until the clams open and the fish flakes easily. Discard any clams that do not open. Garnish and serve immediately.

Sweet & Sour Seafood

18 live mussels
6 large scallops
200 g/7 oz baby squid, cleaned
2 shallots, finely chopped
6 raw tiger prawns, peeled and
deveined
¼ cucumber
1 carrot, peeled
¼ head Chinese leaves,
shredded

DRESSING
4 tbsp lime juice
2 garlic cloves, finely chopped
2 tbsp Thai fish sauce
1 tsp sesame oil
1 tbsp soft light brown sugar
2 tbsp chopped fresh mint
¼ tsp pepper
salt

❊ Scrub and debeard the mussels. Discard any damaged mussels or open ones that do not close when firmly tapped. Steam them in just the water that clings to them for 1–2 minutes until opened. Lift out with a slotted spoon, reserving the liquid in the pan. Discard any mussels that have not opened.

❊ Separate the corals from the scallops and cut the whites in half horizontally. Cut the tentacles from the squid and slice the body cavities into rings.

❊ Add the shallots to the liquid in the pan and simmer over a high heat until the liquid is reduced to about 3 tablespoons. Add the scallops, squid and prawns and stir for 2–3 minutes until cooked. Remove and spoon the mixture into a wide bowl.

❊ Cut the cucumber and carrot in half lengthways, then thinly slice on a diagonal angle to make long, pointed slices. Toss with the Chinese leaves.

❊ To make the dressing, place all the ingredients in a screw-top jar and shake well until evenly combined. Season to taste with salt.

❊ Toss the vegetables and seafood together. Spoon the dressing over the vegetables and seafood and serve immediately.

Spiced Balti Seafood

1 garlic clove, crushed	3 tbsp chopped fresh coriander
2 tsp freshly grated root ginger	500 g/1 lb 2 oz cooked peeled
2 tsp ground coriander	king prawns
2 tsp ground cumin	2 tbsp oil
1/2 tsp ground cardamom	2 small onions, sliced
1/4 tsp chilli powder	1 fresh green chilli, chopped
2 tbsp tomato purée	salt
5 tbsp water	

❊ Put the garlic, ginger, ground coriander, cumin, cardamom, chilli powder, tomato purée, 4 tablespoons of the water and 2 tablespoons of the fresh coriander into a bowl. Mix all the ingredients together.

❊ Add the prawns to the bowl and leave to marinate for 2 hours.

❊ Heat the oil in a karahi or wok, add the onions and stir-fry until golden brown.

❊ Add the prawns, marinade and the chilli and stir-fry over a medium heat for 5 minutes. Add salt, and the remaining tablespoon of water if the mixture is very dry. Stir-fry over a medium heat for a further 5 minutes.

❊ Serve the prawns immediately, garnished with the remaining chopped coriander.

Mussel Casserole

1 kg/2 lb 4 oz mussels	1 red chilli, finely chopped
150 ml/5 fl oz white wine	100 g/3 1/2 oz passata
1 tbsp oil	1 tbsp chopped marjoram
1 onion, finely chopped	toast or crusty bread, to serve
3 garlic cloves, chopped	

❊ Scrub and debeard the mussels and rinse under cold running water. Discard any mussels that do not close when they are tapped.

❊ Place the mussels in a large saucepan. Pour in the wine and cook for 5 minutes, shaking the pan occasionally until the shells open. Remove and discard any mussels that do not open.

❊ Remove the mussels from the pan with a slotted spoon. Strain the cooking liquid through a fine sieve set over a bowl, reserving the liquid.

❊ Heat the oil in a large frying pan. Add the onion, garlic and chilli and cook for 4–5 minutes or until just softened.

❊ Add the reserved cooking liquid to the pan and cook for 5 minutes or until reduced, stirring.

❊ Stir in the passata, marjoram and mussels and cook until hot, about 3 minutes.

❊ Transfer to serving bowls and serve with the toast.

Balti Scallops

750 g/1 lb 10 oz shelled
scallops
2 tbsp oil
2 onions, chopped
3 tomatoes, quartered
2 fresh green chillies, sliced
4 lime wedges, to garnish

MARINADE
3 tbsp chopped fresh coriander
2.5-cm/1-inch piece of root
ginger, grated
1 tsp ground coriander
3 tbsp lemon juice
grated rind of 1 lemon
$1/4$ tsp pepper
$1/2$ tsp salt
$1/2$ tsp ground cumin
1 garlic clove, crushed

❖ To make the marinade, mix all the ingredients together in a bowl.

❖ Put the scallops into a bowl. Add the marinade and turn the scallops until they are well coated,   then cover and leave to marinate for 1 hour or overnight in the fridge.

❖ Heat the oil in a Balti pan or wok, add the onions and stir-fry until softened.

❖ Add the tomatoes and chillies and stir-fry for 1 minute.

❖ Add the scallops and stir-fry for 6–8 minutes until the scallops are cooked through, but still succulent inside.

❖ Serve garnished with the lime wedges.

Mushroom & Bean Chilli

4 tbsp olive oil
225 g/8 oz small button mushrooms
1 large onion, chopped
1 garlic clove, chopped
1 green pepper, deseeded and cut into strips
1 tsp each paprika, ground coriander and ground cumin
1/4–1/2 tsp chilli powder
400 g/14 oz canned chopped tomatoes
150 ml/5 fl oz vegetable stock
1 tbsp tomato purée
400 g/14 oz canned red kidney beans, drained and rinsed
2 tbsp chopped fresh coriander
salt and pepper

❈ Heat 1 tablespoon of the oil in a large frying pan. Add the mushrooms and stir-fry until golden. Remove with a slotted spoon and reserve until required.

❈ Add the remaining oil to the pan. Add the onion, garlic and green pepper and fry for 5 minutes. Stir in the paprika, ground coriander, cumin and chilli powder and cook for a further minute.

❈ Add the tomatoes, stock and tomato purée, stir well, then cover and cook for 20 minutes.

❈ Add the reserved mushrooms and kidney beans and cook, covered, for a further 20 minutes. Season to taste with salt and pepper and stir in the fresh coriander. Serve immediately.

Mexican Chilli Corn Pie

1 tbsp corn oil
2 garlic cloves, crushed
1 red pepper, seeded and diced
1 green pepper, seeded and diced
1 celery stick, diced
1 tsp hot chilli powder
400 g/14 oz canned chopped tomatoes
325 g/11 1/2 oz canned sweetcorn, drained
215 g/7 1/2 oz canned kidney beans, drained and rinsed
2 tbsp chopped coriander
salt and pepper
sprigs of fresh coriander, to garnish
tomato and avocado salad, to serve

TOPPING
125 g/4 1/2 oz polenta
1 tbsp plain flour
1/2 tsp salt
2 tsp baking powder
1 egg, beaten
6 tbsp milk
1 tbsp corn oil
125 g/4 1/2 oz grated mature Cheddar cheese

❈ Heat the oil in a large frying pan and gently fry the garlic, peppers and celery for 5–6 minutes until just softened.

❈ Stir in the chilli powder, tomatoes, sweetcorn, beans and seasoning. Bring to the boil and simmer for 10 minutes. Stir in the chopped coriander and spoon into an ovenproof dish.

❈ To make the topping, mix together the polenta, flour, salt and baking powder. Make a well in the centre, add the egg, milk and oil and beat until a smooth batter is formed.

❈ Spoon over the pepper and sweetcorn mixture and sprinkle with the cheese. Bake in a preheated oven, 220°C/425°F/Gas Mark 7, for 25–30 minutes until golden and firm.

❈ Garnish with the sprigs of coriander and serve immediately with the tomato and avocado salad.

Kidney Bean Kiev

GARLIC BUTTER
100 g/3 1/2 oz butter
3 garlic cloves, crushed
1 tbsp chopped parsley

BEAN PATTIES
675 g/1 lb 8 oz canned red
kidney beans
150 g/5 1/2 oz fresh white
breadcrumbs

25 g/1 oz butter
1 leek, chopped
1 celery stick, chopped
1 tbsp chopped parsley
1 egg, beaten
salt and pepper
vegetable oil, for shallow frying

❖ To make the garlic butter, put the butter, garlic and parsley in a bowl and blend together with a wooden spoon. Place the garlic butter on a sheet of baking paper, roll into a cigar shape and wrap in the baking paper. Chill in the refrigerator until required.

❖ Using a potato masher, mash the red kidney beans in a mixing bowl and stir in 75 g/2 3/4 oz of the breadcrumbs until thoroughly blended.

❖ Melt the butter in a heavy-based frying pan. Add the leek and celery and sauté over a low heat, stirring constantly,for 3–4 minutes. Add the bean mixture to the pan, together with the parsley, season to taste with salt and pepper and mix thoroughly. Remove from the heat and set aside to cool. Divide the kidney bean mixture into 4 equal portions and shape them into ovals.

❖ Slice the garlic butter into 4 pieces and place a slice in the centre of each bean patty. With your hands, mould the bean mixture around the garlic butter to encase it completely.

❖ Dip each bean patty into the beaten egg to coat and then roll in the remaining breadcrumbs.

❖ Heat a little oil in a frying pan and fry the patties, turning once, for 7–10 minutes or until golden brown. Serve immediately.

Brazil Nut & Mushroom Pie

PASTRY
225 g/8 oz plain
wholemeal flour
100 g/3 1/2 oz margarine,
cut into small pieces
4 tbsp water
milk, to glaze

FILLING
25 g/1 oz margarine
1 onion, chopped

1 garlic clove, finely chopped
125 g/4 1/2 oz button
mushrooms, sliced
1 tbsp plain flour
150 ml/5 fl oz vegetable stock
175 g/6 oz Brazil nuts
1 tbsp tomato purée
75 g/2 3/4 oz fresh wholemeal
breadcrumbs
2 tbsp chopped parsley
1/2 tsp pepper

❖ To make the pastry, place the flour in a mixing bowl and rub in the margarine with your fingertips until the mixture resembles fine breadcrumbs. Stir in the water and bring together to form a smooth dough. Knead lightly, then wrap and chill in the refrigerator for 30 minutes.

❖ To make the filling, melt half of the margarine in a pan. Add the onion, garlic and mushrooms and fry over a medium heat, stirring occasionally, for 5 minutes,until soft. Add the flour and cook for 1 minute, stirring frequently. Gradually add the stock, stirring until the sauce is smooth and beginning to thicken. Chop the Brazil nuts. Stir in the tomato purée, nuts, breadcrumbs, parsley and pepper. Set aside to cool slightly.

❖ On a lightly floured surface, roll out two-thirds of the pastry and use to line a 20-cm/8-inch loose-based flan tin or pie dish. Spread the filling in the pastry case. Brush the edges of the pastry with milk. Roll out the remaining pastry to fit the top of the pie. Seal the edges, make a slit in the top of the pastry and brush with milk to glaze.

❖ Bake in a preheated oven, 200°C/400°F/Gas Mark 6, for 30–40 minutes, until golden brown. Serve immediately.

Chickpea Roast

450 g/1 lb canned chickpeas,
drained
1 tsp yeast extract
150 g/5^1/$_2$ oz chopped walnuts
150 g/5^1/$_2$ oz fresh white
breadcrumbs
1 onion, finely chopped
100 g/3^1/$_2$ oz mushrooms,
sliced
50 g/1^3/$_4$ oz canned sweetcorn,
drained
2 garlic cloves, crushed
2 tbsp dry sherry
2 tbsp vegetable stock
1 tbsp chopped fresh coriander
225 g/8 oz puff pastry
1 egg, beaten
2 tbsp milk
salt and pepper

SAUCE
1 tbsp vegetable oil
1 leek, thinly sliced
4 tbsp dry sherry
150 ml/5 fl oz vegetable stock

❖ Blend the chickpeas, yeast extract, nuts and breadcrumbs in a food processor for 30 seconds. In a frying pan, sauté the onion and mushrooms in their own juices for 3–4 minutes. Stir in the chickpea mixture, corn and garlic. Add the sherry, stock, coriander and seasoning and bind the mixture together. Remove from the heat and allow to cool.

❖ Roll out the pastry on a floured surface to form a 35.5 x 30-cm/14 x 12-inch rectangle. Shape the chickpea mixture into a loaf shape and wrap the pastry around it, sealing the edges. Place seam side down on a dampened baking tray and score the top in a criss-cross pattern. Mix the egg and milk and brush over the pastry. Cook in a preheated oven, 200°C/400°F/Gas Mark 6, for 25–30 minutes.

❖ To make the sauce, heat the oil in a saucepan and sauté the leek for 5 minutes. Add the sherry and stock, bring to the boil and simmer for 5 minutes. Pour over the chickpea roast and serve.

Almond & Sesame Nut Roast

2 tbsp sesame or olive oil
1 small onion, finely chopped
60 g/2 oz arborio rice
300 ml/10 fl oz vegetable stock
1 large carrot, grated
1 large leek, finely chopped
2 tsp sesame seeds, toasted
90 g/3 oz chopped almonds,
  toasted
60 g/2 oz ground almonds
90 g/3 oz grated mature
  Cheddar cheese
2 eggs, beaten

1 tsp dried mixed herbs
salt and pepper
sprigs of fresh flat-leaf parsley,
  to garnish
fresh vegetables, to serve

SAUCE
25 g/1 oz butter
1 small onion, finely chopped
125 g/4¹/₂ oz mushrooms,
  finely chopped
25 g/1 oz plain flour
300 ml/10 fl oz vegetable stock

❄ Heat the oil in a large frying pan and fry the onion gently for 2–3 minutes. Add the rice and cook gently for 5–6 minutes, stirring frequently.

❄ Add the stock, bring to the boil, reduce the heat and simmer for 15 minutes, or until the rice is tender. Add a little extra water if necessary. Remove from the heat and transfer to a large mixing bowl.

❄ Add the carrot, leek, sesame seeds, almonds, cheese, eggs and herbs. Mix well and season with salt and pepper. Transfer the mixture to a greased 500-g/1 lb 2-oz loaf tin, levelling the surface. Bake in a preheated oven, 180°C/350°F/Gas Mark 4, for 1 hour, until set and firm. Leave in the tin for 10 minutes.

❄ To make the sauce, melt the butter in a small saucepan and fry the onion until dark golden brown. Add the mushrooms and cook for 2 minutes. Stir in the flour, cook gently for 1 minute, then gradually add the stock. Bring to the boil, stirring, until thickened and blended. Season to taste.

❄ Turn out the nut roast, slice and serve, garnished with parsley, with the fresh vegetables, accompanied by the sauce.

Nutty Harvest Loaf

25 g/1 oz butter, plus extra
  for greasing
450 g/1 lb floury potatoes,
  diced
1 onion, chopped
2 garlic cloves, crushed
125 g/4¹/₂ oz unsalted peanuts
75 g/2³/₄ oz fresh
  white breadcrumbs
1 egg, beaten
2 tbsp chopped coriander

150 ml/5 fl oz vegetable stock
75 g/2³/₄ oz sliced mushrooms
50 g/1³/₄ oz sun-dried
  tomatoes, sliced
salt and pepper

SAUCE
150 ml/5 fl oz crème fraîche
2 tsp tomato purée
2 tsp clear honey
2 tbsp chopped coriander

❄ Grease a 450-g/1-lb loaf tin. Bring a saucepan of lightly salted water to the boil, add the potatoes and cook for 10 minutes until cooked through. Drain well, mash and set aside.

❄ Melt half the butter in a frying pan. Add the onion and garlic and fry gently for 2–3 minutes until soft. Finely chop the nuts or process them in a food processor for 30 seconds with the breadcrumbs.

❄ Mix the chopped nuts and breadcrumbs into the potatoes with the egg, coriander and stock. Stir in the onion and garlic and mix well.

❄ Melt the remaining butter in the frying pan, add the sliced mushrooms and cook for 2–3 minutes.

❄ Press half the potato mixture into the base of the loaf tin. Spoon the mushrooms on top and sprinkle with the sun-dried tomatoes. Spoon the remaining potato mixture on top and smooth the surface. Cover with foil and bake in a preheated oven, 190°C/350°F/Gas Mark 5, for 1 hour or until firm to the touch.

❄ Meanwhile, mix the sauce ingredients together. Cut the nutty harvest loaf into slices and serve with the sauce.

Winter Vegetable Casserole

1 tbsp olive oil	6 tbsp dry white wine
1 red onion, halved and sliced	400 g/14 oz canned chickpeas,
3 garlic cloves, crushed	drained
225 g/8 oz spinach	1 bay leaf
1 fennel bulb, cut into eighths	1 tsp ground coriander
1 red pepper, deseeded and	1/2 tsp paprika
cubed	salt and pepper
1 tbsp plain flour	fennel fronds, to garnish
450 ml/16 fl oz vegetable stock	

❖ Heat the olive oil in a large flameproof casserole. Add the onion and garlic and sauté over a low heat, stirring frequently, for 1 minute. Add the spinach and cook, stirring occasionally, for 4 minutes or until wilted.

❖ Add the fennel and red pepper and cook, stirring constantly, for 2 minutes.

❖ Stir in the flour and cook, stirring constantly, for 1 minute.

❖ Add the stock, wine, chickpeas, bay leaf, coriander and paprika, cover and simmer for 30 minutes. Season to taste with salt and pepper, garnish with the fennel fronds and serve immediately, straight from the casserole.

Cold Weather Casserole

55 g/2 oz butter or	600 ml/1 pint vegetable stock
margarine	2 tbsp tomato purée
2 leeks, sliced	1 tsp dried thyme
2 carrots, sliced	2 bay leaves
2 potatoes, cut into bite-sized	salt and pepper
pieces	
1 swede, cut into bite-sized	**DUMPLINGS**
pieces	115 g/4 oz self-raising flour
2 courgettes, sliced	pinch of salt
1 fennel bulb, halved and sliced	55 g/2 oz suet
2 tbsp plain flour	2 tbsp chopped fresh parsley
425 g/15 oz canned butter	about 4 tbsp water
beans	

❖ Melt the butter in a large heavy-based saucepan over a low heat. Add the leeks, carrots, potatoes, swede, courgettes and fennel and cook, stirring occasionally, for 10 minutes. Stir in the flour and cook, stirring constantly, for 1 minute. Stir in the can juice from the beans, the stock, tomato purée, thyme and bay leaves and season to taste with salt and pepper. Bring to the boil, stirring constantly, then cover and simmer for 10 minutes.

❖ Meanwhile, make the dumplings. Sift the flour and salt into a bowl. Stir in the suet and parsley, then add enough water to bind to a soft dough. Divide the dough into 8 pieces and roll into balls.

❖ Add the butter beans and dumplings to the pan, cover and simmer for a further 30 minutes. Remove and discard the bay leaf before serving.

Chinese Vegetable Casserole

4 tbsp vegetable oil
2 carrots, sliced
1 courgette, sliced
4 baby sweetcorn cobs, halved
lengthways
125 g/4$\frac{1}{2}$ oz cauliflower florets
1 leek, sliced
125 g/4$\frac{1}{2}$ oz water chestnuts,
halved
225 g/8 oz firm tofu, cubed
300 ml/10 fl oz vegetable stock
1 tsp salt
2 tsp dark brown sugar
2 tsp dark soy sauce
2 tbsp dry sherry
1 tbsp cornflour
2 tbsp water
1 tbsp chopped fresh coriander,
to garnish

❖ Heat the oil in a preheated wok until it is almost smoking. Reduce the heat slightly, add the carrots, courgette, sweetcorn, cauliflower and leek to the wok and stir-fry for 2–3 minutes.

❖ Stir in the water chestnuts, tofu, stock, salt, sugar, soy sauce and sherry and bring to the boil. Reduce the heat, cover the pan and simmer for 20 minutes.

❖ Blend the cornflour with the water to form a smooth paste.

❖ Stir the cornflour mixture into the wok. Bring the sauce to the boil and cook, stirring constantly, until it thickens and clears.

❖ Transfer the casserole to a warmed serving dish, sprinkle with the coriander and serve immediately.

Italian Vegetable Stew

1 red onion, sliced
2 leeks, sliced
4 garlic cloves, finely chopped
1 small acorn squash, diced
1 aubergine, sliced
1 small celeriac, diced
2 turnips, sliced
2 plum tomatoes, chopped
1 carrot, sliced
1 courgette, sliced
2 red peppers, deseeded and
cut into strips
1 fennel bulb, sliced
175 g/6 oz chard or spinach
beet, chopped
2 bay leaves

^{1}/$_2$ tsp fennel seeds
^{1}/$_2$ tsp chilli powder
pinch of dried thyme
pinch of dried oregano
pinch of sugar
125 ml/4 fl oz extra virgin
olive oil
225 ml/8 fl oz vegetable stock
25 g/1 oz fresh basil leaves,
torn
4 tbsp chopped fresh flat-leaf
parsley
salt and pepper
2 tbsp freshly grated Parmesan
cheese, to serve (optional)

❊ Put the onion, leeks, garlic, squash, aubergine, celeriac, turnips, tomatoes, carrot, courgette, peppers, fennel, chard, bay leaves, fennel seeds, chilli powder, thyme, oregano, sugar, oil, stock and half the basil leaves in a large heavy-based saucepan. Mix well and bring to the boil.

❊ Reduce the heat, cover the pan and leave the vegetables to simmer for about 30 minutes, until tender.

❊ Sprinkle in the remaining basil and the parsley and season to taste with salt and pepper. Serve immediately, sprinkled with the cheese, if using.

Mushroom Stroganoff

1 onion
25 g/1 oz butter
450 g/1 lb closed-cup
mushrooms
1 tsp tomato purée
1 tsp coarse grain mustard

150 ml/5 fl oz crème fraîche
1 tsp paprika
salt and pepper
chopped fresh parsley,
to garnish

❊ Finely chop the onion. Heat the butter in a large heavy-based frying pan. Add the onion and cook gently for 5–10 minutes, until soft. Meanwhile, trim and quarter the mushrooms.

❊ Add the mushrooms to the frying pan and stir-fry for a few minutes until they begin to soften. Stir in the tomato purée and mustard, then add the crème fraîche. Cook gently, stirring constantly, for 5 minutes.

❊ Stir in the paprika and season to taste with salt and pepper. Garnish with the parsley and serve immediately.

Gnocchi with Tomato Sauce

350 g/12 oz floury potatoes, halved
85 g/3 oz self-raising flour, plus extra for dusting
2 tsp dried oregano
2 tbsp vegetable oil
1 large onion, chopped
2 garlic cloves, chopped
400 g/14 oz canned chopped tomatoes
1/2 vegetable stock cube dissolved in 100 ml/31/2 fl oz boiling water
2 tbsp fresh basil, shredded, plus whole leaves to garnish
salt and pepper
freshly grated Parmesan cheese, to serve

❖ Bring a large saucepan of water to the boil. Add the potatoes and cook for 12–15 minutes or until tender. Drain and set aside to cool.

❖ Peel and then mash the potatoes with the salt and pepper, sifted flour and oregano. Mix together with your hands to form a dough.

❖ Heat the oil in a saucepan. Add the onions and garlic and cook for 3–4 minutes. Add the tomatoes and stock and cook, uncovered, for 10 minutes. Season to taste with salt and pepper.

❖ Roll the potato dough into a sausage about 2.5 cm/ 1 inch in diameter. Cut the sausage into 2.5-cm/1-inch lengths. Flour your hands, then press a fork into each piece to create a series of ridges on one side and the indent of your index finger on the other.

❖ Bring a large saucepan of water to the boil, add the gnocchi in batches and cook for 2–3 minutes. They should rise to the surface when cooked. Remove from the pan with a slotted spoon, drain well and keep warm while you cook the remaining batches.

❖ Stir the basil into the tomato sauce and pour over the gnocchi. Garnish with basil leaves and season to taste with pepper. Sprinkle with the cheese and serve immediately.

Potato-Topped Lentil Bake

TOPPING	FILLING
675 g/1 lb 8 oz floury potatoes, diced	225 g/8 oz red lentils
25 g/1 oz butter	60 g/2 oz butter
1 tbsp milk	1 leek, sliced
50 g/13/4 oz chopped pecan nuts	2 garlic cloves, crushed
2 tbsp chopped thyme	1 celery stick, chopped
sprigs of fresh thyme, to garnish	125 g/41/2 oz broccoli florets
	175 g/6 oz smoked tofu, cubed
	2 tsp tomato purée
	salt and pepper

❖ To make the topping, bring a saucepan of lightly salted water to the boil and cook the potatoes for 10–15 minutes or until cooked through. Drain well, add the butter and milk and mash thoroughly. Stir in the pecan nuts and chopped thyme and set aside.

❖ Cook the lentils in boiling water for 20–30 minutes, or until tender. Drain and set aside.

❖ Melt the butter in a frying pan. Add the leek, garlic, celery and broccoli. Fry over a medium heat, stirring frequently, for 5 minutes until soft. Add the tofu cubes. Stir in the lentils, together with the tomato purée. Season to taste with salt and pepper, then turn the mixture into the base of a shallow ovenproof dish.

❖ Spoon the mashed potato on top of the lentil mixture, spreading to cover it completely.

❖ Cook in a preheated oven, 200°C/400°F/Gas Mark 6, for about 30–35 minutes or until the topping is golden. Garnish with the sprigs of thyme and serve hot.

Four Cheese & Potato Layer

900 g/2 lb unpeeled waxy potatoes, cut into wedges
25 g/1 oz butter
1 red onion, halved and sliced
2 garlic cloves, crushed
25 g/1 oz plain flour
600 ml/1 pint milk
400 g/14 oz canned artichoke hearts in brine, drained and halved
150 g/5^{1}/$_{2}$ oz frozen mixed vegetables, thawed
125 g/4^{1}/$_{2}$ oz grated Gruyère cheese
125 g/4^{1}/$_{2}$ oz grated mature Cheddar cheese
50 g/1^{3}/$_{4}$ oz crumbled Gorgonzola
25 g/1 oz grated Parmesan cheese
225 g/8 oz tofu, sliced
2 tbsp chopped thyme
salt and pepper
sprigs of fresh thyme, to garnish

❋ Bring a saucepan of lightly salted water to the boil and cook the potato wedges for 10 minutes. Drain thoroughly.

❋ Meanwhile, melt the butter in a saucepan. Add the sliced onion and garlic and fry over a low heat, stirring frequently, for 2–3 minutes.

❋ Stir the flour into the pan and cook for 1 minute. Gradually add the milk and bring to the boil, stirring constantly.

❋ Reduce the heat and add the artichoke hearts, mixed vegetables, half of each of the 4 cheeses and the tofu to the pan, mixing well. Stir in the chopped thyme and season to taste with salt and pepper.

❋ Arrange a layer of parboiled potato wedges in the base of a shallow ovenproof dish. Spoon the vegetable mixture over the top and cover with the remaining potato wedges. Sprinkle the rest of the 4 cheeses over the top.

❋ · Cook in a preheated oven, 200°C/400°F/Gas Mark 6, for 30 minutes or until the potatoes are cooked and the top is golden brown. Serve the layer garnished with the sprigs of thyme.

Potato & Vegetable Layer

500 g/1 lb 2 oz waxy potatoes, sliced
1 tbsp vegetable oil
1 onion, chopped
2 garlic cloves, crushed
500 g/1 lb 2 oz tofu, diced
2 tbsp tomato purée
2 tbsp plain flour
300 ml/10 fl oz vegetable stock
2 large tomatoes, sliced
1 aubergine, sliced
2 tbsp chopped fresh thyme
450 ml/16 fl oz natural yogurt
2 eggs, beaten
salt and pepper
salad, to serve

❉ Bring a saucepan of lightly salted water to the boil and cook the potatoes for 10 minutes until tender, but not breaking up. Drain and set aside.

❉ Heat the oil in a frying pan. Add the onion and garlic and fry, stirring occasionally, for 2–3 minutes.

❉ Add the tofu, tomato purée and flour and cook for 1 minute. Gradually stir in the stock and bring to the boil, stirring. Reduce the heat and simmer for 10 minutes.

❉ Arrange a layer of the potato slices in the base of a deep ovenproof dish. Spoon the tofu mixture evenly on top. Layer the sliced tomatoes, then the aubergine and, finally, the remaining potato slices on top of the tofu mixture, making sure that it is completely covered. Sprinkle with the thyme.

❉ Mix the yogurt and eggs together in a bowl and season to taste with salt and pepper. Spoon the yogurt topping over the sliced potatoes to cover them completely.

❉ Bake in a preheated oven, 190°C/375°F/Gas Mark 5, for about 35–45 minutes or until the topping is brown. Serve with a crisp salad.

Curried Vegetables

2 tbsp olive oil
1 onion, diced
1 tbsp garam masala
1/2 tsp ground cumin
1 tsp ground turmeric
400 g/14 oz canned chopped tomatoes in tomato juice
300 ml/10 fl oz vegetable stock
450 g/1 lb new potatoes, cut into chunks
280 g/10 oz cauliflower florets
55 g/2 oz flaked almonds
250 g/9 oz baby spinach leaves
naan bread, to serve

❉ Heat the oil in a saucepan over a medium–low heat, add the onion and spices and cook, stirring constantly, for 2–3 minutes, taking care not to burn the spices as they are cooking in a small amount of oil. Add the tomatoes and stock and bring to the boil, then reduce the heat, cover and simmer for 25 minutes.

❉ Meanwhile, put the potatoes into a separate saucepan, cover with cold water and bring to the boil. Reduce the heat, cover and simmer for 15 minutes. Add the cauliflower and return to the boil, then reduce the heat, cover and simmer for a further 10 minutes, or until just tender.

❉ While the vegetables are cooking, preheat the grill to medium. Spread the almonds out in a single layer on a baking tray and toast under the preheated grill, turning to brown evenly, for 1–2 minutes – watch constantly as they brown very quickly. Tip the almonds into a small dish and set aside.

❉ Add the spinach to the potatoes and cauliflower, stir into the water and simmer for 1 minute. Drain the vegetables and return to the pan. Stir in the curried tomato sauce. Transfer to a warmed serving dish, sprinkle over the toasted almonds and serve immediately with the naan bread.

Coconut Vegetable Curry

1 large aubergine, cut into
2.5-cm/1-inch cubes
2 tbsp salt
2 tbsp vegetable oil
2 garlic cloves, crushed
1 fresh green chilli,
deseeded and finely chopped
1 tsp grated root ginger
1 onion, finely chopped
2 tsp garam masala
8 cardamom pods
1 tsp ground turmeric
1 tbsp tomato purée

700 ml/1¼ pints vegetable
stock
1 tbsp lemon juice
225 g/8 oz potatoes, diced
225 g/8 oz small cauliflower
florets
225 g/8 oz okra, trimmed
225 g/8 oz frozen peas
150 ml/5 fl oz coconut milk
salt and pepper
flaked coconut, to garnish
naan bread, to serve

❖ Layer the aubergine cubes in a bowl, sprinkling with salt as you go. Set aside for 30 minutes.

❖ Rinse well under cold running water to remove all the salt. Drain and pat dry with kitchen paper. Set aside.

❖ Heat the oil in a large saucepan. Add the garlic, chilli, ginger, onion and spices and fry over a medium heat, stirring occasionally, for 4–5 minutes, until lightly browned.

❖ Stir in the tomato purée, stock, lemon juice, potatoes and cauliflower and mix well. Bring to the boil, reduce the heat, cover and simmer for 15 minutes.

❖ Stir in the aubergine, okra, peas and coconut milk and season to taste with salt and pepper. Return to the boil and continue to simmer, uncovered, for a further 10 minutes, or until tender. Remove and discard the cardamom pods.

❖ Pile on to a warmed serving platter, garnish with the flaked coconut and serve immediately with the naan bread.

Chickpea Curry

6 tbsp vegetable oil
2 onions, sliced
1 tsp finely chopped root
ginger
1 tsp ground cumin
1 tsp ground coriander
1 tsp fresh garlic, crushed
1 tsp chilli powder

2 fresh green chillies
1 tbsp fresh coriander leaves
150 ml/5 fl oz water
300 g/10½ oz potatoes
400 g/14 oz canned chickpeas,
drained and rinsed
1 tbsp lemon or lime juice
chapatis, to serve (optional)

❖ Heat the oil in a large saucepan over a medium heat.

❖ Add the onions to the pan and fry, stirring occasionally, until they are golden brown.

❖ Reduce the heat, add the ginger, ground cumin, ground coriander, garlic, chilli powder, chillies and fresh coriander to the pan and stir-fry for 2 minutes.

❖ Add the water to the mixture in the pan and stir to mix.

❖ Using a sharp knife, cut the potatoes into small cubes.

❖ Add the potatoes and chickpeas to the mixture in the pan, cover and simmer, stirring occasionally, for 5–7 minutes.

❖ Sprinkle the lemon juice over the curry.

❖ Transfer the chickpea curry to serving dishes. Serve the curry hot with the chapatis, if using.

Mixed Vegetable Balti

225 g/8 oz split yellow peas
3 tbsp vegetable oil
1 tsp onion seeds
2 onions, sliced
115 g/4 oz courgettes, sliced
115 g/4 oz potatoes, cut into
1-cm/^{1}/$_2$-inch cubes
115 g/4 oz carrots, sliced
1 small aubergine, sliced
225 g/8 oz tomatoes, chopped
300 ml/10 fl oz water
3 garlic cloves, chopped
1 tsp ground cumin
1 tsp ground coriander
1 tsp salt
2 fresh green chillies, deseeded
and sliced
^{1}/$_2$ tsp garam masala
2 tbsp chopped fresh coriander

✢ Put the split peas into a pan and cover with lightly salted water. Bring to the boil and simmer for 30 minutes. Drain the peas and keep warm.

✢ Heat the oil in a balti pan or wok, add the onion seeds and fry until they start popping.

✢ Add the onions and stir-fry over a medium heat until golden brown.

✢ Add the courgettes, potatoes, carrots and aubergine to the pan. Stir-fry the vegetables for about 2 minutes.

✢ Stir in the tomatoes, water, garlic, cumin, ground coriander, salt, chillies, garam masala and reserved split peas.

✢ Bring to the boil, then reduce the heat and simmer for 15 minutes until all the vegetables are tender.

✢ Stir the fresh coriander into the vegetables. Transfer to a warmed serving dish and serve immediately.

Spiced Cashew Nut Curry

❖ **SERVES 4** ❖

250 g/9 oz unsalted cashew
nuts
1 tsp coriander seeds
1 tsp cumin seeds
2 cardamom pods
1 tbsp sunflower oil
1 onion, thinly sliced
1 garlic clove, crushed
1 small fresh green chilli,
deseeded and chopped
1 cinnamon stick
1/4 tsp ground turmeric
4 tbsp coconut cream
300 ml/10 fl oz hot vegetable
stock
3 kaffir lime leaves, finely
shredded
salt and pepper
boiled jasmine rice, to serve

❖ Soak the cashew nuts in cold water overnight. Drain
thoroughly. Crush the coriander seeds, cumin seeds and
cardamom pods with a pestle and mortar.

❖ Heat the oil and stir-fry the onion and garlic for 2–3
minutes until soft but not brown. Add the chilli, crushed
spices, cinnamon stick and turmeric and stir-fry for a
further minute.

❖ Add the coconut cream and the hot stock to the pan.
Bring to the boil, then add the cashew nuts and lime leaves.

❖ Cover the pan, reduce the heat and simmer for about
20 minutes. Serve hot, accompanied by the jasmine rice.

Red Curry with Cashew Nuts

❖ **SERVES 4** ❖

250 ml/9 fl oz coconut milk
1 kaffir lime leaf
1/4 tsp light soy sauce
4 baby sweetcorn cobs, halved
lengthways
115 g/4 oz broccoli florets
115 g/4 oz French beans, cut
into pieces
4 tbsp cashew nuts
15 fresh basil leaves
1 tbsp chopped fresh coriander
1 tbsp chopped roasted
peanuts, to garnish

RED CURRY PASTE
7 fresh red chillies, deseeded
and blanched
2 tsp cumin seeds
2 tsp coriander seeds
2.5-cm/1-inch piece of
galangal, chopped
1/2 lemon grass stalk, chopped
1 tsp salt
grated rind of 1 lime
4 garlic cloves, chopped
3 shallots, chopped
2 kaffir lime leaves, shredded
1 tbsp vegetable oil

❖ To make the curry paste, grind all the ingredients in
a large mortar with a pestle or in a grinder. Alternatively,
process briefly in a food processor. (The quantity of red curry
paste is more than is required for this recipe. Store for up to
3 weeks in a sealed jar in the refrigerator.)

❖ Put a wok or large heavy-based frying pan over a high
heat, add 3 tablespoons of the red curry paste and stir until
it gives off its aroma. Reduce the heat to medium.

❖ Add the coconut milk, kaffir lime leaf, soy sauce, baby
sweetcorn, broccoli, French beans and cashew nuts. Bring
to the boil and simmer for about 10 minutes until the
vegetables are cooked but still crunchy.

❖ Remove and discard the lime leaf and stir in the basil
leaves and coriander. Transfer to a warmed serving dish,
garnish with the peanuts and serve.

Mixed Bean Stir-Fry

❖ SERVES 4 ❖

400 g/14 oz canned red kidney
beans
400 g/14 oz canned cannellini
beans
6 spring onions
200 g/7 oz canned pineapple
rings or pieces in natural
juice, chopped
2 tbsp pineapple juice
3–4 pieces of stem ginger
2 tbsp ginger syrup from
the jar

thinly pared rind of 1/2 lime
or lemon, cut into julienne
strips
2 tbsp lime or lemon juice
2 tbsp soy sauce
1 tsp cornflour
1 tbsp sesame oil
115 g/4 oz French beans, cut
into 4-cm/11/2-inch lengths
225 g/8 oz canned bamboo
shoots
salt and pepper

❖ Drain all the beans, rinse under cold water and drain again very thoroughly.

❖ Cut 4 spring onions into narrow diagonal slices. Thinly slice the remainder and reserve for a garnish.

❖ Combine the pineapple and juice, ginger and syrup, lime rind and juice, soy sauce and cornflour in a bowl.

❖ Heat the oil in the wok, swirling it around until really hot. Add the diagonally sliced spring onions and stir-fry for about a minute, then add the French beans. Drain and thinly slice the bamboo shoots, add to the pan and continue to stir-fry for 2 minutes.

❖ Add the pineapple and ginger mixture and bring just to the boil. Add the canned beans and stir until very hot – for about 1 minute.

❖ Season to taste with salt and pepper, sprinkle with the reserved spring onions and serve.

Green Lentil Pan-Fry

❖ SERVES 4 ❖

150 g/51/2 oz green lentils
4 tbsp butter or margarine
2 garlic cloves, crushed
2 tbsp olive oil
1 tbsp cider vinegar
1 red onion, cut into 8 pieces
55 g/2 oz baby sweetcorn cobs,
halved lengthways

1 yellow pepper, deseeded and
cut into strips
1 red pepper, deseeded and cut
into strips
55 g/2 oz French beans, halved
125 ml/4 fl oz vegetable stock
2 tbsp clear honey
salt and pepper
crusty bread, to serve

❖ Soak the lentils in a large saucepan of cold water for 25 minutes. Bring to the boil, reduce the heat and simmer for 20 minutes. Drain thoroughly.

❖ Add 1 tablespoon of the butter, 1 garlic clove, 1 tablespoon of the oil and the vinegar to the lentils and mix well.

❖ Melt the remaining butter and oil in a frying pan and stir-fry the remaining garlic, the onion, baby sweetcorn, peppers and French beans for 3–4 minutes.

❖ Add the stock and bring to the boil. Simmer for about 10 minutes or until the liquid has evaporated.

❖ Add the honey and season to taste. Stir in the lentil mixture and cook for 1 minute. Spoon on to warmed serving plates and serve with the bread.

Butternut Squash Stir-Fry

1 kg/2 lb 4 oz butternut squash,
peeled
3 tbsp groundnut oil
1 onion, sliced
2 cloves garlic, crushed
1 tsp coriander seeds
1 tsp cumin seeds
2 tbsp chopped fresh coriander
150 ml/5 fl oz coconut milk
100 ml/3½ fl oz water
100 g/3½ oz salted cashew
nuts

TO GARNISH
freshly grated lime rind
fresh coriander
lime wedges

❊ Slice the butternut squash into small bite-sized cubes, using a sharp knife.

❊ Heat the groundnut oil in a large preheated wok.

❊ Add the butternut squash, onion and garlic to the wok and stir-fry for 5 minutes.

❊ Stir in the coriander seeds, cumin seeds and chopped coriander, and stir-fry for
1 minute.

❊ Add the coconut milk and water to the wok and bring to the boil. Cover the wok and
leave to simmer for 10–15 minutes, or until the squash is tender.

❊ Add the cashew nuts and stir to combine thoroughly.

❊ Transfer to warmed serving dishes and garnish with the lime rind, fresh coriander and
lime wedges. Serve immediately.

Winter Vegetable Stir-Fry

❊ **SERVES 4** ❊

3 tbsp sesame oil
25 g/1 oz blanched almonds
1 large carrot, cut into thin strips
1 large turnip, cut into thin strips
1 onion, finely sliced
1 garlic clove, crushed
3 celery sticks, finely sliced
125 g/4½ oz Brussels sprouts, topped, tailed and halved
125 g/4½ oz cauliflower florets
125 g/4½ oz white cabbage, shredded
2 tsp sesame seeds
1 tsp grated root ginger
½ tsp chilli powder
1 tbsp chopped fresh coriander
1 tbsp light soy sauce
salt and pepper
sprigs of fresh coriander, to garnish

❊ Heat the oil in a wok or large frying pan. Stir-fry the almonds until lightly browned, then lift them out and drain on absorbent kitchen paper.

❊ Add all the vegetables, except the cabbage, to the wok and stir-fry briskly for 3–4 minutes.

❊ Add the cabbage, sesame seeds, ginger and chilli powder and cook, stirring, for 2 minutes.

❊ Stir in the chopped coriander, soy sauce and almonds. Season to taste. Serve the vegetables garnished with the sprigs of coriander.

Tofu Stir-Fry

❊ **SERVES 4** ❊

225 g/8 oz firm tofu
1 tbsp groundnut or sunflower oil
2 spring onions, chopped
1 garlic clove, finely chopped
115 g/4 oz mangetout
115 g/4 oz baby sweetcorn cobs, halved
115 g/4 oz shiitake mushrooms, thinly sliced
2 tbsp finely chopped coriander leaves

MARINADE
2 tbsp dark soy sauce
1 tbsp Chinese rice wine
2 tsp brown sugar
½ tsp Chinese five-spice powder
1 fresh red chilli, deseeded and finely chopped
2 spring onions, finely chopped
1 tbsp grated root ginger

❊ Combine all the marinade ingredients in a shallow non-metallic dish, whisking well to mix. Cut the tofu into bite-sized pieces, add to the marinade and turn to coat. Cover with clingfilm and set aside in the refrigerator to marinate for 2 hours, turning the tofu once or twice.

❊ Drain the tofu and reserve the marinade. Heat the oil in a wok. Add the tofu and stir-fry for 2–3 minutes, until golden. Remove and set aside. Add the spring onions and garlic and stir-fry for 2 minutes, then add the baby sweetcorn and stir-fry for 1 minute. Add the mangetout and mushrooms and stir-fry for 2 minutes.

❊ Return the tofu to the wok and add the marinade. Cook gently for 1–2 minutes until heated through. Sprinkle with the chopped coriander and serve immediately.

Sweet & Sour Tofu

❈ SERVES 4 ❈

2 celery sticks
1 carrot
1 green pepper, deseeded
75 g/2¾ oz mangetout
2 tbsp vegetable oil
2 garlic cloves, crushed
8 baby sweetcorn cobs
125 g/4½ oz beansprouts
450 g/1 lb tofu, cubed
rice or noodles, to serve

SAUCE
2 tbsp light brown sugar
2 tbsp wine vinegar
225 ml/8 fl oz vegetable stock
1 tsp tomato purée
1 tbsp cornflour

❈ Using a sharp knife, thinly slice the celery, cut the carrot into thin strips, dice the pepper and cut the mangetout in half diagonally.

❈ Heat the vegetable oil in a preheated wok until it is almost smoking. Reduce the heat slightly, add the crushed garlic, celery, carrot, pepper, mangetout and sweetcorn and stir-fry for 3–4 minutes.

❈ Add the bean sprouts and tofu to the wok and cook for 2 minutes, stirring well.

❈ To make the sauce, combine the sugar, vinegar, stock, tomato purée and cornflour, stirring well to mix. Stir into the wok, bring to the boil and cook, stirring, until the sauce thickens and clears. Continue to cook for 1 minute. Serve with the rice.

Vegetable Sesame Stir-Fry

❈ SERVES 4 ❈

2 tbsp vegetable oil
3 garlic cloves, crushed
1 tbsp sesame seeds, plus
   extra to garnish
2 celery sticks, sliced
2 baby sweetcorn cobs, sliced
60 g/2 oz button mushrooms
1 leek, sliced
1 courgette, sliced
1 small red pepper, deseeded
   and sliced
1 fresh green chilli, deseeded
   and sliced
60 g/2 oz Chinese leaves,
   shredded
rice or noodles, to serve

SAUCE
½ tsp Chinese curry powder
2 tbsp light soy sauce
1 tbsp Chinese rice wine or dry
   sherry
1 tsp sesame oil
1 tsp cornflour
4 tbsp water

❈ Heat the vegetable oil in a preheated wok or heavy-based frying pan, swirling the oil around the base of the wok until it is almost smoking.

❈ Reduce the heat slightly, add the garlic and sesame seeds to the wok and stir-fry for 30 seconds.

❈ Add the celery, baby sweetcorn, mushrooms, leek, courgette, pepper, chilli and Chinese leaves and stir-fry for 4–5 minutes, until the vegetables are just beginning to soften.

❈ To make the sauce, mix together the Chinese curry powder, light soy sauce, Chinese rice wine, sesame oil, cornflour and water.

❈ Add the sauce mixture to the wok and stir thoroughly to combine with the other ingredients.

❈ Bring the mixture to the boil and cook, stirring constantly, until the sauce thickens and clears.

❈ Cook the vegetables and sauce for 1 minute, spoon into a warmed serving dish and garnish with sesame seeds. Serve the stir-fry immediately with the rice.

Sweet & Sour Cauliflower

450 g/1 lb cauliflower florets
2 tbsp sunflower oil
1 onion, sliced
225 g/8 oz carrots, sliced
100 g/3$\frac{1}{2}$ oz mangetout
1 ripe mango, sliced
100 g/3$\frac{1}{2}$ oz beansprouts
3 tbsp chopped fresh coriander
3 tbsp fresh lime juice
1 tbsp clear honey
6 tbsp coconut milk

❖ Bring a large saucepan of water to the boil. Add the cauliflower to the pan and cook for 2 minutes. Drain the cauliflower thoroughly.

❖ Heat the sunflower oil in a large preheated wok. Add the onion and carrots to the wok and stir-fry for about 5 minutes.

❖ Add the drained cauliflower and mangetout to the wok and stir-fry for 2–3 minutes.

❖ Add the mango and beansprouts to the wok and stir-fry for about 2 minutes.

❖ Mix together the coriander, lime juice, honey and coconut milk in a bowl.

❖ Add the coriander and coconut mixture to the wok and stir-fry for about 2 minutes or until the juices are bubbling.

❖ Transfer the sweet and sour cauliflower stir-fry to serving dishes and serve immediately.

Simple
pasta, noodles & rice

Basil & Tomato Pasta

1 tbsp olive oil
2 sprigs rosemary
2 cloves garlic
450 g/1 lb tomatoes, halved
1 tbsp sun-dried tomato paste
12 fresh basil leaves, plus extra
to garnish
675 g/1 lb 8 oz fresh farfalle or
350 g/12 oz dried farfalle
salt and pepper

❉ Place the oil, rosemary, garlic and tomatoes, skin side up, in a shallow roasting tin.

❉ Drizzle with a little oil and cook under a preheated grill for 20 minutes or until the tomato skins are slightly charred.

❉ Peel the skin from the tomatoes. Roughly chop the tomato flesh and place in a saucepan.

❉ Squeeze the pulp from the garlic cloves and mix with the tomato flesh and sun-dried tomato paste.

❉ Roughly tear the fresh basil leaves into smaller pieces and then stir them into the sauce. Season to taste with a little salt and pepper. Set aside.

❉ Cook the farfalle in a saucepan of boiling water for 8–10 minutes or until it is tender but still firm to the bite. Drain well.

❉ Gently reheat the tomato and basil sauce, stirring constantly.

❉ Transfer the farfalle to serving plates and pour over the basil and tomato sauce. Serve at once.

Wild Mushroom Linguine

225 g/8 oz mixed wild
mushrooms
450 g/1 lb dried linguine
55 g/2 oz butter
1 garlic clove, crushed
250 g/9 oz mascarpone cheese
2 tbsp milk
1 tsp chopped fresh sage
salt and pepper
freshly grated Parmesan cheese,
to serve

❉ Slice the mushrooms. Bring a large saucepan of lightly salted water to the boil and cook the pasta for 10–12 minutes or according to the packet instructions, until tender but still firm to the bite.

❉ Meanwhile, melt the butter in a separate large saucepan. Add the garlic and sliced mushrooms and cook for 3–4 minutes.

❉ Reduce the heat and stir in the mascarpone cheese, milk and sage. Season to taste with salt and pepper.

❉ Drain the pasta thoroughly and add to the mushroom sauce. Toss until the pasta is well coated with the sauce. Transfer to warmed dishes and serve immediately with the Parmesan cheese.

Tomato & Olive Fettuccine

4 plum tomatoes, peeled, deseeded and chopped
4 garlic cloves, finely chopped
8 black olives, stoned and finely chopped
1 fresh red chilli, deseeded and finely chopped
2 tbsp chopped fresh flat-leaf parsley
2 tbsp extra virgin olive oil
1 tbsp lemon juice
280 g/10 oz dried fettuccine
salt and pepper

❄ Place the tomatoes in a large non-metallic sieve set over a bowl. Cover and set aside in the refrigerator for 30 minutes.

❄ Combine the garlic, olives, chilli, parsley, oil and lemon juice in a separate bowl. Season to taste with salt and pepper. Cover and set aside in the refrigerator until required.

❄ Add the tomatoes to the garlic mixture, discarding the drained juice.

❄ Bring a large saucepan of lightly salted water to the boil. Add the fettuccine, return to the boil and cook for 8–10 minutes or until tender but still firm to the bite. Drain, then tip into a serving bowl. Add the garlic and tomato mixture and toss well. Serve immediately.

Spinach & Mushroom Pasta

300 g/10½ oz dried penne or pasta shape of your choice
2 tbsp olive oil
250 g/9 oz mushrooms, sliced
1 tsp dried oregano
250 ml/9 fl oz vegetable stock
1 tbsp lemon juice
6 tbsp cream cheese
200 g/7 oz frozen spinach leaves
salt and pepper

❄ Bring a large saucepan of lightly salted water to the boil and cook the pasta according to the packet instructions. Drain, reserving 175 ml/6 fl oz of the cooking liquid.

❄ Meanwhile, heat the oil in a large heavy-based frying pan over a medium heat, add the mushrooms and cook, stirring frequently, for 8 minutes, or until almost crisp. Stir in the oregano, stock and lemon juice and cook for 10–12 minutes, or until the sauce is reduced by half.

❄ Stir in the cream cheese and spinach and cook over a medium–low heat for 3–5 minutes. Add the reserved cooking liquid, then the cooked pasta. Stir well, season to taste with salt and pepper and heat through before serving.

Sicilian Spaghetti

❖ **SERVES 6** ❖

150 ml/5 fl oz olive oil, plus extra for brushing
2 aubergines
350 g/12 oz minced beef
1 onion, chopped
2 garlic cloves, crushed
2 tbsp tomato purée
400 g/14 oz canned chopped tomatoes
1 tsp Worcestershire sauce
1 tsp chopped fresh marjoram or oregano, or $1/2$ tsp dried marjoram or oregano
60 g/2 oz stoned black olives, sliced
1 green, red or yellow pepper, cored, deseeded and chopped
175 g/6 oz dried spaghetti
115 g/4 oz freshly grated Parmesan cheese
salt and pepper
sprigs of fresh oregano or parsley, to garnish

❖ Brush a 20-cm/8-inch loose-based round cake tin with oil, line the base with baking paper and brush with oil.

❖ Slice the aubergines. Heat a little oil in a frying pan and fry the aubergines in batches for 3–4 minutes or until brown on both sides. Add more oil, as necessary. Drain on kitchen paper.

❖ Put the minced beef, onion and garlic in a saucepan and cook over a medium heat, stirring occasionally, until brown. Add the tomato purée, tomatoes, Worcestershire sauce, marjoram and salt and pepper to taste. Leave to simmer, stirring occasionally, for 10 minutes. Add the olives and chopped pepper and cook for a further 10 minutes.

❖ Bring a saucepan of lightly salted water to the boil. Add the spaghetti and 1 tablespoon of the oil and cook for 8–10 minutes until tender but still firm to the bite. Drain and turn the spaghetti into a bowl. Add the meat mixture and cheese and toss with 2 forks.

❖ Arrange aubergine slices over the base and up the sides of the cake tin. Add the spaghetti, pressing down firmly, then cover with the rest of the aubergine slices. Bake in a preheated oven, 200°C/400°F/Gas Mark 6, for 40 minutes. Leave to stand for 5 minutes, then invert on to a serving dish. Discard the baking paper. Garnish with the fresh herbs and serve.

Aubergine Pasta

150 ml/5 fl oz vegetable stock
150 ml/5 fl oz white wine
vinegar
2 tsp balsamic vinegar
3 tbsp olive oil
sprig of fresh oregano
450 g/1 lb aubergines, peeled
and thinly sliced
400 g/14 oz dried linguine

MARINADE
2 tbsp extra virgin olive oil
2 garlic cloves, crushed
2 tbsp chopped fresh oregano
2 tbsp finely chopped roasted
almonds
2 tbsp diced red pepper
2 tbsp lime juice
grated rind and juice of
1 orange
salt and pepper

❄ Put the stock, wine vinegar and balsamic vinegar into a saucepan and bring to the boil over a low heat. Add 2 teaspoons of the olive oil and the sprig of oregano and simmer gently for about 1 minute.

❄ Add the aubergine slices to the pan, remove from the heat and set aside for 10 minutes.

❄ Meanwhile make the marinade. Combine the oil, garlic, oregano, almonds, red pepper, lime juice, orange rind and orange juice in a large bowl and season to taste.

❄ Carefully remove the aubergine from the saucepan with a slotted spoon, and drain well. Add the aubergine slices to the marinade, mixing well, and set aside in the refrigerator for about 12 hours.

❄ Bring a large saucepan of lightly salted water to the boil. Add half of the remaining oil and the linguine and cook for 8–10 minutes until just tender. Drain the pasta thoroughly and toss with the remaining oil while still warm. Arrange the pasta on a serving plate with the aubergine slices and the marinade and serve.

Green Garlic Tagliatelle

2 tbsp walnut oil
1 bunch spring onions, sliced
2 garlic cloves, thinly sliced
225 g/8 oz mushrooms, sliced
500 g/1 lb 2 oz fresh green and
white tagliatelle
225 g/8 oz frozen chopped leaf
spinach, thawed and drained
125 g/4 oz full-fat soft cheese
with garlic and herbs

4 tbsp single cream
60 g/2 oz chopped, unsalted
pistachio nuts
2 tbsp shredded fresh basil
salt and pepper
sprigs of fresh basil, to garnish
Italian bread, to serve

❄ Gently heat the oil in a wok or frying pan and fry the spring onions and garlic for 1 minute or until just softened. Add the mushrooms, stir well, cover and cook gently for 5 minutes or until softened.

❄ Meanwhile, bring a large saucepan of lightly salted water to the boil and cook the pasta for 3–5 minutes or until just tender. Drain the pasta thoroughly and return to the pan.

❄ Add the spinach to the mushrooms and heat through for 1–2 minutes. Add the cheese and allow to melt slightly. Stir in the cream and continue to heat without allowing to boil.

❄ Pour the mixture over the pasta, season to taste and mix well. Heat gently, stirring, for 2–3 minutes.

❄ Pile into a warmed serving bowl and sprinkle over the pistachio nuts and shredded basil. Garnish with the sprigs of basil and serve with the bread.

Tagliatelle with Pumpkin

❊ SERVES 4 ❊

500 g/1 lb 2 oz pumpkin or
butternut squash
2 tbsp olive oil
1 onion, finely chopped
2 garlic cloves, crushed
4–6 tbsp chopped fresh parsley
good pinch of ground or freshly
grated nutmeg
about 250 ml/9 fl oz chicken or
vegetable stock

125 g/4$\frac{1}{2}$ oz Parma ham,
cut into narrow strips
275 g/9 oz tagliatelle, green or
white (fresh or dried)
150 ml/5 fl oz double cream
salt and pepper
freshly grated Parmesan
cheese, to serve

❊ Peel the pumpkin and scoop out the seeds and the membrane. Cut the flesh into 1-cm/$\frac{1}{2}$-inch dice.

❊ Heat the olive oil in a saucepan and gently fry the onion and garlic until soft. Add half the parsley and fry for 1–2 minutes.

❊ Add the pumpkin and continue to cook for 2–3 minutes. Season well with salt and pepper and nutmeg.

❊ Add half the stock, bring to the boil, cover and simmer for about 10 minutes or until the pumpkin is tender, adding more stock as necessary. Add the ham and continue to cook for 2 minutes, stirring frequently.

❊ Meanwhile, bring a large saucepan of lightly salted water to the boil and cook the tagliatelle, allowing 3–4 minutes for fresh pasta or 8–10 minutes for dried. Drain thoroughly and turn into a warmed dish.

❊ Add the cream to the ham mixture and heat gently. Season and spoon over the pasta. Sprinkle with the remaining parsley and serve, handing around the cheese separately.

Creamy Pasta with Peas

❊ SERVES 4 ❊

450 g/1 lb mixed plain and
green dried tagliarini or
spaghetti
55 g/2 oz unsalted butter
900 g/2 lb fresh peas, shelled
200 ml/7 fl oz double cream

55 g/2 oz freshly grated
pecorino cheese, plus extra
to serve
pinch of freshly grated nutmeg
salt and pepper

❊ Bring a large saucepan of lightly salted water to the boil. Add the pasta, bring back to the boil and simmer for 8–10 minutes until tender but still firm to the bite.

❊ Meanwhile, melt the butter in a wok or heavy-based saucepan. Add the peas and cook over a low heat, stirring frequently, for 4–5 minutes. Pour in 150 ml/5 fl oz of the cream, bring to the boil and simmer for 1 minute.

❊ When the pasta is cooked, drain well and add to the peas. Pour in the remaining cream, add the cheese and season to taste with nutmeg and salt and pepper. Toss well, then transfer to a warmed serving dish and serve immediately, handing around the grated cheese separately.

Stuffed Cannelloni

❖ SERVES 4 ❖

8 dried cannelloni tubes
1 tbsp olive oil
25 g/1 oz freshly grated
Parmesan cheese
sprigs of fresh herbs, to
garnish

FILLING
25 g/1 oz butter
300 g/10^1/$_2$ oz frozen spinach,
thawed and chopped
115 g/4 oz ricotta cheese
25 g/1 oz freshly grated
Parmesan cheese
60 g/2 oz chopped ham
pinch of freshly grated nutmeg
2 tbsp double cream
2 eggs, lightly beaten
salt and pepper

SAUCE
25 g/1 oz butter
25 g/1 oz plain flour
300 ml/10 fl oz milk
2 bay leaves
pinch of freshly grated nutmeg

❖ To make the filling, melt the butter in a saucepan and stir-fry the spinach for 2–3 minutes. Remove from the heat and stir in the ricotta and Parmesan cheeses and the ham. Season to taste with nutmeg and salt and pepper. Beat in the cream and eggs to make a thick paste.

❖ Bring a saucepan of lightly salted water to the boil. Add the pasta and the oil and cook for 10–12 minutes or until almost tender. Drain and set aside to cool.

❖ To make the sauce, melt the butter in a saucepan. Stir in the flour and cook, stirring, for 1 minute. Gradually stir in the milk. Add the bay leaves and simmer, stirring, for 5 minutes. Add the nutmeg and salt and pepper to taste. Remove from the heat and discard the bay leaves.

❖ Spoon the filling into a piping bag and fill the cannelloni.

❖ Spoon a little sauce into the base of an ovenproof dish. Arrange the cannelloni in the dish in a single layer and pour over the remaining sauce. Sprinkle over the Parmesan cheese and bake in a preheated oven, 190°C/375°F/Gas Mark 5, for 40–45 minutes. Garnish with the herbs and serve.

Basil & Pine Kernel Pesto

about 40 fresh basil leaves, washed and dried
3 garlic cloves, crushed
25 g/1 oz pine kernels
50 g/1¾ oz Parmesan cheese, finely grated
2–3 tbsp extra virgin olive oil
675 g/1 lb 8 oz fresh pasta or 350 g/12 oz dried pasta
salt and pepper

❊ Put the basil, garlic, pine kernels and cheese into a food processor and blend for about 30 seconds or until smooth. Alternatively, pound all of the ingredients by hand, using a mortar and pestle.

❊ If you are using a food processor, keep the motor running and slowly add the olive oil. Alternatively, add the oil drop by drop while stirring briskly. Season to taste with salt and pepper.

❊ Bring a large saucepan of lightly salted water to the boil and cook the pasta, allowing 3–4 minutes for fresh pasta or 8–10 minutes for dried, or until it is cooked through but still firm to the bite. Drain the pasta thoroughly in a colander.

❊ Transfer the pasta to a serving plate and add the pesto. Toss to mix well and serve hot.

Spinach & Ricotta Shells

400 g/14 oz dried lumache rigate grande
5 tbsp olive oil
60 g/2 oz fresh white breadcrumbs
125 ml/4 fl oz milk
300 g/10½ oz frozen spinach, thawed and drained
225 g/8 oz ricotta cheese
pinch of freshly grated nutmeg
400 g/14 oz canned chopped tomatoes, drained
1 garlic clove, crushed
salt and pepper

❊ Bring a large saucepan of lightly salted water to the boil. Add the pasta and 1 tablespoon of the olive oil and cook for 8–10 minutes until just tender, but still firm to the bite. Drain the pasta, refresh under cold water and set aside until required.

❊ Put the breadcrumbs, milk and 3 tablespoons of the remaining olive oil in a food processor and work to combine.

❊ Add the spinach and ricotta cheese to the food processor and work to a smooth mixture. Transfer to a bowl, stir in the nutmeg and season to taste with salt and pepper.

❊ Mix together the tomatoes, garlic and the remaining oil and spoon the mixture into the base of a large ovenproof dish.

❊ Using a teaspoon, fill the lumache with the spinach and ricotta mixture and arrange on top of the tomato mixture in the dish. Cover and bake in a preheated oven, 180°C/350°F/Gas Mark 4, for 20 minutes. Serve hot.

Tagliarini with Gorgonzola

❖ SERVES 4 ❖

25 g/1 oz butter
225 g/8 oz Gorgonzola cheese, roughly crumbled
150 ml/5 fl oz double cream
2 tbsp dry white wine
1 tsp cornflour

4 sprigs fresh sage, finely chopped
400 g/14 oz dried tagliarini
2 tbsp olive oil
salt and white pepper

❖ Melt the butter in a heavy-based saucepan. Stir in 175 g/6 oz of the cheese and melt, over a low heat, for about 2 minutes.

❖ Add the cream, wine and cornflour and beat with a whisk until fully incorporated.

❖ Stir in the sage and season to taste with salt and pepper. Bring to the boil over a low heat, whisking constantly, until the sauce thickens. Remove from the heat and set aside while you cook the pasta.

❖ Bring a large saucepan of lightly salted water to the boil. Add the tagliarini and 1 tablespoon of the olive oil. Cook the pasta for 8–10 minutes or until just tender, drain thoroughly and toss in the remaining olive oil. Transfer the pasta to a serving dish and keep warm.

❖ Reheat the sauce over a low heat, whisking constantly. Spoon the Gorgonzola sauce over the tagliarini, generously sprinkle over the remaining cheese and serve immediately.

Golden Macaroni Cheese

❖ SERVES 4 ❖

200 g/7 oz dried elbow macaroni
1 onion, sliced
4 hard-boiled eggs, quartered
4 cherry tomatoes, halved
3 tbsp dried breadcrumbs
2 tbsp finely grated Red Leicester cheese

CHEESE SAUCE
40 g/1½ oz butter
5 tbsp plain flour
600 ml/1 pint milk
140 g/5 oz Red Leicester cheese, grated
salt and cayenne pepper

❖ Preheat the grill to medium. Bring a large, heavy-based saucepan of lightly salted water to the boil. Add the macaroni and sliced onion, return to the boil and cook for 8–10 minutes, or until the pasta is tender but still firm to the bite. Drain well and tip the macaroni and onion into an ovenproof dish.

❖ To make the cheese sauce, melt the butter in a saucepan. Stir in the flour and cook, stirring constantly, for 1–2 minutes. Remove the saucepan from the heat and gradually whisk in the milk. Return the saucepan to the heat and bring to the boil, whisking constantly. Simmer for 2 minutes or until the sauce is thick and glossy. Remove the saucepan from the heat, stir in the cheese and season to taste with salt and cayenne pepper.

❖ Pour the sauce over the macaroni, add the eggs and mix lightly. Arrange the tomato halves on top. Mix the breadcrumbs with the finely grated cheese and sprinkle over the surface. Cook under the preheated hot grill for 3–4 minutes, or until the topping is golden and bubbling. Serve immediately.

Spicy Tomato Tagliatelle

50 g/1¾ oz butter
1 onion, finely chopped
1 garlic clove, crushed
2 small red chillies,
deseeded and diced
450 g/1 lb fresh tomatoes,
peeled, deseeded and diced
200 ml/7 fl oz vegetable stock
2 tbsp tomato purée
1 tsp sugar
675 g/1 lb 8 oz fresh green and
white tagliatelle, or
350 g/12 oz dried tagliatelle
salt and pepper

❖   Melt the butter in a large saucepan. Add the onion and garlic and cook for 3–4 minutes or until soft.

❖   Add the chillies to the pan and continue cooking for about 2 minutes.

❖   Add the tomatoes and stock, reduce the heat and leave to simmer for 10 minutes, stirring.

❖   Pour the sauce into a food processor and blend for 1 minute until smooth. Alternatively, push the sauce through a sieve.

❖   Return the sauce to the pan and add the tomato purée, sugar and salt and pepper to taste. Gently reheat over a low heat, until piping hot.

❖   Bring a saucepan of lightly salted water to the boil and cook the tagliatelle for 8–10 minutes or until it is tender but still firm to the bite. Drain the tagliatelle, transfer to serving plates and serve with the tomato sauce.

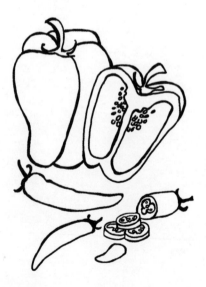

Pasta with Nuts & Cheese

225 g/8 oz pine kernels
350 g/12 oz dried pasta shapes
2 courgettes, sliced
225 g/8 oz broccoli,
broken into florets
200 g/7 oz full-fat soft cheese
150 ml/5 fl oz milk
1 tbsp chopped fresh basil

125 g/4½ oz button
mushrooms, sliced
90 g/3 oz blue cheese,
crumbled
salt and pepper
sprigs of fresh basil, to garnish
green salad, to serve

❄ Scatter the pine kernels on a baking tray and grill, turning occasionally, until lightly browned all over. Set aside.

❄ Bring a large saucepan of lightly salted water to the boil and cook the pasta for 8–10 minutes or until just tender but still firm to the bite.

❄ Meanwhile, bring a saucepan of lightly salted water to the boil and cook the courgettes and broccoli for about 5 minutes or until just tender.

❄ Put the soft cheese into a saucepan and heat gently, stirring constantly. Add the milk and stir to mix. Add the basil and mushrooms and cook gently for 2–3 minutes. Stir in the blue cheese and season to taste.

❄ Drain the pasta and the vegetables and mix together. Pour over the cheese and mushroom sauce and add the pine kernels. Toss gently to mix. Garnish with the sprigs of basil and serve with the green salad.

Penne with Walnut Sauce

25 g/1 oz butter
3 tbsp olive oil
2 red onions, thinly sliced
450 g/1 lb courgettes, thinly
sliced
375 g/12 oz dried penne
55 g/2 oz chopped walnuts

3 tbsp chopped fresh flat-leaf
parsley
2 tbsp crème fraîche
salt and pepper
2 tbsp freshly grated Parmesan
cheese, for sprinkling

❄ Melt the butter with the oil in a large heavy-based frying pan. Add the onions, cover and cook over a low heat, stirring occasionally, for 5 minutes until soft. Add the courgettes to the pan, cover and cook, stirring occasionally, for 15–20 minutes until the vegetables are very tender.

❄ Bring a large saucepan of lightly salted water to the boil. Add the pasta, bring back to the boil and simmer for 8–10 minutes, until the pasta is tender, but still firm to the bite.

❄ Meanwhile, stir the walnuts, parsley and crème fraîche into the courgette mixture and add salt and pepper to taste.

❄ Drain the pasta and tip into a serving dish. Add the courgette mixture and toss well. Sprinkle over the cheese and serve the pasta immediately.

Fettuccine all' Alfredo

❊ **SERVES 4** ❊

2 tbsp butter
200 ml/7 fl oz double cream
450 g/1 lb fresh fettuccine
85 g/3 oz freshly grated
Parmesan cheese, plus extra
to serve

pinch of freshly grated nutmeg
salt and pepper
sprig of fresh flat-leaf parsley,
to garnish

❊ Put the butter and 150 ml/5 fl oz of the cream into a large saucepan and bring the mixture to the boil over a medium heat. Reduce the heat, then simmer gently for 1¹/₂ minutes, or until the cream has thickened slightly.

❊ Meanwhile, bring a large saucepan of lightly salted water to the boil over a medium heat. Add the pasta and cook for 2–3 minutes or until tender but still firm to the bite. Drain thoroughly and return to the pan, then pour over the cream sauce.

❊ Toss the pasta in the sauce over a low heat, stirring with a wooden spoon, until coated thoroughly.

❊ Add the remaining cream, the cheese and the nutmeg to the pasta mixture and season to taste with salt and pepper. Toss the pasta in the mixture while heating through.

❊ Transfer the pasta mixture to a warmed serving plate and garnish with the parsley. Serve immediately with Parmesan cheese.

Parsley Chicken Spaghetti

❊ **SERVES 4** ❊

1 tbsp olive oil
thinly pared rind of 1 lemon,
cut into julienne strips
1 tsp finely chopped fresh
root ginger
1 tsp sugar
225 ml/8 fl oz chicken stock
250 g/9 oz dried spaghetti

55 g/2 oz butter
225 g/8 oz skinless, boneless
chicken breasts, diced
1 red onion, finely chopped
leaves from 2 bunches of
flat-leaf parsley
salt

❊ Heat the oil in a heavy-based saucepan. Add the lemon rind and cook over a low heat, stirring frequently, for 5 minutes. Stir in the ginger and sugar, season to taste with salt and cook, stirring constantly, for a further 2 minutes. Pour in the stock, bring to the boil, then cook for 5 minutes or until the liquid has reduced by half.

❊ Meanwhile, bring a large heavy-based saucepan of lightly salted water to the boil. Add the pasta, return to the boil and cook for 8–10 minutes or until tender but still firm to the bite.

❊ Meanwhile, melt half the butter in a frying pan. Add the chicken and onion and cook, stirring frequently, for 5 minutes or until the chicken is lightly browned all over. Stir in the lemon and ginger mixture and cook for 1 minute. Stir in the parsley leaves and cook, stirring constantly, for a further 3 minutes.

❊ Drain the pasta and transfer to a warmed serving dish, then add the remaining butter and toss well. Add the chicken sauce, toss again and serve.

Chicken Lasagne

❊ SERVES 4 ❊

350 g/12 oz fresh lasagne
(about 9 sheets) or
150 g/5$\frac{1}{2}$ oz dried lasagne
(about 9 sheets)
1 tbsp olive oil
1 red onion, finely chopped
1 garlic clove, crushed
100 g/3$\frac{1}{2}$ oz mushrooms,
wiped and sliced
350 g/12 oz chicken breast, cut
into chunks
150 ml/5 fl oz red wine,
diluted with 100 ml/3$\frac{1}{2}$ fl oz
water
250 g/9 oz passata
1 tsp sugar
freshly grated Parmesan
cheese, for sprinkling

BÉCHAMEL SAUCE
75 g/2$\frac{3}{4}$ oz butter
50 g/1$\frac{3}{4}$ oz plain flour
600 ml/1 pint milk
1 egg, beaten
75 g/2$\frac{3}{4}$ oz freshly grated
Parmesan cheese
salt and pepper

❊   Bring a large saucepan of lightly salted water to the boil and cook the lasagne according to the instructions on the packet. Lightly grease a deep ovenproof dish.

❊   Heat the oil in a pan. Add the onion and garlic and cook for 3–4 minutes. Add the mushrooms and chicken and stir-fry for 4 minutes or until the meat browns.

❊   Add the wine, bring to the boil, then simmer for 5 minutes. Stir in the passata and sugar and cook for 3–5 minutes until the meat is tender and cooked through. The sauce should have thickened, but still be quite runny.

❊   To make the sauce, melt the butter in a saucepan, stir in the flour and cook for 2 minutes. Remove the pan from the heat and gradually add the milk, mixing to form a smooth sauce. Return the pan to the heat and bring to the boil, stirring until thickened. Leave to cool slightly, then beat in the egg and half the cheese. Season to taste.

❊   Place 3 sheets of lasagne in the base of the dish and spread with half of the chicken mixture. Repeat the layers. Top with the last 3 sheets of lasagne, pour over the sauce and sprinkle with the cheese. Bake in a preheated oven, 190°C/375°F/Gas Mark 5, for 30 minutes until golden and the pasta is cooked.

Orecchiette with Chicken

800 g/1 lb 12 oz canned chopped tomatoes
4 dried red chillies
3 tbsp olive oil
1 onion, chopped
115 g/4 oz skinless, boneless chicken breast, cut into thin strips
350 g/12 oz mushrooms, sliced
3 garlic cloves, finely chopped
90 g/3 oz black olives
125 ml/4 fl oz dry white wine
450 g/1 lb dried orecchiette
2 tbsp chopped fresh flat-leaf parsley
salt and pepper

❊   Place the tomatoes and their can juices in a large heavy-based pan with the chillies. Bring to the boil, then simmer gently for 20 minutes, or until reduced.

❊   Meanwhile, heat 2 tablespoons of the olive oil in a heavy-based frying pan. Add the onion and cook over a low heat, stirring occasionally, for 5 minutes or until softened. Add the chicken and cook, stirring frequently, for 8 minutes or until golden brown. Add the mushrooms and garlic and cook, stirring frequently, for an additional 5 minutes. Add the olives and wine and cook for 3–5 minutes, or until reduced.

❊   While the chicken mixture is cooking, bring a saucepan of lightly salted water to the boil. Add the pasta, return to the boil, and cook for 8–10 minutes, or until tender but still firm to the bite. Rub the tomato and chilli mixture through a sieve into a bowl and set aside.

❊   Drain the pasta well and transfer to a warmed serving dish. Stir the reserved tomato sauce into the chicken mixture with the parsley, season to taste with salt and pepper and spoon over the pasta. Toss lightly and serve.

Artichoke Chicken Linguine

4 chicken breasts, skinned
finely grated rind and juice of 1 lemon
2 tbsp olive oil
2 garlic cloves, crushed
400 g/14 oz canned artichoke hearts, drained and sliced
250 g/9 oz baby plum tomatoes
300 g/10$\frac{1}{2}$ oz dried linguine
chopped fresh parsley and freshly grated Parmesan cheese, to serve

❊   Put each chicken breast in turn between 2 pieces of clingfilm and bash with a rolling pin to flatten. Put the chicken into a shallow non-metallic dish with the lemon rind and juice and 1 tablespoon of the oil and turn to coat in the marinade. Cover and leave to marinate in the refrigerator for 30 minutes.

❊   Heat the remaining oil in a frying pan over a low heat, add the garlic and cook for 1 minute, stirring frequently. Add the artichokes and tomatoes and cook for 5 minutes, stirring occasionally. Add about half the marinade from the chicken and cook over a medium heat for a further 5 minutes.

❊   Meanwhile, preheat the grill to high. Remove the chicken from the remaining marinade and arrange on the grill pan. Cook the chicken under the preheated grill for 5 minutes each side until thoroughly cooked through.

❊   Meanwhile, bring a large saucepan of lightly salted water to the boil, add the linguine to the boiling water and cook for 7–9 minutes or until just tender. Drain the pasta and return to the saucepan, pour over the artichoke and tomato mixture and slice in the cooked chicken.

❊   Divide between 4 warmed plates and scatter over the parsley and cheese.

Mustard Baked Chicken

8 chicken pieces (about   1 tsp paprika
115 g/4 oz each)   3 tbsp poppy seeds
60g/2 oz butter, melted   400 g/14 oz fresh pasta shells
4 tbsp mild mustard   1 tbsp olive oil
2 tbsp lemon juice   salt and pepper
1 tbsp brown sugar

❊ Arrange the chicken pieces in a single layer in a large ovenproof dish.

❊ Mix together the butter, mustard, lemon juice, sugar and paprika in a bowl and season to taste with salt and pepper. Brush half the mixture over the upper surfaces of the chicken pieces and bake in a preheated oven, 200°C/400°F/Gas Mark 6, for 15 minutes.

❊ Remove the dish from the oven and carefully turn over the chicken pieces. Coat the upper surfaces of the chicken with the remaining mustard mixture, sprinkle the chicken pieces with the poppy seeds and return to the oven for a further 15 minutes.

❊ Meanwhile, bring a large saucepan of lightly salted water to the boil. Add the pasta shells and olive oil and cook for 3–4 minutes or until the pasta is tender, but still firm to the bite.

❊ Drain the pasta thoroughly and arrange on a warmed serving dish. Top the pasta with the chicken, pour over the sauce and serve immediately.

Grilled Chicken with Lemon

4 chicken quarters   2 sprigs fresh thyme
grated rind and juice of 2 lemons   14 oz/400 g dried tagliatelle
4 tbsp olive oil   salt and pepper
2 garlic cloves, crushed

❊ Prick the skin of the chicken quarters all over with a fork. Put the chicken pieces in a dish, add the lemon juice, oil, garlic, thyme, salt and pepper and mix well. Cover and leave to marinate in the fridge for at least 2 hours.

❊ To cook the chicken, preheat the grill. Put the chicken in a grill pan and baste with the marinade. Cook for 30–40 minutes, basting and turning occasionally, until the chicken is tender. (To test if the chicken is cooked, pierce the thickest part of the chicken pieces with a skewer. If the juices run clear the chicken is cooked.)

❊ Meanwhile, bring a large saucepan of lightly salted water to the boil. Add the tagliatelle and olive oil and cook for 8–10 minutes or until the pasta is tender but still firm to the bite.

❊ Drain the pasta thoroughly and arrange on a warmed serving dish. Top the pasta with the chicken, spoon over any remaining marinade and garnish with the lemon rind.

Chicken with Orange Sauce

❖ SERVES 4 ❖

2 tbsp rapeseed oil
3 tbsp olive oil
4 x 225 g/8 oz chicken
suprêmes
150 ml/5 fl oz orange brandy
15 g/^{1}/$_{2}$ oz plain flour
150 ml/5 fl oz freshly squeezed
orange juice
25 g/1 oz courgette, cut into
matchsticks
25 g/1 oz red pepper, cut into
matchsticks
25 g/1 oz leek, finely shredded
400 g/14 oz dried wholemeal
spaghetti
3 large oranges, peeled and cut
into segments
rind of 1 orange, cut into very
fine strips
2 tbsp chopped fresh tarragon
150 g/4 oz fromage frais or
ricotta cheese
salt and pepper
fresh tarragon leaves,
to garnish

❖ Heat the rapeseed oil and 1 tablespoon of the olive oil in a frying pan. Add the chicken and cook quickly until golden brown. Add the orange brandy and cook for 3 minutes. Sprinkle over the flour and cook for 2 minutes.

❖ Reduce the heat and add the orange juice, courgette, pepper and leek and season. Simmer for 5 minutes until the sauce has thickened.

❖ Meanwhile, bring a saucepan of lightly salted water to the boil. Add the spaghetti and 1 tablespoon of the olive oil and cook for 10 minutes. Drain the spaghetti, transfer to a serving dish and drizzle over the remaining oil.

❖ Add half the orange segments, half the orange rind, the tarragon and fromage frais to the sauce in the pan and cook for 3 minutes.

❖ Place the chicken on top of the pasta, pour over a little sauce, and garnish with the orange segments, orange rind and tarragon. Serve immediately.

Lasagne Verde

1 tbsp butter, for greasing	1 large onion, chopped
14 sheets precooked lasagne	1 celery stick, diced
850 ml/1½ pints béchamel	4 garlic cloves, crushed
sauce (see page 247)	25 g/1 oz plain flour
85 g/3 oz grated mozzarella	300 ml/10 fl oz beef stock
cheese	150 ml/5 fl oz red wine
sprig of fresh basil, to garnish	1 tbsp chopped fresh parsley
	1 tsp chopped fresh marjoram
MEAT SAUCE	1 tsp chopped fresh basil
2 tbsp olive oil	2 tbsp tomato purée
450 g/1 lb minced beef	salt and pepper

❊ To make the meat sauce, heat the oil in a large frying pan over a medium heat. Add the minced beef and fry, stirring frequently, until browned all over. Add the onion, celery and garlic and cook for 3 minutes.

❊ Sprinkle over the flour and cook, stirring, for 1 minute. Gradually stir in the stock and wine, season with salt and pepper and add the herbs. Bring to the boil and simmer for 35 minutes. Add the tomato purée and simmer for 10 minutes.

❊ Lightly grease an ovenproof dish with the butter. Arrange sheets of lasagne over the base, spoon over a layer of meat sauce, then béchamel sauce. Put another layer of lasagne on top and repeat, finishing with a layer of béchamel sauce. Sprinkle over the mozzarella cheese.

❊ Bake the lasagne in a preheated oven, 190°C/375°F/Gas Mark 5, for about 35 minutes or until the top is golden brown and bubbling. Garnish with a the sprig of basil and serve immediately.

Creamed Strips of Beef

75 g/3 oz butter	150 ml/5 fl oz double cream
450 g/1 lb sirloin steak,	salt and pepper
trimmed and cut into	4 slices hot toast, cut into
thin strips	triangles, to serve
175 g/6 oz button mushrooms,	
sliced	**PASTA**
1 tsp mustard	450 g/1 lb dried rigatoni
pinch of freshly grated root	2 tbsp olive oil
ginger	2 sprigs fresh basil
2 tbsp dry sherry	115 g/4 oz butter

❊ Melt the butter in a large frying pan and gently fry the steak over a low heat, stirring frequently, for 6 minutes. Using a slotted spoon, transfer the steak to an ovenproof dish and keep warm.

❊ Add the sliced mushrooms to the pan and cook for 2–3 minutes in the juices remaining in the pan. Add the mustard, ginger, salt and pepper. Cook for 2 minutes, then add the sherry and cream. Cook for a further 3 minutes, then pour the cream sauce over the steak.

❊ Bake the steak and cream mixture in a preheated oven, 190°C/375°F/Gas Mark 5, for 10 minutes.

❊ Meanwhile, cook the pasta. Bring a large saucepan of lightly salted water to the boil. Add the rigatoni, olive oil and 1 of the basil sprigs and boil rapidly for 10 minutes until the pasta is tender but still firm to the bite. Drain the pasta and transfer to a warmed serving plate. Toss the pasta with the butter and garnish with a sprig of basil.

❊ Serve the creamed steak strips with the pasta and toast triangles.

Meatballs in Red Wine Sauce

150 ml/5 fl oz milk
150 g/5¹/₂ oz fresh white breadcrumbs
2 tbsp butter
9 tbsp olive oil
225 g/8 oz oyster mushrooms, sliced
2¹/₂ tbsp wholemeal flour
200 ml/7 fl oz beef stock
150 ml/5 fl oz red wine
4 tomatoes, peeled and chopped
1 tbsp tomato purée
1 tsp brown sugar
1 tbsp finely chopped fresh basil
12 shallots, chopped
450 g/1 lb minced steak
1 tsp paprika
450 g/1 lb dried egg tagliatelle
salt and pepper
sprigs of fresh basil, to garnish

❊ Pour the milk into a bowl, add the breadcrumbs and set aside to soak for 30 minutes.

❊ Heat half the butter and 4 tablespoons of the oil in a saucepan. Fry the mushrooms for 4 minutes, then stir in the flour and cook for 2 minutes. Add the stock and wine and simmer for 15 minutes. Add the tomatoes, tomato purée, sugar and basil. Season and simmer for 30 minutes.

❊ Mix the shallots, steak and paprika with the breadcrumbs and season to taste. Shape the mixture into 14 meatballs.

❊ Heat 4 tablespoons of the remaining oil and the rest of the butter in a large frying pan. Fry the meatballs, turning frequently, until brown all over. Transfer to a deep casserole, pour over the red wine and mushroom sauce, cover and bake in a preheated oven, 180°C/350°F/Gas Mark 4, for 30 minutes.

❊ Bring a saucepan of lightly salted water to the boil. Add the pasta and the remaining oil, bring back to the boil and cook for 8–10 minutes or until tender but still firm to the bite. Drain and transfer to a serving dish. Remove the casserole from the oven and cool for 3 minutes. Pour the meatballs and sauce over the pasta, garnish with the basil and serve.

Classic Tagliatelle Bolognese

4 tbsp olive oil, plus extra for drizzling
85 g/3 oz pancetta or rindless streaky bacon, diced
1 onion, chopped
1 garlic clove, finely chopped
1 carrot, chopped
1 celery stick, chopped
225 g/8 oz fresh minced beef
115 g/4 oz chicken livers, chopped
2 tbsp passata
125 ml/4 fl oz dry white wine
225 ml/8 fl oz beef stock or water
1 tbsp chopped fresh oregano or marjoram
1 bay leaf
450 g/1 lb dried tagliatelle
salt and pepper
freshly grated Parmesan cheese, to serve

❊ Heat the oil in a large heavy-based saucepan. Add the pancetta and cook over a medium heat, stirring occasionally, for 3–5 minutes, or until turning brown. Add the onion, garlic, carrot and celery and cook, stirring occasionally, for a further 5 minutes.

❊ Add the beef and cook over a high heat, breaking up the meat with a wooden spoon, for 5 minutes or until browned. Stir in the chicken livers and cook, stirring occasionally, for a further 2–3 minutes. Add the passata, wine, beef stock, oregano and bay leaf and season to taste with salt and pepper. Bring to the boil, reduce the heat, cover and simmer for 30–35 minutes.

❊ Meanwhile, bring a large heavy-based saucepan of lightly salted water to the boil. Add the pasta, return to the boil and cook for 8–10 minutes or until tender but still firm to the bite. Drain, transfer to a warmed serving dish, drizzle with a little olive oil and toss well. Remove and discard the bay leaf from the sauce, then pour it over the pasta, toss again and serve with the cheese.

Pasticcio

1 tbsp olive oil
225 g/8 oz dried fusilli, or other
short pasta shapes
4 tbsp double cream
salt
sprigs of fresh rosemary,
to garnish

SAUCE
2 tbsp olive oil, plus extra
for brushing
1 onion, thinly sliced
1 red pepper, deseeded and
chopped
2 garlic cloves, chopped
625 g/1 lb 6 oz lean minced
beef
400 g/14 oz canned chopped
tomatoes
125 ml/4 fl oz dry white wine
2 tbsp chopped fresh parsley
50 g/1¾ oz canned anchovies,
drained and chopped
salt and pepper

TOPPING
300 ml/10 fl oz natural yogurt
3 eggs
pinch of freshly grated nutmeg
55 g/2 oz Parmesan cheese,
freshly grated

❖ To make the sauce, heat the oil in a large frying pan and fry the onion and red pepper for 3 minutes. Stir in the garlic and cook for 1 minute. Add the beef and cook, stirring frequently, until browned.

❖ Add the tomatoes and wine, stir well and bring to the boil. Simmer, uncovered, for 20 minutes or until the sauce is fairly thick. Stir in the parsley and anchovies and season to taste.

❖ Bring a large saucepan of lightly salted water to the boil. Add the oil and pasta, bring back to the boil and cook for 8–10 minutes until the pasta is tender but still firm to the bite. Drain, then transfer to a bowl. Stir in the cream and set aside.

❖ To make the topping, beat the yogurt with the eggs and nutmeg until well combined and season to taste with salt and pepper.

❖ Brush a large, shallow ovenproof dish with oil. Spoon in half the pasta mixture and cover with half the meat sauce. Repeat these layers, then spread the topping evenly over the final layer. Sprinkle the grated cheese evenly on top.

❖ Bake in a preheated oven, 190°C/375°F/Gas Mark 5, for 25 minutes or until the topping is golden brown and bubbling. Garnish with the sprigs of rosemary and serve immediately.

Pasta & Pork in Cream Sauce

450 g/1 lb pork fillet, thinly sliced	1 tbsp lemon juice
4 tbsp olive oil	pinch of saffron
225 g/8 oz button mushrooms, sliced	350 g/12 oz dried orecchioni
200 ml/7 fl oz passata	4 tbsp double cream
	salt
	12 quail eggs, to garnish

❉ Put the pork slices between 2 sheets of clingfilm and pound until wafer thin, then cut into strips.

❉ Heat the oil in a large frying pan over a medium heat. Add the pork strips and stir-fry for 5 minutes. Add the mushrooms to the pan and stir-fry for a further 2 minutes.

❉ Pour over the passata, reduce the heat and simmer gently for 20 minutes.

❉ Meanwhile, bring a large saucepan of lightly salted water to the boil over a medium heat. Add the lemon juice, saffron and pasta and cook for 8–10 minutes, or until the pasta is tender, but still firm to the bite. Drain and keep warm.

❉ Stir the cream into the pan with the pork and heat gently for a few minutes.

❉ Boil the eggs for 3 minutes in a small saucepan of boiling water. Cool in cold water and remove the shells.

❉ Transfer the pasta to a large warmed serving plate, top with the pork and the sauce and garnish with the eggs. Serve immediately.

Baked Fennel Linguine

6 fennel bulbs	40 g/1$\frac{1}{2}$ oz plain flour
150 ml/5 fl oz vegetable stock	7 tbsp double cream
2 tbsp butter	1 tbsp Madeira
6 slices rindless smoked bacon, diced	450 g/1 lb dried linguine
6 shallots, quartered	1 tbsp olive oil
	salt and pepper

❉ Trim the fennel bulbs, then peel off and reserve the outer layer of each. Cut the bulbs into quarters and put them in a large saucepan with the stock and the reserved outer layers. Bring to the boil, reduce the heat and simmer for 5 minutes.

❉ Using a slotted spoon, transfer the fennel to a large dish. Discard the outer layers of the fennel bulbs. Bring the stock to the boil and reduce by half. Set aside.

❉ Melt the butter in a frying pan. Add the bacon and shallots and fry over a medium heat, stirring frequently, for 4 minutes. Add the flour, reduced stock, cream and Madeira and cook, stirring constantly, for 3 minutes or until the sauce is smooth. Season to taste with salt and pepper and pour over the fennel.

❉ Bring a large saucepan of lightly salted water to the boil. Add the pasta and oil, bring back to the boil and cook for 8–10 minutes until the pasta is tender but still firm to the bite. Drain and transfer to a deep ovenproof dish.

❉ Add the fennel and sauce and bake in a preheated oven, 180°C/350°F/Gas Mark 4, for 20 minutes. Serve immediately.

Smoked Ham Linguine

450 g/1 lb dried linguine
450 g/1 lb broccoli florets
225 g/8 oz Italian smoked ham
salt and pepper
Italian bread, such as ciabatta
or focaccia, to serve

ITALIAN CHEESE SAUCE
1 tbsp butter
40 g/1½ oz plain flour
125 ml/4 fl oz milk
1 tbsp single cream
pinch of freshly grated nutmeg
25 g/1 oz grated Cheddar
  cheese
1 tbsp freshly grated Parmesan
  cheese
salt and pepper

❋ First, make the Italian cheese sauce. Melt the butter in a saucepan, stir in the flour and cook for 1 minute. Remove from the heat and gradually whisk in the milk. Stir in the cream and nutmeg and season to taste with salt and pepper. Return to the heat, bring to the boil, stirring constantly, then simmer for 5 minutes. Remove from the heat and stir in the cheeses until melted and thoroughly blended. Set aside.

❋ Bring a large pan of lightly salted water to the boil. Add the pasta and broccoli, bring back to the boil and cook for 8–10 minutes until the pasta is tender but still firm to the bite. Drain well.

❋ Cut the Italian smoked ham into thin strips. Toss the linguine, broccoli and ham into the cheese sauce and gently warm through. Season with pepper and serve with the bread.

Chorizo & Mushroom Pasta

675 g/1 lb 8 oz dried vermicelli
125 ml/4 fl oz olive oil
2 garlic cloves
125 g/4½ oz chorizo, sliced
225 g/8 oz wild mushrooms

3 fresh red chillies, chopped
50 g/1¾ oz freshly grated
  Parmesan cheese
salt and pepper
10 anchovy fillets, to garnish

❋ Bring a large saucepan of lightly salted water to the boil. Add the vermicelli and 1 tablespoon of the oil and cook for 8–10 minutes or until just tender, but still firm to the bite.

❋ Drain the pasta thoroughly, place on a large warmed serving plate and keep warm.

❋ Meanwhile, heat the remaining oil in a large frying pan. Add the garlic and fry for 1 minute.

❋ Add the chorizo and wild mushrooms and cook for 4 minutes,

❋ Add the chopped chillies and cook for a further minute.

❋ Pour the chorizo and wild mushroom mixture over the vermicelli and season with a little salt and pepper.

❋ Sprinkle with the cheese, garnish with a lattice of anchovy fillets and serve immediately.

Pasta Carbonara

1 tbsp olive oil
40 g/1$\frac{1}{2}$ oz butter
100 g/3$\frac{1}{2}$ oz pancetta or
unsmoked bacon, diced
3 eggs, beaten
2 tbsp milk
1 tbsp thyme, stalks removed
675 g/1 lb 8 oz fresh or
350 g/12 oz dried conchiglietti
50 g/1$\frac{3}{4}$ oz Parmesan cheese,
grated
salt and pepper

❄ Heat the oil and butter in a frying pan until the mixture is just beginning to froth.

❄ Add the pancetta to the pan and cook for 5 minutes or until brown all over.

❄ Mix together the eggs and milk in a small bowl. Stir in the thyme and season to taste with salt and pepper.

❄ Bring a saucepan of lightly salted water to the boil and cook the pasta for 8–10 minutes until tender but still firm to the bite. Drain thoroughly.

❄ Add the pasta to the frying pan with the eggs and cook over a high heat for about 30 seconds or until the eggs just begin to cook and set. Do not overcook the eggs or they will become rubbery.

❄ Add half the cheese, stirring to combine.

❄ Transfer the pasta to a serving plate, pour over the sauce and toss to mix well.

❄ Sprinkle the remaining cheese over the top and serve immediately.

Pasta with Bacon & Tomatoes

900 g/2 lb small, sweet tomatoes
6 slices rindless smoked bacon
60 g/2 oz butter
1 onion, chopped
1 garlic clove, crushed
4 fresh oregano sprigs, finely chopped
450 g/1 lb dried orecchiette
1 tbsp olive oil
salt and pepper
freshly grated pecorino cheese, to serve

❖ Blanch the tomatoes in boiling water. Drain, peel and seed the tomatoes, then roughly chop the flesh.

❖ Using a sharp knife, chop the bacon into small dice.

❖ Melt the butter in a saucepan. Add the bacon and fry until golden.

❖ Add the onion and garlic and fry over a medium heat for 5–7 minutes, until just soft.

❖ Add the tomatoes and oregano to the pan and season to taste with salt and pepper. Reduce the heat and simmer for 10–12 minutes.

❖ Bring a large saucepan of lightly salted water to the boil. Add the pasta and oil and cook for 12 minutes until the pasta is just tender but still firm to the bite. Drain the pasta and transfer to a warmed serving dish or bowl.

❖ Spoon the bacon and tomato sauce over the pasta, toss to coat and serve with the cheese.

Spinach & Anchovy Pasta

❖ SERVES 4 ❖

900 g/2 lb fresh, young spinach leaves
400 g/14 oz dried fettuccine
6 tbsp olive oil
3 tbsp pine kernels
3 garlic cloves, crushed
8 canned anchovy fillets, drained and chopped
salt

❖ Trim off any tough spinach stalks. Rinse the spinach leaves and place them in a large saucepan with only the water that is clinging to them after washing. Cover and cook over a high heat, shaking the pan from time to time, until the spinach has wilted but retains its colour. Drain well, set aside and keep warm.

❖ Bring a large saucepan of lightly salted water to the boil. Add the fettuccine and 1 tablespoon of the oil and cook for 8–10 minutes until the pasta is just tender but still firm to the bite.

❖ Heat 4 tablespoons of the remaining oil in a saucepan. Add the pine kernels and fry until golden. Remove the pine kernels from the pan and set aside until required.

❖ Add the garlic to the pan and fry until golden. Add the anchovies and stir in the spinach. Cook, stirring, for 2–3 minutes, until heated through. Return the pine kernels to the pan.

❖ Drain the fettuccine, toss in the remaining olive oil and transfer to a warmed serving dish. Spoon the anchovy and spinach sauce over the fettucine, toss lightly and serve immediately.

Pasta Puttanesca

3 tbsp extra virgin olive oil
1 large red onion, finely chopped
4 canned anchovy fillets, drained
pinch of chilli flakes
2 garlic cloves, finely chopped
400 g/14 oz canned chopped tomatoes
2 tbsp tomato purée

225 g/8 oz dried spaghetti
25 g/1 oz stoned black olives, roughly chopped
25 g/1 oz stoned green olives, roughly chopped
1 tbsp capers, rinsed and drained
4 sun-dried tomatoes in oil, drained and roughly chopped
salt and pepper

❈ Heat the oil in a saucepan and cook the onion, anchovies and chilli flakes for 10 minutes until soft. Add the garlic and cook for 30 seconds. Stir in the tomatoes and tomato purée and bring to the boil. Simmer gently for 10 minutes.

❈ Meanwhile, bring a saucepan of lightly salted water to the boil. Add the pasta, bring back to the boil and cook for 8–10 minutes until tender but still firm to the bite.

❈ Add the olives, capers and sun-dried tomatoes to the sauce. Simmer for a further 2–3 minutes. Season to taste.

❈ Drain the pasta well and stir in the sauce. Toss thoroughly to mix. Transfer to a serving dish and serve hot.

Prawn &Tuna Pasta Bake

225 g/8 oz tricolour pasta shapes
1 tbsp vegetable oil
175 g/6 oz button mushrooms, sliced
1 bunch of spring onions, trimmed and chopped
400 g/14 oz canned tuna in brine, drained and flaked
175 g/6 oz peeled prawns, thawed, if frozen

2 tbsp cornflour
425 ml/15 fl oz milk
4 medium tomatoes, thinly sliced
25 g/1 oz fresh breadcrumbs
25 g/1 oz grated low-fat Cheddar cheese
salt and pepper
wholemeal bread and fresh salad, to serve

❈ Bring a large saucepan of lightly salted water to the boil. Add the pasta, bring back to the boil and cook for 8–10 minutes until tender but still firm to the bite. Drain well.

❈ Meanwhile, heat the oil in a large frying pan. Add the mushrooms and all but a handful of the spring onions and cook over a low heat, stirring occasionally, for 4–5 minutes until soft.

❈ Place the cooked pasta in a bowl and stir in the mushroom mixture, tuna and prawns.

❈ Blend the cornflour with a little milk to make a paste. Pour the remaining milk into a saucepan and stir in the paste. Heat, stirring, until the sauce begins to thicken. Season. Stir the sauce into the pasta mixture. Transfer to an ovenproof dish and place on a baking tray.

❈ Arrange the tomato slices over the pasta and sprinkle with the breadcrumbs and cheese. Bake in a preheated oven, 190°C/375°F/Gas Mark 5, for 25–30 minutes until golden. Serve sprinkled with the reserved spring onions and accompanied by the bread and salad.

Macaroni & Tuna Layer

125–150 g/4^1/$_2$–5^1/$_2$ oz dried macaroni
2 tbsp oil
1 garlic clove, crushed
60 g/2 oz button mushrooms, sliced
^{1}/$_2$ red pepper, thinly sliced
200 g/7 oz canned tuna in brine, drained and flaked
^{1}/$_2$ tsp dried oregano
salt and pepper

SAUCE
25 g/1 oz butter or margarine
1 tbsp plain flour
250 ml/9 fl oz milk
2 tomatoes, sliced
2 tbsp dried breadcrumbs
25 g/1 oz mature Cheddar or Parmesan cheese, grated

❉ Bring a saucepan of lightly salted water to the boil and cook the macaroni, with 1 tablespoon of the oil added, for 10–12 minutes or until the pasta is tender but still firm to the bite. Drain, rinse and drain thoroughly.

❉ Heat the remaining oil in a saucepan or frying pan and fry the garlic, mushrooms and red pepper until soft. Add the tuna, oregano and seasoning, and heat through.

❉ Grease a 1-litre/1^3/$_4$-pint ovenproof dish, and add half the cooked macaroni. Cover with the tuna mixture and then add the remaining macaroni.

❉ To make the sauce, melt the butter in a saucepan, stir in the flour and cook for 1 minute. Add the milk gradually and bring to the boil. Simmer for 1–2 minutes, stirring continuously, until thickened. Season to taste. Pour the sauce over the macaroni.

❉ Lay the sliced tomatoes over the sauce and sprinkle with the breadcrumbs and cheese.

❉ Place in a preheated oven, 200°C/400°F/Gas Mark 6, for about 25 minutes, or until piping hot and the top is well browned.

Spaghetti with Tuna

200 g/7 oz canned tuna, drained
60 g/2 oz canned anchovies, drained
250 ml/9 fl oz olive oil
60 g/2 oz roughly chopped flat-leaf parsley
150 ml/5 fl oz crème fraîche
450 g/1 lb dried spaghetti
25 g/1 oz butter
salt and pepper
black olives, to garnish
crusty bread, to serve

❖ Put the tuna into a food processor or blender, together with the anchovies, 225 ml/8 fl oz of the olive oil and the flat-leaf parsley. Process until the sauce is very smooth.

❖ Spoon the crème fraîche into the food processor or blender and process again for a few seconds to blend thoroughly. Season to taste with salt and pepper.

❖ Bring a large saucepan of lightly salted water to the boil. Add the spaghetti and the remaining olive oil and cook for 8–10 minutes until the spaghetti is tender but still firm to the bite.

❖ Drain the spaghetti, return to the pan and place over a medium heat. Add the butter and toss well to coat. Spoon in the sauce and quickly toss into the spaghetti, using 2 forks.

❖ Remove the pan from the heat and divide the spaghetti between 4 warmed individual serving plates. Garnish with the olives and serve immediately with the bread.

Linguine with Sardines

8 sardines, filleted
1 fennel bulb
4 tbsp olive oil
3 garlic cloves, sliced
1 tsp chilli flakes
350 g/12 oz dried linguine
$1/2$ tsp finely grated lemon rind
1 tbsp lemon juice
25 g/1 oz pine kernels, toasted
2 tbsp chopped fresh parsley
salt and pepper

❖ Wash the sardine fillets and pat dry on kitchen paper. Roughly chop them into large pieces and set aside. Trim the fennel bulb and slice very thinly.

❖ Heat 2 tablespoons of the olive oil in a large heavy-based frying pan and add the garlic and chilli flakes. Cook for 1 minute, then add the fennel slices. Cook over a medium–high heat, stirring occasionally, for 4–5 minutes until soft. Reduce the heat, add the sardine pieces and cook for a further 3–4 minutes until just cooked.

❖ Meanwhile, bring a saucepan of lightly salted water to the boil. Add the pasta, bring back to the boil and cook for 8–10 minutes until tender but still firm to the bite. Drain well and return to the pan.

❖ Add the lemon rind, lemon juice, pine kernels and parsley to the sardines and toss together. Season to taste with salt and pepper. Add to the pasta with the remaining olive oil and toss together gently. Transfer to a warmed serving dish and serve immediately.

Spaghettini with Crab

1 dressed crab, 450 g/1 lb, including the shell	2 garlic cloves, finely chopped
350 g/12 oz dried spaghettini	3 tbsp chopped fresh parsley
6 tbsp extra virgin olive oil	2 tbsp lemon juice
1 fresh red chilli, deseeded and finely chopped	1 tsp finely grated lemon rind
	salt and pepper
	lemon wedges, to garnish

❊ Scoop the meat from the crab shell into a bowl. Lightly mix the white and brown meat together and set aside.

❊ Bring a large saucepan of lightly salted water to the boil. Add the pasta, bring back to the boil and cook for 8–10 minutes until tender but still firm to the bite. Drain well and return to the pan.

❊ Meanwhile, heat 2 tablespoons of the oil in a frying pan. Add the chilli and garlic. Cook for 30 seconds, then add the crabmeat, parsley, lemon juice and lemon rind. Stir-fry over a low heat for a further minute until the crab is just heated through.

❊ Add the crab mixture to the pasta with the remaining oil and season to taste with salt and pepper. Toss together thoroughly, transfer to a warmed serving dish and serve immediately, garnished with the lemon wedges.

Smoked Salmon Spaghetti

	SMOKED SALMON SAUCE
450 g/1 lb dried buckwheat spaghetti	300 ml/10 fl oz double cream
2 tbsp olive oil	150 ml/5 fl oz whisky or brandy
90 g/3 oz feta cheese, crumbled	125 g/4$\frac{1}{2}$ oz smoked salmon
	cayenne pepper
salt	pepper
fresh coriander or parsley leaves, to garnish	2 tbsp chopped fresh coriander or parsley, to garnish

❊ Bring a large saucepan of lightly salted water to the boil. Add the spaghetti and 1 tablespoon of the olive oil and cook for 8–10 minutes until tender but still firm to the bite. Drain the spaghetti, return to the pan and sprinkle over the remaining oil. Cover, shake the pan, set aside and keep warm.

❊ To make the sauce, pour the cream into a small saucepan and bring to simmering point, but do not let it boil. Pour the whisky into another small saucepan and bring to simmering point, but do not allow it to boil. Remove both saucepans from the heat and mix together the cream and whisky.

❊ Cut the smoked salmon into thin strips and add to the cream mixture. Season to taste with cayenne pepper and pepper. Just before serving, stir in the chopped coriander.

❊ Transfer the spaghetti to a warmed serving dish, pour over the sauce and toss thoroughly with 2 large forks. Scatter over the crumbled feta cheese, garnish with the coriander leaves and serve immediately.

Poached Salmon with Penne

4 x 275-g/9¹/₂-oz fresh salmon
steaks
60 g/2 oz butter
175 ml/6 fl oz dry white wine
sea salt
8 peppercorns
sprig of fresh dill
sprig of fresh tarragon
1 lemon, sliced
450 g/1 lb dried penne
2 tbsp olive oil
lemon slices and fresh
watercress, to garnish

LEMON & WATERCRESS SAUCE
25 g/1 oz butter
25 g/1 oz plain flour
150 ml/5 fl oz warm milk
juice and finely grated rind of
2 lemons
60 g/2 oz watercress, chopped
salt and pepper

❖ Put the salmon in a large non-stick saucepan. Add the butter, wine, a pinch of sea salt, the peppercorns, dill, tarragon and lemon. Cover, bring to the boil and simmer for 10 minutes.

❖ Using a fish slice, carefully remove the salmon. Strain and reserve the cooking liquid. Remove and discard the salmon skin and centre bones. Place on a warmed dish, cover and keep warm.

❖ Meanwhile, bring a saucepan of lightly salted water to the boil. Add the penne and 1 tablespoon of the oil and cook for 8–10 minutes until tender but still firm to the bite. Drain and sprinkle over the remaining oil. Place on a warmed serving dish, top with the salmon steaks and keep warm.

❖ To make the sauce, melt the butter and stir in the flour for 2 minutes. Stir in the milk and about 7 tablespoons of the reserved cooking liquid. Add the lemon juice and rind and cook, stirring, for a further 10 minutes.

❖ Add the watercress to the sauce, stir gently and season to taste with salt and pepper.

❖ Pour the sauce over the salmon and penne, garnish with the slices of lemon and the watercress and serve.

262

Pasta with Clams

675 g/1 lb 8 oz fresh clams or
290 g/10 oz canned clams,
drained
2 tbsp olive oi
2 garlic cloves, finely chopped
400 g/14 oz mixed seafood,
such as prawns, squid and
mussels, thawed, if frozen

150 ml/5 fl oz white wine
150 ml/5 fl oz fish stock
675 g/1 lb 8 oz fresh pasta or
350 g/12 oz dried pasta
2 tbsp chopped tarragon
salt and pepper

❄ If you are using fresh clams, scrub them clean and discard any that are already open.

❄ Heat the oil in a large frying pan. Add the garlic and the clams to the pan and cook for 2 minutes, shaking the pan to ensure that all of the clams are coated in the oil.

❄ Add the remaining seafood mixture to the pan and cook for a further 2 minutes.

❄ Pour the wine and stock over the mixed seafood and garlic and bring to the boil. Cover the pan, reduce the heat and leave to simmer for 8–10 minutes or until the shells open. Discard any clams or mussels that do not open.

❄ Meanwhile, bring a saucepan of lightly salted water to the boil and cook the pasta for 8–10 minutes or until it is cooked through but still firm to the bite. Drain the pasta thoroughly.

❄ Stir the tarragon into the sauce and season to taste with salt and pepper.

❄ Transfer the pasta to a serving plate and pour over the sauce. Serve immediately.

Mussel & Scallop Spaghetti

225 g/8 oz dried wholemeal
spaghetti
60 g/2 oz rindless lean back
bacon, chopped
2 shallots, finey chopped
2 celery sticks, finely
chopped
150 ml/5 fl oz dry white wine

150 ml/5 fl oz fresh fish stock
500 g/1 lb 2 oz fresh mussels,
prepared
225 g/8 oz shelled queen or
China bay scallops
1 tbsp chopped fresh parsley
salt and pepper

❄ Bring a saucepan of lightly salted water to the boil and cook the spaghetti according to the packet instructions, until the pasta is tender but still firm to the bite – about 10 minutes.

❄ Meanwhile, gently dry-fry the bacon in a large non-stick frying pan for 2–3 minutes. Stir in the shallots, celery and wine. Simmer gently, uncovered, for 5 minutes until softened.

❄ Add the stock, mussels and scallops, cover and cook for a further 6–7 minutes. Discard any mussels that remain unopened.

❄ Drain the spaghetti and add to the frying pan. Add the parsley, season to taste with salt and pepper and toss together. Continue to cook for 1–2 minutes to heat through. Pile on to warmed serving plates, spooning over the cooking juices.

Pasta Shells with Mussels

400 g/14 oz dried pasta shells
1 tbsp olive oil

SAUCE
3.5 litres/6 pints mussels, scrubbed
250 ml/9 fl oz dry white wine
2 large onions, chopped
125 g/4^1/2 oz unsalted butter
6 large garlic cloves, finely chopped
5 tbsp chopped fresh parsley
300 ml/10 fl oz double cream
salt and pepper
crusty bread, to serve

❈ Debeard the mussels and rinse well in several changes of water. Discard any mussels that refuse to close when tapped. Put the mussels in a large saucepan with the wine and half the onions. Cover the pan, shake and cook over a medium heat for 2–3 minutes until the mussels open.

❈ Remove the pan from the heat, lift out the mussels with a slotted spoon, reserving the liquor, and set aside until they are cool enough to handle. Discard any mussels that have not opened.

❈ Melt the butter in a saucepan over a medium heat and fry the remaining onion for 3–4 minutes or until translucent. Stir in the garlic and cook for 1 minute. Gradually pour on the reserved cooking liquor, stirring to blend thoroughly. Stir in the parsley and cream. Season to taste with salt and pepper and bring to simmering point. Taste and adjust the seasoning if necessary.

❈ Bring a large saucepan of lightly salted water to the boil, add the oil and pasta and cook for 8–10 minutes or until the pasta is tender but still firm to the bite. Drain in a colander, return to the pan, cover and keep warm.

❈ Remove the mussels from their shells, reserving a few shells for garnish. Stir the mussels into the cream sauce. Tip the pasta into a warmed serving dish, pour over the sauce and toss it together well. Garnish with a few of the reserved mussel shells. Serve hot with the bread.

Saffron Mussel Tagliatelle

1 kg/2 lb 4 oz mussels
150 ml/5 fl oz white wine
1 medium onion, finely chopped
25 g/1 oz butter
2 garlic cloves, crushed
2 tsp cornflour
300 ml/10 fl oz double cream
pinch of saffron threads or saffron powder
juice of ^{1}/2 lemon
1 egg yolk
450 g/1 lb dried tagliatelle
1 tbsp olive oil
salt and pepper
3 tbsp chopped fresh parsley, to garnish

❈ Debeard the mussels and rinse well under cold running water. Discard any that do not close when sharply tapped. Put the mussels in a saucepan with the wine and onion. Cover and cook over a high heat, shaking the pan, for 5–8 minutes, until the shells open.

❈ Drain and reserve the cooking liquid. Discard any mussels that are still closed. Reserve a few mussels for the garnish and remove the remainder from their shells.

❈ Strain the cooking liquid into a pan. Bring to the boil and reduce by about half. Remove the pan from the heat.

❈ Melt the butter in a saucepan. Add the garlic and cook, stirring frequently, for 2 minutes until golden brown. Stir in the cornflour and cook, stirring, for 1 minute. Gradually stir in the cooking liquid and the cream. Crush the saffron threads and add to the pan. Season to taste with salt and pepper and simmer over a low heat for 2–3 minutes until thickened. Stir in the egg yolk, lemon juice and shelled mussels. Do not allow the mixture to boil.

❈ Meanwhile, bring a saucepan of lightly salted water to the boil. Add the pasta and oil and cook for 8–10 minutes until tender but still firm to the bite. Drain and transfer to a serving dish. Add the mussel sauce and toss. Garnish with the parsley and reserved mussels and serve.

Vermicelli with Clams

400 g/14 oz dried vermicelli,
spaghetti or other long pasta
2 tbsp olive oil
25 g/1 oz butter
2 onions, chopped
2 garlic cloves, chopped
400 g/14 oz clams in brine
125 ml/4 fl oz white wine
4 tbsp chopped fresh parsley
$\frac{1}{2}$ tsp dried oregano
pinch of freshly grated nutmeg
salt and pepper
2 tbsp Parmesan cheese
shavings and sprigs of fresh
basil, to garnish

❖ Bring a large saucepan of lightly salted water to the boil. Add the pasta and half the olive oil and cook for 8–10 minutes until the pasta is tender but still firm to the bite. Drain, return to the pan and add the butter. Cover the pan, shake well and keep warm.

❖ Heat the remaining oil in a saucepan over a medium heat. Add the onions and fry until they are translucent. Stir in the garlic and cook for 1 minute.

❖ Strain the liquid from half the clams and add the liquid to the pan with the wine. Stir, bring to simmering point and simmer for 3 minutes. Drain the remaining clams and discard the liquid.

❖ Add the clams, parsley and oregano to the pan and season with pepper and nutmeg. Reduce the heat and cook until the sauce is heated through.

❖ Transfer the pasta to a warmed serving dish and pour over the sauce. Sprinkle with the cheese and basil and serve immediately.

Chow Mein

500 g/1 lb 2 oz egg noodles
4 tbsp vegetable oil
1 onion, thinly sliced
2 carrots, cut into matchsticks
125 g/4^1/$_2$ oz button
mushrooms, quartered
125 g/4^1/$_2$ oz mangetout
^{1}/$_2$ cucumber, cut into sticks

125 g/4^1/$_2$ oz spinach, shredded
125 g/4^1/$_2$ oz beansprouts
2 tbsp dark soy sauce
1 tbsp sherry
1 tsp salt
1 tsp sugar
1 tsp cornflour
1 tsp sesame oil

❖ Cook the noodles according to the instructions on the packet. Drain and rinse under cold running water until cool. Set aside.

❖ Heat 3 tablespoons of the vegetable oil in a preheated wok or frying pan. Add the onion and carrots, and stir-fry for 1 minute. Add the mushrooms, mangetout and cucumber and stir-fry for 1 minute.

❖ Stir in the remaining vegetable oil and add the drained noodles, together with the spinach and beansprouts.

❖ Blend together all the remaining ingredients and pour over the noodles and vegetables.

❖ Stir-fry until the noodle mixture is thoroughly heated through, transfer to a warmed serving dish and serve.

Vegetables with Noodles

1.2 litres/2 pints vegetable
stock
1 garlic clove, crushed
1-cm/^{1}/$_2$-inch piece of root
ginger, finely chopped
225 g/8 oz dried medium egg
noodles
1 red pepper, deseeded and
sliced
85 g/3 oz frozen peas
115 g/4 oz broccoli florets
85 g/3 oz shiitake mushrooms,
sliced

2 tbsp sesame seeds
225 g/8 oz canned water
chestnuts, drained and
halved
225 g/8 oz canned bamboo
shoots, drained
280 g/10 oz Chinese leaves,
sliced
140 g/5 oz beansprouts
3 spring onions, sliced
1 tbsp dark soy sauce
pepper

❖ Bring the stock, garlic and ginger to the boil in a large saucepan. Stir in the noodles, red pepper, peas, broccoli and mushrooms and return to the boil. Reduce the heat, cover and simmer for 5–6 minutes or until the noodles are tender.

❖ Meanwhile, preheat the grill to medium. Spread out the sesame seeds in a single layer on a baking tray and toast under the preheated grill, turning to brown evenly – watch constantly as they brown very quickly. Tip the sesame seeds into a small dish and set aside.

❖ Once the noodles are tender, add the water chestnuts, bamboo shoots, Chinese leaves, beansprouts and spring onions to the pan. Return the stock to the boil, stir to mix the ingredients and simmer for a further 2–3 minutes to heat through thoroughly.

❖ Carefully drain off 300 ml/10 fl oz of the stock into a small heatproof jug and reserve. Drain and discard any remaining stock and turn the noodles and vegetables into a warmed serving dish. Quickly mix the soy sauce with the reserved stock and pour over the noodles and vegetables. Season to taste with pepper and serve immediately.

Oriental Vegetable Noodles

❖ **SERVES 6** ❖

175 g/6 oz green thread noodles or multi-coloured spaghetti	1 large carrot, grated
	125 g/4½ oz cucumber, finely shredded
1 tsp sesame oil	1 bunch spring onions, finely shredded
2 tbsp crunchy peanut butter	
2 tbsp light soy sauce	1 tbsp dry-roasted peanuts, crushed
1 tbsp white wine vinegar	
1 tsp clear honey	grated carrot and shredded spring onion, to garnish
125 g/4½ oz mooli, grated	

❖ Bring a large saucepan of water to the boil, add the noodles or spaghetti and cook according to the packet instructions. Drain well and rinse in cold water. Leave in a bowl of cold water until required.

❖ To make the peanut butter sauce, put the sesame oil, peanut butter, soy sauce, vinegar and honey into a small screw-top jar. Seal and shake well to mix thoroughly.

❖ Drain the noodles well, place in a large serving bowl and mix in half the peanut sauce.

❖ Using 2 forks, toss in the mooli, carrot, cucumber and spring onions. Sprinkle with the crushed peanuts and garnish with the grated carrot and shredded spring onion. Serve the noodles with the remaining peanut sauce.

Spicy Fried Noodles

❖ **SERVES 4** ❖

500 g/1 lb 2 oz medium egg noodles	1 garlic clove, crushed
60 g/2 oz beansprouts	4 fresh green chillies, deseeded, sliced and soaked in 2 tbsp rice vinegar
15 g/½ oz chives	
3 tbsp sunflower oil	salt

❖ Place the noodles in a bowl, cover with boiling water and soak for 10 minutes. Drain and set aside.

❖ Pick over the beansprouts and soak in cold water while you cut the chives into 2.5-cm/1-inch pieces. Set a few chives aside for the garnish. Drain the beansprouts thoroughly.

❖ Heat the oil in a preheated wok or large heavy-based frying pan. Add the crushed garlic and stir; then add the chillies and stir-fry for about 1 minute, until fragrant.

❖ Add the beansprouts, stir and then add the noodles. Stir in salt to taste and add the chives. Using 2 spoons or a wok scoop, lift and toss the noodles for 1 minute.

❖ Transfer the noodles to a warmed serving dish, garnish with the reserved chives and serve immediately.

Noodles with Mushrooms

225 g/8 oz rice stick noodles
2 tbsp groundnut oil
1 garlic clove, finely chopped
2-cm/³/₄-inch piece of root
ginger, finely chopped
4 shallots, thinly sliced
70 g/2¹/₂ oz shiitake
mushrooms, sliced
100 g/3¹/₂ oz firm tofu, cut into
1.5-cm/⁵/₈-inch dice
2 tbsp light soy sauce
1 tbsp rice wine
1 tbsp Thai fish sauce
1 tbsp smooth peanut butter
1 tsp chilli sauce
2 tbsp toasted peanuts, chopped
shredded fresh basil leaves,
to serve

❄   Soak the rice stick noodles in hot water for 15 minutes or according to the package directions. Drain well.

❄   Heat the oil in a saucepan. Add the garlic, ginger and shallots and stir-fry for 1–2 minutes until soft and lightly browned.

❄   Add the mushrooms and stir-fry over a medium heat for a further 2–3 minutes. Stir in the tofu and toss gently to brown.

❄   Mix together the soy sauce, rice wine, fish sauce, peanut butter and chilli sauce, then stir into the pan.

❄   Stir in the rice noodles and toss to coat evenly in the sauce. Scatter with the peanuts and shredded basil and serve hot.

Hot & Sour Noodles

250 g/9 oz dried medium egg
noodles
1 tbsp sesame oil
1 tbsp chilli oil
1 garlic clove, crushed
2 spring onions, finely chopped
55 g/2 oz button mushrooms,
sliced
40 g/1½ oz dried Chinese
black mushrooms, soaked,
drained and sliced

2 tbsp lime juice
3 tbsp light soy sauce
1 tsp sugar
shredded Chinese leaves,
to serve
2 tbsp chopped fresh coriander
and 2 tbsp chopped, toasted
peanuts, to garnish

❖ Cook the noodles according to the package instructions.
Drain well, return to the pan, toss with the sesame oil, and
set aside.

❖ Heat the chilli oil in a large frying pan or wok and
quickly stir-fry the garlic, onions and button mushrooms
for 2 minutes until just soft.

❖ Add the black mushrooms, lime juice, soy sauce and
sugar and continue stir-frying until boiling. Add the noodles
and toss to mix.

❖ Make a bed of shredded Chinese leaves on a serving
platter and spoon the noodle mixture on top. Garnish with
the coriander and peanuts and serve immediately.

Garlic Chilli Chicken

6 garlic cloves, finely chopped
5-cm/2-inch piece of root
ginger, peeled and finely
chopped
1 fresh red chilli, deseeded and
finely chopped
4 skinless boneless chicken
breasts, about 140 g/5 oz each,
cut into thin strips
175 g/6 oz dried medium egg
noodles

2 tsp sesame oil
2 tbsp chopped fresh coriander
grated rind and juice of 1 lime
2 tbsp groundnut oil
1 bunch of spring onions,
chopped
55 g/2 oz beansprouts
2 tbsp dark soy sauce
salt and pepper

❖ Combine the garlic, ginger and chilli in a dish. Add
the chicken, turning to coat. Cover and marinate in the
refrigerator for 2 hours.

❖ Bring a saucepan of lightly salted water to the boil, add
the noodles and cook, according to the packet instructions,
until tender. Drain and toss with the sesame oil, coriander
and lime rind and juice and season to taste with salt and
pepper.

❖ Heat the groundnut oil in a preheated wok or frying pan.
Add the chicken and stir-fry for 5–6 minutes, or until tender
and lightly coloured. Remove with a slotted spoon. Add the
spring onions and beansprouts to the wok and stir-fry for
2 minutes.

❖ Return the chicken to the wok and add the noodles and
soy sauce. Cook, stirring and tossing, for 2–3 minutes, or
until heated through, and serve.

Chicken Chop Suey

4 tbsp light soy sauce	350 g/12 oz beansprouts
2 tsp light brown sugar	3 tsp sesame oil
500 g/1 lb 2 oz skinless,	1 tbsp cornflour
boneless chicken breasts	3 tbsp water
3 tbsp vegetable oil	425 ml/15 fl oz chicken stock
2 onions, quartered	shredded leek, to garnish
2 garlic cloves, crushed	

❄ Mix the soy sauce and sugar together, stirring until the sugar has dissolved.

❄ Trim any fat from the chicken and cut into thin strips. Place the meat in a shallow dish and spoon over the soy mixture, turning to coat. Marinate in the refrigerator for 20 minutes.

❄ Heat the oil in a wok and stir-fry the chicken for 2–3 minutes, until golden brown. Add the onions and garlic and cook for a further 2 minutes. Add the beansprouts, cook for 4–5 minutes, then add the sesame oil.

❄ Mix the cornflour and water to form a smooth paste. Pour the stock into the wok, add the cornflour paste and bring to the boil, stirring until the sauce is thickened and clear. Serve, garnished with the shredded leek.

Chicken & Noodle One-Pot

1 tbsp sunflower oil	2 tbsp mild curry paste
1 onion, sliced	450 ml/16 fl oz coconut milk
1 garlic clove, crushed	300 ml/10 fl oz chicken stock
2.5-cm/1-inch piece of root	250 g/9 oz Chinese egg noodles
ginger, peeled and grated	2 tsp lime juice
1 bunch spring onions, sliced	salt and pepper
diagonally	sprigs of fresh basil,
500 g/1 lb 2 oz chicken breast	to garnish
fillet, skinned and cut into	
bite-sized pieces	

❄ Heat the oil in a wok or large heavy-based frying pan.

❄ Add the onion, garlic, ginger and spring onions to the wok and stir-fry for 2 minutes until soft.

❄ Add the chicken and curry paste and stir-fry for 4 minutes or until the vegetables and chicken are golden brown. Stir in the coconut milk, stock and salt and pepper to taste, and mix well.

❄ Bring to the boil, break the noodles into large pieces, if necessary, add to the wok, cover and simmer for about 6–8 minutes until the noodles are just tender, stirring occasionally.

❄ Add the lime juice and adjust the seasoning, if necessary.

❄ Serve the chicken and noodle one-pot at once in deep soup bowls, garnished with the sprigs of basil.

Oyster Sauce Noodles

250 g/9 oz egg noodles
450 g/1 lb chicken thighs
2 tbsp groundnut oil
100 g/3¹/₂ oz carrots, sliced
3 tbsp oyster sauce
2 eggs
3 tbsp cold water

❊ Place the egg noodles in a large bowl or dish. Pour enough boiling water over the noodles to cover and leave to stand for 10 minutes.

❊ Meanwhile, remove the skin from the chicken thighs. Cut the chicken flesh into small pieces, using a sharp knife.

❊ Heat the oil in a large preheated wok or frying pan, swirling the oil around the base of the wok until it is really hot.

❊ Add the pieces of chicken and the carrot slices to the wok and stir-fry for about 5 minutes.

❊ Drain the noodles thoroughly. Add the noodles to the wok and stir-fry for a further 2–3 minutes or until the noodles are heated through.

❊ Beat together the oyster sauce, eggs and water. Drizzle the mixture over the noodles and stir-fry for a further 2–3 minutes or until the eggs set.

❊ Transfer the mixture in the wok to warmed serving bowls and serve hot.

Speedy Peanut Pan-Fry

300 g/10½ oz courgettes
250 g/9 oz baby sweetcorn
250 g/9 oz thread egg noodles
2 tbsp corn oil
1 tbsp sesame oil
8 boneless chicken thighs or
4 breasts, sliced thinly
300 g/10½ oz button
mushrooms

350 g/12 oz beansprouts
4 tbsp smooth peanut butter
2 tbsp soy sauce
2 tbsp lime or lemon juice
60 g/2 oz roasted peanuts
salt and pepper
fresh coriander, to garnish

❊ Using a sharp knife, trim and thinly slice the courgettes and baby sweetcorn. Set aside until required.

❊ Bring a saucepan of lightly salted water to the boil and cook the noodles for 3–4 minutes.

❊ Meanwhile, heat the corn oil and sesame oil in a large wok or frying pan and fry the chicken over a fairly high heat for 1 minute.

❊ Add the courgettes, corn and mushrooms and stir-fry for 5 minutes.

❊ Add the beansprouts, peanut butter, soy sauce and lime juice, season with pepper, then cook for a further 2 minutes.

❊ Drain the noodles thoroughly. Scatter with the roasted peanuts and serve with the noodles. Garnish with the coriander.

Chicken on Crispy Noodles

225 g/8 oz skinless, boneless
chicken breasts, shredded
1 egg white
5 tsp cornflour
225 g/8 oz thin egg noodles
300 ml/10 fl oz vegetable oil
600 ml/1 pint chicken stock
2 tbsp dry sherry

2 tbsp oyster sauce
1 tbsp light soy sauce
1 tbsp hoisin sauce
1 red pepper, deseeded and
very thinly sliced
2 tbsp water
3 spring onions, chopped

❊ Mix together the chicken, egg white and 2 teaspoons of the cornflour in a bowl. Leave to stand for at least 30 minutes.

❊ Blanch the noodles in boiling water for 2 minutes, then drain thoroughly.

❊ Heat the vegetable oil in a preheated wok. Add the noodles, spreading them to cover the base of the wok. Cook over a low heat for about 5 minutes, until the noodles are brown on the underside. Flip the noodles over and brown on the other side. Remove from the wok when crisp and brown, place on a serving plate and keep warm. Drain the oil from the wok.

❊ Add half the stock to the wok. Remove from the heat and add the chicken, stirring well so that it does not stick. Return to the heat and cook for 2 minutes. Drain, discarding the stock.

❊ Wipe the wok with kitchen paper and return to the heat. Add the sherry, sauces, pepper and the remaining stock and bring to the boil. Blend the remaining cornflour with the water and stir it into the mixture.

❊ Return the chicken to the wok and cook over a low heat for 2 minutes. Place the chicken on top of the noodles and sprinkle with the spring onions.

Quick Chicken Noodles

175 g/6 oz Chinese thread egg noodles
2 tbsp sesame or vegetable oil
25 g/1 oz peanuts
1 bunch spring onions, sliced
1 green pepper, deseeded and cut into thin strips
1 large carrot, cut into matchsticks
125 g/4½ oz cauliflower, broken into small florets
350 g/12 oz skinless, boneless chicken, cut into strips
250 g/9 oz mushrooms, sliced
1 tsp finely grated root ginger
1 tsp Chinese five-spice powder
1 tbsp chopped fresh coriander
1 tbsp light soy sauce
salt and pepper
fresh chives, to garnish

❖ Put the noodles in a large bowl and cover with boiling water. Leave to soak for 6 minutes.

❖ Heat the oil in a wok and stir-fry the peanuts for 1 minute until brown. Remove from the wok and leave to drain.

❖ Add the spring onions, pepper, carrot, cauliflower and chicken to the pan. Stir-fry over a high heat for 4–5 minutes.

❖ Drain the noodles thoroughly and add to the wok. Add the mushrooms and stir-fry for 2 minutes. Add the ginger, five-spice powder and coriander and stir-fry for 1 minute.

❖ Season with the soy sauce and salt and pepper. Sprinkle with the peanuts, garnish with the chives and serve.

Yellow Bean Noodles

175 g/6 oz cellophane noodles
1 tbsp groundnut oil
1 leek, sliced
2 garlic cloves, crushed
450 g/1 lb minced chicken
425 ml/15 fl oz chicken stock
1 tsp chilli sauce
2 tbsp yellow bean sauce
4 tbsp light soy sauce
1 tsp sesame oil
chopped chives, to garnish

❖ Place the noodles in a bowl, pour over boiling water and soak for 15 minutes.

❖ Drain the noodles thoroughly and cut into short lengths with kitchen scissors.

❖ Heat the groundnut oil in a wok or frying pan and stir-fry the leek and garlic for 30 seconds.

❖ Add the chicken to the wok and stir-fry for 4–5 minutes until the chicken is completely cooked through.

❖ Add the chicken stock, chilli sauce, yellow bean sauce and soy sauce to the wok and cook for 3–4 minutes.

❖ Add the noodles and sesame oil to the wok and cook, tossing to mix well, for 4–5 minutes.

❖ Spoon the mixture into warmed serving bowls, sprinkle with the chives and serve immediately.

Crispy Duck with Noodles

3 duck breast portions, total
weight about 400 g/14 oz
2 garlic cloves, crushed
1½ tsp chilli paste
1 tbsp honey
3 tbsp dark soy sauce
½ tsp five-spice powder
250 g/9 oz rice stick noodles
1 tsp vegetable oil
1 tsp sesame oil
2 spring onions, sliced
100 g/3½ oz mangetout
2 tbsp tamarind juice
sesame seeds, to garnish

❧ Prick the duck breast skin all over with a fork and place in a deep dish.

❧ Combine the garlic, chilli, honey, soy sauce and five-spice powder, then pour over the duck. Turn over the breast portions to coat them evenly, then cover and set aside to marinate in the refrigerator for at least 1 hour.

❧ Meanwhile, soak the noodles in hot water for 15 minutes or according to the packet instructions. Drain well.

❧ Drain the duck breast portions from the marinade and grill on a rack under a high heat for about 10 minutes, turning them over occasionally, until they become a rich golden brown. Remove and slice thinly.

❧ Heat the vegetable and sesame oils in a pan and stir-fry the spring onions and mangetout for 2 minutes. Stir in the reserved marinade and the tamarind juice and bring to the boil.

❧ Add the sliced duck and noodles and toss to heat thoroughly. Transfer to warmed serving plates and serve immediately, sprinkled with the sesame seeds.

Hoisin Pork with Noodles

250 g/9 oz dried thick Chinese egg noodles, or Chinese wholemeal egg noodles
450 g/1 lb pork fillet, thinly sliced
1 tsp sugar
1 tbsp groundnut or sunflower oil
4 tbsp rice vinegar
4 tbsp white wine vinegar
4 tbsp bottled hoisin sauce
2 spring onions, sliced diagonally
about 2 tbsp garlic-flavoured sunflower oil
2 large garlic cloves, thinly sliced
chopped fresh coriander, to garnish

❄ Cook the noodles according to the packet instructions. Drain well, rinse under cold water to stop the cooking and drain again, then set aside.

❄ Meanwhile, sprinkle the pork slices with the sugar and use your hands to toss together. Heat a wok or large frying pan over a high heat. Add the oil and heat until it shimmers. Add the pork and stir-fry for about 3 minutes until the pork is cooked through and is no longer pink. Use a slotted spoon to remove the pork from the wok and keep warm. Add both vinegars to the wok and boil until they are reduced to about 5 tablespoons. Pour in the hoisin sauce with the spring onions and leave to bubble until reduced by half. Add to the pork and stir together.

❄ Quickly wipe out the pan and reheat. Add the garlic-flavoured oil and heat until it shimmers. Add the garlic slices and stir around for about 30 seconds until they are golden and crisp, then use a slotted spoon to scoop them out of the wok and set aside.

❄ Add the noodles to the wok and stir them around to warm them through. Divide the noodles between 4 plates, top with the pork and onion mixture, sprinkle with the fried garlic slices and garnish with the coriander.

Garlic Pork & Noodles

250 g/9 oz packet medium egg noodles
3 tbsp vegetable oil
2 garlic cloves, crushed
350 g/12 oz pork fillet, cut into strips
4 tbsp dried prawns, or 125 g/4 1/2 oz peeled prawns
1 bunch spring onions, finely chopped
90 g/3 oz chopped roasted and shelled unsalted peanuts
3 tbsp fish sauce
1 1/2 tsp palm or demerara sugar
1–2 small red chillies, deseeded and finely chopped
3 tbsp lime juice
3 tbsp chopped fresh coriander

❄ Place the noodles in a large saucepan of boiling water, then immediately remove from the heat. Cover and leave to stand for 6 minutes, stirring once halfway through the time. After 6 minutes the noodles will be perfectly cooked. Alternatively, follow the instructions on the packet. Drain and keep warm.

❄ Heat the oil in a wok, add the garlic and pork and stir-fry until the pork strips are browned, about 2–3 minutes.

❄ Add the prawns, spring onions, peanuts, fish sauce, sugar, chillies to taste and lime juice. Stir-fry for a further minute.

❄ Add the noodles and coriander and stir-fry until heated through, about 1 minute. Serve the stir-fry immediately.

Pad Thai Noodles

❖ SERVES 4 ❖

250 g/9 oz rice stick noodles
3 tbsp groundnut oil
3 garlic cloves, finely chopped
115 g/4 oz pork fillet, chopped into 5-mm/¼-inch pieces
200 g/7 oz cooked peeled prawns
1 tbsp sugar
3 tbsp Thai fish sauce
1 tbsp tomato ketchup
1 tbsp lime juice
2 eggs, beaten
115 g/4 oz beansprouts

TO GARNISH
1 tsp dried red chilli flakes
2 spring onions, thickly sliced
2 tbsp chopped fresh coriander

❖ Soak the rice noodles in hot water for about 10 minutes or according to the packet instructions. Drain thoroughly and set aside.

❖ Heat the groundnut oil in a large frying pan or wok, add the garlic and fry over a high heat for 30 seconds. Add the pork and stir-fry for 2–3 minutes until brown all over.

❖ Stir in the prawns, then add the sugar, fish sauce, ketchup and lime juice, and continue stir-frying for a further 30 seconds.

❖ Stir in the eggs and stir-fry until lightly set. Stir in the noodles, then add the beansprouts and stir-fry for a further 30 seconds to cook lightly.

❖ Turn out on to a warmed serving dish and scatter with the chilli flakes, spring onion slices and coriander. Serve hot.

Drunken Noodles

❖ SERVES 4 ❖

175 g/6 oz rice stick noodles
2 tbsp vegetable oil
1 garlic clove, crushed
2 small fresh green chillies, chopped
1 small onion, thinly sliced
150 g/5½ oz lean minced pork or chicken
1 small green pepper, deseeded and finely chopped
4 kaffir lime leaves, finely shredded
1 tbsp dark soy sauce
1 tbsp light soy sauce
½ tsp sugar
1 tomato, cut into thin wedges
2 tbsp fresh basil leaves, finely shredded, to garnish

❖ Soak the noodles in hot water for 15 minutes or according to the package directions. Drain well.

❖ Heat the oil in a wok and stir-fry the garlic, chillies and onion for 1 minute.

❖ Stir in the pork or chicken and stir-fry over a high heat for a further minute, then add the green pepper and continue stir-frying for a further 2 minutes.

❖ Stir in the lime leaves, soy sauces and sugar. Add the noodles and tomato and toss well to heat thoroughly.

❖ Sprinkle with the basil and serve hot.

Egg Noodles with Beef

❋ **SERVES 4** ❋

285 g/10 oz egg noodles
3 tbsp walnut oil
2.5-cm/1-inch piece of root
ginger, cut into thin strips
5 spring onions, finely
shredded
2 garlic cloves, finely chopped
1 red pepper, deseeded and
thinly sliced
100 g/3½ oz button
mushrooms, thinly sliced
350 g/12 oz fillet steak, cut into
thin strips
1 tbsp cornflour
5 tbsp dry sherry
3 tbsp soy sauce
1 tsp soft brown sugar
225 g/8 oz beansprouts
1 tbsp sesame oil
salt and pepper
strips of spring onion,
to garnish

❋ Bring a large saucepan of water to the boil. Add the egg noodles and cook according to the instructions on the packet. Drain the noodles, rinse under cold running water, drain thoroughly again and set aside.

❋ Heat the walnut oil in a preheated wok until it is really hot.

❋ Add the ginger, spring onions and garlic and stir-fry for 45 seconds.

❋ Add the sliced pepper, mushrooms and steak and stir-fry for 4 minutes. Season to taste with salt and pepper.

❋ Mix together the cornflour, sherry and soy sauce in a small jug to form a paste, and pour into the wok. Sprinkle over the sugar and stir-fry all of the ingredients for a further 2 minutes.

❋ Add the beansprouts, noodles and sesame oil to the wok, stir and toss together for 1 minute.

❋ Transfer the stir-fry to warmed serving dishes, garnish with the strips of spring onion and serve.

Beef with Beansprouts

1 bunch spring onions, thinly
sliced lengthways
2 tbsp sunflower oil
1 garlic clove, crushed
1 tsp finely chopped root ginger
500 g/1 lb 2 oz tender beef,
cut into thin strips
1 large red pepper, deseeded
and sliced
1 small fresh red chilli,
deseeded and chopped

350 g/12 oz fresh beansprouts
1 small lemon grass stalk,
finely chopped
2 tbsp smooth peanut butter
4 tbsp coconut milk
1 tbsp rice vinegar
1 tbsp soy sauce
1 tsp soft light brown sugar
250 g/9 oz medium egg
noodles
salt and pepper

❈ Set aside some of the sliced spring onions for the garnish. Heat the sunflower oil in a frying pan or wok over a high heat. Add the remaining spring onions, the garlic and ginger and stir-fry for 2–3 minutes until soft. Add the beef strips and stir-fry for 4–5 minutes until evenly browned.

❈ Add the red pepper and stir-fry for a further 3–4 minutes. Add the chilli and beansprouts and stir-fry for 2 minutes. Combine the lemon grass, peanut butter, coconut milk, vinegar, soy sauce and sugar, then stir the mixture into the wok.

❈ Meanwhile, cook the noodles according to the packet instructions. Drain and stir into the frying pan, tossing to mix evenly.

❈ Season to taste with salt and pepper. Sprinkle the reserved spring onion slices over the stir-fry and serve hot.

Beef with Lemon Grass

500 g/1 lb 2 oz lean beef fillet
2 tbsp vegetable oil
1 garlic clove, finely chopped
1 lemon grass stalk, finely
shredded
2 tsp finely chopped
root ginger

1 red pepper, deseeded and
thickly sliced
1 green pepper, deseeded and
thickly sliced
1 onion, thickly sliced
2 tbsp lime juice
salt and pepper
boiled noodles or rice, to serve

❈ If you have time, place the beef in the freezer for 30 minutes beforehand. This helps to firm it up, which makes it easier to slice very thinly. Cut the beef into long, thin strips, cutting across the grain.

❈ Heat the oil in a large frying pan or wok over a high heat. Add the garlic and stir-fry for 1 minute.

❈ Add the beef and stir-fry for a further 2–3 minutes until lightly coloured. Stir in the lemon grass and ginger and remove the pan or wok from the heat.

❈ Remove the beef from the pan or wok and set aside. Add the peppers and onion to the pan or wok and stir-fry over a high heat for 2–3 minutes until the onions are just turning golden brown and slightly soft.

❈ Return the beef to the pan, stir in the lime juice and season to taste with salt and pepper. Serve immediately with the noodles.

Steak with Crisp Noodle Cakes

115 g/4 oz thin dried Chinese
egg noodles
2 spring onions, sliced
diagonally
about 5 tbsp groundnut or
sunflower oil
1 large onion, sliced
1 large steak, such as sirloin
or rump, weighing about
300 g/10 1/2 oz in total and
1 cm/1/2 inch thick

6 tbsp bottled Thai red curry
paste
55 g/2 oz block creamed
coconut, dissolved in 100 ml/
3 1/2 fl oz boiling water
salt and pepper

❄ Cook the noodles according to the packet instructions, drain well and set aside until they are no longer wet. Do not rinse them, because you want the starch to stick them together. Put in a bowl, add the spring onions and toss.

❄ Heat a large frying pan over a high heat. Add 1 tablespoon of the oil and heat until it shimmers. Add half the noodles and press down firmly to form a flat pancake. Reduce the heat to medium and fry for 4 minutes, or until crusty on the bottom. Slide the noodle cake on to a rimless baking tray. Invert the pan over the noodles and flip both the baking tray and the pan, so the noodles drop into the pan. Add another tablespoon of the oil to the pan and continue frying for 3–4 minutes until crisp. Drain on kitchen paper, then keep warm in a low oven while you fry the remaining noodles the same way.

❄ Wipe out the pan and add 1 tablespoon of the oil. Add the onion and fry for about 3 minutes until soft. Season the steak with salt and pepper, add to the pan and fry for 2 minutes. Turn over the steak, add the red curry paste and stir in the creamed coconut. Let the steak cook in the sauce for a further 2 minutes for medium-rare, then remove. Boil the sauce for 1–2 minutes until it thickens.

❄ Thinly slice the steak diagonally, arrange on the noodle cakes and spoon the sauce over.

Cantonese Fried Noodles

350 g/12 oz egg noodles
3 tbsp vegetable oil
675 g/1 lb 8 oz lean beef steak,
cut into thin strips
125 g/4 1/2 oz green cabbage,
shredded
75 g/2 3/4 oz bamboo shoots
6 spring onions, sliced

25 g/1 oz French beans, halved
1 tbsp dark soy sauce
2 tbsp beef stock
1 tbsp dry sherry
1 tbsp muscovado sugar
2 tbsp chopped parsley,
to garnish

❄ Cook the noodles in a saucepan of boiling water for 2–3 minutes. Drain well, rinse under cold running water and drain thoroughly again.

❄ Heat 1 tablespoon of the oil in a preheated wok or frying pan, swirling it around until it is really hot.

❄ Add the noodles and stir-fry for 1–2 minutes. Drain the noodles and set aside until required.

❄ Heat the remaining oil in the wok. Add the beef and stir-fry for 2–3 minutes. Add the cabbage, bamboo shoots, spring onions and beans to the wok and stir-fry for 1–2 minutes.

❄ Add the soy sauce, stock, sherry and sugar to the wok, stirring to mix well.

❄ Stir the noodles into the mixture in the wok, tossing to mix well. Transfer to serving bowls, garnish with the parsley and serve immediately.

Beef with Crispy Noodles

225 g/8 oz medium egg noodles
350 g/12 oz beef fillet
2 tbsp sunflower oil
1 tsp ground ginger
1 clove garlic, crushed
1 red chilli, deseeded and very
finely chopped
100 g/3¹/2 oz carrots, cut into
matchsticks
6 spring onions, sliced
2 tbsp lime marmalade
2 tbsp soy sauce
oil, for frying

❊   Place the noodles in a large dish or bowl. Pour over enough boiling water to cover the noodles and leave to stand for about 10 minutes while you stir-fry the rest of the ingredients.

❊   Using a sharp knife, thinly slice the beef.

❊   Heat the sunflower oil in a large preheated wok or frying pan.

❊   Add the beef and ginger to the wok or frying pan and stir-fry for about 5 minutes.

❊   Add the garlic, chilli, carrots and spring onions to the wok and stir-fry for a further 2–3 minutes.

❊   Add the lime marmalade and soy sauce to the wok and allow to bubble for 2 minutes. Remove the chilli beef and ginger mixture, set aside and keep warm until required.

❊   Heat the oil for frying in the wok or frying pan.

❊   Drain the noodles thoroughly and pat dry with absorbent kitchen paper. Carefully lower the noodles into the hot oil and cook for 2–3 minutes or until crispy. Drain the noodles on absorbent kitchen paper.

❊   Divide the noodles between 4 warmed serving plates and top with the chilli beef and ginger mixture. Serve immediately.

Lamb with Noodles

150 g/5½ oz cellophane noodles
2 tbsp groundnut oil
450 g/1 lb lean lamb, thinly sliced
2 garlic cloves, crushed
2 leeks, sliced
3 tbsp dark soy sauce
250 ml/9 fl oz lamb stock
dash of chilli sauce
strips of red chilli, to garnish

❖ Bring a large saucepan of water to the boil. Add the cellophane noodles and cook for 1 minute. Drain the noodles well, place in a sieve, rinse under cold running water and drain thoroughly again. Set aside until required.

❖ Heat the groundnut oil in a preheated wok or frying pan, swirling the oil around until it is really hot.

❖ Add the lamb to the wok and stir-fry for about 2 minutes.

❖ Add the garlic and leeks to the wok and stir-fry for a further 2 minutes.

❖ Stir in the soy sauce, stock and chilli sauce and cook for 3–4 minutes, stirring frequently, until the meat is cooked through.

❖ Add the noodles to the wok and cook for about 1 minute, stirring, until heated through.

❖ Transfer the lamb and noodles to serving plates, garnish with the chilli strips and serve.

Twice-Cooked Lamb

250 g/9 oz packet egg noodles
450 g/1 lb lamb loin fillet, thinly sliced
2 tbsp soy sauce
2 tbsp sunflower oil
2 cloves garlic, crushed
1 tbsp caster sugar
2 tbsp oyster sauce
175 g/6 oz baby spinach

❖ Place the egg noodles in a large bowl and cover with boiling water. Leave to soak for about 10 minutes.

❖ Bring a large saucepan of water to the boil. Add the lamb and cook for 5 minutes. Drain thoroughly.

❖ Place the slices of lamb in a bowl and mix with the soy sauce and 1 tablespoon of the oil.

❖ Heat the remaining oil in a large preheated wok, swirling the oil around until it is really hot.

❖ Add the lamb and garlic to the wok and stir-fry for about 5 minutes or until the meat is just beginning to brown.

❖ Add the sugar and oyster sauce to the wok and stir well to combine.

❖ Drain the noodles thoroughly. Add the noodles to the wok and stir-fry for a further 5 minutes.

❖ Add the spinach to the wok and cook for 1 minute or until the leaves just wilt. Transfer the lamb and noodles to serving bowls and serve hot.

Teriyaki Salmon with Noodles

4 salmon fillets, about 200 g/7 oz each
125 ml/4 fl oz teriyaki marinade
1 shallot, sliced
2-cm/³⁄₄-inch piece of root ginger, finely chopped
2 carrots, sliced
115 g/4 oz closed-cup mushrooms, sliced
1.2 litres/2 pints vegetable stock
250 g/9 oz dried medium egg noodles
115 g/4 oz frozen peas
175 g/6 oz Chinese leaves, shredded
4 spring onions, sliced

❄ Wipe off any fish scales from the salmon skin. Arrange the salmon fillets, skin side up, in a dish just large enough to fit them in a single layer. Mix the teriyaki marinade with the shallot and ginger in a small bowl and pour over the salmon. Cover and leave to marinate in the refrigerator for 1 hour, turning the salmon over halfway through.

❄ Put the carrots, mushrooms and stock into a large saucepan. Arrange the salmon, skin side down, on a shallow baking tray. Pour the fish marinade into the pan of vegetables and stock and bring to the boil. Reduce the heat, cover and simmer for 10 minutes.

❄ Meanwhile, preheat the grill to medium. Cook the salmon under the preheated grill for 10–15 minutes, depending on the thickness of the fillets, until the flesh turns pink and flakes easily. Remove from the grill and keep warm.

❄ Add the noodles and peas to the stock and return to the boil. Reduce the heat, cover and simmer for 5 minutes or until the noodles are tender. Stir in the Chinese leaves and spring onions and heat through for 1 minute.

❄ Carefully drain off 300 ml/10 fl oz of the stock into a small heatproof jug and reserve. Drain and discard the remaining stock. Divide the noodles and vegetables between 4 warmed serving bowls and top each with a salmon fillet. Pour the reserved stock over each meal and serve immediately.

Trout with Sesame & Chilli

2 tbsp sesame seeds
250 ml/9 fl oz fish stock
8 trout fillets, about 150 g/5¹⁄₂ oz each
250 g/9 oz dried fine egg noodles
juice of ¹⁄₂ lime
1 fresh red chilli, deseeded and thinly sliced
1 tbsp sesame oil, plus extra for drizzling
1 tbsp vegetable oil
1 tsp Thai fish sauce
1 bunch watercress and 4 lime wedges, to serve

❄ Heat a non-stick frying pan over a medium heat, add the sesame seeds and cook, turning, until they begin to colour. Tip on to a plate and set aside.

❄ Put the stock into a large frying pan and bring to a simmer. Add the trout fillets and poach gently for 7–10 minutes, or until just cooked.

❄ Meanwhile, bring a large saucepan of water to the boil, add the noodles and cook for 3 minutes. Drain and toss with the sesame seeds, lime juice, chilli, oils and fish sauce. Keep warm.

❄ To serve, pile an equal quantity of noodles on each of 4 serving plates and top with 2 trout fillets, some watercress and a lime wedge. Drizzle with a little more sesame oil.

Coconut Noodles with Prawns

2 tbsp vegetable oil
1 small red pepper, deseeded and diced
200 g/7 oz pak choi, stalks thinly sliced and leaves chopped
2 large garlic cloves, chopped
1 tsp ground turmeric
2 tsp garam masala
1 tsp chilli powder (optional)
125 ml/4 fl oz hot vegetable stock
2 heaped tbsp smooth peanut butter
350 ml/12 fl oz coconut milk
1 tbsp tamari (wheat-free soy sauce)
250 g/9 oz thick rice noodles
280 g/10 oz cooked peeled large prawns
2 spring onions, finely shredded, and 1 tbsp sesame seeds, to garnish

❖ Heat the oil in a wok or large heavy-based frying pan over a high heat. Add the red pepper, pak choi stalks and garlic and stir-fry for 3 minutes. Add the turmeric, garam masala, chilli powder, if using, and pak choi leaves and stir-fry for a further minute.

❖ Mix the hot stock and peanut butter together in a heatproof bowl until the peanut butter has dissolved, then add to the stir-fry with the coconut milk and tamari. Cook for 5 minutes over a medium heat, or until reduced and thickened.

❖ Meanwhile, immerse the noodles in a bowl of just boiled water. Leave for 4 minutes, then drain and refresh the noodles under cold running water. Add the cooked noodles and prawns to the coconut curry and cook for a further 2–3 minutes, stirring frequently, until heated through.

❖ Serve the noodle dish sprinkled with the spring onions and sesame seeds.

Sweet & Sour Noodles

❈ **SERVES 4** ❈

3 tbsp fish sauce
2 tbsp distilled white vinegar
2 tbsp caster or palm sugar
2 tbsp tomato purée
2 tbsp sunflower oil
3 cloves garlic, crushed
350 g/12 oz rice noodles, soaked in boiling water for 5 minutes

8 spring onions, sliced
175 g/6 oz carrots, grated
150 g/5$\frac{1}{2}$ oz beansprouts
2 eggs, beaten
225 g/8 oz peeled king prawns
50 g/1$\frac{3}{4}$ oz chopped peanuts
1 tsp chilli flakes, to garnish

❈ Mix together the fish sauce, vinegar, sugar and tomato purée.

❈ Heat the oil in a large preheated wok.

❈ Add the garlic to the wok and stir-fry for 30 seconds.

❈ Drain the noodles thoroughly and add them to the wok together with the fish sauce and tomato purée mixture. Mix well to combine.

❈ Add the spring onions, carrot and beansprouts to the wok and stir-fry for 2–3 minutes.

❈ Move the contents of the wok to one side, add the beaten eggs to the empty part of the wok and cook until the egg sets. Add the noodles, prawns and peanuts to the wok and mix well. Transfer to warmed serving dishes and garnish with the chilli flakes. Serve hot.

Noodles with Chilli & Prawns

❈ **SERVES 4** ❈

250 g/9 oz thin glass noodles
2 tbsp sunflower oil
1 onion, sliced
2 red chillies, deseeded and very finely chopped
4 lime leaves, thinly shredded

1 tbsp fresh coriander
2 tbsp palm or caster sugar
2 tbsp fish sauce
450 g/1 lb raw tiger prawns, peeled

❈ Place the noodles in a large bowl. Pour over enough boiling water to cover the noodles and leave to stand for 5 minutes. Drain thoroughly and set aside until required.

❈ Heat the sunflower oil in a large preheated wok or frying pan until it is really hot.

❈ Add the onion, chillies and lime leaves to the wok and stir-fry for 1 minute.

❈ Add the coriander, sugar, fish sauce and prawns to the wok and stir-fry for a further 2 minutes or until the prawns turn pink.

❈ Add the noodles to the wok, toss to mix well and stir-fry for 1–2 minutes or until heated through.

❈ Transfer the noodles and prawns to warmed serving bowls and serve immediately.

Seafood Chow Mein

❈ SERVES 4 ❈

90 g/3 oz squid, cleaned
3–4 fresh scallops
90 g/3 oz raw prawns, shelled
1/2 egg white, lightly beaten
1 tbsp cornflour paste
275 g/9 1/2 oz egg noodles
5-6 tbsp vegetable oil
2 tbsp light soy sauce
60 g/2 oz mangetout
1/2 tsp salt
1/2 tsp sugar
1 tsp Chinese rice wine
2 spring onions, finely shredded
a few drops of sesame oil

❈ Open up the squid and score the inside in a criss-cross pattern, then cut into pieces about the size of a postage stamp. Soak the squid in a bowl of boiling water until all the pieces curl up. Rinse in cold water and drain.

❈ Cut each scallop into 3–4 slices. Cut the prawns in half lengthways if large. Mix the scallops and prawns with the egg white and cornflour paste.

❈ Cook the noodles in boiling water according to the packet instructions, then drain and rinse under cold water. Drain well, then toss with about 1 tablespoon of the oil.

❈ Heat 3 tablespoons of the oil in a preheated wok. Add the noodles and 1 tablespoon of the soy sauce and stir-fry for 2–3 minutes. Remove to a large serving dish.

❈ Heat the remaining oil in the wok and add the mangetout and seafood. Stir-fry for about 2 minutes, then add the salt, sugar, wine, remaining soy sauce and about half the spring onions. Blend well and add a little stock or water if necessary. Pour the seafood mixture over the noodles and sprinkle with sesame oil. Garnish with the remaining spring onions and serve.

Spiced Basmati Pilau

❈ SERVES 6 ❈

500 g/1 lb 2 oz basmati rice
175 g/6 oz broccoli, trimmed
6 tbsp vegetable oil
2 large onions, chopped
225 g/8 oz sliced mushrooms
2 garlic cloves, crushed
6 cardamom pods, split
6 whole cloves
8 black peppercorns
1 cinnamon stick or piece of cassia bark
1 tsp ground turmeric
1.2 litres/2 pints boiling vegetable stock or water
60 g/2 oz seedless raisins
60 g/2 oz unsalted pistachio nuts, coarsely chopped
salt and pepper

❈ Place the rice in a sieve and wash well under cold running water. Drain. Trim off most of the broccoli stalk and cut into small florets, then quarter the stalk lengthways and cut diagonally into 1-cm/1/2-inch pieces.

❈ Heat the oil in a large saucepan. Add the onions and broccoli stalks and cook over a low heat, stirring frequently, for 3 minutes. Add the mushrooms, rice, garlic and spices and cook for 1 minute, stirring, until the rice is coated in oil.

❈ Add the boiling stock and season to taste with salt and pepper. Stir in the broccoli florets and return the mixture to the boil. Cover, reduce the heat and cook over a low heat for 15 minutes without uncovering the pan.

❈ Remove from the heat and leave to stand for 5 minutes without uncovering. Add the raisins and pistachios and gently fork through to fluff up the grains. Serve hot.

Lentil & Vegetable Biryani

125 g/4$\frac{1}{2}$ oz continental lentils
4 tbsp vegetable ghee or oil
2 onions, quartered and sliced
2 garlic cloves, crushed
2.5-cm/1-inch piece of root
ginger, chopped
1 tsp ground turmeric
$\frac{1}{2}$ tsp chilli powder
1 tsp ground coriander
2 tsp ground cumin
3 tomatoes, peeled and
chopped
1 aubergine, trimmed and
cut into 1-cm/$\frac{1}{2}$-inch pieces
1.75 litres/3 pints boiling
vegetable stock
1 red or green pepper,
deseeded and diced
350 g/12 oz basmati rice
125 g/4$\frac{1}{2}$ oz French beans,
halved
225 g/8 oz cauliflower florets
125 g/4$\frac{1}{2}$ oz mushrooms,
sliced or quartered
60 g/2 oz unsalted cashew nuts
3 hard-boiled eggs, shelled and
cut into wedges, and sprigs of
fresh coriander, to garnish

❈ Rinse the lentils under cold running water and drain. Heat the ghee or oil in a saucepan, add the onions and fry gently for 2 minutes. Stir in the garlic, ginger and spices and fry gently, stirring frequently, for 1 minute.

❈ Add the lentils, tomatoes, aubergine and 600 ml/1 pint of the stock, mix well, then cover and simmer gently for 20 minutes.

❈ Add the diced pepper and cook for a further 10 minutes or until the lentils are tender and all the liquid has been absorbed.

❈ Meanwhile, rinse the rice under cold running water. Drain and place in another pan with the remaining stock. Bring to the boil, add the French beans, cauliflower and mushrooms, then cover and cook gently for 15 minutes or until the rice and vegetables are tender. Remove from the heat and set aside, covered, for 10 minutes.

❈ Add the lentil mixture and the cashew nuts to the cooked rice and mix lightly together. Pile on to a warmed serving platter and garnish with the wedges of hard-boiled egg and the coriander sprigs. Serve hot.

Garlic Rice

❄ **SERVES 6** ❄

500 ml/18 fl oz chicken stock
3 tbsp olive oil
1 Spanish onion, finely chopped
4 garlic cloves, finely chopped
225 g/8 oz long-grain rice

3 tbsp chopped fresh parsley
1 tbsp finely grated lemon rind
1 bay leaf
salt and pepper

❄ Preheat the oven to 200°C/400°F/Gas Mark 6. Pour the stock into a saucepan and bring to the boil.

❄ Meanwhile, heat the oil in a flameproof casserole dish. Add the onion and garlic and cook over a low heat, stirring occasionally, for 10 minutes or until golden. Add the rice and stir until the grains are coated in oil. Stir in the stock, parsley, lemon rind and bay leaf and season to taste with salt and pepper.

❄ Bring to the boil, then cover and cook in the oven for 35–45 minutes, or until tender. Stir the rice occasionally during cooking to prevent it from sticking to the casserole. Discard the bay leaf before serving.

Baked Tomato Rice

❄ **SERVES 4** ❄

2 tbsp vegetable oil
1 onion, coarsely chopped
1 red pepper, deseeded and
chopped
2 garlic cloves, finely chopped
1/2 tsp dried thyme
300 g/10 1/2 oz long-grain rice
1 litre/1 3/4 pints chicken or
vegetable stock
225 g/8 oz canned chopped
tomatoes

1 bay leaf
2 tbsp shredded fresh basil
175 g/6 oz mature Cheddar
cheese, grated
2 tbsp chopped fresh chives
4 herbed pork sausages,
cooked and cut into
1-cm/1/2-inch pieces
2–3 tbsp freshly grated
Parmesan cheese

❄ Heat the oil in a large flameproof casserole over a medium heat. Add the onion and red pepper and cook, stirring frequently, for about 5 minutes until soft and lightly coloured. Stir in the garlic and thyme and cook for a further minute.

❄ Add the rice and cook, stirring frequently, for about 2 minutes until the rice is well coated and translucent. Stir in the stock, tomatoes and bay leaf. Bring to the boil and simmer vigorously for 5 minutes until the stock is almost completely absorbed.

❄ Stir in the basil, Cheddar cheese, chives and pork sausages and bake, covered, in a preheated oven, 180°C/350°F/Gas Mark 4, for about 25 minutes.

❄ Sprinkle with the Parmesan cheese and return to the oven, uncovered, for 5 minutes until the top is golden. Serve hot, straight from the casserole.

Stir-Fried Rice with Egg

❄ **SERVES 4** ❄

2 tbsp groundnut oil
1 egg, beaten with 1 tsp water
1 garlic clove, finely chopped
1 small onion, finely chopped
1 tbsp Thai red curry paste
250 g/9 oz long-grain rice,
    cooked

55 g/2 oz cooked peas
1 tbsp Thai fish sauce
2 tbsp tomato ketchup
2 tbsp chopped fresh coriander
fresh red chillies and
    cucumber slices, to garnish

❄ To make chilli flowers for the garnish, hold the stem of each chilli with your fingertips and use a small sharp pointed knife to cut a slit down the length from near the stem end to the tip. Turn the chilli about a quarter turn and make another cut. Repeat to make a total of 4 cuts, then scrape out the seeds. Cut each petal again, in half or into quarters, to make 8–16 petals. Place the chilli in iced water.

❄ Heat about 1 teaspoon of the oil in a wok. Pour in the egg mixture, swirling it to coat the wok evenly and make a thin layer. When set and golden, remove the egg from the wok and roll up. Set aside.

❄ Add the remaining oil to the wok and stir-fry the garlic and onion for 1 minute. Add the curry paste, then stir in the rice and peas. Stir until heated through.

❄ Stir in the fish sauce, ketchup and coriander. Remove the wok from the heat and pile the rice on to a warmed serving dish.

❄ Slice the egg roll into spiral strips, without unrolling, and use to garnish the rice. Add the cucumber slices and chilli flowers. Serve hot.

Rocket & Tomato Risotto

❄ **SERVES 4–6** ❄

2 tbsp olive oil
2 tbsp unsalted butter
1 large onion, finely chopped
2 garlic cloves, finely chopped
350 g/12 oz arborio rice
125 ml/4 fl oz dry white vermouth
1.5 litres/2¾ pints chicken or
    vegetable stock, simmering
6 vine-ripened or Italian plum
    tomatoes, deseeded and
    chopped

125 g/4½ oz wild rocket
handful of fresh basil leaves
115 g/4 oz freshly grated
    Parmesan cheese
225 g/8 oz mozzarella cheese,
    coarsely grated or diced
salt and pepper

❄ Heat the oil and half the butter in a large frying pan. Add the onion and cook for about 2 minutes until just beginning to soften. Stir in the garlic and rice and cook, stirring frequently, until the rice is translucent and well coated.

❄ Pour in the vermouth; it will evaporate almost immediately. Add a ladleful (about 225 ml/8 fl oz) of the stock and cook, stirring, until it is absorbed.

❄ Continue adding the stock, about half a ladleful at a time, allowing each addition to be absorbed before adding the next. Just before the rice is tender, stir in the chopped tomatoes and rocket. Shred the basil leaves and immediately stir into the risotto. Continue to cook, adding more stock, until the risotto is creamy and the rice is tender, but still firm to the bite.

❄ Remove from the heat and stir in the remaining butter, and the Parmesan and mozzarella cheeses. Season to taste with salt and pepper. Remove the pan from the heat, cover and leave to stand for about 1 minute. Serve immediately, before the mozzarella cheese melts completely.

Easy Cheese Risotto

4–6 tbsp unsalted butter
1 onion, finely chopped
300 g/10^1/$_2$ oz arborio or
carnaroli rice
125 ml/4 fl oz dry white
vermouth or white wine
1.2 litres/2 pints chicken or
vegetable stock, simmering
85 g/3 oz freshly grated
Parmesan cheese, plus extra
for sprinkling
salt and pepper

❖ Heat about 2 tablespoons of the butter in a large heavy-based saucepan over a medium heat. Add the onion and cook for about 2 minutes until just beginning to soften. Add the rice and cook, stirring frequently, for about 2 minutes until translucent and well coated with the butter.

❖ Pour in the vermouth: it will bubble and steam rapidly and evaporate almost instantly. Add a ladleful (about 225 ml/8 fl oz) of the simmering stock and cook, stirring constantly, until the stock is completely absorbed.

❖ Continue adding the stock, about half a ladleful at a time, allowing each addition to be absorbed before adding the next – never allow the rice to cook dry. This should take 20–25 minutes. The risotto should have a creamy consistency and the rice grains should be tender, but still firm to the bite.

❖ Switch off the heat and stir in the remaining butter and the cheese. Season to taste with salt and pepper. Cover, leave to stand for about 1 minute, then serve with Parmesan cheese, for sprinkling.

Butternut Squash Risotto

600 g/1 lb 5 oz butternut
squash or pumpkin, peeled
and cut into bite-sized pieces
4 tbsp olive oil
1 tsp clear honey
25 g/1 oz fresh basil
25 g/1 oz fresh oregano

1 tbsp margarine
2 onions, finely chopped
450 g/1 lb arborio rice
175 ml/6 fl oz dry white wine
1.2 litres/2 pints vegetable stock
salt and pepper

❊ Preheat the oven to 200°C/400°F/Gas Mark 6. Put the squash into a roasting tin. Mix 1 tablespoon of the oil with the honey and spoon over the squash. Turn the squash to coat it in the mixture. Roast in the preheated oven for 30–35 minutes or until tender.

❊ Meanwhile, put the basil and oregano into a food processor with 2 tablespoons of the remaining oil and process until finely chopped and blended. Set aside.

❊ Heat the margarine and remaining oil in a large heavy-based saucepan over a medium heat. Add the onions and fry, stirring occasionally, for 8 minutes or until soft and golden. Add the rice and cook for 2 minutes, stirring to coat the grains in the oil mixture.

❊ Pour in the wine and bring to the boil. Reduce the heat slightly and cook until the wine is almost absorbed. Add the stock, a little at a time, and cook over a medium–low heat, stirring constantly, for 20 minutes.

❊ Gently stir in the herb oil and squash until thoroughly mixed into the rice and cook for a further 5 minutes or until the rice is creamy and cooked but still firm to the bite. Season well with salt and pepper before serving.

Mushroom & Sage Risotto

15 g/$\frac{1}{2}$ oz dried ceps
300 ml/10 fl oz hot water
850 ml/1$\frac{1}{2}$ pints vegetable
stock
85 g/3 oz butter
1 onion, finely chopped
2 garlic cloves, chopped
200 g/7 oz mixed wild
mushrooms

150 ml/5 fl oz dry white wine
350 g/12 oz arborio rice
1 tbsp chopped fresh sage
55 g/2 oz freshly grated
Parmesan cheese
salt and pepper

❊ Place the mushrooms in a bowl and cover with the water. Leave to soak for 15 minutes. Drain the mushrooms and strain the liquid into a saucepan. Pour in the stock and heat. Simmer gently to keep it hot.

❊ Heat half the butter in a large heavy-based saucepan. Add the onion and garlic and cook gently for 10 minutes until soft.

❊ Add the dried and fresh mushrooms and cook for a few minutes until just soft. Stir in the wine. Boil rapidly until reduced by one-third, then add the rice and sage. Stir in the hot stock, a little at a time, and wait until it has been absorbed before adding more.

❊ Continue until all the stock has been added and the liquid has been absorbed. Stir in the remaining butter, salt and pepper to taste and the cheese and serve immediately.

Sun-Dried Tomato Risotto

❖ SERVES 4 ❖

1 tbsp olive oil	8 sun-dried tomatoes,
25 g/1 oz butter	cut into strips
1 large onion, finely chopped	100 g/3½ oz frozen peas,
350 g/12 oz arborio rice,	thawed
washed	50 g/1¾ oz Parma ham,
about 15 strands of saffron	shredded
150 ml/5 fl oz white wine	75 g/2¾ oz freshly grated
850 ml/1½ pints hot vegetable	Parmesan cheese, plus extra
or chicken stock	to serve

❖ Heat the oil and butter in a large frying pan. Add the onion and cook for 4–5 minutes or until softened.

❖ Add the rice and saffron to the frying pan, stirring well to coat the rice in the oil, and cook for 1 minute.

❖ Add the wine and stock slowly to the rice mixture in the pan, a ladleful at a time, stirring and making sure that all the liquid is absorbed before adding the next ladleful.

❖ About halfway through adding the stock, stir in the sun-dried tomatoes.

❖ When all of the wine and stock has been absorbed, the rice should be cooked. Test by tasting a grain – if it is still crunchy, add a little more water and continue cooking. It should take 15–20 minutes to cook.

❖ Stir in the peas, ham and cheese. Cook for 2–3 minutes, stirring, until hot. Serve with extra cheese.

Risotto-Stuffed Peppers

❖ SERVES 4 ❖

4 red or orange peppers	50 g/1¾ oz butter
1 tbsp olive oil	50 g/1¾ oz pecorino cheese,
1 large onion, finely chopped	grated
350 g/12 oz arborio rice,	50 g/1¾ oz Italian sausage,
washed	such as felino salame or
about 15 strands of saffron	other coarse Italian salame,
150 ml/5 fl oz white wine	chopped
850 ml/1½ pints hot vegetable	200 g/7 oz mozzarella cheese,
or chicken stock	sliced

❖ Cut the peppers in half, retaining some of the stalk. Remove the seeds.

❖ Place the peppers, cut side up, under a preheated grill for 12–15 minutes or until soft and charred.

❖ Meanwhile, heat the oil in a large frying pan. Add the onion and cook for 3–4 minutes or until softened. Add the rice and saffron, stirring to coat in the oil, and cook for 1 minute.

❖ Add the wine and stock slowly, a ladleful at a time, making sure that all of the liquid has been absorbed before adding the next ladleful of liquid. When all of the liquid has been absorbed, the rice should be cooked. Test by tasting a grain – if it is still crunchy add a little more water and continue cooking. It should take at least 15 minutes to cook.

❖ Stir in the butter, pecorino cheese and sausage.

❖ Spoon the risotto into the peppers. Top with a slice of mozzarella cheese and grill for 4–5 minutes or until the cheese is bubbling. Serve hot.

Creamy Chicken Curry

2 tbsp vegetable oil
4 skinless, boneless chicken
breasts, about 800 g/
1 lb 12 oz in total, cut into
2.5-cm/1-inch pieces
1½ tsp cumin seeds
1 large onion, grated
2 fresh green chillies,
finely chopped
2 large garlic cloves, grated
1 tbsp grated root ginger
1 tsp ground turmeric
1 tsp ground coriander
1 tsp garam masala
300 ml/10 fl oz coconut milk
250 ml/9 fl oz canned chopped
tomatoes
2 tsp lemon juice
salt
cooked jasmine rice, to serve
2 tbsp chopped fresh coriander,
to garnish

❖ Heat the oil in a large heavy-based saucepan over a medium heat. Add the chicken and cook for 5–8 minutes, turning frequently, until lightly browned and cooked through. Remove from the pan and set aside. Add the cumin seeds and cook until they begin to darken and sizzle. Stir in the onion, partially cover and cook over a medium–low heat, stirring frequently, for 10 minutes or until soft and golden. Add the chillies, garlic, ginger, turmeric, ground coriander and garam masala and cook for 1 minute.

❖ Return the chicken to the pan and stir in the coconut milk and tomatoes. Partially cover and cook over a medium heat for 15 minutes until the sauce has reduced and thickened. Stir in the lemon juice and season to taste with salt.

❖ Serve the curry with the jasmine rice, garnished with the coriander.

Chicken Jambalaya

400 g/14 oz skinless, boneless chicken breasts, diced
1 red onion, diced
1 garlic clove, crushed
600 ml/1 pint chicken stock
400 g/14 oz canned chopped tomatoes in tomato juice
280 g/10 oz brown rice
1–2 tsp hot chilli powder
1/2 tsp paprika
1 tsp dried oregano
1 red pepper, deseeded and diced
1 yellow pepper, deseeded and diced
85 g/3 oz frozen sweetcorn kernels
85 g/3 oz frozen peas
3 tbsp chopped fresh parsley
pepper
crisp green salad, to serve

❊ Put the chicken, onion, garlic, stock, tomatoes and rice into a large heavy-based saucepan. Add the chilli powder, paprika and oregano and stir well. Bring to the boil, then reduce the heat, cover and simmer for 25 minutes.

❊ Add the peppers, sweetcorn and peas to the rice mixture and return to the boil. Reduce the heat, cover and simmer for a further 10 minutes or until the rice is just tender (brown rice retains a nutty texture when cooked) and most of the stock has been absorbed but is not completely dry.

❊ Stir in 2 tablespoons of the parsley and season to taste with pepper. Transfer the jambalaya to a warmed serving dish, garnish with the remaining parsley and serve with the green salad.

Chicken Biryani

1 1/2 tsp finely chopped root ginger
1 1/2 tsp fresh garlic, crushed
1 tbsp garam masala
1 tsp chilli powder
1/2 tsp ground turmeric
2 tsp salt
20 green/white cardamom seeds, crushed
300 ml/10 fl oz natural yogurt
1.5 kg/3 lb 5 oz chicken, skinned and cut into 8 pieces
150 ml/5 fl oz milk
saffron strands
6 tbsp ghee
2 onions, sliced
450 g/1 lb basmati rice
2 cinnamon sticks
4 black peppercorns
1 tsp black cumin seeds
4 fresh green chillies
fresh coriander leaves, finely chopped
4 tbsp lemon juice

❊ Blend together the ginger, garlic, garam masala, chilli powder, turmeric, 1 teaspoon of the salt and the cardamom seeds and mix with the yogurt and chicken pieces. Set aside to marinate for 3 hours.

❊ Pour the milk into a saucepan and bring to the boil. Pour over the saffron and set aside.

❊ Heat the ghee in a saucepan and cook the onions until golden brown. Remove half of the onions and ghee from the pan and set aside.

❊ Place the rice, cinnamon sticks, 4 peppercorns and the black cumin seeds in a saucepan of water. Bring the rice to the boil and remove from the heat when half-cooked. Drain and place in a bowl. Mix with the remaining salt.

❊ Add the chicken mixture to the pan with the onions and ghee. Deseed the chillies, if wished, and finely chop. Add half each of the chillies, coriander, lemon juice and saffron. Add the rice and then the rest of the ingredients. Cover tightly so no steam escapes. Cook over a low heat for 1 hour. Check that the meat is cooked through before serving. If the meat is not cooked, return to the heat and cook for a further 15 minutes. Mix thoroughly before serving hot.

Spanish Lemon Chicken

❈ **SERVES 4** ❈

1 tbsp plain flour	2 preserved lemons, cut into
4 chicken quarters, skin on	quarters
2 tbsp olive oil	250 g/9 oz brown basmati rice
2 garlic cloves, crushed	white pepper
1 large Spanish onion,	12 pimiento-stuffed green
thinly sliced	olives
750 ml/1¼ pints chicken stock	chopped fresh parsley,
½ tsp saffron strands	to garnish
2 yellow peppers, deseeded	green salad, to serve
and cut into chunks	

❈ Preheat the oven to 180°C/350°F/Gas Mark 4. Put the flour into a large polythene bag. Add the chicken, close the top of the bag and shake to coat with flour.

❈ Heat the oil in a large frying pan over a low heat, add the garlic and cook for 1 minute, stirring constantly.

❈ Add the chicken to the pan and cook over a medium heat, turning frequently, for 5 minutes, or until the skin has lightly browned, then remove to a plate.

❈ Add the onion to the pan and cook, stirring occasionally, for 10 minutes until soft.

❈ Meanwhile, put the stock and saffron into a saucepan over a low heat and heat through.

❈ Transfer the chicken and onion to a large casserole dish, add the peppers, lemons and rice, then pour over the stock. Mix well and season to taste with pepper.

❈ Cover and cook in the preheated oven for 50 minutes, or until the chicken is cooked through and tender. Reduce the oven temperature to 160°C/325°F/Gas Mark 3. Add the olives to the casserole and cook for a further 10 minutes.

❈ Serve garnished with the parsley and accompanied by the green salad.

Chicken & Rice Casserole

❈ **SERVES 4** ❈

150 g/5½ oz long-grain rice	850 ml/1½ pints chicken stock
1 tbsp dry sherry	2 open-cup mushrooms, sliced
2 tbsp light soy sauce	60 g/2 oz water chestnuts,
2 tbsp dark soy sauce	halved
2 tsp dark brown sugar	75 g/2¾ oz broccoli florets
1 tsp salt	1 yellow pepper, sliced
1 tsp sesame oil	4 tsp grated root ginger
900 g/2 lb skinless, boneless	whole chives, to garnish
chicken meat, diced	

❈ Cook the rice in a saucepan of boiling water for about 15 minutes. Drain well, rinse under cold water and drain again thoroughly.

❈ Mix together the sherry, soy sauces, sugar, salt and oil.

❈ Stir the chicken into the soy mixture, turning to coat the chicken well. Leave to marinate for about 30 minutes.

❈ Bring the stock to the boil in a saucepan or preheated wok. Add the chicken with the marinade, mushrooms, water chestnuts, broccoli, sliced pepper and ginger.

❈ Stir in the rice, reduce the heat, cover and cook for 25–30 minutes until the chicken and vegetables are cooked through. Transfer to serving plates, garnish with the chives and serve.

Sage Chicken with Rice

1 large onion, chopped
1 garlic clove, crushed
2 sticks celery, sliced
2 carrots, diced
2 sprigs fresh sage
300 ml/10 fl oz chicken stock
350 g/12 oz boneless, skinless chicken breasts
225 g/8 oz mixed brown and wild rice
400 g/14 oz canned chopped tomatoes
dash of Tabasco sauce
2 medium courgettes, trimmed and thinly sliced
100 g/3 1/2 oz lean ham, diced
salt and pepper
fresh sage leaves, to garnish
salad leaves and fresh crusty bread, to serve

❖ Place the onion, garlic, celery, carrots and sprigs of sage in a large saucepan and pour in the stock.

❖ Bring to the boil, cover the pan and simmer for 5 minutes.

❖ Cut the chicken into 2.5-cm/1-inch cubes and stir into the pan with the vegetables. Cover the pan and continue to cook for a further 5 minutes.

❖ Stir in the mixed brown and wild rice and the tomatoes.

❖ Add a dash of Tabasco sauce to taste and season well. Bring to the boil, cover and simmer for 25 minutes.

❖ Stir in the courgettes and ham and continue to cook, uncovered, for a further 10 minutes, stirring occasionally, until the rice is just tender.

❖ Remove and discard the sprigs of sage.

❖ Garnish with the sage leaves and serve with the salad and bread.

Chicken Basquaise

1.35 kg/3 lb chicken, cut into 8 pieces	1 tbsp tomato purée
flour, for dusting	200 g/7 oz long-grain rice
3 tbsp olive oil	450 ml/16 fl oz chicken stock
1 Spanish onion, thickly sliced	1 tsp crushed dried chillies
2 red or yellow peppers, deseeded and cut lengthways into thick strips	$1/2$ tsp dried thyme
2 garlic cloves	120 g/4 oz Bayonne or other air-dried ham, diced
150 g/5 oz spicy chorizo sausage, peeled and cut into 1-cm/$1/2$-inch pieces	12 dry-cured black olives
	2 tbsp chopped fresh flat-leaf parsley
	salt and pepper

❊ Pat the chicken pieces dry with kitchen paper. Put 2 tablespoons flour in a polythene bag, season with salt and pepper and add the chicken pieces. Seal the bag and shake to coat the chicken.

❊ Heat 2 tablespoons of the oil in a large flameproof casserole over a medium–high heat. Add the chicken and cook, turning frequently, for about 15 minutes until well browned all over. Transfer to a plate.

❊ Heat the remaining oil in the casserole and add the onion and peppers. Reduce the heat to medium and stir-fry until beginning to colour and soften. Add the garlic, chorizo and tomato purée and cook, stirring constantly, for about 3 minutes. Add the rice and cook, stirring to coat, for about 2 minutes until the rice is translucent.

❊ Add the stock, crushed chillies and thyme, season to taste with salt and pepper and stir well. Bring to the boil. Return the chicken to the casserole, pressing it gently into the rice. Cover and cook over a very low heat for 45 minutes until the chicken is cooked through and the rice is tender.

❊ Gently stir the ham, olives and half the parsley into the rice mixture. Re-cover and heat through for a further 5 minutes. Sprinkle with the remaining parsley and serve.

Golden Glazed Chicken

6 skinless boneless chicken breast portions	2 tbsp sunflower oil
1 tsp ground turmeric	350 g/12 oz long-grain rice
1 tbsp wholegrain mustard	1 orange
300 ml/10 fl oz orange juice	3 tbsp chopped fresh mint
2 tbsp clear honey	salt and pepper
	sprigs of fresh mint, to garnish

❊ With a sharp knife, mark the surface of the chicken breasts in a diamond pattern and place in a single layer in a shallow dish.

❊ Combine the turmeric, mustard, orange juice and honey and pour the mixture over the chicken. Season to taste with salt and pepper. Chill until required.

❊ Lift the chicken from the marinade and pat dry on kitchen paper. Reserve the marinade.

❊ Heat the oil in a wide pan, add the chicken and sauté until golden, turning once. Drain off any excess oil. Pour the marinade into the pan, cover and simmer for 10–15 minutes until the chicken is tender.

❊ Bring a saucepan of lightly salted water to the boil and cook the rice for 15–20 minutes until tender, then drain well. Finely grate the orange rind and stir it into the rice with the mint.

❊ Remove the peel and white pith from the orange and cut the flesh into segments.

❊ Serve the chicken with the orange and mint rice, garnished with the orange segments and sprigs of mint.

Onion Rice & Spiced Chicken

1 tbsp Chinese five-spice powder	3 tbsp groundnut oil
2 tbsp cornflour	1 onion, diced
350 g/12 oz skinless boneless chicken breast portions, diced	225 g/8 oz long-grain rice
	1/2 tsp ground turmeric
	600 ml/1 pint chicken stock
	2 tbsp snipped fresh chives

❖ Place the five-spice powder and cornflour in a large bowl. Add the chicken pieces and toss to coat all over.

❖ Heat 2 tablespoons of the oil in a large preheated wok. Add the chicken pieces to the wok and stir-fry for 5 minutes. Using a slotted spoon, remove the chicken and reserve.

❖ Add the remaining oil to the wok.

❖ Add the onion to the wok and stir-fry for 1 minute.

❖ Add the rice, turmeric and stock to the wok and gently bring to the boil.

❖ Return the chicken pieces to the wok, reduce the heat and simmer for 10 minutes, or until the liquid has been absorbed and the rice is tender.

❖ Add the chives, stir to mix and serve hot.

Chinese Chicken Rice

350 g/12 oz long-grain rice	1 green chilli, deseeded and finely chopped
1 tsp turmeric	1 medium carrot, coarsely grated
2 tbsp sunflower oil	
350 g/12 oz skinless, boneless chicken breasts or thighs, sliced	150 g/5 1/2 oz beansprouts
1 red pepper, deseeded and sliced	6 spring onions, sliced, plus extra to garnish
1 green pepper, deseeded and sliced	2 tbsp soy sauce
	salt

❖ Place the rice and turmeric in a large saucepan of lightly salted water and cook until the grains of rice are just tender, about 10 minutes. Drain the rice thoroughly and press out any excess water with kitchen paper.

❖ Heat the oil in a large preheated wok or frying pan.

❖ Add the strips of chicken to the wok or frying pan and stir-fry over a high heat until the chicken is just beginning to turn a golden colour.

❖ Add the sliced peppers and chilli to the wok and stir-fry for 2–3 minutes.

❖ Add the rice to the wok, a little at a time, tossing well after each addition until well combined and the grains of rice are separated.

❖ Add the carrot, beansprouts and spring onions to the wok and stir-fry for a further 2 minutes.

❖ Drizzle with the soy sauce and toss to combine.

❖ Transfer the Chinese chicken rice to a warmed serving dish, garnish with spring onions and serve at once.

Orange Turkey with Rice

❊ SERVES 4 ❊

1 tbsp olive oil
1 onion, chopped
450 g/1 lb skinless lean turkey,
cut into thin strips
300 ml/10 fl oz unsweetened
orange juice
1 bay leaf
225 g/8 oz small broccoli florets
1 large courgette, diced
1 large orange
350 g/12 oz cooked brown rice
salt and pepper
tomato and onion salad,
to serve
25 g/1 oz stoned black olives in
brine, drained and quartered,
and shredded basil leaves,
to garnish

❊ Heat the oil in a large frying pan and fry the onion and turkey, stirring, for 4–5 minutes until lightly browned.

❊ Pour in the orange juice and add the bay leaf and seasoning. Bring to the boil and simmer for 10 minutes.

❊ Meanwhile, bring a large saucepan of lightly salted water to the boil and cook the broccoli florets, covered, for 2 minutes. Add the courgette, bring back to the boil, cover and cook for a further 3 minutes (do not overcook). Drain and set aside.

❊ Using a sharp knife, peel off the skin and white pith from the orange.

❊ Thinly slice down the orange to make round slices, then halve each slice.

❊ Stir the broccoli, courgette, rice and orange slices into the turkey mixture. Gently mix together and season, then heat through for a further 3–4 minutes until piping hot.

❊ Transfer the turkey rice to warmed serving plates and garnish with the olives and basil. Serve the turkey with the fresh tomato and onion salad.

Chinese Risotto

2 tbsp groundnut oil	225 g/8 oz carrots, diced
1 onion, sliced	1 green pepper, deseeded and
2 cloves garlic, crushed	diced
1 tsp Chinese five-spice	275 g/9^1/$_2$ oz risotto rice
powder	850 ml/1^1/$_2$ pints vegetable or
225 g/8 oz Chinese sausage,	chicken stock
sliced	1 tbsp fresh chives

❊ Heat the groundnut oil in a large preheated wok or heavy-based frying pan.

❊ Add the onion, garlic and five-spice powder to the wok and stir-fry for 1 minute.

❊ Add the sausage, carrots and diced pepper to the wok and stir to combine.

❊ Stir in the risotto rice and cook for 1 minute.

❊ Gradually add the stock, a little at a time, stirring constantly, until the liquid has been completely absorbed and the rice grains are tender.

❊ Snip the chives with scissors and stir into the wok with the last of the stock.

❊ Transfer the risotto to warmed serving bowls and serve immediately.

Spicy Pork & Rice

275 g/9^1/$_2$ oz long-grain rice	1 onion, peeled and diced
600 ml/1 pint cold water	2 cloves garlic, crushed
350 g/12 oz pork fillet	100 g/3^1/$_2$ oz carrots, diced
2 tsp Chinese five-spice	1 red pepper, deseeded and
powder	diced
25 g/1 oz cornflour	100 g/3^1/$_2$ oz peas
3 large eggs, beaten	15 g/^{1}/$_2$ oz butter
25 g/1 oz demerara sugar	salt
2 tbsp sunflower oil	

❊ Place the rice in a large saucepan, add the cold water and a pinch of salt. Bring to the boil, cover, then reduce the heat and leave to simmer for about 9 minutes, or until all of the liquid has been absorbed and the rice is tender.

❊ Meanwhile, slice the pork into very thin even-sized pieces, using a sharp knife. Set the pork strips aside until required.

❊ Whisk together the five-spice powder, cornflour, 1 egg and the sugar. Toss the pork in the mixture until coated.

❊ Heat the sunflower oil in a large wok or frying pan. Add the pork and cook over a high heat until the pork is cooked through and crispy. Remove the pork from the wok with a slotted spoon and set aside until required.

❊ Add the onion, garlic, carrots, pepper and peas to the wok and stir-fry for 5 minutes.

❊ Return the pork to the wok together with the cooked rice and stir-fry for 5 minutes.

❊ Heat the butter in a frying pan. Add the remaining beaten eggs and cook until set. Turn out on to a clean board and slice thinly. Toss the strips of egg into the rice mixture and serve immediately.

Sweet Chilli Pork Fried Rice

❅ **SERVES 4** ❅

450 g/1 lb pork fillet
2 tbsp sunflower oil
2 tbsp sweet chilli sauce, plus extra to serve
1 onion, sliced
175 g/6 oz carrots, cut into matchsticks
175 g/6 oz courgettes, cut into sticks

100 g/3 1/2 oz canned bamboo shoots, drained
275 g/9 1/2 oz cooked long-grain rice
1 egg, beaten
1 tbsp chopped fresh parsley

❅ Using a sharp knife, cut the pork into thin slices.

❅ Heat the sunflower oil in a large preheated wok or frying pan.

❅ Add the pork to the wok and stir-fry for 5 minutes.

❅ Add the chilli sauce to the wok and allow to bubble, stirring, for 2–3 minutes or until syrupy.

❅ Add the onion, carrots, courgettes and bamboo shoots to the wok and stir-fry for a further 3 minutes.

❅ Add the cooked rice and stir-fry for 2–3 minutes or until the rice is heated through.

❅ Drizzle the beaten egg over the top of the fried rice and cook, tossing the ingredients in the wok with two spoons, until the egg sets.

❅ Scatter with the parsley and serve immediately, with sweet chilli sauce.

Caribbean Pork

❅ **SERVES 4** ❅

4 pork loin chops
4 tbsp muscovado sugar
4 tbsp orange or pineapple juice
2 tbsp Jamaican rum
1 tbsp desiccated coconut
1/2 tsp ground cinnamon
mixed salad leaves, to serve

COCONUT RICE
225 g/8 oz basmati rice
450 ml/16 fl oz water
150 ml/5 fl oz coconut milk
4 tbsp raisins
4 tbsp roasted peanuts or cashew nuts
salt and pepper
2 tbsp desiccated coconut, toasted, for sprinkling

❅ Trim any excess fat from the pork and place it in a non-metallic dish.

❅ Combine the sugar, orange juice, rum, coconut and cinnamon in a bowl, stirring until the sugar dissolves. Pour the mixture over the pork and set aside to marinate in the refrigerator for at least 2 hours or preferably overnight.

❅ Remove the pork, reserving the marinade for basting. Cook under a hot grill for 15–20 minutes, basting with the marinade.

❅ Meanwhile, make the coconut rice. Place the rice in a saucepan with the water and coconut milk and gradually bring to the boil. Stir, cover and reduce the heat. Simmer gently for 12 minutes or until the rice is tender and the liquid has been absorbed. Fluff up with a fork.

❅ Stir the raisins and nuts into the rice, season to taste with salt and pepper and sprinkle with the coconut. Transfer the pork and rice to warmed serving plates and serve with the salad leaves.

Indonesian Fried Rice

1 large onion, chopped
2–3 garlic cloves
1 tsp prawn paste
2 fresh red chillies, deseeded
and chopped
about 125 ml/4 fl oz vegetable oil
3 eggs, lightly beaten
450 g/1 lb beef rump steak,
about 1 cm/$\frac{1}{2}$ inch thick
2 carrots, cut into thin batons
175 g/6 oz Chinese long beans
or French beans, cut into
2.5-cm/1-inch pieces
6 small spring onions, cut into
1-cm/$\frac{1}{2}$-inch pieces
250 g/9 oz raw shelled prawns
750 g/1 lb 10 oz cooked
long-grain rice, at room
temperature
6 tbsp dark soy sauce

TO GARNISH

4 tbsp ready-fried onion flakes
10-cm/4-inch piece of
cucumber, deseeded and cut
into thin sticks
2 tbsp chopped fresh coriander

❊ Put the onion, garlic, prawn paste and chillies into a food processor and process until a paste forms. Add a little oil and process until smooth. Set aside.

❊ Heat 1–2 tablespoons of the oil in a large non-stick frying pan. Pour in the egg to form a thin layer and cook for 1 minute until just set. Turn and cook for 5 seconds on the other side. Slide out and cut in half. Roll up each half, then slice into 5-mm/$\frac{1}{4}$-inch strips. Set aside.

❊ Heat 2 tablespoons of the oil in the same pan over a high heat and add the steak. Cook for 2 minutes on each side to brown and seal, but do not cook completely. Cool, then cut into thin strips and reserve.

❊ Heat 2 tablespoons of the oil in a large wok over a medium–high heat. Add the reserved chilli paste and cook, stirring frequently, for about 3 minutes. Add 2 tablespoons of the oil, the carrots and the beans. Stir-fry for about 2 minutes. Add the spring onions, prawns and beef strips and stir-fry until the prawns have turned pink.

❊ Stir in the rice, half the sliced omelette, 2 tablespoons of the soy sauce and 50 ml/2 fl oz water. Cover and steam for 1 minute. Spoon into a warmed serving dish, top with the remaining omelette and drizzle with the remaining soy sauce. Sprinkle with the onion flakes, cucumber and coriander and serve immediately.

Sweet Potato & Coconut Beef

2 tbsp vegetable oil	2 tbsp red curry paste
2 cloves garlic	300 ml/10 fl oz coconut milk
1 onion	3 lime leaves
350 g/12 oz rump steak	cooked jasmine rice, to serve
350 g/12 oz sweet potato	

❋ Heat the oil in a large preheated wok or heavy-based frying pan.

❋ Peel the garlic cloves and crush them in a pestle with a mortar. Thinly slice the onions.

❋ Using a sharp knife, thinly slice the beef. Add the beef to the wok and stir-fry for about 2 minutes or until sealed on all sides.

❋ Add the garlic and the onion to the wok and stir-fry for a further 2 minutes.

❋ Using a sharp knife, peel and dice the sweet potato.

❋ Add the sweet potato to the wok with the red curry paste, coconut milk and lime leaves and bring to a rapid boil. Reduce the heat, cover and leave to simmer for about 15 minutes or until the potatoes are tender.

❋ Remove and discard the lime leaves and transfer the stir-fry to warmed serving bowls. Serve hot with the jasmine rice.

Seven-Spice Beef

225 g/8 oz long-grain rice	2 tbsp groundnut oil
600 ml/1 pint water	1 onion, diced
350 g/12 oz beef fillet	225 g/8 oz carrots, diced
2 tbsp dark soy sauce	100 g/3$\frac{1}{2}$ oz frozen peas
2 tbsp tomato ketchup	2 eggs, beaten
1 tbsp seven-spice seasoning	2 tbsp cold water

❋ Place the rice in a saucepan with the water, bring to the boil, cover and simmer for 12 minutes until tender. Turn out the cooked rice on to a tray and leave to cool.

❋ Using a sharp knife, thinly slice the beef fillet and place in a large shallow dish.

❋ Mix together the soy sauce, tomato ketchup and seven-spice seasoning. Spoon over the beef and toss well to coat.

❋ Heat the oil in a preheated wok. Add the slices of beef and stir-fry for 3–4 minutes.

❋ Add the onion, carrots and peas to the wok and stir-fry for a further 2–3 minutes. Add the cooked rice to the wok and mix together.

❋ Beat the eggs with 2 tablespoons of cold water. Drizzle the egg mixture over the rice and stir-fry for 3–4 minutes, or until the rice is heated through and the egg has set. Transfer the rice and beef to a warmed serving bowl and serve immediately.

Fish with Coconut & Basil

2 tbsp vegetable oil
450 g/1 lb skinless cod fillet
25 g/1 oz seasoned flour
1 clove garlic, crushed
2 tbsp red curry paste
1 tbsp fish sauce
300 ml/10 fl oz coconut milk
175 g/6 oz cherry tomatoes,
halved
20 fresh basil leaves
fragrant rice, to serve

❊ Heat the vegetable oil in a large preheated wok.

❊ Using a sharp knife, cut the fish into large cubes, removing any bones with a pair of clean tweezers.

❊ Place the seasoned flour in a bowl. Add the cubes of fish and mix until well coated.

❊ Add the coated fish to the wok and stir-fry over a high heat for 3–4 minutes or until the fish just begins to brown at the edges.

❊ In a small bowl, mix together the garlic, curry paste, fish sauce and coconut milk. Pour the mixture over the fish and bring to the boil.

❊ Add the tomatoes to the mixture in the wok and leave to simmer for 5 minutes.

❊ Roughly chop or tear the fresh basil leaves. Add the basil to the wok and stir carefully to combine, taking care not to break up the cubes of fish.

❊ Transfer to serving plates and serve hot with the rice.

Rice with Crab & Mussels

❊ SERVES 4 ❊

300 g/10$\frac{1}{2}$ oz long-grain rice
175 g/6 oz white crabmeat,
fresh, canned or frozen, or
8 crab sticks, thawed,
if frozen
2 tbsp sesame or sunflower oil
2.5-cm/1-inch piece of fresh
ginger root, grated
4 spring onions, thinly sliced
diagonally
125 g/4$\frac{1}{2}$ oz mangetout,
cut into 2–3 pieces
$\frac{1}{2}$ tsp turmeric
1 tsp ground cumin
400 g/14 oz mussels in brine,
well drained, or 350 g/12 oz
frozen mussels, thawed
425 g/15 oz canned bean
sprouts, well drained
salt and pepper

❊ Place the rice in a saucepan with 475 ml/16 fl oz lightly salted water, bring to the boil, cover and simmer for 12 minutes.

❊ Extract the crabmeat, if using fresh crab. Flake the crabmeat or cut the crab sticks into 3 or 4 pieces.

❊ Heat the oil in a preheated wok and stir-fry the ginger and spring onions for a minute or so. Add the mangetout and continue to cook for a further minute. Sprinkle the turmeric, cumin and seasoning over the vegetables and mix well.

❊ Add the crabmeat and mussels and stir-fry for 1 minute. Stir in the cooked rice and beansprouts and stir-fry for 2 minutes or until hot and well mixed.

❊ Adjust the seasoning to taste and serve immediately.

Aromatic Seafood Rice

225 g/8 oz basmati rice
2 tbsp ghee or vegetable oil
1 onion, peeled and chopped
1 garlic clove, peeled and
crushed
1 tsp cumin seeds
$1/2$–1 tsp chilli powder
4 cloves
1 cinnamon stick or a piece of
cassia bark
2 tsp curry paste
225 g/8 oz peeled prawns
500g/1 lb 2 oz white fish fillets
(such as monkfish, cod or
haddock), skinned and boned
and cut into bite-sized pieces
600 ml/1 pint boiling water
60 g/2 oz frozen peas
60 g/2 oz frozen sweetcorn
kernels
1–2 tbsp lime juice
2 tbsp toasted desiccated
coconut
salt and pepper
sprigs of fresh coriander and
slices of lime, to garnish

❄ Place the rice in a sieve and wash well under cold running water until the water runs clear, then drain well.

❄ Heat the ghee in a saucepan, add the onion, garlic, spices and curry paste and fry very gently for 1 minute.

❄ Stir in the rice and mix well until coated in the spiced oil. Add the prawns and white fish and season well with salt and pepper. Lightly stir, then pour in the boiling water.

❄ Cover and cook gently for 10 minutes, without uncovering the pan. Add the peas and corn, cover and continue cooking for a further 8 minutes. Remove from the heat and allow to stand for 10 minutes.

❄ Uncover the pan, fluff up the rice with a fork and transfer to a warmed serving platter.

❄ Sprinkle the dish with the lime juice and toasted coconut, and serve garnished with the coriander and the lime slices.

Quick Seafood Rice

2 tbsp oil
1 large onion, chopped
1 garlic clove, finely chopped
8 large tomatoes, peeled, deseeded and chopped
225 g/8 oz paella or risotto rice
850 ml/1½ pints fish stock
400 g/14 oz mixed seafood mixture, thawed

450 g/1 lb fresh mussels, cleaned
175 g/6 oz petit pois, cooked
2 tbsp chopped fresh parsley
salt and pepper
fresh crusty bread, to serve

❖ Heat the oil in a preheated wok or large frying pan. Add the onion and fry until just soft. Add the garlic and half the tomatoes and stir together well. Add the rice and stir-fry for 2–3 minutes before adding half the stock and bringing to the boil. Simmer for 12–15 minutes, adding more stock as necessary.

❖ Add the seafood mixture, mussels and petit pois. Season to taste with salt and pepper and cook for a further 3–4 minutes, until hot, the mussels have opened and the liquid has been mostly absorbed. Discard any mussels that remain closed.

❖ Stir in the remaining tomatoes and the parsley, taste and adjust the seasoning, if necessary, and serve immediately with the bread.

Fried Rice with Prawns

300 g/10½ oz long-grain rice
2 eggs
4 tsp cold water
salt and pepper
3 tbsp sunflower oil
4 spring onions, thinly sliced diagonally
1 garlic clove, crushed
125 g/4½ oz closed-cup or button mushrooms, thinly sliced

2 tbsp oyster or anchovy sauce
200 g/7 oz canned water chestnuts, drained and sliced
250 g/9 oz peeled prawns, thawed, if frozen
½ bunch watercress, roughly chopped
sprigs of fresh watercress, to garnish (optional)

❖ Place the rice in a saucepan with 475 ml/16 fl oz lightly salted water, bring to the boil, cover and simmer for 12 minutes.

❖ Beat each egg separately with 2 teaspoons of the water and salt and pepper.

❖ Heat 2 teaspoons of the oil in a wok or large frying pan, swirling it around until really hot. Pour in the first egg, swirl it around and leave to cook undisturbed until set. Remove to a plate or board and repeat with the second egg. Cut the omelettes into 2.5-cm/1-inch squares.

❖ Heat the remaining oil in the wok and, when really hot, add the spring onions and garlic and stir-fry for 1 minute. Add the mushrooms and continue to cook for a further 2 minutes.

❖ Stir in the oyster sauce and seasoning, add the water chestnuts and prawns and stir-fry for 2 minutes.

❖ Stir in the rice and stir-fry for 1 minute, then add the watercress and omelette squares and stir-fry for a further 1–2 minutes until piping hot. Serve at once, garnished with the watercress, if using.

Thai Prawn & Mushroom Rice

8 pieces dried Chinese black
mushrooms
175 g/6 oz long-grain rice
350 ml/12 fl oz water
2 tbsp oil
1 small onion, finely chopped
2 garlic cloves, finely chopped
2 fresh red chillies, deseded
and cut into thin strips

85 g/3 oz bamboo shoots, cut
into matchsticks
1 tbsp Thai fish sauce
175 g/6 oz cooked peeled
prawns
2 tbsp chopped fresh coriander

❊ Place the mushrooms in a bowl, pour over enough boiling water to cover and leave to soak for 30 minutes. Drain and chop.

❊ Meanwhile, rinse the rice in several changes of water and drain thoroughly. Place in a saucepan with the water. Bring to the boil and stir once. Reduce the heat to a gentle simmer, then cover the saucepan and cook for 12 minutes or until the rice is cooked and the water has been absorbed. Fluff up the rice with a fork.

❊ Heat the oil in a preheated wok. Add the onion and garlic and cook, stirring occasionally, until soft. Add the chillies and stir-fry for 2 minutes. Stir in the bamboo shoots, mushrooms and fish sauce.

❊ Continue to stir-fry for 2 minutes, then stir in the rice and prawns. Stir gently for a few minutes until completely heated through. Stir in the coriander and serve immediately.

Cellophane Noodles & Prawns

175 g/6 oz cellophane noodles
1 tbsp vegetable oil
1 garlic clove, crushed
2 tsp grated root ginger
24 raw tiger prawns, peeled
and deveined
1 red pepper, deseeded and
thinly sliced
1 green pepper, deseeded and
thinly sliced

1 onion, chopped
2 tbsp light soy sauce
juice of 1 orange
2 tsp wine vinegar
pinch of brown sugar
150 ml/5 fl oz fish stock
1 tbsp cornflour
2 tsp water
slices of orange, to garnish

❊ Bring a saucepan of lightly salted water to the boil and cook the noodles for 1 minute. Drain well, rinse under cold water and then drain again.

❊ Heat the oil in a wok and stir-fry the garlic and ginger for 30 seconds.

❊ Add the prawns and stir-fry for 2 minutes. Remove with a slotted spoon and keep warm.

❊ Add the peppers and onion to the wok and stir-fry for 2 minutes. Stir in the soy sauce, orange juice, vinegar, sugar and stock. Return the prawns to the wok and cook for 8–10 minutes, until cooked through.

❊ Blend the cornflour with the water and stir into the wok. Bring to the boil, add the noodles and cook for 1–2 minutes. Garnish with the slices of orange and serve.

Crab-Fried Rice

150 g/5$\frac{1}{2}$ oz long-grain rice
2 tbsp groundnut oil
125 g/4$\frac{1}{2}$ oz canned white
crabmeat, drained
1 leek, sliced
150 g/5$\frac{1}{2}$ oz beansprouts
2 eggs, beaten
1 tbsp light soy sauce
2 tsp lime juice
1 tsp sesame oil
salt
slices of lime, to garnish

❋ Bring a saucepan of lightly salted water to the boil and cook the rice for 15 minutes. Drain well, rinse under cold running water and drain again thoroughly.

❋ Heat the groundnut oil in a preheated wok until it is really hot.

❋ Add the crabmeat, leek and beansprouts to the wok and stir-fry for 2–3 minutes. Remove the mixture from the wok with a slotted spoon and set aside until required.

❋ Add the eggs to the wok and cook, stirring occasionally, for 2–3 minutes until they begin to set.

❋ Stir the rice and the crabmeat, leek and beansprout mixture into the eggs in the wok.

❋ Add the soy sauce and lime juice to the mixture in the wok. Cook for 1 minute, stirring to combine, and sprinkle with the sesame oil.

❋ Transfer the crab-fried rice to a serving dish, garnish with the slices of lime and serve immediately.

Simple
desserts & baking

Family Apple Pie

225 g/8 oz plain flour,
plus 2 tbsp for dusting
pinch of salt
55 g/2 oz butter
55 g/2 oz vegetable shortening
2–3 tbsp cold water, to mix
700 g/1 lb 9 oz cooking apples,
peeled, cored and finely
sliced

115 g/4 oz caster sugar,
plus 1 tsp for sprinkling
1 tsp ground cinnamon
1/4 nutmeg, freshly grated
55 g/2 oz raisins
1 tbsp semolina
2 tsp milk
custard or ice cream, to serve

❊ Place the flour and salt in a bowl. Gently rub in the butter and shortening until the mixture resembles breadcrumbs. Sprinkle in the cold water and stir well using a palette knife. Continue to mix until you have a smooth dough. Wrap in clingfilm and leave to rest in the refrigerator for 1–2 hours.

❊ Preheat the oven to 190°C/375°F/Gas Mark 5. In a mixing bowl, combine the apples, sugar, spices, raisins and semolina.

❊ Divide the dough into two pieces, one piece slightly larger than the other. On a lightly floured work surface, roll out the larger piece of pastry into a circle just larger than a 23-cm/9-inch (top diameter) pie tin, and use it to line the ungreased tin. Press the pastry down well and make sure no air is trapped.   Put the fruit filling into the pastry case.

❊ Roll out the remaining pastry to a circle just larger than the top of the tin. Moisten the pastry round the rim of the tin with water, and lay the rolled out pastry on top. Press down well round the rim to seal, and cut any excess pastry away. Crimp the edges of the pastry with your fingers or use a fork. Glaze with a little milk and sprinkle with sugar.

❊ Put the tin on a baking tray and bake near the top of the preheated oven for 30–35 minutes until golden brown. Serve whilst still hot with the custard.

Forest Fruit Pie

FILLING	PASTRY
250 g/9 oz blueberries	200 g/7 oz plain flour,
250 g/9 oz raspberries	plus extra for dusting
250 g/9 oz blackberries	25 g/1 oz ground hazelnuts
3 tbsp caster sugar	100 g/3 1/2 oz butter, cut into
2 tbsp icing sugar, to decorate	small pieces, plus extra for
whipped cream, to serve	greasing
	5 tbsp caster sugar
	finely grated rind of 1 lemon
	1 egg yolk, beaten
	4 tbsp milk

❊ Put the fruit in a saucepan with the caster sugar and simmer, stirring frequently, for 5 minutes. Remove the pan from the heat.

❊ Sift the flour into a bowl, then add the hazelnuts. Rub in the butter with the fingertips until the mixture resembles breadcrumbs, then sift in the sugar. Add the lemon rind, egg yolk and 3 tablespoons of the milk and mix. Turn out onto a lightly floured work surface and knead briefly. Wrap and chill in the refrigerator for 30 minutes.

❊ Preheat the oven to 190°C/375°F/Gas Mark 5. Grease a 20-cm/8-inch pie dish with butter. Roll out two-thirds of the pastry to a thickness of 5 mm/1/4 inch and use it to line the base and sides of the dish. Spoon the fruit into the pastry case.

❊ Brush the rim with water, then roll out the remaining pastry and use it to cover the pie. Trim and crimp round the edge, then make 2 small slits in the top and decorate with 2 leaf shapes cut out from the dough trimmings. Brush all over with the remaining milk. Bake for 40 minutes. Remove from the oven, sprinkle with the icing sugar and serve with the whipped cream.

Peach & Ginger Tarte Tatin

❊ SERVES 6 ❊

250 g/9 oz ready-made puff pastry, thawed, if frozen
6–8 just-ripe peaches
75 g/3 oz golden caster sugar
50 g/1¾ oz unsalted butter
3 pieces stem ginger in syrup, chopped
1 tbsp ginger syrup from the stem ginger jar
1 egg, beaten
thick cream or ice cream, to serve

❊ Preheat the oven to 190°C/375°F/Gas Mark 5. Plunge the peaches into boiling water then drain and peel. Cut each in half. Put the sugar in a 25-cm/10-inch heavy ovenproof frying pan and heat it gently until it caramelizes. Don't stir, just shake the pan if necessary. Once the sugar turns a dark caramel colour, remove from the heat and drop 25 g/1 oz of the butter into it.

❊ Place the peaches, cut side up, on top of the caramel, packing them as close together as possible and tucking the ginger into any gaps. Dot with the remaining butter and drizzle with the ginger syrup. Return to a gentle heat while you roll out the pastry in a circle larger than the pan you are using. Drape the pastry over the peaches and tuck it in well around the edges, brush with the beaten egg and bake for 20–25 minutes until the pastry is browned and puffed up.

❊ Remove from the oven and leave to rest for 5 minutes then invert on to a serving plate and serve with thick cream or ice cream.

Buttery Lemon Tart

❊ SERVES 8 ❊

PASTRY	FILLING
150 g/5½ oz plain flour	150 ml/5 fl oz double cream
25 g/1 oz caster sugar	100 g/3½ oz caster sugar
125 g/4½ oz butter, cut into small pieces	4 eggs
1 tbsp water	grated rind of 3 lemons
	12 tbsp lemon juice
	icing sugar, for dusting

❊ To make the pastry, place the flour and sugar in a bowl and rub in the butter using your fingers. Add the water and mix until a soft pastry has formed. Wrap and leave to chill for 30 minutes.

❊ On a lightly floured surface, roll out the dough and line a 24-cm/9½-inch loose-based tart tin. Prick the pastry with a fork and leave to chill for 30 minutes.

❊ Line the pastry case with foil and baking beans and bake in a preheated oven, 190°C/375°F/Gas Mark 5, for 15 minutes. Remove the foil and baking beans and cook for a further 15 minutes.

❊ To make the filling, whisk the cream, sugar, eggs, lemon rind and juice together. Place the pastry case, still in its tin, on a baking tray and pour in the filling.

❊ Bake in the oven for about 20 minutes, or until just set. Leave to cool, then lightly dust with icing sugar before serving.

Apricot, Cranberry & Almond Tart

❖ **SERVES 8–10** ❖

PASTRY
150 g/5¹/2 oz plain flour
125 g/4¹/2 oz caster sugar
125 g/4¹/2 oz butter,
cut into small pieces
1 tbsp water

FILLING
200 g/7 oz unsalted butter
200g/7 oz caster sugar
1 egg
2 egg yolks
40 g/1¹/2 oz plain flour, sifted
175 g/6 oz ground almonds
4 tbsp double cream
410 g/14¹/2 oz canned apricot
halves, drained
125 g/4¹/2 oz fresh cranberries

❖ To make the pastry, place the flour and sugar in a bowl and rub in the butter with your fingers. Add the water and work the mixture together until a soft pastry has formed. Wrap and leave to chill for 30 minutes.

❖ On a lightly floured surface, roll out the dough and line a 24-cm/9¹/2-inch loose-based flan tin. Prick the pastry with a fork and leave to chill for 30 minutes.

❖ Line the pastry case with foil and baking beans and bake in a preheated oven, 190°C/375°F/Gas Mark 5, for 15 minutes. Remove the foil and baking beans and cook for a further 10 minutes.

❖ To make the filling, cream together the butter and sugar until light and fluffy. Beat in the egg and egg yolks, then stir in the flour, almonds and cream.

❖ Place the apricot halves and cranberries on the bottom of the pastry case and spoon the filling over the top.

❖ Bake in the oven for about 1 hour, or until the topping is just set. Leave to cool slightly, then serve warm or cold.

Treacle Tart

250 g/9 oz ready-made shortcrust pastry dough, thawed, if frozen
plain flour, for dusting
350 g/12 oz golden syrup
125 g/4$^{1}/_{2}$ oz fresh white breadcrumbs

125 ml/4 fl oz double cream
finely grated rind of $^{1}/_{2}$ lemon or orange
2 tbsp lemon or orange juice
home-made custard, to serve

❄ Roll out the pastry on a lightly floured work surface and use it to line a 20-cm/8-inch loose-based flan tin, reserving the pastry trimmings. Prick the base of the pastry with a fork and leave to chill in the refrigerator for 30 minutes.

❄ Cut out small shapes from the reserved pastry trimmings, such as leaves, stars or hearts, to decorate the top of the tart.

❄ Mix the syrup, breadcrumbs, cream, grated lemon rind and lemon juice together in a bowl.

❄ Pour the mixture into the pastry case and decorate the edges of the tart with the pastry cut-outs.

❄ Bake in a preheated oven, 190°C/375°F/Gas Mark 5, for about 35–40 minutes or until the filling is just set.

❄ Leave the tart to cool slightly in the tin. Turn out and serve warm with the custard.

Sweet Potato Pie

❄ SERVES 8 ❄

PASTRY	FILLING
175 g/6 oz plain flour, plus extra for dusting	500 g/1 lb 2 oz sweet potatoes, cooked and diced
$^{1}/_{2}$ tsp salt	3 eggs, beaten
$^{1}/_{4}$ tsp caster sugar	100 g/3$^{1}/_{2}$ oz soft light brown sugar
50 g/1$^{3}/_{4}$ oz butter, cut into small pieces	350 ml/12 fl oz canned evaporated milk
40 g/1$^{1}/_{2}$ oz white vegetable fat, cut into small pices	40 g/1$^{1}/_{2}$ oz butter, melted
1–2$^{1}/_{2}$ tbsp cold water	2 tsp vanilla extract
	1 tsp ground cinnamon
	1 tsp ground nutmeg or freshly grated nutmeg
	$^{1}/_{2}$ tsp salt
	whipped cream, to serve

❄ To make the pastry, sift the flour, salt and sugar into a bowl. Add the butter and vegetable fat and rub in with the fingertips until the mixture resembles breadcrumbs. Add the water and mix with a fork to make a soft dough. Wrap the dough and chill in the refrigerator for at least 1 hour.

❄ Put the sweet potatoes in a bowl and beat in the eggs and brown sugar until very smooth. Beat in the remaining ingredients, then set aside until required.

❄ Preheat the oven to 220°C/425°F/Gas Mark 7. Roll out the pastry on a lightly floured work surface into a thin 28-cm/11-inch round and use to line a deep 23-cm/9-inch pie plate. Trim the excess pastry and press a floured fork around the edge. Prick the base all over with the fork. Line with baking paper and fill with baking beans. Bake for 12 minutes.

❄ Remove from the oven and take out the paper and beans. Pour the filling into the pastry case and return to the oven for a further 10 minutes. Reduce the oven temperature to 160°C/325°F/Gas Mark 3 and bake for a further 35 minutes, or until a knife inserted into the centre comes out clean. Leave to cool on a wire rack. Serve warm or at room temperature with the whipped cream.

Fruit Crumble Tart

PASTRY
150 g/5¹/2 oz plain flour, plus
 extra for dusting
25 g/1 oz caster sugar
125 g/4¹/2 oz butter, diced
1 tbsp water

FILLING
250 g/9 oz raspberries
450 g/1 lb plums, halved,
 stoned and roughly chopped
3 tbsp demerara sugar

CRUMBLE TOPPING
125 g/4¹/2 oz plain flour
75 g/2³/4 oz demerara sugar
100 g/3¹/2 oz butter, diced
100 g/3¹/2 oz chopped mixed
 nuts
1 tsp ground cinnamon
single cream or ice cream,
 to serve

❖ To make the pastry, place the flour, sugar and butter in a bowl and rub in the butter with your fingertips until the mixture resembles breadcrumbs. Add the water and bring together with your fingers to form a soft dough. Wrap the dough in clingfilm and chill in the refrigerator for 30 minutes.

❖ Roll out the pastry on a lightly floured work surface and use it to line the base of a 24-cm/9¹/2-inch loose-based flan tin. Prick the pastry with a fork and chill in the refrigerator for about 30 minutes.

❖ To make the filling, toss the raspberries and plums together with the sugar and spoon into the pastry case.

❖ To make the crumble topping, mix the flour, sugar and butter together in a bowl. Rub in the butter with your fingertips until the mixture resembles breadcrumbs. Stir in the nuts and cinnamon.

❖ Sprinkle the topping over the fruit and press down gently with the back of a spoon. Bake in a preheated oven, 200°C/400°F/Gas Mark 6, for 20–25 minutes until the topping is golden brown. Serve the tart with the cream.

Pear & Chocolate Tart

100 g/3¹/2 oz plain flour
25 g/1 oz ground almonds
70 g/2¹/2 oz block margarine
 about 3 tbsp water

FILLING
400 g/14 oz canned pear halves
 in fruit juice
55 g/2 oz butter
4 tbsp caster sugar
2 eggs, beaten
100 g/3¹/2 oz ground almonds

2 tbsp cocoa powder
few drops of almond essence
icing sugar, for dusting

CHOCOLATE SAUCE
4 tbsp caster sugar
3 tbsp golden syrup
90 ml/3¹/4 fl oz water
175 g/6 oz plain chocolate,
 broken into pieces
25 g/1 oz butter

❖ Grease a 20-cm/8-inch flan tin. Sift the flour into a mixing bowl and stir in the almonds. Rub in the margarine with your fingertips until the mixture resembles breadcrumbs. Add enough water to mix to a soft dough. Cover, chill in the freezer for 10 minutes, then roll out and use to line the tin. Prick the base and chill again.

❖ Meanwhile, make the filling. Drain the pears well. Beat the butter and sugar until light and fluffy. Beat in the eggs. Fold in the almonds, cocoa powder and almond essence. Spread the chocolate mixture in the pastry case and arrange the pears on top, pressing down lightly. Bake in the centre of a preheated oven, 200°C/400°F/Gas Mark 6, for 30 minutes or until the filling has risen. Cool slightly and transfer to a serving dish, if liked. Dust with sugar.

❖ To make the chocolate sauce, place the sugar, syrup and water in a saucepan and heat gently, stirring until the sugar dissolves. Boil gently for 1 minute. Remove from the heat, add the chocolate and butter and stir until melted and well combined. Serve the sauce with the flan.

Mississippi Mud Pie

225 g/8 oz plain flour
2 tbsp cocoa powder
150 g/5½ oz butter
2 tbsp caster sugar
about 2 tbsp cold water

FILLING
175 g/6 oz butter
350 g/12 oz dark muscovado
sugar
4 eggs, lightly
beaten
4 tbsp cocoa powder, sifted
150 g/5½ oz plain chocolate
300 ml/10 fl oz single cream
1 tsp chocolate essence

TOPPING
425 ml/15 fl oz double cream,
whipped
chocolate flakes

❧ To make the pastry, sift the flour and cocoa powder into a mixing bowl. Rub in the butter with your fingertips until the mixture resembles fine breadcrumbs. Stir in the sugar and enough cold water to mix to a soft dough. Chill for 15 minutes.

❧ Roll out the dough on a lightly floured work surface and use to line a deep 23-cm/ 9-inch loose-based flan tin or ceramic flan dish. Line with foil and baking beans. Bake blind in a preheated oven, 190°C/375°F/Gas Mark 5, for 15 minutes. Remove the beans and foil and cook for a further 10 minutes until crisp.

❧ Meanwhile, make the filling. Beat the butter and sugar in a bowl and gradually beat in the eggs with the cocoa powder. Melt the chocolate and beat it into the mixture with the single cream and the chocolate essence.

❧ Pour the mixture into the cooked pastry case and bake at 160°C/325°F/Gas Mark 3 for 45 minutes or until the filling is set.

❧ Leave to cool completely, then transfer the pie to a serving plate, if preferred. Cover with the whipped cream and leave to chill.

❧ Decorate the pie with the chocolate flakes and chill before serving.

Key Lime Pie

70 g/2¹/₂ oz butter, melted

CRUMB CRUST
175 g/6 oz digestive or
gingernut biscuits
2 tbsp caster sugar
¹/₂ tsp ground cinnamon

FILLING
butter, for greasing
400 ml/14 fl oz canned
condensed milk
125 ml/4 fl oz freshly squeezed
lime juice
finely grated rind of 3 limes
4 egg yolks
whipped cream, to serve

❖ Preheat the oven to 160°C/325°F/Gas Mark 3. Lightly grease a 23-cm/9-inch pie plate, about 4 cm/1¹/₂ inches deep.

❖ To make the crumb crust, put the biscuits, sugar and cinnamon in a food processor and process until fine crumbs form – do not overprocess to a powder. Add the melted butter and process again until moistened.

❖ Tip the crumb mixture into the pie plate and press over the base and up the sides. Place the pie plate on a baking tray and bake in the oven for 5 minutes.

❖ Meanwhile, beat the condensed milk, lime juice, lime rind and egg yolks together in a bowl until well blended.

❖ Remove the crumb crust from the oven, pour the filling into the crumb crust and spread out to the edge. Return to the oven for a further 15 minutes, or until the filling is set around the edge but still wobbly in the centre.

❖ Leave to cool completely on a wire rack, then cover and chill for at least 2 hours. Serve spread thickly with the whipped cream.

Lemon Meringue Pie

PASTRY
155 g/5¹/₂ oz plain flour, plus
extra for dusting
85 g/3 oz butter, cut into
small pieces, plus extra for
greasing
35 g/1¹/₄ oz icing sugar, sifted
finely grated rind of ¹/₂ lemon
¹/₂ egg yolk, beaten
1¹/₂ tbsp milk

FILLING
3 tbsp cornflour
300 ml/10 fl oz water
juice and grated rind of
2 lemons
175 g/6 oz caster sugar
2 eggs, separated

❖ To make the pastry, sift the flour into a bowl. Rub in the butter with your fingertips until the mixture resembles fine breadcrumbs. Mix in the remaining ingredients. Knead briefly on a lightly floured work surface. Rest for 30 minutes.

❖ Preheat the oven to 180°C/350°F/Gas Mark 4. Grease a 20-cm/8-inch pie dish with butter. Roll out the pastry to a thickness of 5 mm/¹/₄ inch; use it to line the base and sides of the dish. Prick all over with a fork, line with baking paper and fill with baking beans. Bake for 15 minutes. Remove the pastry case from the oven and take out the paper and beans. Reduce the temperature to 150°C/300°F/Gas Mark 2.

❖ To make the filling, mix the cornflour with a little of the water. Put the remaining water in a saucepan. Stir in the lemon juice and rind and the cornflour paste. Bring to the boil, stirring. Cook for 2 minutes. Cool a little. Stir in 5 tablespoons of the sugar and the egg yolks and pour into the pastry case.

❖ Whisk the egg whites in a clean, grease-free bowl until stiff. Gradually whisk in the remaining sugar and spread over the pie. Bake for a further 40 minutes. Remove from oven, cool and serve.

Chocolate Nut Strudel

❈ **SERVES 6** ❈

150 g/5½ oz unsalted butter, plus extra for greasing
200 g/7 oz mixed chopped nuts
115 g/4 oz plain chocolate, chopped
115 g/4 oz milk chocolate, chopped
115 g/4 oz white chocolate, chopped
200 g/7 oz filo pastry, thawed, if frozen
3 tbsp golden syrup
55 g/2 oz icing sugar
cream, to serve

❈ Preheat the oven to 190°C/375°F/Gas Mark 5. Lightly grease a baking tray with butter. Reserve 1 tablespoon of the nuts. Mix the 3 types of chocolate together.

❈ Place 1 sheet of filo on a clean tea towel. Melt the butter and brush the sheet of filo with the butter, drizzle with a little syrup and sprinkle with some nuts and chocolate. Place another sheet of filo on top and repeat until you have used all the nuts and chocolate.

❈ Use the tea towel to help you to carefully roll up the strudel and place on the baking tray, drizzle with a little more syrup and sprinkle with the reserved nuts. Bake in the preheated oven for 20–25 minutes. If the nuts start to brown too much, cover the strudel with a sheet of foil.

❈ Sprinkle the strudel with the icing sugar, slice and serve with the cream.

Strawberry Cheesecake

❈ **SERVES 8** ❈

BASE
55 g/2 oz unsalted butter
225 g/8 oz crushed digestive biscuits
55 g/2 oz chopped walnuts

FILLING
450 g/1 lb mascarpone cheese
2 eggs, beaten
3 tbsp caster sugar

250 g/9 oz white chocolate, broken into pieces
225 g/8 oz strawberries, hulled and quartered

TOPPING
175 g/6 oz mascarpone cheese
chocolate caraque
16 whole strawberries

❈ To make the base, melt the butter over a low heat and stir in the crushed biscuits and the nuts. Spoon the mixture into a 23-cm/9-inch loose-based cake tin and press evenly over the base with the back of a spoon. Set aside.

❈ Preheat the oven to 150°C/300°F/Gas Mark 2. To make the filling, beat the cheese until smooth, then beat in the eggs and sugar. Put the chocolate in the top of a double boiler or in a heatproof bowl set over a saucepan of barely simmering water. Stir over a low heat until melted. Remove from the heat and cool slightly, then stir into the cheese mixture. Finally, stir in the strawberries.

❈ Spoon the mixture into the cake tin, spread out evenly and smooth the surface. Bake in the preheated oven for 1 hour until the filling is just firm. Turn off the oven but leave the cheesecake in it until completely cold.

❈ Transfer the cheesecake to a serving plate and spread the mascarpone cheese on top. Decorate with the chocolate caraque and whole strawberries.

Marbled Chocolate Cheesecake

❊ SERVES 10–12 ❊

BASE
225 g/8 oz toasted oat cereal
50 g/1¾ oz toasted hazelnuts, chopped
50 g/1¾ oz butter
25 g/1 oz plain chocolate

FILLING
350 g/12 oz full-fat soft cheese
100 g/3½ oz caster sugar
200 ml/7 fl oz thick yogurt
300 ml/10 fl oz double cream
1 sachet gelatine
3 tbsp water
175 g/6 oz plain chocolate, melted
175 g/6 oz white chocolate, melted

❊ To make the base, place the toasted oat cereal in a polythene bag and crush with a rolling pin. Pour the crushed cereal into a mixing bowl and stir in the hazelnuts.

❊ Melt the butter and chocolate together over a low heat and stir into the cereal mixture, stirring until well coated.

❊ Using the bottom of a glass, press the mixture into the base and up the sides of a 20-cm/8-inch springform tin.

❊ To make the filling, beat together the cheese and sugar with a wooden spoon until smooth. Beat in the yogurt. Whip the cream until just holding its shape and fold into the mixture. Sprinkle the gelatine over the water in a heatproof bowl and leave to go spongy. Place over a pan of hot water and stir until dissolved. Stir into the mixture.

❊ Divide the mixture in half and beat the plain chocolate into one half and the white chocolate into the other half.

❊ Place alternate spoonfuls of mixture on top of the cereal base. Swirl the filling together with the tip of a knife to give a marbled effect. Level the top with a scraper or a palette knife. Leave to chill until set before serving.

317

Ricotta-Lemon Cheesecake

55 g/2 oz sultanas	2 tbsp candied orange peel,
3 tbsp Marsala or grappa	finely chopped
butter, for greasing	finely grated rind of 2 large
2 tbsp semolina, plus extra for	lemons
dusting	
350 g/12 oz ricotta cheese,	**TO DECORATE**
drained	icing sugar
3 large egg yolks, beaten	sprigs of fresh mint
100 g/3¹/₂ oz caster sugar	redcurrants or berries
3 tbsp lemon juice	(optional)

❋ Soak the sultanas in the Marsala in a small bowl for about 30 minutes until the liquid has been absorbed and the fruit is swollen.

❋ Meanwhile, cut out a circle of baking paper to fit a loose-based 20-cm/8-inch round cake tin, about 5 cm/ 2 inches deep. Grease and base-line the tin. Lightly dust with semolina and tip out the excess.

❋ Using a wooden spoon, press the ricotta cheese though a nylon sieve into a bowl. Add the egg yolks, sugar, semolina and lemon juice and beat well until blended.

❋ Fold in the sultanas, candied orange peel and lemon rind. Pour into the tin and smooth the surface.

❋ Bake the cheesecake in the centre of a preheated oven, 180°C/350°F/Gas Mark 4, for 30–40 minutes until firm when you press the top and coming away slightly from the sides of the tin.

❋ Turn off the oven and open the door. Leave the cheesecake to cool in the oven for 2–3 hours. To serve, remove from the pan and transfer to a plate. Sift over a layer of icing sugar to dust the top and sides lightly. Decorate with the mint and redcurrants, if wished.

Peach Cobbler

FILLING	PIE TOPPING
6 peaches, peeled and sliced	175 g/6 oz plain flour
4 tbsp caster sugar	115 g/4 oz caster sugar
¹/₂ tbsp lemon juice	1¹/₂ tsp baking powder
1¹/₂ tsp cornflour	¹/₂ tsp salt
¹/₂ tsp almond or vanilla	85 g/3 oz butter, diced
essence	1 egg
vanilla or pecan ice cream,	5–6 tbsp milk
to serve	

❋ Preheat the oven to 220°C/425°F/Gas Mark 7. Put the peaches in a 23-cm/9-inch square ovenproof dish that is also suitable for serving. Add the sugar, lemon juice, cornflour and almond essence and toss together. Bake the peaches in the oven for 20 minutes.

❋ Meanwhile, to make the topping, sift the flour, all but 2 tablespoons of the sugar, the baking powder and salt into a bowl. Rub in the butter with your fingertips until the mixture resembles breadcrumbs. Mix the egg and 5 tablespoons of the milk in a jug, then mix into the dry ingredients with a fork until a soft, sticky dough forms. If the dough seems too dry, stir in the extra tablespoon of milk.

❋ Reduce the oven temperature to 200°C/400°F/Gas Mark 6. Remove the peaches from the oven and drop spoonfuls of the topping over the surface, without smoothing. Sprinkle with the remaining sugar, return to the oven and bake for a further 15 minutes, or until the topping is golden brown and firm – the topping will spread as it cooks. Serve hot or at room temperature with the ice cream.

Hot Chocolate Soufflé

100 g/3¹/₂ oz plain chocolate
300 ml/10 fl oz milk
25 g/1 oz butter
4 large eggs, separated
1 tbsp cornflour
4 tbsp caster sugar
¹/₂ tsp vanilla essence
100 g/3¹/₂ oz plain chocolate chips
caster and icing sugar, for dusting

CHOCOLATE CUSTARD
2 tbsp cornflour
1 tbsp caster sugar
450 ml/16 fl oz milk
50 g/1³/₄ oz plain chocolate

❊ Grease an 850-ml/1¹/₂-pint soufflé dish and sprinkle with caster sugar. Break the chocolate into pieces.

❊ Heat the milk with the butter in a saucepan until almost boiling. Mix the egg yolks, cornflour and caster sugar in a bowl and pour on some of the hot milk, whisking. Return to the pan and cook gently, stirring constantly until thickened. Add the chocolate and stir until melted. Remove from the heat and stir in the vanilla essence.

❊ Whisk the egg whites until standing in soft peaks. Fold half of the egg whites into the chocolate mixture. Fold in the rest with the chocolate chips. Pour into the dish and bake in a preheated oven, 180°C/350°F/Gas Mark 4, for 40–45 minutes until well risen.

❊ Meanwhile, make the custard. Put the cornflour and sugar in a small bowl and mix to a smooth paste with a little of the milk. Heat the remaining milk until almost boiling. Pour a little of the hot milk on to the cornflour, mix well, then pour back into the saucepan. Cook gently, stirring until thickened. Break the chocolate into pieces and add to the custard, stirring until melted.

❊ Dust the soufflé with sugar and serve immediately with the chocolate custard.

Mixed Fruit Pavlova

3 egg whites
pinch of salt
175 g/6 oz caster sugar
300 ml/10 fl oz double cream, lightly whipped
fresh fruit of your choice (raspberries, strawberries, peaches, passion fruit, cape gooseberries)

❊ Carefully line a baking tray with a sheet of baking paper.

❊ Whisk the egg whites with the salt in a large bowl until they form soft peaks.

❊ Whisk in the sugar a little at a time, whisking well after each addition until all of the sugar has been incorporated.

❊ Spoon three-quarters of the meringue on to the baking tray, forming a round 20 cm/8 inches in diameter.

❊ Place spoonfuls of the remaining meringue all around the edge of the round so they join up to make a nest shape.

❊ Bake in a preheated oven, 140°C/ 275°F/Gas Mark 1, for 1¹/₄ hours.

❊ Turn the heat off, but leave the pavlova in the oven until it is completely cold.

❊ To serve, place the pavlova on a serving dish. Spread with the lightly whipped cream, then arrange the fresh fruit on top.

Layered Meringue Gâteau

❄ **SERVES 8** ❄

6 egg whites
140 g/5 oz caster sugar
175 g/6 oz icing sugar
2 tbsp cornflour

FILLING
225 ml/8 fl oz double cream
140 g/5 oz plain chocolate,
broken into small pieces
4 tsp dark rum

TO DECORATE
150 ml/5 fl oz double cream
4 tsp caster sugar
1–2 tsp cocoa powder,
for dusting

❄ Prepare 5 sheets of baking paper by drawing an 18-cm/7-inch circle on each. Use them to line baking trays.

❄ Whisk the egg whites until they form soft peaks. Mix the sugars and cornflour together and sift into the egg whites, a little at a time, whisking until firm peaks form.

❄ Spoon the meringue mixture into a piping bag fitted with a round nozzle. Starting from the centre, carefully pipe a spiral, measuring 18 cm/7 inches, on each of the prepared pieces of baking paper.

❄ Bake in a preheated oven, at the lowest possible temperature, with the oven door kept slightly ajar, for 6 hours or overnight.

❄ After baking, carefully peel the meringue spirals from the baking paper and place on wire racks to cool.

❄ To make the filling, pour the cream into a saucepan and place over a low heat. Add the chocolate and stir until melted. Remove from the heat and beat with a hand-held whisk. Beat in the rum, then cover with clingfilm and refrigerate overnight or for as long as the meringues are in the oven.

❄ To assemble the gâteau, beat the filling with an electric mixer until thick and smooth. Place 3 of the meringue layers on a work surface and spread the filling over them. Stack the 3 meringue layers, one on top of the other, and place an uncovered meringue layer on top. Crush the fifth meringue layer into crumbs.

❄ To make the decoration, whip the cream with the sugar until thick. Carefully spread the mixture over the top of the gâteau. Sprinkle the meringue crumbs on top of the cream and dust the centre of the gâteau with cocoa powder. Serve within 1–2 hours.

Banana Cream Profiteroles

❋ SERVES 4 ❋

CHOUX PASTRY
150 ml/5 fl oz water
60 g/2¹/₂ oz butter
85 g/3 oz strong white flour,
sifted
2 eggs

CHOCOLATE SAUCE
100 g/3¹/₂ oz plain chocolate,
broken into pieces

2 tbsp water
4 tbsp icing sugar
25 g/1 oz unsalted butter

FILLING
300 ml/10 fl oz double cream
1 banana
2 tbsp icing sugar
2 tbsp banana-flavoured
liqueur

❋ Lightly grease a baking tray. Place the water in a saucepan, add the butter and heat gently until the butter melts. Bring to a rolling boil, then remove the pan from the heat and add the flour in one go, beating well until the mixture leaves the sides of the saucepan and forms a ball. Leave to cool slightly, then gradually beat in the eggs to form a smooth, glossy mixture. Spoon into a large piping bag fitted with a 1-cm/¹/₂-inch plain nozzle.

❋ Sprinkle the baking tray with a little water. Pipe about 18 small balls of the choux pastry on to the baking tray, allowing enough room for them to expand during cooking. Bake in a preheated oven, 220°C/425°F/Gas Mark 7, for 15–20 minutes until crisp and golden. Remove from the oven and, using a sharp knife, make a small slit in each one for steam to escape. Cool on a wire rack.

❋ To make the chocolate sauce, place all the ingredients in a heatproof bowl set over a saucepan of simmering water and heat until combined to make a smooth, glossy sauce, stirring constantly.

❋ To make the filling, whip the cream until standing in soft peaks. Mash the banana with the sugar and liqueur. Fold into the cream. Place in a piping bag fitted with a 1-cm/¹/₂-inch plain nozzle and carefully pipe into the profiteroles. Serve mounded up on a glass cake stand, with the chocolate sauce poured over.

Chocolate Éclairs

❋ MAKES 10 ❋

CHOUX PASTRY
150 ml/5 fl oz water
70 g/2¹/₂ oz butter, cut into
small pieces
90 g/3 oz strong white flour,
sifted
2 eggs

CRÈME PÂTISSIÈRE
2 eggs, lightly beaten
4 tbsp caster sugar

2 tbsp cornflour
300 ml/10 fl oz milk
¹/₄ tsp vanilla essence

ICING
25 g/1 oz butter
1 tbsp milk
1 tbsp cocoa powder
100 g/3¹/₂ oz icing sugar
a little white chocolate, melted

❋ Lightly grease a baking tray. Place the water in a saucepan, add the butter and heat gently until the butter melts. Bring to a rolling boil, then remove the pan from the heat and add the flour in one go, beating well until the mixture leaves the sides of the saucepan and forms a ball. Leave to cool slightly, then gradually beat in the eggs to form a smooth, glossy mixture. Spoon into a large piping bag fitted with a 1-cm/¹/₂-inch plain nozzle.

❋ Sprinkle the baking tray with a little water. Pipe éclairs 7.5-cm/3-inch long, spaced well apart. Bake in a preheated oven, 200°C/400°F/Gas Mark 6, for 30–35 minutes or until crisp and golden. Make a small slit in each one to let the steam escape. Cool on a wire rack.

❋ Meanwhile, make the crème pâtissière. Whisk the eggs and sugar until thick and creamy, then fold in the cornflour. Heat the milk until almost boiling and pour on to the eggs, whisking. Transfer to the saucepan and cook over a low heat, stirring until thick. Remove from the heat and stir in the vanilla essence. Cover with baking paper and cool.

❋ To make the icing, melt the butter with the milk in a saucepan, remove from the heat and stir in the cocoa powder and sugar. Split the éclairs lengthways and pipe in the crème pâtissière. Spread the icing over the top of the éclairs. Spoon over the white chocolate, swirl in and leave to set.

Traditional Tiramisù

20–24 sponge fingers, about 150 g/5^1/$_2$ oz	350 g/12 oz mascarpone cheese
2 tbsp cold black coffee	2 tsp lemon juice
2 tbsp coffee essence	250 ml/9 fl oz double cream
2 tbsp Amaretto	1 tbsp milk
4 egg yolks	25 g/1 oz flaked almonds, lightly toasted
90 g/3 oz caster sugar	
few drops of vanilla essence	2 tbsp cocoa powder
grated rind of ^{1}/$_2$ lemon	1 tbsp icing sugar

❈ Arrange almost half of the sponge fingers in the base of a glass bowl or serving dish.

❈ Combine the black coffee, coffee essence and Amaretto together and sprinkle a little more than half the mixture over the sponge fingers.

❈ Put the egg yolks into a heatproof bowl with the sugar, vanilla essence and lemon rind. Stand the bowl over a saucepan of gently simmering water and whisk the mixture until very thick and creamy and the whisk leaves a very heavy trail when lifted from the bowl.

❈ Put the mascarpone cheese in a separate bowl with the lemon juice and beat until smooth. Combine the egg and mascarpone cheese mixtures and when evenly blended pour half over the sponge fingers and spread out evenly.

❈ Add another layer of sponge fingers, sprinkle with the remaining coffee and Amaretto mixture, then cover with the rest of the cheese and egg mixture. Chill the tiramisù for at least 2 hours or overnight.

❈ To serve, whip the cream and milk together until fairly stiff and spread or pipe over the dessert. Sprinkle with the flaked almonds and then sift an even layer of cocoa powder so the top is completely covered. Finally, sift a light layer of icing sugar over the cocoa.

Traditional Italian Zabaglione

4 egg yolks	125 ml/4 fl oz Marsala
50 g/1^3/$_4$ oz caster sugar	cocoa powder, to dust
50 g/1^3/$_4$ oz plain chocolate	

❈ In a large glass mixing bowl, whisk together the egg yolks and caster sugar, using electric beaters, until you have a very pale mixture.

❈ Finely grate the chocolate and fold into the egg mixture. Fold in the wine.

❈ Place the mixing bowl over a saucepan of gently simmering water. Cook gently, whisking constantly until the mixture thickens; take care not to overcook or the mixture will curdle.

❈ Spoon the hot mixture into warmed individual glass dishes and dust lightly with cocoa powder. Serve the zabaglione as soon as possible so that it is warm, light and fluffy.

Panna Cotta

1 tbsp vegetable oil
1 vanilla pod
600 ml/1 pint double cream
4 tbsp caster sugar
2 tsp powdered gelatine
3 tbsp cold water
6 sprigs fresh mint and
about 18 strawberries, sliced,
to decorate

❖ Use the oil to grease 6 x 125-ml/4-fl oz dariole moulds or ramekins well. Split the vanilla pod with a sharp knife and scrape out all the seeds. Put the pod and the seeds in a saucepan with the cream and sugar and stir well over a low heat. Carefully bring to simmering point and simmer gently for 2–3 minutes. Remove from the heat and leave to cool a little.

❖ Soak the gelatine in 3 tablespoons of cold water in a small, heatproof bowl. Place the bowl over a saucepan of hot water and heat gently until the gelatine is dissolved and clear.

❖ Remove the vanilla pod from the cream and stir in the gelatine. Pour the mixture into the prepared moulds, cover with clingfilm and chill for at least 3 hours, or overnight, until set.

❖ To serve, dip the moulds up to the rim (do not immerse completely) in hot water for 2 seconds, then turn out on to serving plates. Serve decorated with the mint and strawberries.

Spanish Flan

butter, for greasing	500 ml/18 fl oz milk
175 g/6 oz caster sugar	1 vanilla pod
4 tbsp water	2 large eggs
juice of 1/2 lemon	2 large egg yolks

❄ Lightly butter a 1.2-litre/2-pint soufflé dish. To make the caramel, put 75 g/2¾ oz sugar with the water in a pan over a medium–high heat and cook, stirring constantly, until the sugar dissolves. Boil until the syrup turns a deep golden brown.

❄ Immediately remove from the heat and add a few drops of lemon juice. Pour into the soufflé dish and swirl around. Set aside.

❄ Pour the milk into a pan. Slit the vanilla pod lengthways and add it to the milk. Bring to the boil, remove the pan from the heat and stir in the remaining sugar, stirring until it dissolves. Set aside.

❄ Beat the eggs and egg yolks together in a bowl. Pour the milk mixture over them, whisking. Remove the vanilla pod. Strain the egg mixture into a bowl, then transfer to the soufflé dish.

❄ Place the dish in a roasting tin filled with enough boiling water to come two-thirds up the side.

❄ Bake in a preheated oven, 160°C/325°F/Gas Mark 3, for 1¼–1½ hours until a knife inserted in the centre comes out clean. Leave to cool completely. Cover with clingfilm and refrigerate for at least 24 hours.

❄ Run a round-bladed knife around the edge of the dish. Place an upturned, rimmed serving plate on top, then invert the plate and dish, giving a sharp shake halfway over. Lift off the dish and serve.

Yogurt Ambrosia

300 ml/10 fl oz double cream	6 tbsp dark muscovado sugar
300 ml/10 fl oz thick Greek yogurt	

❄ In a large basin, use a balloon whisk to beat the cream until thick. Add the yogurt and mix together well. Pour into a large shallow serving dish (about 20 cm/8 inches in diameter) or 6 small ramekins.

❄ Sprinkle the sugar over the surface of the mixture in quite a thick layer. Cover with clingfilm and chill in the refrigerator overnight. The sugar will dissolve, leaving a luscious toffee layer.

Mint Chocolate Desserts

300 ml/10 fl oz double cream
150 ml/5 fl oz creamy fromage
frais
25 g/1 oz icing sugar

1 tbsp crème de menthe
175 g/6 oz plain chocolate
chocolate, to decorate

❄ Place the cream in a large mixing bowl and whisk until standing in soft peaks.

❄ Fold in the fromage frais and icing sugar, then place about one-third of the mixture in a smaller bowl. Stir the crème de menthe into the smaller bowl. Melt the chocolate and stir it into the larger bowl.

❄ Place alternate spoonfuls of the 2 mixtures into serving glasses, then swirl the mixture together to give a decorative effect. Leave to chill until required.

❄ To make the piped chocolate decorations, melt a small amount of chocolate and place in a paper piping bag.

❄ Place a sheet of baking paper on a board and pipe squiggles, stars or flower shapes with the melted chocolate. Alternatively, to make curved decorations, pipe decorations on to a long strip of baking paper, then carefully place the strip over a rolling pin, securing with sticky tape. Leave the chocolate to set, then carefully remove from the baking paper.

❄ Decorate each dessert with piped chocolate decorations and serve. Alternatively, the desserts can be decorated and then chilled, if preferred.

Quick Chocolate Mousse

300 ml/10 fl oz single cream
200 g/7 oz continental plain
chocolate (should have at
least 52% cocoa solids)

2 eggs, lightly beaten
2 tbsp Marsala
2 tbsp grated white chocolate,
to decorate

❄ Heat the cream in a saucepan over a low heat for about 3–4 minutes until almost boiling.

❄ Break up or chop the plain chocolate into small pieces and place in a blender.

❄ Pour the hot cream into the blender and then blend together until smooth.

❄ Pour in the eggs and blend again until well mixed. Add the Marsala and give the mixture a final blend.

❄ Pour into 6 ramekin dishes and allow to cool. Cover with clingfilm and chill for about 2 hours. Serve decorated with the grated white chocolate.

Champagne Mousse

SPONGE
25 g/1 oz butter, melted, plus
extra for greasing
4 eggs
100 g/3^1/$_2$ oz caster sugar
75 g/2^3/$_4$ oz self-raising flour
2 tbsp cocoa powder

MOUSSE
1 sachet gelatine
3 tbsp water
300 ml/10 fl oz champagne
300 ml/10 fl oz double cream
2 egg whites
6 tbsp caster sugar
55 g/2 oz plain chocolate-
flavoured cake covering,
melted, to decorate

❊ Line a 38 x 25-cm/15 x 10-inch Swiss roll tin with greased baking paper. Place the eggs and sugar in a bowl and beat with an electric mixer until the mixture is very thick and the whisk leaves a trail when lifted. If using a balloon whisk, stand the bowl over a saucepan of hot water whilst whisking. Sift the flour and cocoa together and fold into the egg mixture. Fold in the butter. Pour into the tin and bake in a preheated oven, 200°C/400°F/Gas Mark 6, for 8 minutes or until springy to the touch. Cool for 5 minutes, then turn out on to a wire rack until cold. Meanwhile, line 4 x 10-cm/4-inch baking rings. Line the sides with 2.5-cm/ 1-inch strips of cake and the base with circles.

❊ To make the mousse, sprinkle the gelatine over the water and leave to go spongy. Place the bowl over a saucepan of hot water and stir until dissolved. Stir in the champagne.

❊ Whip the cream until just holding its shape. Fold in the champagne mixture. Leave in a cool place until on the point of setting, stirring. Whisk the egg whites until standing in soft peaks, add the sugar and whisk until glossy. Fold into the setting mixture. Spoon into the sponge cases, allowing the mixture to go above the sponge. Chill for 2 hours. Pipe the cake covering in squiggles on a piece of baking paper, leave them to set, then use them to decorate the mousses.

Chocolate Marshmallow Cake

85 g/3 oz unsalted butter,
plus 1 tbsp for greasing
225 g/8 oz caster sugar
1/2 tsp vanilla essence
2 eggs, lightly beaten
85 g/3 oz plain chocolate,
broken into pieces
150 ml/5 fl oz buttermilk
175 g/6 oz self-raising flour
1/2 tsp bicarbonate of soda

pinch of salt
55 g/2 oz milk chocolate,
grated, to decorate

ICING
175 g/6 oz white marshmallows
1 tbsp milk
2 egg whites
2 tbsp caster sugar

❋ Grease an 850-ml/1 1/2-pint ovenproof pudding basin with butter. Cream the butter, sugar and vanilla together until very pale and fluffy, then gradually beat in the eggs.

❋ Melt the plain chocolate in a heatproof bowl over a saucepan of simmering water. When the chocolate has melted, stir in the buttermilk gradually, until well combined. Remove the pan from the heat and cool slightly.

❋ Sift the flour, bicarbonate of soda and salt into a bowl.

❋ Add the chocolate mixture and the flour mixture alternately to the creamed mixture, a little at a time. Spoon the creamed mixture into the prepared basin and smooth the surface. Bake in a preheated oven, 160°C/325°F/Gas Mark 3, for 50 minutes. Turn out on to a wire rack to cool.

❋ Meanwhile, make the icing. Put the marshmallows and milk in a small saucepan and heat very gently until the marshmallows have melted. Remove the pan from the heat and leave to cool.

❋ Whisk the egg whites until soft peaks form, then add the sugar and whisk until stiff peaks form. Fold the egg white into the cooled marshmallow mixture and set aside.

❋ When the cake is cool, cover the top and sides with the marshmallow icing. Sprinkle over the grated chocolate.

Oranges in Spiced Caramel

4 large juicy oranges
4–6 tbsp shelled pistachio nuts,
chopped, to decorate

SPICED CARAMEL
250 g/9 oz caster sugar
5 black peppercorns, lightly
crushed
4 cloves
1 green cardamom pod, lightly
crushed
300 ml/10 fl oz water

❋ To make the spiced caramel, put the sugar, peppercorns, cloves, cardamom pod and 150 ml/5 fl oz of the water in a saucepan and stir to dissolve the sugar over a medium heat. When the sugar has dissolved, turn up the heat and boil, without stirring, until the syrup thickens and turns a deep caramel colour. Use a wet pastry brush to brush down the side of the pan if necessary.

❋ Very carefully, pour in another 150 ml/5 fl oz of the water, standing back because it will splatter. Remove the pan from the heat and, using a long-handled wooden spoon, stir until all the caramel has dissolved. Set aside to cool.

❋ Pare off the orange rind and pith, cutting carefully so the oranges retain their shape. Either leave the oranges whole, or, working over a bowl, cut them into segments, cutting the flesh away from the membranes.

❋ Pour the caramel syrup with the spices over the oranges and stir together gently. Cover and chill until ready to serve. Serve in individual bowls with the chopped pistachio nuts sprinkled over the tops at the last minute.

Aztec Oranges

6 oranges
1 lime
2 tbsp tequila
2 tbsp orange-flavoured liqueur

dark soft brown sugar, to taste
fine lime rind strips, to decorate

❄ Using a sharp knife, cut a slice off the top and bottom of the oranges, then remove the peel and pith, cutting downwards and taking care to retain the shape of the oranges.

❄ Holding the oranges on their sides, cut them horizontally into slices.

❄ Place the oranges in a bowl. Cut the lime in half and squeeze over the oranges. Sprinkle with the tequila and liqueur, then sprinkle over sugar to taste.

❄ Cover with clingfilm and chill in the refrigerator until ready to serve, then transfer to a serving dish and garnish with the lime strips.

Cinnamon Pears

1 lemon
4 firm ripe pears
300 ml/10 fl oz dry cider or unsweetened apple juice
1 cinnamon stick, broken in half
fresh mint leaves, to decorate

MAPLE RICOTTA CREAM
125 g/4$\frac{1}{2}$ oz ricotta cheese
125 g/4$\frac{1}{2}$ oz natural fromage frais
$\frac{1}{2}$ tsp ground cinnamon
$\frac{1}{2}$ tsp grated lemon rind
1 tbsp maple syrup
lemon rind, to decorate

❄ Using a swivel vegetable peeler, remove the lemon rind and put it in a non-stick frying pan. Squeeze the lemon and pour the juice into a shallow bowl.

❄ Peel, halve and core the pears. Toss them in the lemon juice to prevent discoloration. Add them to the frying pan and pour over the lemon juice remaining in the bowl.

❄ Add the cider and the cinnamon stick. Gently bring to the boil, then reduce the heat and simmer for 10 minutes. Carefully remove the pears using a slotted spoon, and reserve the cooking juice. Put the pears in a warmed heatproof serving dish, cover with foil and keep warm in a low oven.

❄ Return the pan to the heat, bring to the boil, then simmer for about 8–10 minutes, until reduced by half. Spoon over the pears.

❄ To make the maple ricotta cream, mix together all the ingredients. Decorate with the lemon rind and serve with the pears.

Poached Pears in Chocolate

6 firm ripe pears
100 g/3½ oz caster sugar
2 cinnamon sticks
rind of 1 orange
2 cloves
1 bottle rosé wine

CHOCOLATE SAUCE
175 g/6 oz plain chocolate
250 g/9 oz mascarpone cheese
2 tbsp orange-flavoured liqueur

❖ Carefully peel the pears, leaving the stalks intact.

❖ Place the sugar, cinnamon sticks, orange rind, cloves and wine in a saucepan large enough to hold the pears.

❖ Heat gently until the sugar has dissolved, then add the pears and bring to a simmer. Cover the pan and poach the pears gently for 20 minutes. If serving them cold, leave the pears to cool in the liquid and chill until required. If serving hot, leave the pears in the hot liquid whilst preparing the sauce.

❖ To make the sauce, melt the chocolate. Beat together the mascarpone cheese and the liqueur. Beat the cheese mixture into the melted chocolate.

❖ Remove the pears from the poaching liquid and place on a serving plate. Add a spoonful of sauce on the side and serve the remainder separately. Alternatively, pipe a rosette of the sauce on each plate.

Exotic Fruit Salad

❊ **SERVES 6** ❊

3 passion fruit   1 mango
125 g/4 oz caster sugar   10 lychees, canned or fresh
150 ml/5 fl oz water   1 star fruit

❊ Halve the passion fruit and press the flesh through a sieve into a saucepan.

❊ Add the sugar and water to the pan and bring to a gentle boil, stirring.

❊ Put the mango on a chopping board and cut a thick slice from either side, cutting as near to the stone as possible. Cut away as much flesh as possible in large chunks from the stone section.

❊ Take the 2 side slices and make 3 cuts through the flesh but not the skin, and 3 more at right angles to make a lattice pattern.

❊ Push the mango skin inside out so that the cubed flesh is exposed and you can easily cut it off.

❊ Peel and stone the lychees and cut the star fruit into 12 slices.

❊ Add all the mango flesh, the lychees and the star fruit to the passion-fruit syrup and poach gently for 5 minutes. Remove the fruit with a slotted spoon.

❊ Bring the syrup to the boil and cook for 5 minutes until it thickens slightly.

❊ To serve, transfer all the fruit to individual serving glasses, pour over the sugar syrup and serve warm.

Mango & Passion Fruit Salad

❊ **SERVES 4** ❊

1 large mango
2 oranges
4 passion fruit
2 tbsp orange-flavoured liqueur, such as Grand Marnier
fresh mint or geranium leaves, to decorate

MASCARPONE CREAM
125 g/4 1/2 oz mascarpone cheese
1 tbsp clear honey
4 tbsp Greek yogurt
few drops vanilla essence

❊ Using a sharp knife, cut the mango in half lengthways as close to the stone as possible. Remove the stone, using a sharp knife.

❊ Peel off the mango skin, cut the flesh into slices and place in a large bowl.

❊ Peel the oranges, removing all the pith, and cut into segments. Add to the bowl with any juices.

❊ Halve the passion fruit, scoop out the flesh and add to the bowl with the orange-flavoured liqueur. Mix together all the ingredients in the bowl.

❊ Cover the bowl with clingfilm and chill in the refrigerator for 1 hour. Turn into individual glass serving dishes.

❊ To make the mascarpone cream, blend the mascarpone cheese and honey together. Add the yogurt and the vanilla essence and stir until thoroughly blended.

❊ Serve the fruit salad with the mascarpone cream, decorated with the mint.

Fruit Salad with Ginger Syrup

2.5-cm/1-inch piece of root
ginger, peeled
and chopped
60 g/2 oz caster sugar
150 ml/5 fl oz water
grated rind and juice of 1 lime
4 tbsp ginger wine
1 pineapple, peeled, cored and
cut into bite-sized pieces
2 mangoes, peeled, stoned
and diced
4 kiwi fruit, peeled and sliced

1 paw-paw, peeled, deseeded
and diced
2 passion fruit, halved and
flesh removed
350 g/12 oz lychees, peeled
and stoned
1/4 fresh coconut, grated
60 g/2 oz Cape gooseberries,
to decorate (optional)
coconut ice cream, to serve
(optional)

❖ Place the ginger, sugar, water and lime juice in a saucepan and bring slowly to the boil. Simmer for 1 minute, remove from the heat and allow to cool slightly.

❖ Strain the syrup, add the ginger wine and mix well. Cool completely.

❖ Place the prepared fruit in a serving bowl. Add the cold syrup and mix well. Cover and chill the fruit in the refrigerator for 2–4 hours.

❖ Just before serving, add half the grated coconut to the salad and mix well. Sprinkle the remainder on top.

❖ If using Cape gooseberries to decorate the salad, peel back each calyx to form a flower. Wipe the berries clean, then arrange them around the side of the fruit salad before serving.

Piña Colada Pineapple

1 small pineapple
2 tbsp unsalted butter
25 g/1 oz light muscovado
sugar

55 g/2 oz fresh coconut, grated
2 tbsp coconut-flavoured
liqueur or rum

❖ Using a very sharp knife, cut the pineapple into quarters and then remove the tough core from the centre, leaving the leaves attached.

❖ Carefully cut the pineapple flesh away from the skin. Remove any eyes with small sharp knife. Make horizontal cuts across the flesh of the pineapple quarters.

❖ Gently heat the butter in a saucepan until melted, stirring constantly. Brush the melted butter over the pineapple and sprinkle with the sugar.

❖ Cover the pineapple leaves with foil to prevent them burning, transfer the pineapple quarters to a grill rack and place under a preheated medium grill.

❖ Grill the pineapple for about 10 minutes.

❖ Sprinkle the coconut over the pineapple and grill, cut side up, for a further 5–10 minutes or until the pineapple is piping hot.

❖ Transfer the pineapple to serving plates and remove the foil from the leaves. Spoon a little coconut-flavoured liqueur or rum over the pineapple and serve immediately.

Banana Fritters

70 g/2¹/₂ oz plain flour
2 tbsp rice flour
1 tbsp caster sugar
1 egg, separated
150 ml/5 fl oz coconut milk
4 large bananas
sunflower oil, for deep-frying

TO DECORATE
1 tsp icing sugar
1 tsp ground cinnamon
lime wedges

❖ Sift the plain flour, the rice flour and the sugar into a mixing bowl and make a well in the centre. Add the egg yolk and coconut milk.

❖ Beat the mixture until a smooth, thick batter forms. Whisk the egg white in a clean, dry bowl until it is stiff enough to hold soft peaks. Fold it into the batter lightly and evenly.

❖ Heat a 6-cm/2¹/₂-inch depth of oil in a large pan to 180°C/350°F or until a cube of bread browns in 30 seconds. Cut the bananas in half crossways, then dip them quickly into the batter to coat them.

❖ Drop the bananas carefully into the hot oil and fry them, in batches, for 2–3 minutes until they are golden brown, turning once.

❖ Drain on kitchen paper. Sprinkle with icing sugar and cinnamon and serve immediately, with the lime wedges for squeezing juice as desired.

Caramel Apple Wedges

115 g/4 oz flour	2^1/$_2$ tbsp sesame seeds
1 egg	250 g/9 oz caster sugar
125 ml/4 fl oz water	2 tbsp vegetable oil, plus extra
4 crisp dessert apples	for deep-frying

✻ Place the flour, egg and water in a bowl and whisk well until a smooth, thick batter forms.

✻ Core the apples and cut each into 8 wedges. Drop into the batter and stir in the sesame seeds.

✻ Put the sugar and oil in a heavy-based saucepan and heat, stirring, until the sugar dissolves. Continue until the syrup begins to turn golden. Remove from the heat but keep warm.

✻ Heat the oil for frying in a wok or deep saucepan to 180°C/350°F/Gas Mark 4 or until a cube of bread turns golden in 30 seconds. Lift the apple pieces one by one from the batter, using tongs or chopsticks, and lower into the hot oil. Fry for 2–3 minutes until golden brown and crisp.

✻ Remove with a slotted spoon and dip very quickly into the sugar mixture. Dip the apple wedges briefly into iced water and drain on non-stick paper. Serve immediately.

Crêpes with Apples

✶ **SERVES 4** ✶

125 g/4^1/$_2$ oz plain flour	**FILLING**
pinch of salt	225 g/8 oz Bramley apples,
1 tsp finely grated lemon rind	peeled, cored and sliced
1 egg	2 tbsp sultanas
300 ml/10 fl oz milk	
1–2 tbsp vegetable oil, plus	**SAUCE**
extra for greasing	85 g/3 oz butter
pared lemon rind, to decorate	3 tbsp golden syrup
	85 g/3 oz light muscovado
	sugar
	1 tbsp rum or brandy (optional)
	1 tbsp lemon juice

✻ Sift the flour and salt into a bowl. Add the lemon rind, egg and milk and whisk to make a smooth batter.

✻ Heat a little oil in a heavy-based frying pan. Make 8 thin pancakes, using extra oil as required. Stack the cooked pancakes, layering them with kitchen paper.

✻ To make the filling, cook the apples with the sultanas in a little water until soft. Divide the mixture evenly between the pancakes and roll up or fold into triangles. Brush an ovenproof dish with a little oil and arrange the pancakes in it. Bake in a preheated oven, 160°C/325°F/Gas Mark 3, for 15 minutes until the pancakes are warmed through.

✻ To make the sauce, melt the butter, syrup and sugar together in a pan, stirring well. Add the rum or brandy, if using, and the lemon juice. Do not allow the mixture to boil.

✻ Serve the pancakes on warmed plates, with a little sauce poured over and decorated with lemon rind.

Stuffed Nectarines

85 g/3 oz plain continental chocolate, finely chopped
55 g/2 oz amaretti biscuit crumbs
1 tsp finely grated lemon rind
1 large egg white
6 tbsp Amaretto liqueur

6 nectarines, halved and stoned
300 ml/10 fl oz white wine
55 g/2 oz milk chocolate, grated
whipped cream or vanilla or chocolate ice cream, to serve

❄ Mix the chocolate, amaretti crumbs and lemon rind together in a bowl. Lightly beat the egg white and add it to the mixture with half the Amaretto liqueur. Using a small sharp knife, slightly enlarge the cavities in the nectarines. Add the removed nectarine flesh to the chocolate and crumb mixture and mix well.

❄ Preheat the oven to 190°C/375°F/Gas Mark 5. Place the nectarines, cut side up, in an ovenproof dish just large enough to hold them in a single layer. Pile the chocolate and crumb mixture into the cavities, dividing it equally between them. Mix the wine and remaining Amaretto and pour it into the dish around the nectarines.

❄ Bake in the preheated oven for 40–45 minutes until the nectarines are tender. Transfer 2 nectarine halves to each individual serving plate and spoon over a little of the cooking juices. Sprinkle over the grated milk chocolate and serve the nectarines immediately with the whipped cream.

Rich Chocolate Brownies

100 g/3½ oz unsalted butter, plus extra for greasing
175 g/6 oz caster sugar
75 g/2¾ oz dark muscovado sugar
125 g/4½ oz plain chocolate
1 tbsp golden syrup

2 eggs
1 tsp chocolate or vanilla essence
100 g/3½ oz plain flour
2 tbsp cocoa powder
½ tsp baking powder

❄ Lightly grease a 20-cm/8-inch shallow square cake tin with a little butter and base-line with baking paper.

❄ Place the butter, sugars, chocolate and golden syrup in a heavy-based saucepan and heat gently, stirring, until the mixture is well blended and smooth. Remove from the heat and leave to cool.

❄ Beat together the eggs and flavouring. Whisk in the cooled chocolate mixture.

❄ Sift together the flour, cocoa powder and baking powder and fold carefully into the egg and chocolate mixture, using a metal spoon or a spatula.

❄ Spoon the mixture into the prepared tin and bake in a preheated oven, 180°C/350°F/Gas Mark 4, for 25 minutes or until the top is crisp and the edge of the cake is beginning to shrink away from the tin. The inside of the cake mixture will still be quite stodgy and soft to the touch.

❄ Leave the cake to cool completely in the tin, then cut it into squares to serve.

Iced Chocolate & Cream Cheese Brownies

100 g/3$\frac{1}{2}$ oz butter, plus extra
for greasing
200 g/7 oz low-fat soft cheese
$\frac{1}{2}$ tsp vanilla essence
2 eggs
250 g/9 oz caster sugar
3 tbsp cocoa powder
100 g/3$\frac{1}{2}$ oz self-raising flour,
sifted
50 g/1$\frac{3}{4}$ oz pecan nuts,
chopped

FUDGE ICING
50 g/1$\frac{3}{4}$ oz butter
1 tbsp milk
100 g/3$\frac{1}{2}$ oz icing sugar
2 tbsp cocoa powder
pecan nuts, to decorate
(optional)

✤ Lightly grease a 20-cm/8-inch square shallow cake tin with a little butter and base-line with baking paper.

✤ Beat together the cheese, vanilla essence and 25 g/1 oz of the caster sugar until smooth, then set aside.

✤ Beat the eggs and remaining caster sugar together until light and fluffy. Place the butter and cocoa powder in a small saucepan and heat gently, stirring until the butter melts and the mixture combines, then stir it into the egg mixture. Fold in the flour and nuts.

✤ Pour half of the brownie mixture into the tin and level the top. Carefully spread the soft cheese over it, then cover it with the remaining brownie mixture. Bake in a preheated oven, 180°C/350°F/Gas Mark 4, for 40–45 minutes. Leave to cool in the tin.

✤ To make the icing, melt the butter in the milk. Stir in the icing sugar and cocoa powder. Spread the icing over the brownies and decorate with the pecan nuts, if using. Leave the icing to set, then cut into squares to serve.

335

Chocolate Caramel Squares

125 g/4½ oz butter, cut into small pieces, plus extra for greasing
175 g/6 oz plain flour
50 g/1¾ oz soft brown sugar, sifted

TOPPING
50 g/1¾ oz butter
50 g/1¾ oz soft brown sugar
400 g/14 oz canned condensed milk
150 g/5½ oz milk chocolate

❄ Lightly grease a 23-cm/9-inch square cake tin with a little butter.

❄ Sift the flour into a mixing bowl and rub in the butter with your fingers until the mixture resembles fine breadcrumbs. Add the sugar and mix to form a firm dough.

❄ Press the dough into the bottom of the prepared tin and prick all over with a fork.

❄ Bake in a preheated oven, 190°C/375°F/Gas Mark 5, for 20 minutes or until lightly golden. Leave to cool in the tin.

❄ To make the topping, place the butter, sugar and condensed milk in a non-stick saucepan and cook over a gentle heat, stirring constantly, until the mixture comes to the boil.

❄ Reduce the heat and cook for 4–5 minutes or until the caramel is pale golden and thick and is coming away from the sides of the pan. Pour the topping over the shortbread base and leave to cool.

❄ When the caramel topping is firm, melt the chocolate in a heatproof bowl set over a saucepan of simmering water. Spread the melted chocolate over the topping, leave to set in a cool place, then cut the shortbread into squares to serve.

Chocolate & Apricot Squares

125 g/4½ oz butter, plus extra for greasing
175 g/6 oz white chocolate, chopped
4 eggs
125 g/4½ oz caster sugar

200 g/7 oz plain flour, sifted
1 tsp baking powder
pinch of salt
100 g/3½ oz dried apricots, chopped

❄ Lightly grease a 20-cm/8-inch square cake tin with a little butter and base-line with baking paper.

❄ Melt the butter and chocolate in a heatproof bowl set over a saucepan of simmering water. Stir frequently with a wooden spoon until the mixture is smooth and glossy. Leave the mixture to cool slightly.

❄ Beat the eggs and caster sugar into the butter and chocolate mixture until well combined.

❄ Fold in the flour, baking powder, salt and chopped dried apricots and mix together well so all the ingredients are combined.

❄ Pour the mixture into the prepared tin and bake in a preheated oven, 180°C/350°F/Gas Mark 4, for about 25–30 minutes.

❄ The centre of the cake may not be completely firm, but it will set as it cools. Leave in the tin to cool.

❄ When the cake is completely cold turn it out and slice into squares to serve.

Hazelnut Bites

❖ **MAKES 16** ❖

100 g/3¹/₂ oz butter, cut into small pieces, plus extra for greasing
150 g/5¹/₂ oz plain flour
pinch of salt
1 tsp baking powder
150 g/5¹/₂ oz soft brown sugar

1 egg, beaten
4 tbsp milk
100 g/3¹/₂ oz hazelnuts, halved
demerara sugar, for sprinkling (optional)

❖ Lightly grease a 23-cm/9-inch square cake tin with a little butter and base-line with baking paper.

❖ Sift the flour, salt and baking powder into a large mixing bowl.

❖ Rub in the butter with your fingers until the mixture resembles fine breadcrumbs. Stir in the brown sugar.

❖ Add the egg, milk and nuts to the mixture and stir well until thoroughly combined.

❖ Spoon the mixture into the prepared cake tin and level the surface. Sprinkle with the demerara sugar, if using.

❖ Bake in a preheated oven, 180°C/350°F/Gas Mark 4, for about 25 minutes, or until the mixture is firm to the touch when pressed with a finger.

❖ Leave to cool for 10 minutes, then loosen the edges with a round-bladed knife and turn out on to a wire rack. Cut into squares.

Flapjacks

❖ **MAKES 21** ❖

225 g/8 oz butter
225 g/8 oz light muscovado sugar

85 g/3 oz golden syrup
450 g/1 lb porridge oats

❖ Preheat the oven to 180°C/350°F/Gas Mark 4. Line a 23-cm/9-inch square cake tin with baking paper.

❖ Put the butter, sugar and syrup into a saucepan and heat over a low heat for 2–3 minutes until melted. Mix in the porridge oats and stir well.

❖ Pour the mixture into the prepared tin, press down well and bake in the centre of the preheated oven for 30–35 minutes until golden brown but still moist and slightly soft when pressed.

❖ Remove from the oven and leave to cool in the tin for 5 minutes. Cut into about 21 squares and leave to cool completely for about 30 minutes in the tin.

❖ Carefully remove the flapjacks from the tin and store in an airtight container in a cool place for up to 3–4 days.

Lemon Cream Butterflies

✷ MAKES 12 ✷

125 g/4^1/$_2$ oz soft margarine,
plus extra for greasing
125 g/4^1/$_2$ oz caster sugar
150 g/5^1/$_2$ oz self-raising flour
2 large eggs
2 tbsp cocoa powder
25 g/1 oz plain chocolate,
melted

LEMON BUTTER CREAM
100 g/3^1/$_2$ oz unsalted butter,
softened
225 g/8 oz icing sugar, sifted
grated rind of ^{1}/$_2$ lemon
1 tbsp lemon juice
icing sugar, to dust

✷ Place 12 paper cases in a muffin pan. Place all of the ingredients for the cakes, except the melted chocolate, in a large mixing bowl and beat with electric beaters until the mixture is just smooth. Beat in the chocolate.

✷ Spoon equal amounts of the cake mixture into each paper case, filling them three-quarters full. Bake in a preheated oven, 180°C/350°F/Gas Mark 4, for 15 minutes or until springy to the touch. Transfer the cakes to a wire rack and leave to cool.

✷ To make the lemon butter cream, place the butter in a mixing bowl and beat until fluffy, then gradually beat in the icing sugar. Beat in the lemon rind and gradually add the lemon juice, beating well.

✷ When cold, cut the top off each cake, using a serrated knife. Cut each top in half.

✷ Spread or pipe the butter cream icing over the cut surface of each cake and push the 2 cut pieces of cake top into the icing to form wings. Dust with the icing sugar.

White Chocolate Cakes

100 g/3 1/2 oz butter, softened, plus extra for greasing
100 g/3 1/2 oz caster sugar
2 eggs, lightly beaten
150 g/5 1/2 oz self-raising flour
2 tbsp milk
50 g/1 3/4 oz plain chocolate chips
25 g/1 oz cocoa powder

ICING
225 g/8 oz white chocolate
150 g/5 1/2 oz low-fat soft cheese

❈ Lightly grease an 18-cup muffin tin with a little butter.

❈ Beat together the butter and sugar until pale and fluffy. Gradually add the eggs, beating well after each addition. Add a little of the flour if the mixture begins to curdle. Add the milk, then fold in the chocolate chips.

❈ Sift together the remaining flour and cocoa powder and fold into the mixture with a metal spoon or spatula. Divide the mixture equally between the cups and level the tops.

❈ Bake in a preheated oven, 180°C/350°F/Gas Mark 4, for 20 minutes, or until well risen and springy to the touch. Leave to cool on a wire rack.

❈ To make the icing, melt the chocolate, then leave to cool slightly. Beat the cream cheese until slightly soft, then beat in the melted chocolate. Spread a little of the icing over each cake and chill for 1 hour before serving.

Banana Cinnamon Muffins

150 g/5 1/2 oz margarine, melted, plus extra for greasing
150 g/5 1/2 oz plain flour
1 tsp baking powder
pinch of salt
150 g/5 1/2 oz caster sugar
6 tbsp milk
2 eggs, lightly beaten
2 small bananas, mashed

ICING
50 g/1 3/4 oz cream cheese
2 tbsp margarine
1/4 tsp ground cinnamon
90 g/3 1/4 oz icing sugar

❈ Preheat the oven to 200°C/400°F/Gas Mark 6. Lightly grease a 12-cup muffin tin with a little margarine.

❈ Sift the flour, baking powder and salt together into a mixing bowl. Stir in the sugar.

❈ Whisk the milk, eggs and margarine together in a separate bowl until combined. Slowly stir into the flour mixture without beating. Fold in the mashed bananas.

❈ Spoon the mixture into the cups and bake in the preheated oven for 20 minutes until risen and golden. Turn out on to a wire rack and leave to cool.

❈ To make the icing, beat the cream cheese and margarine together in a bowl, then beat in the cinnamon and icing sugar until smooth and creamy. Chill the icing in the refrigerator for about 15 minutes to firm up, then top each muffin with a spoonful.

Chocolate Chip Muffins

❄ **MAKES 12** ❄

85 g/3 oz soft margarine, plus extra for greasing
280 g/10 oz caster sugar
2 large eggs
150 ml/5 fl oz plain yogurt
5 tbsp milk
400 g/14 oz plain flour
1 tsp bicarbonate of soda
50 g/1³/4 oz plain chocolate chips

❄ Preheat the oven to 200°C/400°F/Gas Mark 6. Lightly grease a 12-cup muffin tin with a little margarine.

❄ Place the margarine and sugar in a mixing bowl and beat with a wooden spoon until light and fluffy. Beat in the eggs, yogurt, and milk until combined.

❄ Sift the flour and baking soda into the batter. Stir until just blended.

❄ Stir in the chocolate chips, then divide the batter evenly between the cups and bake in the oven for 25 minutes, or until risen and golden. Remove the muffins from the oven and let cool in the pan for 5 minutes, then place them on a wire rack to cool completely.

Lime & Poppy Seed Muffins

❄ **MAKES 12** ❄

175 ml/6 fl oz sunflower or groundnut oil, plus extra for oiling
225 g/8 oz plain flour
1 tsp baking powder
¹/2 tsp salt
200 g/7 oz caster sugar
1 large egg
1 large egg white
475 ml/16 fl oz milk
1 tbsp lime juice
1 tbsp grated lime rind
2 tsp poppy seeds
2 tsp grated lime rind and 1–2 tsp poppy seeds, to decorate

❄ Preheat the oven to 190°C/375°F/Gas Mark 5. Oil a 12-cup muffin tin. Sift the flour, baking powder and salt into a mixing bowl. Then add the sugar and stir together.

❄ In a separate bowl, whisk the egg, egg white, oil and the milk together, then stir in the lime juice and lime rind. Add the egg mixture to the flour mixture, then add the poppy seeds and gently stir together. Do not overstir the batter – it is fine for it to be a little lumpy.

❄ Divide the muffin batter evenly between the 12 cups in the muffin tin (they should be about two-thirds full). Sprinkle over the grated lime rind and poppy seeds to decorate, then bake in the oven for 25 minutes or until risen and golden. Remove the muffins from the oven and serve warm, or place them on a wire rack and let cool.

Low-Fat Blueberry Muffins

❉ MAKES 12 ❉

vegetable oil,
for oiling
375 g/13 oz plain flour
1 tsp bicarbonate of soda
¼ tsp salt
1 tsp mixed spice
175 g/6 oz caster sugar
3 large egg whites
3 tbsp low-fat margarine
150 ml/5 fl oz low-fat natural or
blueberry-flavoured yogurt
1 tsp vanilla essence
140 g/5 oz fresh blueberries

❉ Preheat the oven to 190°C/375°F/Gas Mark 5. Oil a 12-cup muffin tin. Sift the flour, bicarbonate of soda, salt and half the mixed spice into a large mixing bowl. Add 6 tablespoons of the sugar and mix together.

❉ In a separate bowl, whisk the egg whites together. Add the margarine, yogurt and vanilla essence and mix together well, then stir in the fresh blueberries until thoroughly mixed. Add the fruit mixture to the flour mixture and then gently stir together until just combined. Do not overstir the batter – it is fine for it to be a little lumpy.

❉ Divide the muffin batter evenly between the 12 cups in the muffin tin (they should be about two-thirds full). Mix the remaining sugar with the remaining mixed spice, then sprinkle the mixture over the muffins. Transfer to the oven and bake for 25 minutes or until risen and golden. Remove the muffins from the oven and serve warm, or place them on a wire rack and let cool.

Raisin & Cherry Morsels

100 g/3^1/2 oz butter, cut into small pieces, plus extra for greasing
200 g/7 oz plain flour
2 tsp baking powder
75 g/2^3/4 oz demerara sugar

100 g/3^1/2 oz sultanas
25 g/1 oz glacé cherries, finely chopped
1 egg, beaten
2 tbsp milk

❄ Lightly grease a baking tray with a little butter.

❄ Sift the flour and baking powder into a mixing bowl. Rub in the butter with your fingers until the mixture resembles breadcrumbs.

❄ Stir in the sugar, sultanas and chopped glacé cherries.

❄ Add the beaten egg and the milk to the mixture and mix to form a soft dough.

❄ Spoon 8 mounds of the mixture on to the baking tray, spacing them well apart as they will spread while they are cooking.

❄ Bake in a preheated oven, 200°C/400°F/Gas Mark 6, for 15–20 minutes or until firm to the touch when pressed with a finger.

❄ Remove from the baking tray. Either serve piping hot from the oven or transfer to a wire rack and leave to cool before serving.

Butter Shortbread Fantails

125 g/4^1/2 oz butter, softened, plus extra for greasing
40 g/1^1/2 oz granulated sugar
25 g/1 oz icing sugar
225 g/8 oz plain flour

pinch of salt
2 tsp orange flower water
caster sugar, for sprinkling

❄ Lightly grease a 20-cm/8-inch shallow round cake tin with a little butter.

❄ In a large mixing bowl, cream together the butter, the granulated sugar and the icing sugar until light and fluffy.

❄ Sift the flour and salt into the creamed mixture. Add the orange flower water and bring everything together to form a soft dough.

❄ On a lightly floured surface, roll out the dough to a 20-cm/8-inch round and place in the tin. Prick the dough well and score into 8 triangles with a round-bladed knife.

❄ Bake in a preheated oven, 150°C/300°F/Gas Mark 2, for 30–35 minutes or until the biscuit is pale golden and crisp.

❄ Sprinkle with caster sugar, then cut along the marked lines to make the fantails.

❄ Leave the shortbread to cool before removing the pieces from the tin. Store in an airtight container.

Vanilla Hearts

❋ **MAKES 12** ❋

150 g/5$\frac{1}{2}$ oz butter, diced, plus extra for greasing

225 g/8 oz plain flour, plus extra for dusting

125 g/4$\frac{1}{2}$ oz caster sugar, plus extra for dusting

1 tsp vanilla essence

❋ Lightly grease a baking tray with a little butter.

❋ Sift the flour into a large mixing bowl and rub in the butter with your fingertips until the mixture resembles fine breadcrumbs.

❋ Stir in the caster sugar and vanilla essence and bring the mixture together with your hands to form a firm dough.

❋ Roll out the dough on a lightly floured work surface to a thickness of 2.5 cm/1 inch. Stamp out 12 hearts with a heart-shaped biscuit cutter measuring about 5 cm/2 inches across and 2.5 cm/1 inch deep.

❋ Arrange the hearts on the prepared baking tray. Bake in a preheated oven, 180°C/350°F/Gas Mark 4, for about 15–20 minutes until light golden.

❋ Transfer the vanilla hearts to a wire rack and leave to cool completely. Dust with a little caster sugar just before serving.

Almond Biscuits

❋ **MAKES 32** ❋

150 g/5$\frac{1}{2}$ oz unblanched almonds

225 g/8 oz butter, softened

6 tbsp icing sugar, plus extra for sifting

275 g/9$\frac{1}{2}$ oz plain flour

2 tsp vanilla essence

$\frac{1}{2}$ tsp almond essence

❋ Line 2 baking trays with baking paper. Using a cook's knife, finely chop the almonds, or process them in a small food processor, taking care not to let them turn into a paste. Set aside.

❋ Put the softened butter in a bowl and beat with an electric mixer until smooth. Sift in the icing sugar and continue beating until the mixture is creamed and smooth.

❋ Sift in the flour, holding the sieve high above the bowl, and gently beat it in until blended. Add the vanilla and almond essences and beat again to form a soft dough. Stir in the chopped almonds.

❋ Using a teaspoon, shape the dough into 32 round balls about the size of walnuts. Place on the prepared baking trays, spacing them well apart. Bake in a preheated oven, 180°C/350°F/Gas Mark 4, for 20–25 minutes until the biscuits are set and just starting to turn brown.

❋ Leave the biscuits to stand on the baking trays for 2 minutes to firm up. Sift a thick layer of icing sugar over them. Transfer to a wire rack and leave to cool completely.

❋ Lightly dust with more icing sugar just before serving. Store the biscuits in an airtight container.

Spiced Biscuits

175 g/6 oz unsalted butter, plus extra for greasing
175 g/6 oz dark muscovado sugar
225 g/8 oz plain flour
pinch of salt
1/2 tsp bicarbonate of soda
1 tsp ground cinnamon
1/2 tsp ground coriander
1/2 tsp ground nutmeg
1/4 tsp ground cloves
2 tbsp dark rum

❖ Lightly grease 2 baking trays with a little butter.

❖ Cream the butter and sugar together in a mixing bowl until light and fluffy.

❖ Sift the flour, salt, bicarbonate of soda, cinnamon, coriander, nutmeg and cloves into the butter and sugar mixture.

❖ Stir the dark rum into the creamed mixture until blended.

❖ Place 12 small mounds of the mixture on the baking trays using 2 teaspoons. Space the mounds well apart to allow room for expansion during cooking. Flatten each one slightly with the back of a spoon.

❖ Bake in a preheated oven, 180°C/350°F/Gas Mark 4, for 10–12 minutes until golden.

❖ Carefully transfer the biscuits to wire racks to cool completely and crispen before serving.

White Chocolate Biscuits

125 g/4½ oz butter, softened,
  plus extra for greasing
125 g/4½ oz soft brown sugar
1 egg, beaten
200 g/7 oz self-raising flour

pinch of salt
125 g/4½ oz white chocolate,
  roughly chopped
50 g/1¾ oz Brazil nuts,
  chopped

❊ Use a little butter to lightly grease 2 or 3 baking trays, enough to accommodate 24 biscuits.

❊ In a large mixing bowl, cream together the butter and sugar until light and fluffy.

❊ Gradually add the beaten egg to the creamed mixture, beating well after each addition.

❊ Sift the flour and salt into the creamed mixture and blend well.

❊ Stir in the white chocolate and the chopped nuts.

❊ Place heaped teaspoons of the white chocolate mixture on the prepared baking trays. Do not put more than 6 teaspoons of the mixture on to each baking tray as the biscuits will spread considerably during cooking.

❊ Bake in a preheated oven, 190°C/375°F/Gas Mark 5, for 10–12 minutes or until just golden brown.

❊ Transfer the biscuits to wire racks and leave until completely cold before serving.

Iced Orange Biscuits

75 g/2¾ oz butter, softened
75 g/2¾ oz caster sugar
1 egg
1 tbsp milk
225 g/8 oz plain flour
25 g/1 oz cocoa powder

ICING
175 g/6 oz icing sugar, sifted
3 tbsp orange juice
a little plain chocolate, melted

❊ Carefully line 2 baking trays with sheets of baking paper.

❊ Beat together the butter and sugar until light and fluffy. Beat in the egg and milk until well combined. Sift together the flour and cocoa powder and gradually mix together to form a soft dough. Use your fingers to incorporate the last of the flour and bring the dough together.

❊ Roll out the dough on a lightly floured surface until 5 mm/¼ inch thick. Using a 5-cm/2-inch fluted round cutter, cut out as many biscuits as you can. Re-roll the dough trimmings and cut out more biscuits.

❊ Place the biscuits on the prepared baking trays and bake in a preheated oven, 180°C/350°F/Gas Mark 4, for 10–12 minutes or until golden.

❊ Leave the biscuits to cool on the baking trays for a few minutes, then transfer to a wire rack to cool completely.

❊ To make the icing, place the icing sugar in a bowl and stir in enough orange juice to form a thin icing that will coat the back of a spoon. Spread the icing over the biscuits and leave to set. Drizzle with the melted chocolate. Allow the chocolate to set before serving.

Chocolate Wheat Biscuits

❄ **MAKES 20** ❄

75 g/2¾ oz butter, plus extra for greasing
100 g/3½ oz demerara sugar
1 egg
25 g/1 oz wheatgerm
125 g/4½ oz wholemeal self-raising flour
60 g/2 oz self raising flour, sifted
125 g/4½ oz milk chocolate

❄ Lightly grease a baking tray with a little butter.

❄ Beat the butter and sugar until fluffy. Add the egg and beat well. Stir in the wheatgerm and flours. Bring the mixture together with your hands.

❄ Roll rounded teaspoons of the mixture into balls and place these on the prepared baking tray, allowing room for the biscuits to spread during cooking.

❄ Flatten the biscuits slightly with the prongs of a fork. Bake in a preheated oven, 180°C/350°F/Gas Mark 4, for 15–20 minutes, or until golden. Leave to cool on the tray for a few minutes before transferring to a wire rack to cool completely.

❄ Melt the chocolate, then dip each biscuit in the chocolate to cover the bases and come a little way up the sides. Leave the excess to drip back into the bowl.

❄ Place the biscuits on a sheet of baking paper and leave to set in a cool place before serving.

Caraway Roundels

❄ **MAKES 36** ❄

100 g/3½ oz butter, cut into small pieces, plus extra for greasing
225 g/8 oz plain flour
pinch of salt
225 g/8 oz caster sugar
1 egg, beaten
2 tbsp caraway seeds
demerara sugar, for sprinkling (optional)

❄ Lightly grease several baking trays with a little butter.

❄ Sift the flour and salt into a mixing bowl. Rub in the butter with your fingers until the mixture resembles fine breadcrumbs. Stir in the caster sugar.

❄ Reserve 1 tablespoon of the beaten egg for brushing the biscuits. Add the rest of the egg to the mixture along with the caraway seeds and bring together to form a soft dough.

❄ On a lightly floured surface, roll out the biscuit dough thinly and then cut out about 36 rounds with a 6-cm/2½-inch biscuit cutter.

❄ Transfer the rounds to the prepared baking trays, brush with the reserved egg and sprinkle with demerara sugar.

❄ Bake in a preheated oven, 160°C/325°F/Gas Mark 3, for 10–15 minutes, or until lightly golden and crisp.

❄ Leave the biscuits to cool on a wire rack and store in an airtight container.

Mixed Fruit Crescents

100 g/3 1/2 oz butter, softened, plus extra for greasing
75 g/2 3/4 oz caster sugar
1 egg, separated
200 g/7 oz plain flour
grated rind of 1 orange
grated rind of 1 lemon
grated rind of 1 lime
2–3 tbsp orange juice
caster sugar, for sprinkling (optional)

❊ Lightly grease 2 baking trays with a little butter.

❊ In a mixing bowl, cream together the butter and sugar until light and fluffy, then gradually beat in the egg yolk.

❊ Sift the flour into the creamed mixture and mix until evenly combined. Add the orange, lemon and lime rinds to the mixture with enough of the orange juice to make a soft dough.

❊ Roll out the dough on a lightly floured surface. Stamp out rounds using a 7.5-cm/3-inch biscuit cutter. Make crescent shapes by cutting away a quarter of each round. Re-roll the trimmings to make about 25 crescents.

❊ Place the crescents on the prepared baking trays. Prick the surface of each crescent with a fork.

❊ Lightly whisk the egg white in a small bowl and brush it over the biscuits. Dust with extra caster sugar, if using.

❊ Bake in a preheated oven, 200°C/400°F/Gas Mark 6, for 12–15 minutes. Leave the biscuits to cool on a wire rack before serving.

Sugared Lemon Biscuits

❋ **MAKES 50** ❋

100 g/3¹/2 oz butter, softened, plus extra for greasing	4 tbsp lemon juice
125 g/4¹/2 oz caster sugar	350 g/12 oz plain flour
grated rind of 1 lemon	1 tsp baking powder
1 egg, beaten	1 tbsp milk
	icing sugar, for dredging

❋ Lightly grease several baking trays with a little butter.

❋ In a mixing bowl, cream together the butter, caster sugar and lemon rind until pale and fluffy.

❋ Add the beaten egg and lemon juice a little at a time, beating well after each addition.

❋ Sift the flour and the baking powder into the creamed mixture and blend together. Add the milk, mixing to form a dough.

❋ Turn out the dough on to a lightly floured work surface and divide into about 50 equal-sized pieces.

❋ Roll each piece into a sausage shape with your hands and twist in the middle to make an 'S' shape.

❋ Place on the prepared baking trays and bake in a preheated oven, 160°C/325°F/Gas Mark 3, for 15–20 minutes. Leave to cool completely on a wire rack. Dredge with icing sugar to serve.

Viennese Chocolate Fingers

❋ **MAKES 18** ❋

125 g/4¹/2 oz unsalted butter, plus extra for greasing	175 g/6 oz self-raising flour, sifted
6 tbsp icing sugar	3 tbsp cornflour
	200 g/7 oz plain chocolate

❋ Lightly grease 2 baking trays with alittle butter. Beat the butter and sugar in a mixing bowl until light and fluffy. Gradually beat in the flour and cornflour.

❋ Melt 75 g/2³/4 oz of the chocolate and beat into the biscuit dough.

❋ Place the mixture in a piping bag fitted with a large star nozzle and pipe fingers 5 cm/2 inches long on to the baking trays, spaced apart to allow the biscuits to spread during cooking.

❋ Bake in a preheated oven, 190°C/375°F/Gas Mark 5, for 12–15 minutes.

❋ Leave the biscuits to cool slightly on the baking trays, then transfer with a spatula to a wire rack and leave to cool completely.

❋ Melt the remaining chocolate and dip one end of each biscuit in the chocolate, allowing the excess to drip back into the bowl.

❋ Place the chocolate-dipped biscuits on a sheet of baking paper and leave to set before serving.

Chequerboard Biscuits

175 g/6 oz butter, softened,
plus extra for greasing
6 tbsp icing sugar
1 teaspoon vanilla essence or
grated rind of 1/2 orange

250 g/9 oz plain flour
25 g/1 oz plain chocolate,
melted
a little beaten egg white

❋ Lightly grease a baking tray with a little butter. Beat the butter and icing sugar in a mixing bowl until they are light and fluffy. Beat in the vanilla essence or the grated orange rind.

❋ Gradually beat in the flour to form a soft dough. Use your fingers to incorporate the last of the flour and to bring the dough together.

❋ Divide the dough in half and beat the melted chocolate into one half. Keep each half of the dough separate, cover and leave to chill for about 30 minutes.

❋ Roll out each piece of dough to a rectangle 7.5 x 20 cm/ 3 x 8 inches long and 3 cm/1 1/2 inches thick. Brush one piece of dough with a little egg white and place the other on top.

❋ Cut the block of dough in half lengthways and turn over one half. Brush the side of one strip with egg white and butt the other up to it, so that it resembles a chequerboard.

❋ Cut the block into thin slices and place each slice flat on the baking tray, allowing enough room between them for them to spread out a little during cooking.

❋ Bake in a preheated oven, 180°C/350°F/Gas Mark 4, for about 10 minutes, until just firm. Leave to cool on the baking trays for a few minutes, before carefully transferring to a wire rack with a spatula. Leave to cool completely.

Chocolate Pretzels

100 g/3 1/2 oz unsalted butter,
plus extra for greasing
100 g/3 1/2 oz caster sugar
1 egg
225 g/8 oz plain flour
2 tbsp cocoa powder

TO DECORATE
15 g/1/2 oz butter
100 g/3 1/2 oz plain chocolate
icing sugar, for dusting

❋ Lightly grease a baking tray with a little butter. Beat together the butter and sugar in a large mixing bowl until light and fluffy. Beat in the egg, ensuring all the ingredients are well combined.

❋ Sift the flour and cocoa powder together and gradually beat into the egg mixture to form a soft dough. Use your fingers to incorporate the last of the flour and bring the dough together. Chill for 15 minutes.

❋ Break pieces from the dough and roll into thin sausage shapes about 10 cm/4 inches long and 5 mm/1/4 inch thick. Carefully twist into pretzel shapes by making a circle, then twist the ends through each other to form a letter 'B'.

❋ Place the chocolate pretzels on the prepared baking tray, spaced slightly apart to allow for expansion during cooking.

❋ Bake in a preheated oven, 190°C/375°F/Gas Mark 5, for 8–12 minutes. Leave the pretzels to cool slightly on the baking tray, then transfer to a wire rack to cool completely.

❋ Melt the butter and chocolate in a bowl set over a saucepan of gently simmering water, stirring.

❋ Dip half of each pretzel into the chocolate and allow the excess chocolate to drip back into the bowl. Place the pretzels on a sheet of baking paper and leave to set.

❋ When set, dust the uncoated side of each pretzel with icing sugar before serving.

Chocolate Biscotti

butter, for greasing
1 egg
100 g/3¹/₂ oz caster sugar
1 tsp vanilla essence
125 g/4¹/₂ oz plain flour
¹/₂ tsp baking powder
1 tsp ground cinnamon
50 g/1³/₄ oz plain chocolate,
roughly chopped
50 g/1³/₄ oz flaked almonds,
toasted
50 g/1³/₄ oz pine kernels

❊   Lightly grease a large baking tray with a little butter. Set aside while you prepare the biscuit mixture.

❊   Whisk the egg, sugar and vanilla essence in a mixing bowl with an electric mixer until it is thick and pale – ribbons of mixture should trail from the whisk as you lift it.

❊   Sift the flour, baking powder and cinnamon into a separate bowl, then sift into the egg mixture and fold in gently. Stir in the chocolate, almonds and pine kernels.

❊   Turn out on to a lightly floured work surface and shape into a flat log, 23 cm/9 inches long and 2 cm/³/₄ inch wide. Transfer to the baking tray.

❊   Bake in a preheated oven, 180°C/350°F/Gas Mark 4, for 20–25 minutes or until golden. Remove from the oven and leave to cool for 5 minutes or until firm.

❊   Transfer the log to a chopping board. Using a serrated bread knife, cut the log on the diagonal into slices about 1 cm/¹/₂ inch thick and arrange them on the baking tray. Cook for 10–15 minutes, turning halfway through the cooking time.

❊   Cool for 5 minutes. Transfer to a wire rack to cool completely.

Dutch Macaroons

rice paper
2 egg whites
225 g/8 oz caster sugar
175 g/6 oz ground almonds
225 g/8 oz plain chocolate

❈ Cover 2 baking trays with rice paper. Whisk the egg whites in a large mixing bowl until stiff, then fold in the sugar and ground almonds.

❈ Place the mixture in a large piping bag fitted with a 1-cm/ 1/2-inch plain nozzle and pipe fingers about 7.5 cm/3 inches long, allowing space between them for the mixture to expand during cooking.

❈ Bake the macaroons in a preheated oven, 180°C/350°F/ Gas Mark 4, for 15–20 minutes until golden. Transfer to a wire rack and leave to cool. Remove the excess rice paper from around the edges.

❈ Melt the chocolate and dip the base of each biscuit into the chocolate. Place the macaroons on a sheet of baking paper and leave to set.

❈ Drizzle any remaining melted chocolate over the top of the biscuits (you may have to reheat the chocolate in order to do this). Leave to set before serving.

Florentines

50 g/1 3/4 oz butter
50 g/1 3/4 oz caster sugar
25 g/1 oz plain flour, sifted
50 g/1 3/4 oz almonds, chopped
50 g/1 3/4 oz chopped mixed peel
25 g/1 oz raisins, chopped
25 g/1 oz glacé cherries, chopped
finely grated rind of 1/2 lemon
125 g/4 1/2 oz plain chocolate, melted

❈ Line 2 large baking trays with baking paper.

❈ Heat the butter and sugar in a small saucepan until the butter has just melted and the sugar dissolved. Remove the pan from the heat.

❈ Stir in the flour and mix well. Stir in the chopped almonds, mixed peel, raisins, cherries and lemon rind. Place teaspoonfuls of the mixture well apart on the baking trays.

❈ Bake in a preheated oven, 180°C/350°F/Gas Mark 4, for 10 minutes or until lightly golden.

❈ As soon as the florentines are removed from the oven, press the edges into neat shapes while still on the baking trays, using a biscuit cutter. Leave to cool on the baking trays until firm, then transfer to a wire rack to cool completely.

❈ Spread the melted chocolate over the smooth side of each florentine. As the chocolate begins to set, mark wavy lines in it with a fork. Leave the florentines until set, chocolate side up.

Chocolate & Coconut Roulade

❁ **SERVES 8** ❁

butter, for greasing
3 eggs
75 g/2¾ oz caster sugar
5½ tbsp self-raising flour
1 tbsp block creamed coconut,
softened with 1 tbsp boiling
water
25 g/1 oz desiccated coconut
6 tbsp raspberry jam
a few fresh raspberries,
to garnish

CHOCOLATE COATING
200 g/7 oz plain chocolate
70 g/2½ oz butter
2 tbsp golden syrup

RASPBERRY COULIS
225 g/8 oz fresh or frozen
raspberries, thawed, if frozen
2 tbsp water
4 tbsp icing sugar

❊ Grease a 23 x 30-cm/9 x 12-inch Swiss roll tin with a little butter and line with baking paper. Whisk the eggs and caster sugar together in a large mixing bowl until the whisk leaves a trail that lasts a few seconds when lifted.

❊ Sift the flour and fold in with a metal spoon or a spatula. Fold in the creamed coconut and desiccated coconut. Pour the mixture into the prepared tin and bake in a preheated oven, 200°C/400°F/Gas Mark 6, for 10–12 minutes or until springy to the touch.

❊ Sprinkle a sheet of baking paper with a little caster sugar and place on top of a damp tea towel. Turn out the cake on to the paper and carefully peel away the lining paper. Spread the jam over the sponge and roll up from the short end, using the tea towel to help you. Place seam side down on a wire rack and leave to cool completely.

❊ Meanwhile, make the coating. Melt the chocolate and butter together, stirring. Stir in the golden syrup. Leave to cool for 5 minutes, then spread over the cooled roulade and leave to set.

❊ To make the coulis, purée the fruit in a food processor with the water and sugar and strain to remove the seeds. Cut the roulade into slices and serve with the raspberry coulis and a few raspberries.

Pecan Nut & Raisin Roulade

❁ **SERVES 8** ❁

butter, for greasing
150 g/5½ oz plain chocolate,
broken into pieces
3 tbsp water
175 g/6 oz caster sugar
5 eggs, separated

25 g/1 oz raisins, chopped
25 g/1 oz pecan nuts, chopped
pinch of salt
300 ml/10 fl oz double cream,
whipped lightly
icing sugar, for dusting

❊ Grease a 30 x 20-cm/12 x 8-inch swiss roll tin with a little butter, line with baking paper and grease the paper.

❊ Melt the chocolate with the water in a small saucepan over a low heat until the chocolate has just melted. Leave to cool.

❊ In a bowl, whisk the sugar and egg yolks for 2–3 minutes with a hand-held electric whisk until thick and pale. Fold in the cooled chocolate, raisins and pecan nuts.

❊ In a separate bowl, whisk the egg whites with the salt. Fold one quarter of the egg whites into the chocolate mixture, then fold in the rest of the whites, working lightly and quickly.

❊ Transfer the mixture to the prepared tin and bake in a preheated oven, 180°C/350°F/Gas Mark 4, for 25 minutes or until risen and just firm to the touch. Leave to cool before covering with a sheet of non-stick baking paper and a damp tea towel. Leave until completely cold.

❊ Turn out the roulade on to another piece of baking paper dusted with icing sugar and then remove the lining paper.

❊ Spread the cream over the roulade. Starting from a short end, roll the sponge away from you, using the paper to guide you. Trim the ends of the roulade to make a neat finish and transfer to a serving plate. Leave to chill in the refrigerator until ready to serve. Dust with the icing sugar before serving.

Rich Chocolate Torte

175 g/6 oz butter, softened, plus extra for greasing
225 g/8 oz plain chocolate, broken into pieces
3 tbsp water
150 g/5^1/$_2$ oz soft brown sugar
25 g/1 oz ground almonds
3 tbsp self-raising flour
5 eggs, separated
100 g/3^1/$_2$ oz blanched almonds, finely chopped
icing sugar, for dusting
double cream, to serve (optional)

❄ Grease a 23-cm/9-inch loose-based cake tin with a little butter and base-line with baking paper.

❄ In a saucepan set over a very low heat, melt the chocolate with the water, stirring until smooth. Add the sugar and stir until dissolved, taking the pan off the heat to prevent it overheating.

❄ Add the butter in small amounts until it has melted into the chocolate. Remove from the heat and lightly stir in the ground almonds and flour. Add the egg yolks one at a time, beating well after each addition.

❄ In a large mixing bowl, whisk the egg whites until they stand in soft peaks, then fold them into the chocolate mixture with a metal spoon. Stir in the chopped almonds. Pour the mixture into the tin and level the surface.

❄ Bake in a preheated oven, 180°C/350°F/Gas Mark 4, for 40–45 minutes or until well risen and firm (the cake will crack on the surface during cooking).

❄ Leave the cake to cool in the tin for 30–40 minutes, then turn it out on to a wire rack to cool completely. Dust with icing sugar and serve in slices with the cream, if using.

Almond & Hazelnut Gâteau

butter, for greasing
4 eggs
100 g/3^1/$_2$ oz caster sugar
50 g/1^3/$_4$ oz ground almonds
50 g/1^3/$_4$ oz ground hazelnuts
5^1/$_2$ tbsp plain flour
50 g/1^3/$_4$ oz flaked almonds

FILLING
100 g/3^1/$_2$ oz plain chocolate
15 g/^{1}/$_2$ oz butter
300 ml/10 fl oz double cream
icing sugar, for dusting

❊ Grease two 18-cm/7-inch round sandwich tins with a little butter and base-line with baking paper.

❊ Whisk the eggs and caster sugar together in a large mixing bowl with an electric mixer for 10 minutes or until the mixture is light and foamy and the whisk leaves a trail that lasts a few seconds when lifted.

❊ Fold in the ground almonds and hazelnuts, sift the flour and fold in with a metal spoon or spatula. Pour into the prepared tins.

❊ Scatter the flaked almonds over the top of one of the cakes. Bake both of the cakes in a preheated oven, 190°C/375°F/Gas Mark 5, for 15–20 minutes or until springy to the touch.

❊ Leave the cakes to cool slightly in the tins. Remove from the tins and transfer to a wire rack to cool completely.

❊ Meanwhile, make the filling. Melt the chocolate, remove from the heat and stir in the butter. Leave to cool slightly. Whip the cream until just holding its shape, then fold in the melted chocolate until mixed.

❊ Place the cake without the extra almonds on a serving plate and spread the filling over it. Leave to set slightly, then place the almond-topped cake on top of the filling and leave to chill for about 1 hour. Dust with icing sugar and serve.

Chocolate Butter Cake

25 g/1 oz butter, melted, plus extra for greasing
4 eggs
125 g/4^1/$_2$ oz caster sugar
125 g/4^1/$_2$ oz plain flour
1 tbsp cocoa powder
75 g/2^3/$_4$ oz plain chocolate, melted
150 g/5^1/$_2$ oz finely chopped walnuts

ICING
75 g/2^3/$_4$ oz plain chocolate
125 g/4^1/$_2$ oz butter
200 g/7 oz icing sugar
2 tbsp milk
walnut halves, to decorate

❊ Grease an 18-cm/7-inch deep round cake tin with a little butter and base-line with baking paper. Place the eggs and caster sugar in a mixing bowl and whisk with electric beaters for 10 minutes, or until the mixture is light and foamy and the whisk leaves a trail that lasts a few seconds when lifted.

❊ Sift together the flour and cocoa powder and fold in with a metal spoon or spatula. Fold in the melted butter and chocolate and the chopped walnuts. Pour into the prepared tin and bake in a preheated oven, 160°C/325°F/Gas Mark 3, and bake for 30–35 minutes or until springy to the touch.

❊ Leave to cool in the tin for 5 minutes, then transfer to a wire rack to cool completely. Cut the cold cake into 2 layers.

❊ To make the icing, melt the chocolate and leave to cool slightly. Beat together the butter, icing sugar and milk in a bowl until the mixture is pale and fluffy. Whisk in the melted chocolate.

❊ Sandwich the 2 cake layers with some of the icing and place on a serving plate. Spread the remaining icing over the top of the cake with a palette knife, swirling it slightly as you do so. Decorate the cake with the walnut halves and serve.

Chocolate Ginger Cake

BASE	2 eggs, separated
250 g/9 oz gingernut biscuits	3 tbsp brandy
75 g/2¾ oz plain chocolate	300 ml/10 fl oz double cream
100 g/3½ oz butter	50 g/1¾ oz caster sugar
FILLING	**TO DECORATE**
225 g/8 oz plain chocolate	100 ml/3½ fl oz double cream
250 g/9 oz mascarpone cheese	chocolate coffee beans

❄ Crush the biscuits in a bag with a rolling pin or in a food processor. Melt the chocolate and butter together and pour over the biscuits. Mix well, then use to line the base and sides of a 23-cm/9-inch loose-based fluted flan tin or springform tin. Leave to chill whilst preparing the filling.

❄ To make the filling, melt the chocolate in a pan, remove from the heat and beat in the mascarpone cheese, egg yolks and brandy.

❄ Lightly whip the cream until just holding its shape and fold in the chocolate mixture.

❄ Whisk the egg whites in a grease-free bowl until standing in soft peaks. Add the caster sugar a little at a time and whisk until thick and glossy. Fold into the chocolate mixture, in 2 batches, until just mixed.

❄ Spoon the mixture into the prepared base and chill for at least 2 hours. Carefully transfer to a serving plate. To decorate, whip the cream and pipe on to the cheesecake and add the chocolate coffee beans.

Citrus Mousse Cake

175 g/6 oz butter, plus extra for greasing	**ORANGE MOUSSE**
175 g/6 oz caster sugar	2 eggs, separated
4 eggs, lightly beaten	50 g/1¾ oz caster sugar
200 g/7 oz self-raising flour	200 ml/7 fl oz freshly squeezed orange juice
1 tbsp cocoa powder	2 tsp gelatine
50 g/1¾ oz plain orange-flavoured chocolate, melted	3 tbsp water
peeled orange slices, to decorate	300 ml/10 fl oz double cream

❄ Grease a 20-cm/8-inch springform cake tin with a little butter and base-line with baking paper. Beat the butter and sugar in a bowl until light and fluffy. Gradually add the eggs, beating well after each addition. Sift together the flour and cocoa and fold into the cake mixture. Fold in the melted chocolate.

❄ Pour into the prepared tin and level the top. Bake in a preheated oven, 180°C/350°F/Gas Mark 4, for 40 minutes or until springy to the touch. Leave to cool for 5 minutes in the tin, then turn out and leave to cool on a wire rack. Cut the cold cake into 2 layers.

❄ To make the orange mousse, beat the egg yolks and sugar until light, then whisk in the orange juice. Sprinkle the gelatine over the water in a small bowl and allow to go spongy, then place over a pan of hot water and stir until dissolved. Stir into the mousse.

❄ Whip the cream until holding its shape, reserve a little for decoration and fold the rest into the mousse. Whisk the egg whites until standing in soft peaks, then fold in. Leave in a cool place until starting to set, stirring occasionally.

❄ Place half of the cake in the tin. Pour in the mousse and press the second cake layer on top. Chill until set. Transfer to a dish, pipe cream rosettes on the top and arrange the orange slices in the centre.

Sachertorte

150 g/5½ oz unsalted butter,
plus extra for greasing
175 g/6 oz plain chocolate
150 g/5½ oz caster sugar
6 eggs, separated
150 g/5½ oz plain flour

ICING AND FILLING
175 g/6 oz plain chocolate
5 tbsp strong black coffee
175 g/6 oz icing sugar
6 tbsp good-quality apricot jam
50 g/1¾ oz plain chocolate,
melted, to decorate

❄ Grease a 23-cm/9-inch springform cake tin with a little butter and base-line with baking paper. Melt the chocolate. Beat together the butter and 75 g/2¾ oz of the sugar until pale and fluffy. Add the egg yolks and beat together well. Add the chocolate in a thin stream, beating well. Sift the flour and fold it into the cake mixture. Whisk the egg whites until they stand in soft peaks. Add the remaining sugar and whisk for 2 minutes by hand, or 45–60 seconds if using an electric mixer, until glossy. Fold half into the chocolate mixture, then fold in the remainder.

❄ Spoon into the prepared tin and smooth the top. Bake in a preheated oven, 150°C/300°F/Gas Mark 2, for 1–1¼ hours, until a skewer inserted into the centre comes out clean. Cool in the tin for 5 minutes, then transfer to a wire rack to cool.

❄ To make the icing, melt the chocolate and beat in the coffee until smooth. Sift the icing sugar into a bowl, then whisk in the melted chocolate mixture to give a thick icing. Halve the cake. Warm the jam, spread over one half of the cake and place the other half on top. Invert the cake on to a wire rack. Spoon the icing over the cake and spread, as smoothly and evenly as possible, to coat the top and sides. Leave to set for 5 minutes, allowing any excess icing to drip through the rack. Transfer to a serving plate and leave to set for 2 hours.

❄ To decorate, spoon the melted chocolate into a small piping bag and carefully pipe the word 'Sacher' or 'Sachertorte' across the top of the cake. Leave the chocolate topping to harden and set completely before serving the cake.

White Chocolate Cake

butter, for greasing
2 eggs
50 g/1¾ oz caster sugar
50 g/1¾ oz plain flour
50 g/1¾ oz white chocolate, melted

TRUFFLE TOPPING
300 ml/10 fl oz double cream
350 g/12 oz white chocolate, broken into pieces
250 g/9 oz Quark or fromage frais

TO DECORATE
plain chocolate curls
cocoa powder, to dust

❊ Grease a 20-cm/8-inch round springform tin with a little butter and base-line with baking paper. Whisk the eggs and caster sugar in a mixing bowl for 10 minutes, or until the mixture is very light and foamy and the whisk leaves a trail that lasts a few seconds when lifted. Sift the flour and fold in with a metal spoon. Fold in the melted white chocolate. Pour into the tin and bake in a preheated oven, 180°C/350°F/Gas Mark 4, for 25 minutes or until springy to the touch. Leave to cool slightly, then transfer to a wire rack until completely cold. Return the cold cake to the tin.

❊ To make the topping, place the cream in a saucepan and bring to the boil, stirring to prevent it sticking to the bottom of the pan. Cool slightly, then add the white chocolate pieces and stir until melted and combined. Remove from the heat and leave until almost cool, stirring, then stir in the Quark. Pour the mixture on top of the cake and chill for 2 hours. Remove the cake from the tin and transfer to a serving plate.

❊ To make the chocolate curls, pour melted chocolate on to a marble or acrylic board and spread it thinly with a palette knife. Leave to set at room temperature. Using a scraper, push through the chocolate at a 25° angle until a large curl forms. Remove each curl as you make it and leave to chill until set. Decorate the cake with chocolate curls and sprinkle with a little cocoa powder.

Chocolate Almond Cake

50 g/1¾ oz butter, melted, plus extra for greasing
7 eggs
200 g/7 oz caster sugar
150 g/5½ oz plain flour
50 g/1¾ oz cocoa powder

FILLING
200 g/7 oz plain chocolate
125 g/4½ oz butter
50 g/1¾ oz icing sugar

TO DECORATE
75 g/2¾ oz toasted flaked almonds, crushed lightly
small chocolate curls or grated chocolate

❊ Grease a deep 23-cm/9-inch square cake tin with a little butter and base-line with baking paper.

❊ Whisk the eggs and caster sugar in a mixing bowl with an electric whisk for about 10 minutes or until the mixture is very light and foamy and the whisk leaves a trail that lasts a few seconds when lifted.

❊ Sift together the flour and cocoa and fold half into the mixture. Drizzle over the melted butter and fold in the rest of the flour and cocoa. Pour into the prepared tin and bake in a preheated oven, 180°C/350°F/Gas Mark 4, for 30–35 minutes or until springy to the touch. Leave to cool slightly, then remove from the tin and cool completely on a wire rack. Wash and dry the tin and return the cake to it.

❊ To make the filling, melt the chocolate and butter together, then remove from the heat. Stir in the icing sugar, leave to cool, then beat until thick enough to spread.

❊ Cut the cake in half to form 2 rectangles and cut each half into 3 layers. Sandwich the layers together with three-quarters of the chocolate filling. Spread the remainder over the cake and mark a wavy pattern on the top. Press the almonds on to the sides. Decorate with chocolate curls or grated chocolate.

Chocolate Rum Cake

75 g/2³/4 oz butter, plus extra
for greasing
75 g/2³/4 oz caster sugar
2 eggs, lightly beaten
75 g/2³/4 oz self-raising flour
¹/2 tsp baking powder
25 g/1 oz cocoa powder
50 g/1³/4 oz ground almonds
Cape gooseberries and
50 g/1³/4 oz plain chocolate,
melted, to decorate

TRUFFLE TOPPING
350 g/12 oz plain chocolate
100 g/3¹/2 oz butter
300 ml/10 fl oz double cream
75 g/2³/4 oz plain cake crumbs
3 tbsp dark rum

❋ Lightly grease a 20-cm/8-inch round springform tin with a little butter and base-line with baking paper. Beat together the butter and sugar until light and fluffy. Gradually add the eggs, beating well after each addition.

❋ Sift together the flour, baking powder and cocoa powder and fold into the mixture along with the ground almonds. Pour into the prepared tin and bake in a preheated oven, 180°C/350°F/Gas Mark 4, for 20–25 minutes or until springy to the touch. Leave to cool slightly in the tin, then transfer to a wire rack to cool completely. Wash and dry the tin and return the cooled cake to the tin.

❋ To make the topping, heat the chocolate, butter and cream in a heavy-based saucepan over a low heat and stir until smooth. Cool, then chill for 30 minutes. Beat well with a wooden spoon and chill for a further 30 minutes. Beat the mixture again, then add the cake crumbs and rum, beating until well combined. Spoon over the sponge base and chill for 3 hours.

❋ Meanwhile, dip the gooseberries in the melted chocolate until partially covered. Leave to set on baking paper. Transfer the cake to a serving plate and decorate with the gooseberries.

Creamy Coffee Cake

butter, for greasing
200 g/7 oz self-raising flour
¹/4 tsp baking powder
4 tbsp cocoa powder
100 g/3¹/2 oz caster sugar
2 eggs
2 tbsp golden syrup
150 ml/5 fl oz sunflower oil
150 ml/5 fl oz milk

FILLING
1 tsp instant coffee
1 tbsp boiling water
300 ml/10 fl oz double cream
25 g/1 oz icing sugar

TO DECORATE
50 g/1³/4 oz grated chocolate
chocolate caraque
icing sugar, to dust

❋ Lightly grease three 18-cm/7-inch cake tins with a little butter.

❋ Sift the flour, baking powder and cocoa powder into a large mixing bowl. Stir in the sugar. Make a well in the centre and stir in the eggs, syrup, oil and milk. Beat with a wooden spoon, gradually mixing in the dry ingredients to make a smooth batter. Divide the mixture between the prepared tins.

❋ Bake in a preheated oven, 180°C/350°F/Gas Mark 4, for 35–45 minutes or until springy to the touch. Leave in the tins for about 5 minutes, then turn out on to a wire rack to cool completely.

❋ Dissolve the instant coffee in the boiling water and place in a bowl with the cream and icing sugar. Whip until the cream is just holding its shape. Use half of the cream to sandwich the cakes together. Spread the remaining cream over the top and sides of the cake. Lightly press the grated chocolate into the cream around the edge of the cake.

❋ Transfer to a serving plate. Lay the caraque over the top of the cake. Cut a few thin strips of baking paper and place them on top of the caraque. Dust lightly with icing sugar, then carefully remove the paper. Serve.

Spiced Apple Ring

175 g/6 oz butter, softened,
plus extra for greasing
175 g/6 oz caster sugar
3 eggs, beaten
175 g/6 oz self-raising flour
1 tsp ground cinnamon
1 tsp ground mixed spice
2 eating apples, cored and
grated
2 tbsp apple juice or milk
25 g/1 oz flaked almonds

❖ Lightly grease a 25-cm/10-inch ovenproof ring mould with a little butter.

❖ In a mixing bowl, cream together the butter and sugar until light and fluffy. Gradually add the beaten eggs, beating well after each addition.

❖ Sift together the flour and spices, then carefully fold them into the creamed mixture.

❖ Stir in the grated apples and the apple juice or milk and mix to a soft dropping consistency.

❖ Sprinkle the flaked almonds around the base of the mould and spoon the cake mixture on top. Level the surface with the back of the spoon.

❖ Bake the cake in a preheated oven, 180°C/350°F/Gas Mark 4, for about 30 minutes until well risen and a fine skewer inserted into the centre comes out clean.

❖ Leave the cake to cool in the tin before turning out and transferring to a wire rack to cool completely. Serve the spiced apple ring cut into slices.

Sweet Pear Sponge Cake

❖ **SERVES 6** ❖

175 g/6 oz butter, softened, plus extra for greasing
175 g/6 oz demerara sugar
3 eggs, beaten
150 g/5$\frac{1}{2}$ oz self-raising flour
15 g/$\frac{1}{2}$ oz cocoa powder
2 tbsp milk
2 small pears, peeled, cored and sliced

❖ Grease a 20-cm/8-inch loose-based cake tin with a little butter and base-line with baking paper.

❖ In a bowl, cream together the butter and sugar until pale and fluffy.

❖ Gradually add the beaten eggs to the creamed mixture, beating well after each addition.

❖ Sift the flour and cocoa powder into the creamed mixture and fold in gently until all of the ingredients are combined.

❖ Stir in the milk, then spoon the mixture into the prepared tin. Level the surface with the back of a spoon or a knife.

❖ Arrange the pear slices on top of the cake mixture, arranging them in a radiating pattern.

❖ Bake in a preheated oven, 180°C/350°F/Gas Mark 4, for about 1 hour or until the cake is just firm to the touch.

❖ Leave the cake to cool in the tin, then transfer to a wire rack to cool completely before serving.

Rich Fruit Cake

❖ **SERVES 4** ❖

1 tbsp butter, for greasing
175 g/6 oz stoned chopped unsweetened dried dates
125 g/4$\frac{1}{2}$ oz prunes, chopped
200 ml/7 fl oz unsweetened orange juice
2 tbsp black treacle
1 tsp finely grated lemon rind
1 tsp finely grated orange rind
225 g/8 oz wholemeal self-raising flour
1 tsp mixed spice
125 g/4$\frac{1}{2}$ oz seedless raisins
125 g/4$\frac{1}{2}$ oz sultanas
125 g/4$\frac{1}{2}$ oz currants
125 g/4$\frac{1}{2}$ oz dried cranberries
3 large eggs, separated

TO DECORATE

1 tbsp apricot jam, warmed
icing sugar
175 g/6 oz sugarpaste
strips of orange rind
strips of lemon rind

❖ Grease a deep 20-cm/8-inch cake tin with the butter and base-line with baking paper. Place the dates and prunes in a saucepan over a low heat, pour over the orange juice and simmer for 10 minutes. Remove from the heat and beat into a purée. Stir in the treacle and citrus rinds and set aside to cool.

❖ Sift the flour and spice into a bowl, adding any bran that remains in the sieve. Add the dried fruits. When the date and prune mixture is cool, whisk in the egg yolks. In a separate bowl, whisk the egg whites until stiff. Add the fruit mixture to the dry ingredients and mix.

❖ Gently fold in the egg whites. Transfer to the prepared tin and bake in a preheated oven, 160°C/325°F/Gas Mark 3, for 1$\frac{1}{2}$ hours. Leave to cool in the tin.

❖ Turn the cake out and brush the top with apricot jam. Dust the work surface with icing sugar and roll out the sugarpaste thinly. Lay the sugarpaste over the top of the cake and trim the edges. Decorate with strips of orange and lemon rind.

Blackberry & Apple Cake

1 tbsp butter, for greasing
350 g/12 oz cooking apples
3 tbsp lemon juice
300 g/10$^{1}/_{2}$ oz wholemeal
    self-raising flour
$^{1}/_{2}$ tsp baking powder
1 tsp ground cinnamon,
    plus extra for dusting
175 g/6 oz prepared
    blackberries, thawed, if
frozen, plus extra to decorate

175 g/6 oz light muscovado
    sugar
1 egg, beaten
200 ml/7 fl oz low-fat fromage
    frais
55 g/2 oz white or brown sugar
    cubes, crushed lightly
sliced eating apple, to decorate

❖ Grease a 900-g/2-lb loaf tin with a little butter and line with baking paper. Core, peel and finely dice the apples. Place them in a saucepan with the lemon juice, bring to the boil, cover and simmer for 10 minutes until soft. Beat into a purée, then leave to cool.

❖ Sift the flour, baking powder and cinnamon into a bowl, adding any bran that remains in the sieve. Stir in 115 g/4 oz of the blackberries and the sugar.

❖ Make a well in the centre of the ingredients and add the egg, fromage frais and cooled apple purée. Mix until thoroughly blended. Spoon the mixture into the prepared loaf tin and level the top with a palette knife.

❖ Sprinkle with the remaining blackberries, pressing them down into the cake mixture, and top with the crushed sugar cubes. Bake in a preheated oven, 190°C/375°F/Gas Mark 5, for 40–45 minutes. Leave to cool in the tin.

❖ Turn the cake out and peel away the lining paper. Serve dusted with cinnamon and decorated with blackberries and apple slices.

Chocolate & Orange Ring

175 g/6 oz butter, softened,
    plus extra for greasing
175 g/6 oz caster sugar
3 eggs, beaten
150 g/5$^{1}/_{2}$ oz self-raising flour,
    sifted

25 g/1 oz cocoa powder, sifted
5–6 tbsp orange juice
grated rind of 1 orange

❖ Lightly grease a 25-cm/10-inch ovenproof ring mould with a little butter.

❖ In a mixing bowl, cream together the butter and sugar with an electric whisk for about 5 minutes.

❖ Add the beaten egg a little at a time, whisking well after each addition.

❖ Using a metal spoon, fold the flour into the creamed mixture carefully, then spoon half the mixture into a separate mixing bowl.

❖ Fold the cocoa powder and half of the orange juice into one bowl and mix gently.

❖ Fold the orange rind and the remaining orange juice into the other bowl and mix gently.

❖ Place spoonfuls of each of the mixtures alternately into the mould, then drag a skewer through the mixture to create a marbled effect.

❖ Bake in a preheated oven, 180°C/350°F/Gas Mark 4, for 30–35 minutes or until well risen and a skewer inserted into the centre comes out clean.

❖ Leave the cake to cool in the mould before turning out on to a wire rack.

Clementine & Almond Butter Cake

175 g/6 oz butter, softened,
plus extra for greasing
2 clementines
175 g/6 oz caster sugar
3 eggs, beaten
175 g/6 oz self-raising flour
3 tbsp ground almonds
3 tbsp single cream

GLAZE AND TOPPING
6 tbsp clementine juice
2 tbsp caster sugar
3 white sugar cubes, crushed

❖   Grease an 18-cm/7-inch round cake tin with a little butter and base-line with baking paper.

❖   Pare the rind from the clementines and finely chop the rind. In a bowl, cream together the butter, sugar and clementine rind until pale and fluffy.

❖   Gradually add the beaten eggs to the mixture, beating well after each addition.

❖   Gently fold in the self-raising flour, followed by the ground almonds and the cream. Spoon the mixture into the prepared tin.

❖   Bake in a preheated oven, 180°C/350°F/Gas Mark 4, for about 55–60 minutes or until a fine skewer inserted into the centre comes out clean. Leave to cool slightly.

❖   Meanwhile, make the glaze. Put the clementine juice into a small saucepan with the caster sugar. Bring to the boil, then reduce the heat and simmer for 5 minutes.

❖   Drizzle the glaze over the cake until it has been absorbed and sprinkle with the crushed sugar cubes.

Carrot & Ginger Cake

butter, for greasing	3 tbsp corn oil
225 g/8 oz plain flour	juice of 1 orange
1 tsp baking powder	
1 tsp bicarbonate of soda	**ICING**
2 tsp ground ginger	225 g/8 oz low-fat soft cheese
½ tsp salt	4 tbsp icing sugar
175 g/6 oz light muscovado	1 tsp vanilla essence
sugar	
225 g/8 oz carrots, grated	**TO DECORATE**
2 pieces chopped stem ginger	grated carrot
25 g/1 oz grated root ginger	finely chopped stem ginger
60 g/2 oz seedless raisins	ground ginger
2 eggs, beaten	

❖ Preheat the oven to 180°C/350°F/Gas Mark 4. Grease a 20-cm/8-inch round cake tin with the butter and base-line with baking paper.

❖ Sift the flour, baking powder, bicarbonate of soda, ground ginger and salt into a bowl. Stir in the sugar, carrots, stem ginger, fresh ginger and raisins. Beat together the eggs, oil and orange juice, then pour into the bowl. Mix the ingredients together well.

❖ Spoon the mixture into the tin and bake in the oven for 1–1¼ hours until firm to the touch or until a fine skewer inserted into the centre of the cake comes out clean.

❖ To make the icing, place the soft cheese in a bowl and beat to soften. Sift in the icing sugar and add the vanilla essence. Mix well.

❖ Remove the cake from the tin and cool. Smooth the icing over the top. Decorate the cake with the carrot and ginger and serve.

Chocolate Cake with Almonds

175 g/6 oz butter, plus extra for	25 g/1 oz toasted flaked
greasing	almonds and 25 g/1 oz plain
175 g/6 oz plain chocolate	chocolate, melted,
125 g/4½ oz caster sugar	to decorate
4 eggs, separated	
¼ tsp cream of tartar	**TOPPING**
50 g/1¾ oz self-raising flour	125 g/4½ oz milk chocolate
125 g/4½ oz ground almonds	25 g/1 oz butter
1 tsp almond essence	4 tbsp double cream

❖ Lightly grease and a 23-cm/9-inch round springform tin with a little butter and base-line with baking paper. Break the chocolate into small pieces and place in a small pan with the butter. Heat gently, stirring until melted and well combined.

❖ Place 100 g/3½ oz of the caster sugar in a bowl with the egg yolks and whisk until pale and creamy. Add the melted chocolate mixture, beating until well combined.

❖ Sift together the cream of tartar and flour and fold into the chocolate mixture with the ground almonds and almond essence.

❖ Whisk the egg whites in a bowl until standing in soft peaks. Add the remaining caster sugar and whisk for about 2 minutes by hand, or 45–60 seconds, if using an electric whisk, until thick and glossy. Fold the egg whites into the chocolate mixture and spoon into the tin. Bake in a preheated oven, 190°C/375°F/Gas Mark 5, for 40 minutes or until just springy to the touch. Leave to cool.

❖ Heat the topping ingredients in a bowl over a saucepan of hot water. Remove from the heat and beat for 2 minutes. Leave to chill for 30 minutes. Transfer the cake to a plate and spread with the topping. Scatter with the almonds and drizzle with melted chocolate. Leave to set for 2 hours before serving.

Chocolate Sandwich Cake

125 g/4^1/$_2$ oz soft margarine,
plus extra for greasing
125 g/4^1/$_2$ oz caster sugar
2 eggs
1 tbsp golden syrup
125 g/4^1/$_2$ oz self-raising flour,
sifted
2 tbsp cocoa powder, sifted

FILLING AND TOPPING
50 g/1^3/$_4$ oz icing sugar, sifted
25 g/1 oz butter
100 g/3^1/$_2$ oz white or milk
cooking chocolate
a little milk or white chocolate,
melted (optional)

❉ Lightly grease two 18-cm/7-inch shallow cake tins with a little margarine.

❉ Place all of the ingredients for the cake in a large mixing bowl and beat with a wooden spoon or electric hand whisk to form a smooth mixture.

❉ Divide the mixture between the prepared tins and level the tops. Bake in a preheated oven, 190°C/375F/Gas Mark 5, for 20 minutes or until springy to the touch. Cool for a few minutes in the tins before transferring to a wire rack to cool completely.

❉ To make the filling, beat the icing sugar and butter together in a bowl until light and fluffy. Melt the cooking chocolate and beat half into the icing mixture. Use the filling to sandwich the 2 cakes together.

❉ Spread the remaining melted cooking chocolate over the top of the cake. Pipe circles of contrasting melted milk or white chocolate and feather into the cooking chocolate with a cocktail stick, if liked. Leave to set before serving.

Coconut Cake

100 g/3^1/$_2$ oz butter, diced, plus
extra for greasing
225 g/8 oz self-raising flour
pinch of salt
100 g/3^1/$_2$ oz demerara sugar

100 g/3^1/$_2$ oz desiccated
coconut, plus extra for
sprinkling
2 eggs, beaten
4 tbsp milk

❉ Grease a 900-g/2-lb loaf tin with with a little butter and base-line with baking paper.

❉ Sift the flour and salt into a mixing bowl and rub in the butter with your fingertips until the mixture resembles fine breadcrumbs.

❉ Stir in the sugar, coconut, eggs and milk and mix to a soft dropping consistency.

❉ Spoon the mixture into the prepared loaf tin and level the surface with a palette knife. Bake in a preheated oven, 160°C/325°F/Gas Mark 3, for 30 minutes.

❉ Remove the cake from the oven and sprinkle with the extra coconut. Return to the oven and cook for a further 30 minutes until well risen and golden and a fine metal skewer inserted into the centre comes out clean.

❉ Leave the cake to cool in the tin for 10 minutes. Turn it out and transfer to a wire rack to cool completely before serving.

Yogurt & Pineapple Cake

❊ SERVES 9 ❊

butter, for greasing
150 g/5^1/$_2$ oz low-fat spread
125 g caster sugar
100 g/3^1/$_2$ oz self-raising flour, sifted
3 tbsp cocoa powder, sifted
1^1/$_2$ tsp baking powder
2 eggs
225g/8 oz canned pineapple pieces in natural juice
125 ml/4 fl oz low-fat thick natural yogurt
about 1 tbsp icing sugar
grated chocolate, to decorate

❊ Lightly grease a 20-cm/8-inch square cake tin with the butter.

❊ Place the low-fat spread, caster sugar, flour, cocoa powder, baking powder and eggs in a large mixing bowl. Beat with a wooden spoon or electric hand whisk until smooth.

❊ Pour the cake mixture into the prepared tin and level the surface. Bake in a preheated oven, 190°C/375°F/Gas Mark 5, for 20–25 minutes or until springy to the touch. Leave to cool slightly in the tin before transferring to a wire rack to cool completely.

❊ Drain the pineapple, chop the pineapple pieces and drain again. Reserve a little pineapple for decoration, then stir the rest into the yogurt and sweeten to taste with sugar.

❊ Spread the pineapple and yogurt mixture over the cake and decorate with the reserved pineapple pieces. Sprinkle with the grated chocolate.

Fruit Loaf with Apple Spread

sunflower oil, for brushing
175 g/6 oz porridge oats
100 g/3½ oz light muscovado sugar
1 tsp ground cinnamon
125 g/4½ oz sultanas
175 g/6 oz seedless raisins
2 tbsp malt extract
300 ml/10 fl oz unsweetened apple juice
175 g/6 oz self-raising wholemeal flour

1½ tsp baking powder
whole strawberries and apple wedges, to serve

SPREAD
225 g/8 oz strawberries, washed and hulled
2 eating apples, cored and chopped
300 ml/10 fl oz unsweetened apple juice

❄ Preheat the oven to 180°C/350°F/Gas Mark 4. Oil a 900-g/2-lb loaf tin and base-line with baking paper.

❄ Place the oats, sugar, cinnamon, sultanas, raisins and malt extract in a large bowl. Pour in the apple juice, stir well and leave to soak for 30 minutes.

❄ Sift in the flour and baking powder, adding any husks that remain in the sieve, and fold in using a metal spoon.

❄ Spoon the mixture into the prepared tin and bake in the preheated oven for 1½ hours or until firm and a skewer inserted into the centre comes out clean. Leave to cool in the tin for 10 minutes, then turn out on to a wire rack and leave to cool.

❄ Meanwhile, make the spread. Place the strawberries and apples in a saucepan and pour in the apple juice. Bring to the boil, cover and simmer for 30 minutes. Beat the sauce well and spoon into a clean, warmed jar. Leave to cool, then seal and label. Serve the loaf with 1–2 tablespoons of the spread, the strawberries and the apple wedges.

Chocolate Tea Bread

175 g/6 oz butter, softened, plus extra for greasing
100 g/3½ oz light muscovado sugar
4 eggs, lightly beaten
225 g/8 oz plain chocolate chips

100 g/3½ oz raisins
50 g/1¾ oz chopped walnuts
finely grated rind of 1 orange
225 g/8 oz self-raising flour

❄ Lightly grease a 900-g/2-lb loaf tin with a little butter and base-line with baking paper.

❄ Cream the butter and muscovado sugar together in a bowl until light and fluffy.

❄ Gradually add the eggs, beating well after each addition. If the mixture begins to curdle, beat in 1–2 tablespoons of the flour.

❄ Stir in the chocolate chips, raisins, walnuts and orange rind. Sift the flour and carefully fold it into the mixture.

❄ Spoon the mixture into the prepared loaf tin and make a slight dip in the centre of the top with the back of a spoon.

❄ Bake in a preheated oven, 160°C/325°F/Gas Mark 3, for 1 hour or until a fine skewer inserted into the centre comes out clean.

❄ Leave to cool in the tin for 5 minutes, before carefully turning out and leaving on a wire rack to cool completely.

❄ Serve the tea bread cut into thin slices.

Date & Sesame Loaf

❋ **MAKES 1 LOAF** ❋

butter, for greasing
250 g/9 oz strong white flour
75 g/2¾ oz strong brown flour
½ tsp salt
1 sachet easy-blend dried yeast

200 ml/7 fl oz tepid water
3 tbsp sunflower oil
3 tbsp honey
75 g/2¾ oz dates, chopped
2 tbsp sesame seeds

❋ Grease a 900-g/2-lb loaf tin with the butter. Sift the flours into a large mixing bowl, stir in the salt and dried yeast.

❋ Pour in the water, oil and honey. Mix everything together to form a dough.

❋ Place the dough on a lightly floured surface and knead for about 5 minutes until smooth.

❋ Place the dough in a greased bowl, cover and leave to rise in a warm place for about 1 hour or until doubled in size.

❋ Knead in the dates and sesame seeds. Shape the dough and place in the tin.

❋ Cover and leave in a warm place for a further 30 minutes or until springy to the touch.

❋ Bake in a preheated oven, 220°C/425°F/Gas Mark 7, for 30 minutes or until a hollow sound is heard when the base of the loaf is tapped.

❋ Transfer the loaf to a wire rack and leave to cool. Serve cut into thick slices.

Citrus Bread

❋ **MAKES 1 LOAF** ❋

4 tbsp butter, diced, plus extra for greasing
450 g/1 lb strong white flour, plus extra for dusting
½ tsp salt
50 g/1¾ oz caster sugar
1 sachet easy-blend dried yeast
5–6 tbsp orange juice

4 tbsp lemon juice
3–4 tbsp lime juice
150 ml/5 fl oz tepid water
1 orange
1 lemon
1 lime
2 tbsp clear honey, for glazing

❋ Lightly grease a baking tray with a little butter.

❋ Sift the flour and salt into a large mixing bowl. Stir in the sugar and dried yeast.

❋ Rub the butter into the mixture with your fingertips until the mixture resembles breadcrumbs. Add the lemon and lime juice and the water and bring together with your fingers to form a dough.

❋ Place the dough on a lightly floured work surface and knead for 5 minutes. Place the dough in a greased bowl, cover and leave to rise in a warm place for about 1 hour until doubled in size.

❋ Meanwhile, grate the rind of the orange, lemon and lime. Knead the fruit rinds into the dough.

❋ Divide the dough into 2 balls, making one slightly bigger than the other. Place the larger ball on the baking tray and set the smaller one on top.

❋ Push a floured finger through the centre of the dough. Cover and leave to rise for about 40 minutes or until springy to the touch.

❋ Bake in a preheated oven, 220°C/425°F/Gas Mark 7, for 35 minutes. Remove from the oven and transfer to a wire rack to cool. Glaze with the honey.

Mango Bread with Sultanas

40 g/1¹/₂ oz butter, cut into
small pieces, plus extra
for greasing
450 g/1 lb strong white flour
1 tsp salt
1 sachet easy-blend dried yeast
1 tsp ground ginger
50 g/1³/₄ oz demerara sugar
1 small mango, peeled, cored
and puréed
250 ml/9 fl oz tepid water
2 tbsp clear honey
125 g/4¹/₂ oz sultanas
1 egg, beaten
icing sugar, for dusting

❊ Grease a baking tray with a little butter. Sift the flour and salt into a large mixing bowl, stir in the yeast, ginger and sugar. Rub in the butter with your fingers.

❊ Stir in the mango purée, water and honey and mix together to form a dough.

❊ Place the dough on a lightly floured surface and knead for about 5 minutes until smooth. Alternatively, use an electric mixer with a dough hook. Place the dough in a greased bowl, cover and leave to rise in a warm place for about 1 hour until it has doubled in size.

❊ Knead in the sultanas and shape the dough into 2 sausage shapes, each 25 cm/10 inches long. Carefully twist the 2 pieces together and pinch the ends to seal. Place the dough on the baking tray, cover and leave in a warm place for a further 40 minutes.

❊ Brush the loaf with the egg and bake in a preheated oven, 220°C/425°F/ Gas Mark 7, for 30 minutes or until golden brown. Leave to cool on a wire rack. Dust with the icing sugar before serving.

Chocolate Bread

1 tbsp butter, for greasing
450 g/1 lb strong white flour,
plus extra for dusting
25 g/1 oz cocoa powder
1 tsp salt

1 sachet easy-blend dried yeast
25 g/1 oz demerara sugar
1 tbsp oil
300 ml/10 fl oz hand-hot water

❖ Lightly grease a 900-g/2-lb loaf tin with the butter.

❖ Sift the flour and cocoa powder into a large mixing bowl. Stir in the salt, yeast and sugar.

❖ Pour in the oil with the water and mix the ingredients together to form a dough.

❖ Place the dough on a lightly floured work surface and knead for 5 minutes. Alternatively, use an electric mixer with a dough hook.

❖ Place the dough in a greased bowl, cover and leave to rise in a warm place for about 1 hour or until it has doubled in size.

❖ Knead the dough lightly for about 1 minute to knock it back, then shape it into a loaf. Place it in the prepared tin, cover and leave to rise in a warm place for a further 30 minutes.

❖ Bake in a preheated oven, 200°C/400°F/Gas Mark 6, for 25–30 minutes. When the loaf is cooked it should sound hollow when tapped on the base.

❖ Transfer the bread to a wire rack and leave to cool. Cut into slices and serve.

Yogurt Scones

225 g/8 oz plain flour,
plus extra for dusting
1 tsp salt
1 tbsp baking powder
60 g/2 oz unsalted butter,
chilled, plus extra for greasing

60 g/2 oz sugar
1 egg
6 tbsp low-fat natural yogurt

❖ Preheat the oven to 180°C/350°F/Gas Mark 4.

❖ Sift together the flour, salt and baking powder. Cut the butter into small pieces, and rub it into the dry ingredients until the mixture resembles fine breadcrumbs. Stir in the sugar.

❖ Beat together the egg and yogurt and stir it quickly into the dry ingredients. Mix to form a thick dough and knead until it is smooth and free from cracks.

❖ Lightly flour a pastry board or work surface and a rolling pin and roll out the dough to a thickness of 2 cm/¾ inch.

❖ Cut out rounds with a 5-cm/2-inch pastry cutter, gather up the trimmings and roll them out again. Cut out as many more rounds as possible.

❖ Lightly grease a baking tray with a little butter and heat it in the oven. Transfer the dough rounds to the tray and dust lightly with flour.

❖ Bake the scones in the preheated oven for 10 minutes or until they are risen and golden brown.

❖ Transfer the scones to a wire rack to cool, but serve while still warm.

Rich Apple Scones

❖ **MAKES 8** ❖

175 g/6 oz butter, cut into small pieces, plus extra for greasing
350 g/12 oz self-raising flour
1 tbsp caster sugar
pinch of salt

1 eating apple, peeled, cored and chopped
1 egg, beaten
2 tbsp golden syrup
5 tbsp milk

❖ Lightly grease a baking tray with a little butter.

❖ Sift the flour, sugar and salt into a mixing bowl.

❖ Rub in the butter with your fingers until the mixture resembles fine breadcrumbs.

❖ Stir the chopped apple into the mixture until combined.

❖ Mix the beaten egg, golden syrup and milk together. Add to the dry ingredients to form a soft dough.

❖ On a lightly floured work surface. roll out the dough to a thickness of 2 cm/¾ inch and cut out 8 scones, using a 5-cm/2-inch plain pastry cutter.

❖ Arrange the scones on the prepared baking tray and bake in a preheated oven, 225°/425°F/Gas Mark 7, for 8–10 minutes.

❖ Transfer the scones to a wire rack and cool slightly before serving.

❖ Serve split in half and spread with butter.

Fruit Scones

❖ **MAKES 10–12** ❖

225 g/8 oz self-raising flour, plus extra for dusting
½ tsp salt
1 tsp baking powder
2 tbsp caster sugar
55 g/2 oz butter, plus extra for greasing

55 g/2 oz mixed fruit
150 ml/5 fl oz milk
3 tbsp milk, to glaze
strawberry jam and clotted cream, to serve

❖ Lightly grease a baking tray with a little butter.

❖ Preheat the oven to 220°C/425°F/Gas Mark 7. Sift together the flour, salt, baking powder and sugar into a bowl. Rub in the butter and add the fruit. Stir in the milk, using a round-bladed knife, and make into a soft dough.

❖ Turn the mixture on to a floured surface and lightly flatten the dough until it is of an even thickness, about 1 cm/ ½ inch. Do not be heavy-handed – scones need a light touch.

❖ Using a pastry cutter, cut out the scones and place on the prepared baking tray. Glaze with a little milk.

❖ Bake in the preheated oven for 10–12 minutes until golden and well risen.

❖ Remove from the oven and cool on a wire rack. Serve freshly baked, with strawberry jam and clotted cream. Serve them warm, if possible, but certainly on the same day.

Basic White Bread

450 g/1 lb strong white flour, plus 2 tbsp for dusting
1 tsp salt
❊ one sachet easy-blend dried yeast
1 tbsp vegetable oil or melted butter, plus 1 tsp for greasing
300 ml/10 fl oz warm water

❊ Mix the flour, salt and yeast together in a mixing bowl. Add the oil and water and stir well to form a soft dough.

❊ Turn out the dough on to a lightly floured board and knead well by hand for 5–7 minutes. Alternatively, use a free-standing electric mixer for this and knead the dough with the dough hook for 4–5 minutes. The dough should have a smooth appearance and feel elastic.

❊ Return the dough to the bowl, cover with clingfilm and leave to rise in a warm place for 1 hour. When it has doubled in size, turn it out onto a floured board and knock back for 30 seconds. Knead until smooth.

❊ Shape the dough into a rectangle the length of the tin and three times the width. Grease a 900-g/2-lb loaf tin well, fold the dough into three lengthways and put it in the tin with the join underneath for a well-shaped loaf. Cover and leave to rise in a warm place for 30 minutes until it has risen well above the tin.

❊ Preheat the oven to 220ºC/425ºF/Gas Mark 7. Bake in the centre of the preheated oven for 25–30 minutes until firm and golden brown. Test that the loaf is cooked by tapping it on the base – it should sound hollow. Cool on a cooling rack for 30 minutes. Store in an airtight container in a cool place for 3–4 days.

Walnut & Seed Bread

450 g/1 lb wholemeal flour	2 tsp salt
450 g/1 lb granary flour	2 sachets easy-blend dried
115 g/4 oz strong white flour	yeast
2 tbsp sesame seeds	2 tbsp olive oil or walnut oil
2 tbsp sunflower seeds	700 ml/1¼ pints warm water
2 tbsp poppy seeds	1 tbsp melted butter or oil,
115 g/4 oz walnuts, chopped	for greasing

❄ In a mixing bowl, mix together the flours, seeds, nuts, salt and yeast. Add the oil and warm water and stir well to form a soft dough.

❄ Turn out the dough on to a lightly floured board and knead well for 5–7 minutes. The dough should have a smooth appearance and feel elastic. Return the dough to the bowl, cover with a clean cloth and leave in a warm place for 1–1½ hours to rise. When the dough has doubled in size, turn it out on to a lightly floured board and knead again for 1 minute.

❄ Grease 2 x 450-g/1-lb loaf tins with the butter. Divide the dough into two. Shape each piece into a rectangle the length of the tin and three times the width. Fold the dough into three lengthways. Place in a tin with the join underneath. Repeat with the other piece. Cover and leave to rise in a warm place for 30 minutes until the bread is well risen above the tins.

❄ Preheat the oven to 230°C/450°F/Gas Mark 8. Bake in the centre of the preheated oven for 25–30 minutes. If the loaves are getting too brown, reduce the temperature to 220°C/425°F/Gas Mark 7. To test that the bread is cooked, tap the loaf on the base – it should sound hollow.

❄ Cool on a wire rack for 30 minutes to 1 hour; this enables the steam to escape and prevents a soggy loaf. When cool, seal in a polythene bag and keep in the refrigerator for up to 1 week.

Roasted Pepper Bread

1 tbsp butter, for greasing	1 sachet easy-blend dried yeast
1 red and 1 yellow pepper,	1 tsp granulated sugar
halved and deseeded	300 ml/10 fl oz tepid water
2 sprigs fresh rosemary	450 g/1 lb strong white flour
1 tbsp olive oil, plus extra	1 tsp salt
for oiling	

❄ Grease a 23-cm/9-inch deep round cake tin with the butter.

❄ Place the pepper halves and rosemary in a shallow roasting tin. Pour over the oil and roast in a preheated oven, 200°C/400°F/Gas Mark 6, for 20 minutes, or until slightly charred. Leave to cool slightly, then remove the skins and cut the flesh into slices.

❄ Place the yeast and sugar in a bowl and mix with 100 ml/3½ fl oz of the water. Leave in a warm place for about 15 minutes, or until frothy. Mix the flour and salt together in a large bowl. Stir in the yeast mixture and the remaining water and bring together to form a dough. Knead the dough for 5 minutes until smooth. Cover with oiled clingfilm and leave to rise for about 30 minutes, or until doubled in size.

❄ Cut the dough into 3 equal portions. Roll the portions into rounds slightly larger than the cake tin. Place 1 round in the base of the tin so that it reaches up the sides by about 2 cm/¾ inch. Top with half the pepper mixture. Strip the leaves from the rosemary sprigs and sprinkle half over the top. Place the second round on top, followed by the remaining pepper mixture and rosemary leaves. Top with the last round and push the edges down the sides of the tin.

❄ Cover with oiled clingfilm and leave to rise for 30–40 minutes. Bake for 45 minutes, until golden. When the loaf is cooked it should sound hollow when tapped. Turn out on to a wire rack. Serve warm.

Cheese & Ham Loaf

❊ **MAKES 1 LOAF** ❊

6 tbsp butter, diced, plus extra for greasing
225 g/8 oz self-raising flour
1 tsp salt
2 tsp baking powder
1 tsp paprika
125 g/4^{1}/$_{2}$ oz mature cheese, grated
75 g/2^{3}/$_{4}$ oz smoked ham, chopped
2 eggs, beaten
150 ml/5 fl oz milk

❊ Grease a 450-g/1-lb loaf tin with a little butter and base-line with baking paper.

❊ Sift the flour, salt, baking powder and paprika into a large mixing bowl.

❊ Add the butter and rub it in with your fingertips until the mixture resembles fine breadcrumbs. Stir in the cheese and ham.

❊ Add the beaten eggs and milk to the dry ingredients in the bowl and mix well.

❊ Spoon the cheese and ham mixture into the prepared loaf tin.

❊ Bake in a preheated oven, 180°C/350°F/Gas Mark 4, for about 1 hour or until the loaf is well risen.

❊ Leave the bread to cool in the tin, then turn out and transfer to a wire rack to cool completely.

❊ Cut the bread into thick slices to serve.

Cheese & Chive Bread

❊ **SERVES 8** ❊

butter, for greasing
225 g/8 oz self-raising flour
1 tsp salt
1 tsp mustard powder
115 g/4 oz grated mature cheese
2 tbsp chopped fresh chives
1 egg, beaten
10 g/^{1}/$_{4}$ oz butter, melted
150 ml/5 fl oz milk

❊ Grease a 23-cm/9-inch square cake tin with the butter and base-line with baking paper.

❊ Sift the flour, salt and mustard powder into a large mixing bowl.

❊ Reserve 3 tablespoons of the cheese for sprinkling over the top of the loaf before baking in the oven.

❊ Stir the remaining cheese into the bowl, together with the chives. Mix well.

❊ Add the egg, butter and milk and stir the mixture thoroughly.

❊ Pour the mixture into the prepared tin and spread with a knife. Sprinkle with the reserved cheese.

❊ Bake in a preheated oven, 190°C/375°F/Gas Mark 5, for about 30 minutes.

❊ Let the bread cool slightly in the tin. Turn out the bread on to a wire rack to cool further before serving. Cut into triangles to serve.

Spicy Bread

2 tbsp butter, diced, plus extra
for greasing
225 g/8 oz self-raising flour,
plus extra for dusting
100 g/3¹/₂ oz plain flour
1 tsp baking powder
¹/₄ tsp salt
¹/₄ tsp cayenne pepper
2 tsp curry powder
2 tsp poppy seeds
150 ml/5 fl oz milk
1 egg, beaten

❖ Lightly grease a baking tray with a little butter.

❖ Sift the self-raising flour and the plain flour into a mixing bowl along with the baking powder, salt, cayenne pepper, curry powder and poppy seeds.

❖ Rub in the butter with your fingertips until the mixture resembles breadcrumbs.

❖ Add the milk and beaten egg and bring together with your fingers to form a soft dough.

❖ Turn out the dough on to a lightly floured work surface, then knead lightly for a few minutes.

❖ Shape the dough into a round about 5 cm/2 inches deep, and mark a cross on top with a sharp knife.

❖ Bake in a preheated oven, 190°C/375°F/Gas Mark 5, for 45 minutes.

❖ Remove the bread from the oven, transfer to a wire rack and leave to cool slightly. Serve the bread cut into chunks or slices.

Sage & Garlic Ring

butter, for greasing	2 tsp sea salt
250 g/9 oz strong brown flour	3 garlic cloves, finely chopped
1 sachet easy-blend dried yeast	1 tsp clear honey
3 tbsp chopped fresh sage	150 ml/5 fl oz tepid water

❖ Lightly grease a baking tray with the butter. Sift the flour into a large mixing bowl and stir in the husks that remain in the sieve.

❖ Stir in the dried yeast, sage and half of the sea salt. Reserve 1 teaspoon of the chopped garlic for sprinkling and stir the rest into the bowl. Add the honey with the water and mix together to form a dough.

❖ Turn out the dough on to a lightly floured surface and knead it for about 5 minutes. Alternatively, use an electric mixer with a dough hook.

❖ Place the dough in a greased bowl, cover and leave to rise in a warm place until it has doubled in size.

❖ Knead the dough again for a few minutes, shape it into a circle and place on the baking tray.

❖ Cover and leave to rise for a further 30 minutes, or until springy to the touch. Sprinkle with the rest of the sea salt and garlic.

❖ Bake in a preheated oven, 200°C/400°F/Gas Mark 6, for 25–30 minutes. Leave to cool on a wire rack before serving.

Hazelnut & Raisin Rolls

450 g/1 lb wholemeal flour, plus 3 tbsp for dusting	3 tbsp olive oil or hazelnut oil
225 g/8 oz strong white flour	450 ml/16 fl oz tepid water
1 tsp salt	115 g/4 oz hazelnuts, coarsely chopped
2 sachets easy-blend dried yeast	100 g/3$\frac{1}{2}$ oz raisins

❖ In a mixing bowl, mix together the flours, salt and yeast. Add 2 tablespoons of the oil and all the water and stir well to form a soft dough.

❖ Turn out the dough on to a lightly floured board and knead well for 5–7 minutes. The dough should have a smooth appearance and feel elastic. Add the nuts and raisins and mix well.

❖ Return the dough to the bowl, cover with a clean cloth or some clingfilm, and leave in a warm place for 1–1$\frac{1}{2}$ hours to rise.

❖ When the dough has doubled in size, turn it out onto a lightly floured board and knead again for 1 minute.

❖ Divide the dough into 20–24 even-sized pieces and shape into good rounds. Grease 2 baking trays well with the remaining oil. Place the rolls on the trays, leaving enough space between them to allow for growth whilst they prove.

❖ Cover again and leave to rise for about 30 minutes, until the rolls are risen and have doubled in size.

❖ Preheat the oven to 200°C/400°F/Gas Mark 6. Bake in the preheated oven for about 15 minutes, swapping their positions halfway through. The rolls should be golden brown and their bases should sound hollow when tapped.

❖ Cool on a wire rack and eat on the same day, or store for 2–3 days in a sealed container in the refrigerator.

Sun-Dried Tomato Rolls

❈ MAKES 8 ❈

100 g/3½ oz butter, melted
and cooled slightly, plus
extra for greasing
225 g/8 oz strong white flour
½ tsp salt
1 sachet easy-blend dried yeast

3 tbsp milk, warmed
2 eggs, beaten
50 g/1¾ oz sun-dried
tomatoes in oil, well drained
and finely chopped
milk, for brushing

❈ Lightly grease a baking tray.

❈ Sift the flour and salt into a large mixing bowl. Stir in the yeast, then pour in the butter, milk and eggs. Mix together to form a dough.

❈ Turn out the dough on to a lightly floured surface and knead for about 5 minutes. Alternatively, use an electric mixer with a dough hook.

❈ Place the dough in a greased bowl, cover and leave to rise in a warm place for 1–1½ hours, or until the dough has doubled in size. Knock back the dough by kneading it for a few minutes.

❈ Knead the sun-dried tomatoes into the dough, sprinkling the work surface with extra flour as the tomatoes are quite oily.

❈ Divide the dough into 8 balls and place them on the baking tray. Cover and leave to rise for about 30 minutes, or until the rolls have doubled in size.

❈ Brush the rolls with milk and bake in a preheated oven, 230°C/450°F/Gas Mark 8, for 10–15 minutes or until the rolls are golden brown.

❈ Transfer the rolls to a wire rack and leave to cool slightly before serving.

Mini Focaccia

❈ SERVES 4 ❈

2 tbsp olive oil, plus extra
for greasing
350 g/12 oz strong white flour,
plus extra for dusting
½ tsp salt
1 sachet easy-blend dried yeast
250 ml/9 fl oz tepid water
50 g/1¾ oz stoned green
olives, halved

TOPPING
2 red onions, sliced
50 g/1¾ oz stoned green or
black olives, halved
2 tbsp olive oil
1 tsp sea salt
1 tbsp thyme leaves

❈ Lightly oil several baking trays. Sift the flour and salt into a large mixing bowl, then stir in the yeast. Pour in the olive oil and water and bring together with your fingers to form a dough.

❈ Turn out the dough on to a lightly floured work surface and knead for about 5 minutes. Alternatively, use an electric mixer with a dough hook.

❈ Place the dough in a greased bowl, cover and leave in a warm place for 1–1½ hours or until it has doubled in size.

❈ Knead the dough for 1–2 minutes to knock it back, then knead half of the olives into the dough. Divide the dough into quarters, then shape the quarters into rounds. Place them on the baking trays and push your fingers into the dough rounds to create a dimpled effect.

❈ To make the topping, sprinkle the red onions and the olives over the rounds. Drizzle the oil over the top and sprinkle with the sea salt and thyme leaves. Cover and leave to rise for 30 minutes.

❈ Bake in a preheated oven, 190°C/375°F/Gas Mark 5, for 20–25 minutes or until the focaccia are golden.

❈ Transfer to a wire rack and leave to cool before serving.

Cheese & Mustard Scones

❖ MAKES 8 ❖

4 tbsp butter, diced, plus extra
for greasing
225 g/8 oz self-raising flour,
plus extra for dusting
1 tsp baking powder
125 g/4¹/₂ oz mature cheese,
grated
1 tsp mustard powder
150 ml/5 fl oz milk, plus extra
for brushing
salt and pepper

❖ Lightly grease a baking tray with a little butter.

❖ Sift the flour, baking powder and a pinch of salt into a bowl. Rub in the butter with your fingers until the mixture resembles breadcrumbs.

❖ Stir in the cheese, mustard powder and enough milk to form a soft dough.

❖ Knead the dough very lightly on a lightly floured work surface, then flatten it out with the palm of your hand to a depth of about 2.5 cm/1 inch.

❖ Cut the dough into 8 wedges with a knife. Brush the wedges with a little milk and sprinkle with pepper to taste.

❖ Bake in a preheated oven, 220°C/425°F/Gas Mark 7, for 10–15 minutes, until the scones are golden brown.

❖ Transfer the cheese and mustard scones to a wire rack and leave to cool slightly before serving.

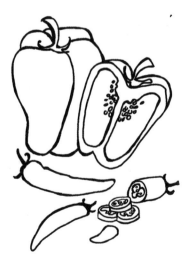

Cheese Muffins

❄ **MAKES 10** ❄

1 tbsp sunflower oil, for oiling
125 g/4 oz self-raising flour
1 tbsp baking powder
1 tsp salt
225 g/8 oz fine polenta
140 g/5 oz grated mature
Cheddar cheese

55 g/2 oz butter, melted
2 large eggs, beaten
1 garlic clove, crushed
300 ml/10 fl oz milk

❄ Preheat the oven to 200°C/400°F/Gas Mark 6. Lightly oil 10 cups of a 12-cup muffin tin. Sift the flour, baking powder and salt into a bowl, then stir in the polenta and two-thirds of the cheese.

❄ Place the butter, eggs, garlic and milk in a separate bowl. Add the wet ingredients to the dry ingredients and mix gently until just combined.

❄ Divide the batter evenly between the cups, sprinkle over the remaining cheese and bake in the oven for 20–25 minutes, or until risen and golden. Remove from the oven and serve warm, or place on a wire rack and leave to cool.

Chive Muffins

❄ **MAKES 12** ❄

1 tbsp sunflower
or groundnut oil, for oiling
350 g/12 oz plain flour
2 tsp baking powder
$1/2$ tsp bicarbonate of soda
25 g/1 oz Cheddar cheese,
grated

35 g/1$1/4$ oz fresh chives, finely
snipped, plus extra to garnish
1 large egg, lightly beaten
225 ml/8 fl oz soured cream
90 ml/3 fl oz natural yogurt
4 tbsp butter, melted

❄ Preheat the oven to 200°C/400°F/Gas Mark 6. Oil a 12-cup muffin tin. Sift the flour, baking powder, and bicarbonate of soda into a large mixing bowl. Add the cheese and chives and mix together well.

❄ In a separate bowl, lightly mix the egg, soured cream, yogurt and melted butter together. Add the soured cream mixture to the flour mixture and then gently stir together until just combined. Do not overstir the batter – it is fine for it to be a little lumpy.

❄ Divide the muffin batter evenly between the 12 cups in the muffin tin (they should be about two-thirds full). Sprinkle over the remaining snipped chives to garnish and transfer to the oven. Bake for 20 minutes, or until risen and golden. Remove the muffins from the oven and serve warm, or place them on a wire rack and leave to cool.

Bacon & Polenta Muffins

1 tbsp sunflower oil, for oiling
150 g/5^1/$_2$ oz pancetta
175 g/6 oz self-raising flour
1 tbsp baking powder
1 tsp salt
280 g/10 oz fine polenta

55 g/2 oz demerara sugar
100 g/3^1/$_2$ oz butter, melted
2 large eggs, beaten
300 ml/10 fl oz milk

❄ Preheat the oven to 200°C/400°F/Gas Mark 6 and preheat the grill to medium. Oil a 12-cup muffin pan. Cook the pancetta under the preheated grill until crisp and then crumble into pieces. Set aside until required.

❄ Sift the flour, baking powder and salt into a bowl, then stir in the polenta and sugar. Place the butter, eggs and milk in a separate bowl. Add the wet ingredients to the dry ingredients and mix until just blended.

❄ Fold in the crumbled pancetta, then divide the muffin batter between the cups and bake in the oven for 20–25 minutes until risen and golden. Remove the muffins from the oven and serve warm, or place them on a wire rack and leave to cool.

Cheese Sablés

150 g/5^1/$_2$ oz butter, diced, plus
extra for greasing
150 g/5^1/$_2$ oz plain flour, plus
extra for dusting

150 g/5^1/$_2$ oz mature cheese,
grated
1 egg yolk
sesame seeds, for sprinkling

❄ Lightly grease several baking trays with a little butter.

❄ Mix the flour and cheese together in a bowl.

❄ Add the butter to the cheese and flour mixture and rub in with your fingertips until the mixture resembles breadcrumbs.

❄ Stir in the egg yolk and mix to form a dough. Wrap in clingfilm. Chill in the refrigerator for 30 minutes.

❄ Roll out the dough thinly on a lightly floured work surface. Stamp out rounds with a 6-cm/2^1/$_2$-inch biscuit cutter, re-rolling the trimmings to make 35 biscuits.

❄ Place the rounds on the prepared baking trays and sprinkle the sesame seeds over the top of them.

❄ Bake in a preheated oven, 200°C/400°F/Gas Mark 6, for 20 minutes until lightly golden.

❄ Carefully transfer the cheese sablés to a wire rack and leave to cool slightly before serving.

Curried Butter & Parmesan Biscuits

100 g/3¹/₂ oz butter, softened,
plus extra for greasing
100 g/3¹/₂ oz plain flour
1 tsp salt
2 tsp curry powder
100 g/3¹/₂ oz Cheshire cheese,
grated
100 g/3¹/₂ oz Parmesan cheese,
grated

❄ Lightly grease about 4 baking trays.

❄ Sift the flour and salt into a mixing bowl.

❄ Stir in the curry powder and the grated Cheshire and Parmesan cheeses. Rub in the softened butter with your fingers until the mixture comes together to form a soft dough.

❄ On a lightly floured surface, roll out the dough thinly to form a rectangle.

❄ Using a .5-cm/2-inch biscuit cutter, cut out 40 round biscuits.

❄ Arrange the biscuits on the baking trays.

❄ Bake in a preheated oven, 180°C/350°F/Gas Mark 4, for 10–15 minutes.

❄ Leave the biscuits to cool slightly on the baking trays. Transfer the biscuits to a wire rack until completely cold and crisp, then serve.

Index

381